Designing Wide Area Networks and Internetworks

Designing Wide Area Networks and Internetworks

A Practical Guide

J. Scott Marcus

Addison-Wesley

An imprint of Addison Wesley Longman, Inc.

Reading, Massachusetts • Harlow, England • Menlo Park, California
Berkeley, California • Don Mills, Ontario • Sydney • Bonn
Amsterdam • Tokyo • Mexico City

Many of the designations used by manufacturers and sellers to distinguish their products are claimed as trademarks. Where those designations appear in this book and Addison-Wesley was aware of a trademark claim, the designations have been printed with an initial capital letter or in all capitals.

The author and publisher have taken care in the preparation of this book, but make no expressed or implied warranty of any kind and assume no responsibility for errors or omissions. No liability is assumed for incidental or consequential damages in connection with or arising out of the use of information or programs contained herein.

The publisher offers discounts on this book when ordered in quantity for special sales. For more information, please contact:

Corporate, Government, and Special Sales
Addison Wesley Longman, Inc.
One Jacob Way
Reading, Massachusetts 01867
(781) 944-3700

Library of Congress Cataloging-in-Publication Data

Marcus, J. Scott.
    Designing wide area networks and internetworks : a
    practical guide / J. Scott Marcus.
        p.   cm.
    Includes bibliographical references.
    ISBN 0-201-69584-7
    1. Wide area networks (Computer networks)   2. Inter-
networking (Telecommunication)   I. Title.
TK5105.87.M37   1999
004.67—dc21   99-30060
                                                              CIP

ISBN 0-201-69584-7
Text printed on recycled and acid-free paper.
1 2 3 4 5 6 7 8 9 10—MA—0302010099
First printing, August 1999

For Peggy,
who kept our family going
while I wrote and edited this book

Contents

Part III   The Management Review Phase   331

Part IV   The Final Design Phase   347

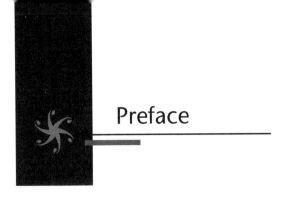

Preface

In the past few years, internetworking has exploded on the scene, thrusting itself into the awareness of the general public. A great many major corporations are finding it necessary to construct private internetworks, or intranets, to facilitate interactions internal to the organization, and many corporations are struggling to develop ways to securely use the public Internet to exchange business information with external customers and suppliers. Telephone companies and Internet service providers (ISPs) are moving quickly to provide cheap and reliable Internet access anywhere in the world.

Unfortunately, the design process for networks of this type is anything but straightforward. Any network that attempts to span a significant area today will represent a significant investment. A comprehensive network covering the entire United States could easily cost tens of millions of dollars a year to operate. Much of this cost is in circuits and services from the telephone companies and in labor.

Routing technology is well understood by a small but steadily growing cadre of gurus. But an understanding of routing technology is not, in and of itself, sufficient to create a cost-effective large-scale internetwork. The difference between a good design and a poor one can represent many millions of dollars of cost a year, one way or the other. For this reason, *cost analysis can be even more important to the design process than is technology analysis.*

Launching a new internetwork today is a daunting task. There are three primary reasons for this:

1. Lack of a well-established design *process*

2. Compartmentalization of knowledge within most organizations or its unavailability to the design team

3. Overwhelming number of alternative techniques, technologies, and vendors and carriers available

In attempting to fill in all three of these gaps, this book provides a workable network design process and presents and synthesizes necessary aspects of the underlying topics in the context of that process. The book attempts to present the economic and performance characteristics of the various technology and carrier service options in a straightforward way, to explain the domain of conditions over which each is optimal, and the options for intermixing technologies and services.

In this book, I have attempted to cover the necessary concepts and skills in an integrated way and to present them at the point in the design process at which they would be used in practice. I did not feel it necessary to duplicate material that is already widely available in the literature; rather, I have provided pointers to suitable references.

Audience

This book is intended for people who design computer internetworks that extend beyond a single building or a single campus. The book will be of particular interest to network designers and planners, network architects, and engineers who design, build, and support wide area internetworks, including people who belong to the information technology or telecommunications staff of a large corporation. The book will also be of value to data network sales and sales support personnel who work for carriers, Internet service providers (ISPs), and systems integrators. Finally, this book will be of interest to anyone wanting to better understand the design process and the underlying cost models for large-scale computer internetworks.

I have attempted to address the needs both of people in large enterprises that use networks and those who build carrier service provider and independent ISP networks to serve broader constituencies. The basic design principles are much the same in both cases, but service providers may tend to work with different transmission technologies and to think about their economics differently.

This book is written for the practitioner, not for the theorist. It attempts to provide the basic underpinnings of network design in a simple, direct, and intuitive way. Technologies are presented at a level of detail consistent with the needs of the network designer, which is to say that many interesting but irrelevant details are omitted.

I had the good fortune to study discrete event simulation at Columbia under the late Ed Ignall. He taught me two important things, both of which are reflected in this text.

- Take the time to understand your problem.
- Use that understanding to simplify your model by eliminating those factors that don't really matter.

Prerequisite Background

I have assumed that you already have a general familiarity with communication protocols in general and with TCP/IP in particular. If that is not the case, I would encourage you to read a good text, such as Andrew Tanenbaum's *Computer Networks,*[1] before you tackle this book.

Mathematical and statistical techniques are presented in terms of their application to the network design problem. No derivations appear in this book. At the same time, a basic understanding of probability and statistics is fundamental to the design process, as these data networks are all based in some degree on statistical multiplexing. I have attempted to provide a nuts-and-bolts review of any necessary aspects of statistics; nonetheless, if you are serious about working in this field, and if you have not already taken the equivalent of a semester course in probability and statistics, you would be well advised to do so.

You do not need a Ph.D. in mathematics to do good work in this field, but you do need to be reasonably good at working with figures. Much network design and most network cost analysis today is done not with sophisticated design tools but with commonplace spreadsheeting tools, such as Microsoft Excel. You will need to be facile with a spreadsheet. With that in mind, a number of illustrative spreadsheets are included. If you have a PC or compatible device with a decent spreadsheeting program, you will find it helpful to work through the examples that we have provided on the Web site for this book (http://www.awl.com/cseng/titles/0-201-69584-7). The formatted versions of the sample spreadsheets are suitable for use by Microsoft Excel; in addition, text versions are provided that should work adequately with any spreadsheeting product that can accommodate comma-delimited text.

This book takes an unabashedly U.S.-centric outlook, at least in terms of the examples that are offered. Yes, I realize that there is a large world out there—as a matter of fact, I spent several years working in Europe. The focus on the United States was intentional and was not based solely on the consideration that internetworking is most advanced in the United States. The deregulation of the carriers is also most advanced at present in the United

---

1. A. Tanenbaum, *Computer Networks*, 3rd ed. (Upper Saddle River, N.J.: Prentice Hall, 1996).

States. It is therefore the United States that poses the greatest opportunity and the greatest challenge for the designer. Deregulation is, however, a worldwide trend, and its pace is accelerating. The techniques that are presented have broad applicability, and the holistic approach that I have emphasized will become increasingly necessary as deregulation progresses.

Organization of This Book

The book begins with Chapter 1, which is a look at internetworking today. Chapter 2 then provides an overview of a suggested network design process, with its four major elements, or phases: definition of requirements, preliminary design, management review, and final design.

Chapter 3 provides more detail on the first phase, definition of requirements, discussing the identification of access locations, performance, availability, and security requirements. Protocol requirements must also be considered in this phase, as well as any needs for realtime voice or video or for transaction processing—needs that typically impose a requirement for deterministic delay. Unit cost requirements must also be considered. These three chapters compose Part I.

Part II drills down into the second phase: preliminary design. It opens with a discussion of the structure of carrier tariffs, as well as the trade-offs and combinations that are possible among them, as this permeates many of the tasks in this phase. Individual chapters then expand on the more complex aspects of the task: selecting an appropriate transmission technology or set of technologies; determining how many levels of hierarchy to use; identifying the number and placement of backbone locations; creating preliminary access, concentration, and backbone topological designs; and laying out the main engineering aspects of the design: routing, naming, addressing, network management, and security. This part concludes with a lengthy chapter on design validation: Have you met your design requirements?

Part III discusses the third phase: management review. Once the preliminary design is complete and the costs are understood, it is usually necessary to take the associated business case to management for review, typically including in-depth financial analysis and a go/no-go decision.

Part IV presents the fourth phase: final design. It is at this point that you will select carriers and equipment vendors. In many cases, you will use a Request for Proposal (RFP) process to obtain competitive price quotations. Once you have made your choices, you will revisit your design assumptions and will fill in the missing details in your design.

Acknowledgments

I am extremely grateful to the numerous reviewers who have contributed in many ways to the value and utility of this book. A few who particularly stand out are Patrick Cain, Ken Dumble, Tom Hicks, Michael Patton, and Daniel Pitt. I also appreciate help provided by Dustin Andrews, Jeffrey Burgan, John Curran, Alan Gatlin, Kathryn Korostoff, and Russell Nelson. I owe a great deal to many fine professionals who taught me a lot about network design along the way, including Dr. Daniel Friedman and Dr. John Ma.

I owe a special debt to Mary Hart, my patient and supportive editor, and to Karen Gettman, Carol Long, and the many fine professionals at Addison Wesley Longman who contributed to this book in ways large and small.

And, finally, I owe an incalculable debt to my wife, Peggy, and to my two sons for enabling me to invest so many hours in this book.

J. Scott Marcus
February 1999

PART

I

Beginning the Internetwork Design Process

1 — Networks and Internetworks

These years closing one millennium and opening the next are an incredibly exciting time for those of us fortunate enough to work with communications technology. Regulatory barriers are falling. The industry is coalescing and rationalizing. Technology is rampant. No longer just a playground for nerds, the Internet has become an essential part of the daily activities of many Americans and is playing an increasingly visible, vital global role. Traditional boundaries between voice and data communications are breaking down. Widespread deployment of fiber optics is demonstrating the potential to drive the cost of telecommunications downward dramatically. And wireless technologies are proliferating.

If you are reading this book, you probably work for an organization that already keenly appreciates the importance of communications technology in today's world. Perhaps you work for a carrier or an Internet service provider (ISP) that earns its livelihood by selling network services; perhaps you work for a commercial organization that depends on internetworking technology for the internal flow of information; perhaps your organization markets or sells its products and services over the Internet. You already understand the key reality of the emerging Internet-based world: *More than anything else, an organization's effectiveness at using network communications determines its overall competitiveness.* Organizations that fail to grasp this key point are destined to fall by the wayside.

This book aims to provide you with a broad and well-integrated understanding, at both a theoretical and a practical level, of the key things you need to understand in order to effectively and efficiently design and deploy wide area internetworks.

In a 1997 e-mail to a public mailing list, Internet guru Noel Chiappa described an engineer as "someone who can build for $25 what any fool can build for $100." When it comes to wide area network design, a poor design can cost vastly more than a good design. I would like you to come away from this book with good engineering skills, including a good understanding of the cost ramifications of your design decisions.

It is a noteworthy challenge to attempt to present the economics of network design in a coherent way; it is easy to lose the reader in the Byzantine details of technology, carrier tariffs and service definitions, and regulatory policy. There are, however, a number of underlying principles that experienced practitioners have instinctively followed for years. I have taken pains to try to codify and organize these principles in order to make the process intelligible to you.

With that said, we can begin! To set the stage for what follows, this chapter addresses a number of questions.

- What exactly is an internetwork?
- Why should your organization want to build an internetwork or to enhance the one it already has?
- How is wide area design different from local area design?
- Why is designing wide area internetworks so difficult?
- How do enterprise networks, internetworks, intranets, extranets, and the Internet differ?
- How do you cope with rapid evolution and change of the network?
- How do you deal with the inevitable political and financial disagreements surrounding any network design?

1.1   Data Communications and Organizational Competitiveness

The importance of data communications in today's world is perhaps so obvious to you as to need no further elaboration. Nonetheless, I would ask that you bear with me while I relate a brief story.

In August 1996, my wife and I were driving through Georgia on our way to the Summer Olympics in Atlanta. We suddenly realized that each of us had assumed that the other had packed our tickets to the Olympic events! After muttering a few choice expletives—too quietly for the kids to hear, I hoped—I reached for my cell phone. After a few tries, I reached a neighbor, who very graciously agreed to help us out. I told him where the tickets were and asked him to take them to Federal Express and to page me with the airbill number.

Consider for a moment: Many organizations offer overnight delivery, including the venerable U.S. Postal Service. Why was I so specific in my instructions? Why did I choose Federal Express and no other?

We arrived in Atlanta that evening. After dinner, I pulled my laptop out of the trunk and dialed in to the Internet. I connected to the Federal Express Web site, typed in my airbill number, and quickly learned that the package had been processed in Boston's Logan airport. The next morning, I dialed in again and saw that the package had processed through Memphis as expected and was on its way to Atlanta (see Figure 1-1). The package showed up at my doorstep shortly after 11:00 A.M.

I had made no special arrangements in advance with Federal Express and had no special software on my laptop beyond a normal Web browser. Yet the reassurance I derived from being able to track the progress of that parcel was incalculable. I very consciously chose an overnight service that could provide me with the timely information that I wanted, solely with tools at hand, in preference to any number of overnight services that could not.

Perhaps the most startling thing about this little tale is that it fails to startle us! We increasingly take for granted communications capabilities that would have been unthinkable just a few years ago. As our expectations evolve over time, however, we are in effect raising the bar for all competitors. Those that make effective and creative use of communications will thrive; the rest are destined to languish over time—some faster, some more slowly.

Note, too, that *the nature of the underlying service has itself evolved* in this example. For services that were always viewed as being tied to data communications, consumer expectations have markedly increased, as we would

```
        <!--BEGIN TRACKING INFORMATION-->
Airbill Number : 1496173840
    ■ Package has been Delivered!
    ■ Delivered To: Recipient
    ■ Delivery Time: 11:06
    ■ Signed For By: D. CTTRELLA
    ■ Cartage Agent:
    ■ Status Exception: Release Signature - not reqd
    ■ Scan Activity:
        • Delivered DECATUR GA 07/27 11:06
        • Delivered with Exception DECATUR GA 07/27 11:06
        • Package on Van DECATUR GA 07/27 09:01
        • Package Left Hub MEMPHIS TN 07/27 04:14
        • Package Left Hub MEMPHIS TN 07/27 04:12
        • Pickup Exception NEWTON MA 07/26 17:10
        • 22 EAST BOSTON MA 07/26 21:05
        • Left Origin Location NEWTON MA 07/26 19:50
<!--END TRACKING INFORMATION-->
```

Figure 1-1: The importance of communications technology today: an example.

expect. Yet consumers are increasingly likely to regard timely and responsive automated customer service as an integral part of the service itself.

We see similar trends within the organization. A few years ago, we all accepted the necessity to play "telephone tag" in order to get hold of an associate, customer, or supplier. Today, we take it for granted that colleagues and collaborators will have e-mail addresses, will frequently check for e-mail, and will make their key documents that are of interest to us accessible on the Web.

1.1.1 Why Build an Internetwork?

Data networking has been steadily evolving for decades now, and many successful networking technologies have emerged. The hallmark of an internetwork, as distinct from a network, is that an internetwork can comprise many networks, where each network might be under independent administration and, possibly, operating with distinct underlying transmission technologies.

We have seen that effective communications is fundamental to success in today's world. Internetworking has consistently shown itself to be an extremely efficient and effective means of constructing data communications systems. *In most cases, internetworking is the best way to do it.* It's just that simple.

An internetworking design can offer numerous advantages, including

- A large base of existing applications
- Availability of those applications on all major computing platforms
- Rapid improvements in the price/performance of internetworking-based technology over time, as vendors make major investments in the technology
- A correspondingly low risk of technological obsolescence
- Media independence, that is, the ability to flexibly intermix many kinds of underlying transmission media
- Robust, automated recovery from failures of one or more components, where economically warranted

This book is relevant to the design of both networks and internetworks but will be of particular interest to the internetwork designer. Internetworking, by virtue of its media independence, gives the designer tremendous flexibility to mix and match various transmission technologies, using each wherever it best fits. This flexibility enables richer and more complex designs; however, doing so calls for a broader perspective on the design process.

1.2 Why Is Building an Internetwork so Challenging?

Designing and building a new large-scale internetwork today is a daunting task. There are three primary reasons for this.

1. There is no well-established *process* for proceeding from concept through design to implementation of an internetwork.

2. The knowledge that would be required to do a good job is too compartmentalized in most organizations or may not be available to the design team at all.

3. The number of alternative techniques, transmission technologies, vendors, and carriers available to the designer is so great as to be bewildering.

We now proceed to consider in turn each of these three problem areas.

1.2.1 Challenge 1: Lack of a Coherent, Comprehensible Design Process for Wide Area Internetworks

A few years ago, my company and our partners were developing a bid for a major modernization of the largest civilian network in the U.S. government. My company invited me to lead a technical team working on this important proposal effort. I accepted cheerfully. I had been designing modern computer communications products for some 15 years and felt confident that the technology required for this particular project was not likely to stretch the state of the art. Designing a network based mostly on off-the-shelf commercially available hardware and software should be, I thought, a snap.

It turned out to be anything but easy. The first hint of trouble came quickly. I attempted to set up a work-breakdown structure for the design effort, in order to schedule engineers to do the work. I immediately hit a brick wall: I was astonished to realize that I did not even understand the steps that a design team would have to follow to go from design to production deployment.

Fortunately, I was able to obtain access to some very talented and experienced network design professionals. They provided me with a great deal of priceless guidance over the next few weeks. Initially, I had hoped to minimize their involvement. I asked them whether they could point to articles or perhaps to a good book about the network design process. They just rolled their eyes and shrugged.

Numerous books deal with network protocols, network applications, and network security, and a few describe network performance analysis. In reality, these are perhaps the best-understood aspects of the network design process. A few highly talented people in the industry know how to do network topological design and how to iterate toward a cost-effective solution, but very little of this know-how is available in printed form to the network designer. Most notably, the *process* of network design is poorly understood and, in general, poorly documented.

This book seeks to address that need by providing a workable internetwork design methodology that can be applied to most internetworking design projects. The book is particularly suitable for large, complex projects; it is equally suitable for designing not only public Internet service provider and carrier networks but also private intranets. I have attempted throughout to present the specific domain knowledge that is required in the context of a *uniform process and methodology for internetwork design*.

1.2.2 Challenge 2: Lack of a Holistic, Integrated View of the Wide Area Internetwork

Once the geographic reach extends beyond a single building or a single campus, the knowledge needed to create an internetwork that delivers good price/performance goes considerably beyond that required to establish an internetwork that merely *works*. At a minimum, you need to understand the following:

- Network protocols in general and the TCP/IP protocol stack in particular
- Supporting application infrastructure, such as Domain Name Service, e-mail, and the World Wide Web
- Network security
- Performance and availability analysis
- The topological design of wide area networks (WANs)
- The cost and performance aspects of services and circuits available from the carriers
- The analysis and comparison of design alternatives, including combinations of carrier services, on the basis of cost and of price/performance
- The operational structures and processes required to design, deploy, and operate a large-scale internetwork

In principle, no single domain of knowledge would appear to pose an insurmountable challenge. The problem is that this knowledge, if it exists at all, tends to be widely dispersed throughout the organization. An understanding of network protocols, servers, and security is likely to exist in a data network engineering group. Familiarity with carrier service offerings and with economic analysis of alternative mixes of offerings might exist only in the corporate telecommunications group. The knowledge of how to do topological design and to analyze performance and availability may not exist at all or may be part of yet another organizational structure. And operations expertise may be elsewhere again.

The problem is further exacerbated by differing vocabularies and mindsets among these individuals and organizations. In many cases, the network engineers are experienced in working with data, whereas the corporate telecommunications people think primarily in terms of voice traffic. The two groups are likely to have a tough time communicating with each other, which can make it surprisingly difficult to knit together a coherent, cohesive team.

1.2.3 Challenge 3: Choosing from among a Potpourri of Data Link Technologies and Carrier Service Options

In today's world, the network designer can select from an extraordinary wealth of options. One of the great strengths of internetworking, as distinct from classical networking, is the *media independence* that it offers. Routers can not only use various kinds of transmission media at the data link layer of the OSI Reference Model but also intermix them flexibly. Today, you can knit together a cost-effective hybrid networking fabric from a mixture of diverse threads.

If you were designing a wide area data network in the United States in, say, 1981, you would have spent very little time determining the best transmission technology. Nearly all networks were built by using conventional private leased lines, with a handful based on public X.25 switched services. Neither would you need to stop and consider who was going to provide your local and long-distance circuits; it would necessarily be the local telephone companies and AT&T.

Today, your data link layer technology choices might include not only leased lines but also ISDN, Frame Relay, SMDS, ATM, or direct transmission of packets over SONET, all of which are described in the chapters to come. Your local carrier choices might include various nontraditional and bypass carriers. Your long-distance carrier choices might include not only AT&T, MCI WorldCom, and Sprint but also many other companies entering the market. As an alternative or an adjunct to all of these, you might consider cryptographically encapsulating your data and sending it over the public Internet.

The carriers are eager to provide information about the capabilities and pricing of their various service offerings. As a designer, you may be deluged with more information than you know what to do with. At the same time, it can be very difficult to obtain the information that you most need.

- What are the typical strengths *and weaknesses* of each transmission technology? For what applications is each best suited?
- Over what domain is each optimal?
- Are any hidden costs associated with each service offering?
- When is it desirable to mix two or more technologies to obtain a hybrid service with better characteristics than either offers individually?

I have not attempted to provide an encyclopedic reference of current carrier offerings, as they are continually changing. I have instead tried to present the *techniques and the thought processes that a network designer might use to identify trade-off points between and among the various technologies and service offerings.* These should prove to be of value over the long haul.

1.3   Enterprise Networks, Intranets, and Extranets

Words mean exactly what I choose them to mean, neither more nor less.

—Humpty Dumpty, in Lewis Carroll, *Through the Looking Glass*

What's in a name? . . . a rose by any other name would smell as sweet.

—William Shakespeare, *Romeo and Juliet*

These days, it seems that every trade publication bombards us with references to intranets and extranets. Just what exactly are they?

Unfortunately, these trendy terms have been so widely used in the trade press, and in so many different ways, that they no longer have a single, clear, widely understood definition. In fact, if you were to ask five experts to define any of these terms, you would probably end up with seven definitions, plus or minus two. The terms have become nearly meaningless.

The pen—or rather, the keyboard—possesses great power. For purposes of this book, we will use *my* definitions of these terms.

1.3.1   Internetworking

To begin with, *internetworking* is a technology at level 3, the network layer of the OSI Reference Model.[1] Internetworking is based on the forwarding of datagrams. In the context of this book, we are concerned primarily with the

---

1. H. Zimmerman, "The OSI Reference Model—The ISO Model of Architecture for Open Systems Interconnection," *IEEE Transactions on Communications,* April 1980. See also A. Tanenbaum, *Computer Networks,* 3rd ed. (Upper Saddle River, N.J.: Prentice Hall, 1996).

forwarding of Internet Protocol (IP) datagrams, as defined in RFC 791[2] and its successors, but a number of other communications protocols also support internetworking.

1.3.2 Intranets

An *intranet* is a network based on internetworking technologies and operated on behalf of a single organization. Typically, an intranet provides for dissemination of information throughout the organization and is based on TCP/IP protocols, particularly on the technologies and protocols surrounding the World Wide Web. An intranet may share resources with other corporate networking assets; however, to the extent that the corporate network does not meet the preceding definition, it is helpful to think of the intranet as being distinct from the corporate network as a whole.

Why might you want an intranet? Intranets tend to do their job cheaply and efficiently. The users of the intranet usually enjoy total platform independence: Web browsers are widely available for the PC Windows environment, the Macintosh, and for most UNIX systems. An intranet is easy to establish because the organization probably already knows how to deal with TCP/IP and can most likely run it over an existing corporate network or internetwork. An intranet can provide economies of scale: You can use a single set of tools and applications to communicate with all of your employees. As we shall see, an *extranet* further extends these economies of scale by using the same methodologies to disseminate information to suppliers, collaborators, stockholders, customers, and other stakeholders.

1.3.3 Enterprise Networks and Enterprise Internetworks

An *enterprise network* is a network operated on behalf of a single organization. In practice, most enterprise networks today are really *enterprise internetworks* as they are based on internetworking technology.

An enterprise network differs from an intranet in a number of respects. First, an enterprise network *might* not be capable of carrying IP traffic, although nearly all can these days. Second, an enterprise network or internetwork is often capable of carrying protocols other than TCP/IP: for instance, SNA, NetWare/IPX, AppleTalk, and so on. An intranet, by contrast, need not deal with protocol suites other than TCP/IP.

As you can see, these definitions begin to blur together. If your organization already has an enterprise internetwork, you will generally want to use it

---

2. J. Postel, Request for Comments (RFC) 791, "Internet Protocol," September 1981.

as a foundation for your intranet; however, the enterprise internetwork may need to be upgraded to meet new requirements.

An intranet uses technologies based on the World Wide Web to disseminate information throughout the organization. An enterprise network or internetwork does not necessarily use the Web or, if it does, does not necessarily use it for *internal* dissemination of information.

1.3.4   The Internet

The *Internet* represents the global public IP-based internetworking system. An intranet is internal to a single organization; the Internet spans tens of millions of individuals and vast numbers of organizations. An intranet serves members (employees) of the organization; the Internet serves the general public.

Your organization probably has an internal telephone network based on some kind of PBX or switchboard. You can think of the relationship between your corporate voice network and the global telephone network as being analogous to that between your intranet and the global Internet. In other words,

Corporate phone system : Global telephone network :: Intranet : Global Internet

In most cases, your intranet will be connected to the public Internet. This is usually done at a small number of physical locations, in the interest of economy and security.

Because the Internet is open to many Internet service providers (ISPs) and a huge customer base, data that traverses the Internet is exposed to numerous security hazards. Data within an intranet, by contrast, is logically within the organization's security perimeter, in general, and thus is subject to corporate security policies. Typically, your organization will position firewalls between your intranet and the Internet, in order to define a security perimeter that does not include the Internet as a whole. This is shown in Figure 1-2.

1.3.5   Extranets

An intranet serves members of an organization; an *extranet,* by contrast, serves those who have a special relationship with the organization—customers, suppliers, collaborators, shareholders, and other stakeholders—but who do not enjoy the level of trust typically associated with an employee. Extranet participants have access to facilities that are not available to the general public but generally do not have access identical to that of employees.

Since communication with external participants is generally outside of the organization's security perimeter, end-to-end security is required. Typically,

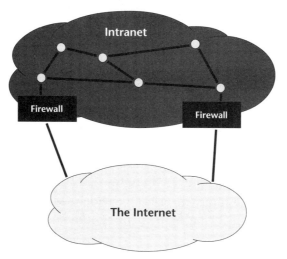

Figure 1-2: An intranet uses firewalls to insulate itself
from the global Internet.

the user's data is *cryptographically encapsulated* (we sometimes say that it is *tunneled*) through the public Internet, as depicted by the dotted lines through the Internet in Figure 1-3.

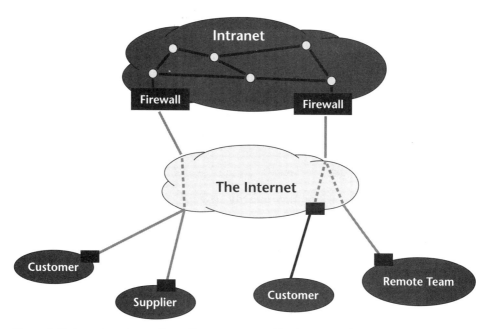

Figure 1-3: An extranet uses firewalls to cryptographically encapsulate traffic that must traverse the global Internet.

What we mean by this is that firewalls—or, alternatively, the end systems themselves—encode the data cryptographically prior to sending it across the public Internet. This is done to prevent third parties from seeing or modifying the data. Typically, the sending firewall encrypts the data, then "wraps it up" (encapsulates it) within an exterior IP datagram, and then sends this IP "sandwich" to a receiving firewall, which reverses the process. This entire process is transparent to the end systems but is essential to ensuring the privacy and integrity of their communications.

Note, incidentally, that although the cryptographic encapsulation is most often performed at the customer's premises (gray), it is also possible to provide it as a part of the Internet service provider's service, at the edge of the lower cloud in Figure 1-3. The figure depicts both possibilities, with firewalls shown in black.

1.3.6 Virtual Private Networks (VPNs) and Internet Virtual Private Networks (iVPNs)

A *virtual private network*, or *VPN*, can mean any of a number of things, depending on the context. These meanings are similar but not quite equivalent.

- In the *voice telephony* world, a VPN generally refers to the use of carrier-provided facilities to provide voice services tailored to an organization's needs, instead of a large number of dedicated circuits.
- In the *data communications* world, a VPN often refers to the use of carrier-provided fast packet, such as Frame Relay, facilities to provide data services tailored to an organization's enterprise networking needs, instead of a large number of dedicated circuits.
- In the *internetworking* world, a VPN generally refers to the use of ISP-provided IP-based facilities to provide data services tailored to an organization's internetworking needs, instead of a large number of dedicated circuits or fast packet services.

Since this book is oriented primarily toward internetworks, we are generally most interested in the third of these definitions. Where the potential for confusion exists, we will refer to the third case as an *Internet virtual private network*, or *iVPN*.

A typical iVPN is depicted in Figure 1-4. Note that the iVPN uses cryptographic encapsulation across the public Internet, just as the extranet does. In this case, however, it is the *intranet* that is being extended with tunneling. The organization's security perimeter (shown in gray) is being extended. Note, however, that the area between the firewalls is not within the organization's

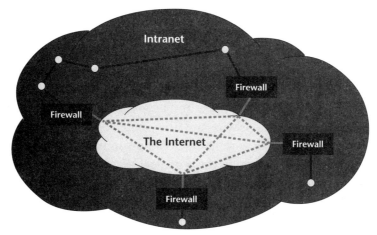

Figure 1-4: An Internet virtual private network (iVPN).

security perimeter; the *tunnels* across the Internet are within the security perimeter, but the Internet itself is not.

Unlike an extranet, the use of an iVPN does not necessarily provide any unique functionality. For dedicated access, an iVPN can be viewed as a direct price/performance alternative to the use of conventional leased lines, Frame Relay, and ATM to carry IP traffic.

To date, relatively few iVPNs have been deployed for dedicated domestic U.S. access. Many analysts predict that iVPNs will become commonplace in the next few years, largely displacing conventional IP over Frame Relay internetworks; my own belief, however, is that dedicated U.S. domestic iVPNs will continue to be a small niche player, for the simple reason that the overall price/performance of the dedicated iVPN, when properly understood, is usually inferior to that of the conventional IP over Frame Relay intranet. Dialup iVPNs and international dedicated iVPNs, by contrast, are likely to be commonplace. We will return to this question in Chapter 6.

1.4   What Changes When You Cross a Street?

Designing an internetwork to function within a building or within a campus of buildings is, at this point, a fairly well-defined and well-understood process. Typically, an organization will deploy a combination of local area networks (LANs), routers, and switches to interconnect the various workstations and servers. The costs are predictable and deterministic, for the most part, and there is no great magic to this process.

The minute that you cross a public thoroughfare—yes, a *street*—the world changes in fundamental ways. Suddenly, you need permits and approvals if you want to string the wires yourself. Moreover, running fiber-optic cable or wire over long distances is capital intensive and requires specialized skill sets.

Most organizations find it simpler and far more cost-effective to let someone else deal with the basics of wire and fiber-optic connectivity. Usually, they leave this to a carrier, a conventional telephone company (*telco*), although it is now possible, in some cases, to use a cable TV company or any of a number of wireless alternatives.

This world is no longer simple and self-contained. Many of the services that you might want to obtain from the telco are tariffed, which is to say that there is a service definition and a price filed with a public authority. Each country has its own procedures for regulating carriers; in the United States, tariffs are usually filed either with a state public utilities commission or with the U.S. *Federal Communications Commission (FCC)*. You may want services that are not tariffed, in which case you must obtain a price quotation from the telco on an *individual case basis (ICB)*.

Wide area circuit and service costs can represent anywhere from 30 percent to 80 percent of the total cost of operation of your network, depending on your individual circumstances. There are strong economic motivations to so design your network as to make efficient use of the services available to you.

1.5   Evolution and Change

Are we not all familiar . . . with the layout of an international airport? As we emerge from the aircraft, we see (over to our right or left) a lofty structure wrapped in scaffolding. Then the air hostess leads us into a hut with an asbestos roof. Nor do we suppose for a moment that it will ever be otherwise. By the time the permanent building is complete the airfield will have been moved to another site. . . .

It is now known that a perfection of planned layout is achieved only by institutions on the point of collapse. . . . perfection of planning is a symptom of decay. During a period of exciting discovery or progress there is no time to plan the perfect headquarters. The time for that comes later, when all the important work has been done. Perfection, we know, is finality; and finality is death.[3]

---

3. C. Northcote Parkinson, *Parkinson's Law and Other Studies in Administration* (Cambridge, Mass.: The Riverside Press, 1957), pp. 60–61.

In the classic "waterfall" model of technology development, one might start with marketing requirements, extrapolated forward over a period of several years, and design a system in a forward-looking way to economically meet all of the anticipated requirements. One would reflect an anticipated growth in traffic and in requirements in general by planning for a phased implementation accommodating all expected needs.

This is how we would like things to work. In reality, none of us are that good! The network designs that can be accomplished with a high degree of confidence and assurance, over a planning horizon extending more than a couple of years, are typically for organizations that are stodgy, static, or moribund.

An enterprise internetwork is likely to undergo rapid growth and evolution. The technology is advancing at a mind-numbing rate. Traffic increases. New devices become available. New applications come into vogue. Traffic increases. New security threats appear. And traffic inexorably increases. Each of these places new demands on the network design.

I used to work with a network that routinely experienced a doubling of traffic *every four months*—an amazing eightfold increase per year! If that trend had continued unabated, traffic for that network would have increased by a factor of 500 in just 3 years. Devices capable of carrying that load without buckling under the strain might not have even existed when I needed them.

Under such conditions, any network design will require continual adaptation and rework in ways that we cannot hope to fully anticipate. The most important thing we can do under such circumstances is to recognize our limitations and to work for a design that is clean, straightforward, and as flexible as possible.

Squeezing needless cost out of the design is always important; however, reducing cost at the expense of the ultimate flexibility or scalability of the system can be a very bad idea. Simpler designs tend to scale better. Reducing cost by increasing complexity will often prove to be penny wise and pound foolish.

1.6   The Real World Impinges

Politics is the art of the possible.

—Otto von Bismarck

This book makes frequent reference to the OSI Reference Model. You are doubtless familiar with this classic seven-layer model of network architecture. In recent years, it has become fashionable to speak with tongue in cheek of a nine-layer model, as in Figure 1-5.

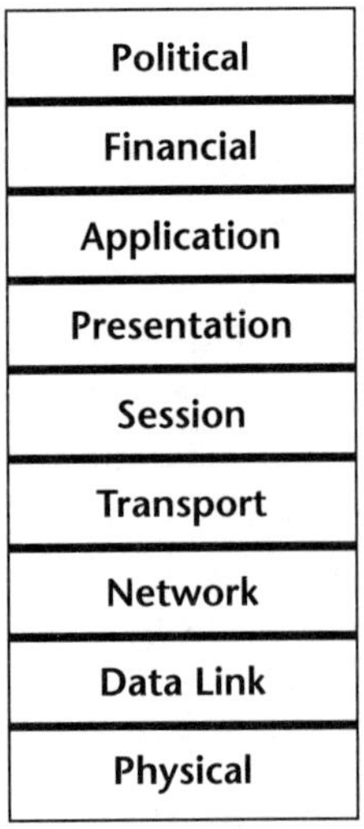

Political
Financial
Application
Presentation
Session
Transport
Network
Data Link
Physical

Figure 1-5: The nine-layer version of the OSI Reference Model.

As you can see, immediately above the classic seven-layer description of network architecture are the financial and the political layers. We have a natural tendency to think of these as being in some sense antithetical to our function as engineers. In fact, political and financial considerations are fundamental to our task.

It is important to bear in mind that no matter how good your design, it will not be built unless certain key decision makers in your organization believe that it is an appropriate and cost-effective solution to perceived organizational needs.

If those needs were articulated with perfect precision, your task might be straightforward. You would attempt to build the best, most cost-effective solution to the stated requirements. In practice, things never happen that way. Networks are designed to meet multiple organizational needs, usually associated with multiple constituencies. The needs of those constituencies are at best imperfectly aligned. Even if your management were able to provide guidance as to how to prioritize conflicting needs, it is unlikely that it would be equipped to translate this guidance into terms explicitly relevant to your network design.

In practice, the network designer often plays a key role in resolving disputes driven by conflicting needs among stakeholders in

> **Law of Network Design**
> No network design exists in a vacuum. The network exists to meet organizational needs.

the network; the network designer is often the individual best able to articulate the inherent trade-offs in various potential design decisions. For this reason, *it is important that you cultivate not only strong technical understanding but also mature business judgment.*

Again, there is a natural tendency to think that the time that we, as engineers, invest in presenting and "selling" the design to our senior management is a distraction from our real job function. In fact, it is the very essence of our task. Throughout this book, I have attempted to treat political and financial issues as an integral part of the design task.

2 The Internetwork Design Process: Overview

How does a modern internetwork progress from concept to realization? There does not appear to be an industry consensus. Indeed, the number of processes that have been attempted is only slightly less than the number of internetworks that have been built or attempted!

There is no single right way to go about the design process. The approach in this book is to describe a workable and adequate process that can be applied to a wide range of situations.

The remainder of the book is organized around this internetwork design process, proceeding in a top-down fashion from greatest abstraction to greatest specificity. In doing so, I have attempted to present specific techniques at the point in the design process at which you would first employ them.

This chapter describes the internetwork process at the highest level of abstraction. It represents a view from the 30,000 feet level—a big picture view, albeit with very little supporting detail. Successive chapters explode each phase of the design process into successively greater levels of detail and specificity.

No organization builds an expensive internetwork for the sheer joy of doing so. At the outset, there must exist a perceived *need*—a business or organizational requirement or opportunity that motivates the entire exercise. In order to fulfill this perceived requirement, we launch a four-phase design effort as follows:

- Phase 1—Definition of requirements: What must this network do?
- Phase 2—Preliminary design: What design can best fulfill the requirements?
- Phase 3—Management review: Now that we understand what the network could do and what it will cost, what are we as an organization willing to deploy?

■ Phase 4—Final design: Based on management guidance, we complete the design and proceed to deployment.

You may find it helpful to think of this design process as an (inverted) tree structure, with the root at the top, very much like an organization chart. The highest levels of the process look like the structure shown in Figure 2-1.

2.1   Phase 1: Definition of Requirements

To accomplish anything in life, you need two things: *resource* and *motive*. In the course of the design process, you will determine how much resource is required, to whatever level of precision you need. But what motivates you to build the network in the first place? What requirements must the network meet to fulfill your needs, and how well must it meet them?

The requirements definition phase of the design process deals with these harder, more fundamental, yet less tangible, questions and attempts to translate your organization's overall communications needs and desires into quantifiable design criteria that are meaningful to an engineer.

■ What business needs are motivating my organization to build or enhance this network?

■ What applications will this network initially serve?

■ What applications is the network likely to need to serve in the future as the network and the user community evolve?

■ What kinds of users must the network serve initially and in the future?

■ What levels of service would the ideal network offer, with particular emphasis on performance, availability, and security requirements?

■ What levels of service would a minimally acceptable network offer?

■ If we sacrifice quality (performance, response time, or reliability) in some specific ways in comparison to the ideal network, such that the network would still meet its minimum requirements, how much business are we likely to forgo (sensitivity analysis)? What is the economic impact to our organization?

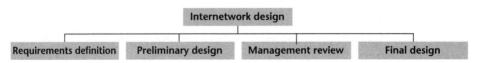

Figure 2-1: The internetwork design process.

During this phase, you will attempt to zero in on workable answers to these questions, with particular emphasis on service locations and on functional, performance, availability, and security requirements. The definition of requirements phase is described in Chapter 3.

2.2 Phase 2: Preliminary Design

What is the most appropriate systems solution for your organization, balancing market and application requirements against cost?

The preliminary design phase provides initial answers to all of the key design questions that determine the nature and the cost of the network. Among the issues that must be considered and resolved are

- Selection of the major transmission technologies to be used in the network
- Determination of the number of levels of hierarchy in the network
- Creation of a preliminary backbone topological design
- Creation of a preliminary access design
- Creation of a preliminary technical design, to include naming and addressing, routing, security, and network management
- Verification that the design meets the requirements

The preliminary design phase is discussed in Chapters 4–16.

2.3 Phase 3: Management Review

The management review phase is critical but little understood. By the end of phase 2, preliminary design, you have developed a moderately detailed design and have reached a good understanding of what that design will cost your organization. Is a network of that quality and that cost going to meet the business needs of your organization? As you read this, you are likely to have a question on the tip of your tongue: "Would any organization do the entire preliminary design without having already made a business judgment to proceed with implementation? Surely the business case would have already been justified before the preliminary design was launched?"

If the network in question represents a fairly minor enhancement to an existing, running network, it is quite possible that the initial business case will reflect meaningful, detailed cost data. For a new or substantially changed network, however, the costs are rarely fully understood when you begin the design process. In many cases, the uncertainty in the estimated cost of the network is likely to be greater than the anticipated profitability of the network (or the change to profitability of an existing network) until roughly the end of the preliminary design phase.

In other words, the initial business case will have been based on very rough costing estimates. These estimates are likely to be off by a wide margin, and experience suggests that they are more likely to be low than high. Until the costing associated with the preliminary design is complete, you have no idea whether your organization will really make money or reduce net costs or otherwise benefit as you hope.

It is my belief that the great majority of networks undergo an extensive management review as soon as the costs have been quantified in moderate detail. This activity may not be planned or scheduled, but it generally happens nonetheless. Many network design projects encounter significant delays at this point, and some never see the light of day as a result of this review. It is my contention that it is better to plan for this activity and to schedule it than to quietly wait for the inevitable.

In a very real sense, this is the "sticker shock" phase of the internetwork design process. In many cases, we are forced to acknowledge that we cannot afford the ideal solution. Your initial definition of requirements should have included considerable sensitivity analysis, to help you to estimate the economic impact of deploying an adequate but less than ideal internetwork. This is the design phase in which we use that sensitivity analysis to reconcile the ideal with the real, wishes with reality. The feasibility analysis phase is described in Chapter 17.

2.4   Phase 4: Final Design

In the course of the final design phase, you attempt to fill in the gaps in the previous work in order to arrive at a deployable and complete design. In part, you will be fleshing out the work done during the preliminary design (phase 2), adapting it to reflect any midcourse corrections that may have emerged as a result of the management review (phase 3). In part, you will be doing new work at a greater level of detail. The key new tasks for the final design phase include

- Selection of carriers
- Selection of equipment vendors
- Optimization of the overall design

- Creation of the physical design
- Creation of the deployment schedule

When these activities are complete, you will once again analyze your costs. The final design phase is described in Chapters 18 and 19. After that, it is time to roll up not your costs but your *sleeves*. The network deployment is ready to begin.

3 Definition of Requirements

In some senses, the definition of requirements, phase 1, is the most critical phase in the network design process, yet this phase is frequently shortchanged. Too often, we are in a hurry to solve a business problem or to close a sale to a customer. We think we understand the answer before we have properly formulated the question.

Every network design must flow organically from business or organizational needs. In the definition of requirements phase, we seek to identify these needs and to abstract them into quantitative terms that a designer can deal with—nothing more and nothing less.

We designers tend to enjoy the engineering and mathematical aspects of the job. Definition of requirements is largely a business problem that may seem somewhat foreign to us. There is, consequently, a tremendous temptation to shortchange this phase, during which we are bored and ill at ease, and to leap ahead to phase 2, the preliminary design, which is perhaps the most intellectually stimulating phase of the project.

The following point cannot be stressed too strongly: *No matter what the technical merits of your design may be, if the design fails to address key needs of your organization, it is a bad design.* Trying to base a good network design on a poor or inadequate understanding of the underlying requirements is exactly like trying to erect a good house on a poor foundation: It is an ultimately futile effort. This chapter describes the key issues that your design needs to consider.

3.1 Identify Access Locations

You are seeking to provide interconnectivity to numerous users and systems. Where are they located?

Your user community is situated at some combination of stationary, permanent, continuously connected locations; stationary, episodically connected locations; and fully mobile locations. These modes of connection are already familiar to us. The first is suitable, for instance, for server systems. The second would be appropriate for telecommuters, who dial in as needed but usually from a constant location. The third would be useful for "road warriors," individuals who dial in as needed from wherever they happen to be. We are just beginning to see an extreme variant of this last option: someone who might want to maintain continuous network access while driving down the highway!

Outside of the United States, you generally need a full street address to obtain service or even to obtain a meaningful price quotation. For domestic locations, you can usually price the circuits with just the NPA (area code) and NXX (exchange, the first three digits of the seven-digit phone number) of the phone line.

3.2 Identify Application Requirements

Your network requirements are ultimately driven by the applications that will use the network. These may be of three types: Internet protocols, transaction processing, and realtime voice or video applications.

3.2.1 Internet versus Non-Internet Protocols

Internet protocols are very much in vogue at the moment; the IP protocol is very suitable for use across a wide area network. However, the Internet protocols do not represent the totality of data networking traffic. If your organization is like most, a significant portion of your networking traffic is still likely to be a mixture of IPX (Novell NetWare), AppleTalk, IBM Systems Network Architecture (SNA), DECnet, NETBIOS, or Banyan Vines. Some of these protocols are overly sensitive to network delay; some, such as SNA and NETBIOS, are not designed to function as routed protocols—at least not in the same sense in which TCP/IP is a routed protocol.

One of the most fundamental decisions you must reach is how to deal with these "legacy" protocols. Possible solutions include

- Prohibiting the use of the protocols across the wide area altogether
- Requiring that legacy protocols be encapsulated in IP before routing them across the wide area
- Routing the legacy protocols in parallel with IP

Each of these approaches has pros and cons, and each has unique pitfalls.

3.2.2   Transaction Processing

Will your network be processing significant numbers of transactions, such as updating the billing records of a major corporation? If so, this is likely to imply stringent response time and reliability requirements and will probably impose additional security requirements as well. Often the network design interacts with the design of the associated application in complex ways—especially as regards database management systems and application program interfaces (APIs).

3.2.3   Realtime Voice or Video

It is becoming increasingly common to transmit voice or video over fast packet technologies, including IP. This places some unusual demands on these protocols.

In delivering voice to a recipient, it is not necessary that every bit be delivered error free; however, it is important that the delay be very predictable and free of variability in delay that would be heard as "jitter." It is easy to delay delivery of an audio signal to a listener in order to give datagrams that were delayed due to statistical multiplexing a little extra time to catch up; however, if the delays get too great, they get in the way of a two-way conversation. If you have ever conducted a transoceanic satellite-link telephone conversation, you are familiar with this phenomenon.

The injection of a large fixed delay might work quite well for video or audio on demand applications, in which a few seconds of initial delay might be perfectly acceptable. Once the transmission gets going, it could be quite smooth. A large fixed delay would be much less satisfactory for two or more parties attempting to converse in realtime.

A great deal of work is going on in this area, particularly in regard to the use of a TCP/IP-based *Resource reSerVation Protocol* (RSVP) and in the diffserv (differentiated services) working group of the IETF. The intent of both efforts is to assure end-to-end delay characteristics for an IP flow—in the case of RSVP, by reserving resources in advance along the path the packets will take. Diffserv takes the more modest approach of marking traffic at the edges of the network and then providing realtime data with favored service within the routers. For the moment, these approaches would have to be viewed as being somewhat avant-garde, and there is considerable doubt that RSVP will ever be suitable for large-scale commercial deployment. Diffserv is simpler and is felt by many to be more scalable and thus more viable. It is moderately likely that diffserv implementations will become widely deployed within the next few years.

A third approach to intermixing realtime voice or video traffic with data traffic would be to use Frame Relay or ATM services, possibly as a means of carrying voice over IP. Further, the design of ATM specifically accommodates the intermixing of constant bit rate (CBR) applications, such as voice and video, with variable bit rate or available bit rate applications (data). The "catch" is that this is useful only if ATM is available on an end-to-end basis to all of the workstations to which you might wish to deliver this service.

There was a time when ATM proponents claimed that we would soon be living in a golden age in which this would be the case; however, very few people would make this claim today. Most of us believe that the world is heterogeneous in regard to data link layer protocols and will remain so for the indefinite future. Under these assumptions, IP-based solutions for carrying realtime voice and video are more interesting than pure ATM-based solutions for many environments.

3.3 Identify Traffic Patterns

A given user population and set of applications is likely to have a certain predictable distribution, or "signature," of traffic across the months of the year, the days of the week, and the hours of the day. Traffic internal to a business enterprise, for instance, tends to occur primarily between 8:00 A.M. and 5:00 P.M. local time, Mondays through Fridays. Traffic from residential consumers, by contrast, tends to be heaviest right after dinner on weekdays, building to a peak at 10:00 P.M. and then tailing off at about 2:00 A.M.

Broad averages of traffic are analytically convenient but are of limited value to the designer. They describe the overall state to which the system might converge over the long run. Your user, sitting at his or her terminal, is not likely to be willing to wait 4 hours for the midday data traffic to die down: The average in the long run is largely irrelevant to this user. In many cases, the shorter-term behavior of your network is more important.

As network designers, we generally have to allocate capacity sufficient to accommodate something close to the peak load that we would normally expect to see. As a result, seasonal, weekly, and diurnal variations are of great importance to us.

3.4 Determine Performance Requirements

We all want good network performance. How good is good enough? Establishing suitable target levels for the performance of the network can avoid a lot of confusion over objectives. The target performance levels that you establish could have a great deal of impact on the price/performance of your network. At what point is it better to save money than to improve the network?

Following is a brief discussion of the performance requirements you will need to understand during phase 1, requirements definition, of your project. These topics are discussed in more depth in Chapter 16.

3.4.1 Throughput and the Traffic Matrix

A *traffic matrix* describes the traffic requirements, in terms of bits per unit time, that we wish to transmit from a given service location in the network to each other service location in the network. A traffic matrix can be structured to show us the average traffic in a network. Alternatively, it may represent a measure of near-peak traffic, such as the average traffic during the busiest hour of the day, or the ninety-fifth percentile of utilization among 10-minute samples for the day. One way or another, our traffic matrix needs to represent a measure of the peak or near-peak load, the load for which the network must be designed. Note, however, that we do not generally design to the absolute maximum possible traffic intensity; that would be too expensive. How would you go about generating such a traffic matrix?

The form of the traffic matrix is straightforward, but the answer to this question is not. Routers provide good instrumentation for monitoring the traffic levels across a link but poor instrumentation when it comes to monitoring traffic to each possible destination. This is due, in part, to router vendors' reluctance to incur the significant processing overhead that would be required to maintain a table reflecting every possible destination. Such a table would also consume a great deal of memory and would consequently need to be dumped or cleared at frequent intervals. This dumping or clearing functionality would add complexity. For all of these reasons, it has been difficult to motivate the router vendors to implement the necessary functionality.

In a few instances, you may be able to infer the traffic matrix from the nature of the underlying applications. If your network is based on a switched technology, you may be able to determine the traffic matrix by querying the switches. Otherwise, you are likely to determine the traffic matrix by monitoring an existing network using an independent probe technology, such as Remote Monitoring Netflow (RMON). My own organization has been very successful in using the capabilities of Cisco routers as a means of developing traffic matrices, but doing so required a significant software development effort on our part.

It is quite possible that you will be unable to directly determine the traffic matrix. In that case, the best you can do is to make some educated guesses, taking all known data, including link traffic levels, into account.

3.4.2 Delay and Latency

If you allocate too little capacity to your links, switches, or routers in comparison to your traffic, you will tend to experience high queuing delays. Thus, your delay requirements are important in that they strongly influence how much bandwidth you will need to allocate to your links.

In an IP-based internetwork, delay and latency are usually not critical; however, this depends heavily on the nature of the applications that are running. If your network will also carry protocols other than TCP/IP, such as SNA or IPX, you should recognize that those protocols can be very sensitive to delay.

The TELNET protocol, for instance, is a TCP/IP-based virtual terminal protocol. UNIX systems have traditionally echoed each character back to the user as soon as he or she types it in, due largely to the need to respond to characters that might initiate specific actions. (As an example, the UNIX vi editor interprets a Control-D character as a request to scroll forward a few lines.) For a TELNET user, delay can be very important: If the delay is too great, the user receives no feedback from the characters that he or she is typing until the echoed character has made its way all the way to the destination and back.

At the opposite end of the spectrum, we have SMTP (Simple Mail Transport Protocol) and NNTP (Network News Transfer Protocol). Mail is an important, high-volume application for most organizations but is not a time-critical application. Mail can operate as a background task, whenever the system and the network have nothing better to do.

Most Web-browsing applications function in the middle of this spectrum. There is no requirement for character-at-a-time responses; however, after initiating an action, the user would like to see the beginnings of a response fairly quickly, preferably within half a second. Most of us have become inured to downloads that take a while, but we like the screen to be refreshed fairly quickly.

For a protocol such as TCP/IP, delay can also serve to limit effective throughput. TCP allocates only so much memory to a connection and associates a *window* with this allocation. The sending TCP will transmit enough data to fill the receiver's window and then must halt until the receiving TCP acknowledges receipt of at least some of the data and reopens the window, thus offering to accept more data. If the network suffers from high latency, the sender will wait a long time for its acknowledgment. This long wait will result in a low effective transmission rate for the session, which may be visible to the user, particularly for file transfers and download operations.

3.4.3 Variability of Delay

Variability of delay could be important for either of two reasons.

■ You may be sending realtime interactive video or interactive audio across the network.

■ Numerous studies have shown that a highly variable delay is far more jarring to users than is a longer but more predictable delay

If you are not planning to carry realtime interactive voice or video over your network, you might well regard variability of delay as being of secondary importance.

3.4.4 Packet Drops

Earlier, we noted the impact that insufficient link, switch, or router capacity can have on queuing delays. Insufficient link or switching capacity can also result in a large number of packets being queued for transmission. If your links are sized too small, for instance, their utilization will tend to be too high. This, in turn, will cause queuing time to go up on the outbound links.

Little's law, a fundamental result from queuing theory, tells us that the size of the queue will be linearly proportionate to the waiting time. As the size of the queue increases, the probability increases that the number of packets queued up will exceed the buffering capacity of the switch or router. At that point, the switch or router has no choice but to drop one or more packets. In most cases, these packet drops will result in far more incremental delay than will the queuing delays.

3.4.5 Misrouted Data

In most cases, the probability of misrouted data in a TCP/IP environment is low enough to be ignored. In any case, the data is unlikely to do harm, since most applications use TCP to deliver the data. TCP requires multiple successful segments with an appropriate sequence of sequence numbers. The likelihood of a random misdelivered datagram causing any damage is negligible. If security is important, and particularly if you have significant use of UDP (User Datagram Protocol), which is not connection oriented, you may want to establish specific quantitative objectives for misrouted data.

3.4.6 Availability

Availability requirements can have a particularly strong impact on network price/performance, yet very few engineers can translate a required availability level into a specific design based on circuits and equipment. Typically, availability is expressed as a percentage. The challenge is to obtain the desired availability, which is often expressed as the "number of nines." For example, there can be a big difference between a network that offers 99.9 percent availability and one that offers 99.99 percent.

In Chapter 16, we'll show you how to use conditional probability to compute the expected availability. For now, you should understand that availability is simply

$$\text{Availability} = \text{Time available} / \text{Time potentially available}$$

Note that time potentially available is usually defined so as to exclude scheduled downtime. Availability can also be computed as

$$\text{Availability} = \text{MTBF} / (\text{MTBF} + \text{MTTR})$$

where MTBF represents the *mean time between failures* (the average time between outages for a given circuit or item of equipment) and MTTR is the *mean time to repair* the circuit or other piece of gear once it's broken. MTBF and MTTR are typically expressed in hours.

3.5 Determine Security Requirements

The uses to which we intend to put the network drive the security requirements for our network, and these strongly influence the security architecture and many elements of the cost of the network. Some networks require very little security; others may require a great deal. Web sites that provide only publicly available advertising material may fall in the former category, while networks that support the national defense or that provide electronic funds transfers will tend to be in the latter category.

It is useful to review the typical security services that a network could offer and to consider how these relate to network design. Security requirements and techniques are discussed in more detail in Chapter 13. The following list simply identifies various aspects of security.

- **Authentication.** This security service unambiguously determines who a user of the network, or party, is. Authentication is a fundamental prerequisite to most other network security services.

   Not every network service requires authentication. As an example, advertising on the Web might be publicly available to all parties, irrespective of who you are or of how you access the network.

Today, many organizations perceive a need for stronger authentication than a multiple-use password can offer. It is just too easy for a malefactor to "snoop" the password and to use it to impersonate an authorized individual. Suitable techniques include "smart cards" with single-use passwords and certificates incorporating cryptographic signatures.

- **Authorization.** This security service determines whether a given party has the right to do something specific. In many cases, authorization and authentication are implemented through a single mechanism. For example, when you log in to a UNIX host, you establish your userid (authentication) and also obtain certain rights, such as the right to read or update files (authorization). In this case, your knowledge of a password confers certain rights on you.

- **Integrity.** This network service ensures that the data received is the same as that which was intended. Integrity means that the data has not been corrupted, either maliciously or inadvertently, while en route. As an example, a software downloading service might use a cryptographic checksum to reduce the risk of "Trojan horse" modifications to the programs.

- **Privacy.** The service that prevents others from knowing what was sent, privacy is generally implemented by using bulk encryption.

- **Nonrepudiation.** This security service is particularly important for financial transactions. If I as a customer order something from an electronic catalog and you as an electronic merchant ship the merchandise to me, you need to be able to bill me for the item. You cannot afford to have me claim that I never ordered the item. You need an electronic signature that I cannot *repudiate,* or disclaim.

Numerous security attacks are possible today. Some may matter to you; others may not.

Denial of service, an increasingly common threat, can be difficult to guard against. Someone may intentionally or inadvertently place service demands on your servers or network that reduce their availability to legitimate users. An example of this is a recent TCP SYN attack; hackers sent a huge number of requests to an ISP's mail server to open TCP connections. These connections never fully opened, but the half-open connections consumed resources on the server, rendering it incapable of performing its mission.

Traffic analysis, by contrast, is a threat that many organizations could safely choose to ignore. A malefactor might be quite interested in knowing with whom you are communicating. This tends to be a significant concern to the military but generally not to commercial users.

3.6 Consider Cost

Cost plays a curious, dual role in the network design process. Consider, for a moment, the mathematical discipline called *mathematical programming* with its better-known subset, *linear programming*. In mathematical programming or linear programming, we seek to minimize an *objective function,* usually a measure of cost, subject to various *constraints* on the variables.

For most purposes, we would tend to think of cost as the objective function of the network design process, the thing that we are trying to minimize subject to our various requirements. Yet cost can also be viewed as a constraint. If cost globally exceeds a particular threshold, the network as a whole becomes commercially infeasible. If certain specific elements of cost exceed relevant thresholds, aspects of the overall business model may be at risk. Therefore, it is useful to think of cost as a constraint, not just as something to minimize or control. In particular, it is helpful to consider in advance the range within which the cost must fall.

The Preliminary Design Phase

4 Preliminary Design: Overview

These are heady times! If you are ready to begin the preliminary design phase, it generally means that you have passed some significant milestones.

- You have achieved enough of a working consensus about requirements to enable you to know what you are building, and why.
- Your management has allocated enough time and money to afford a reasonable prospect of actually delivering the network you are setting out to build.

The preliminary design phase is perhaps the most intellectually stimulating phase of the design process. Designing a modern internetwork is complex, and the potential interactions among the various aspects of the design are complicated, ill-specified, and, in some cases, poorly explained by existing theory. Getting it right can be quite a challenge!

There is no single, well-understood, right way to go about this. In this book, I have simply tried to present a logical sequence of steps, based on significant experience, without claiming that they are either perfect or ideal (see Table 4-1.) In practice, we are all operating in an incredibly fast-paced industry. No seasoned network designer would pretend to have followed a sequence like this with military precision. Events force us to deal with evolving circumstances and to continually revisit assumptions from each aspect of the overall design. Thus, although the sequence of tasks presented here represents a useful model, you should be prepared to adapt it as needed to meet your circumstances.

Table 4-1: Steps of the Preliminary Internetwork Design Process

Step	Objective	Deliverable
Select transmission technologies.	Determine the most appropriate mix of private line, Frame Relay, ATM, and so on.	Contributes to the topological design.
Determine levels of hierarchy.	Determine how many layers of hierarchy your internetwork will use.	Contributes to the topological design.
Identify backbone locations.	Identify the service locations for the backbone.	Contributes to the topological design.
Create access design.	Determine how your end-service locations will be connected to the network.	Contributes to the topological design.
Create access homing design.	Determine how each access layer will be homed to successively higher layers of the internetwork.	Contributes to the topological design.
Create backbone design.	Determine the topology of the backbone itself.	Contributes to the topological design.
Consider names, addresses, and routing.	Decide how you will route data and how you will allocate IP addresses and domain names.	Establishes the naming, addressing, and routing plan.
Create security plan.	Determine how you will mitigate exposure to internal and external hackers and deal with other security hazards.	Devises security plan.
Consider public Internet implications.	Adapt your design if your network is a public Internet provider or if your design is heavily based on the public Internet.	Contributes to the topological design.
Create network management plan.	Determine how you will operate the network: how you will deal with faults, how you will provision service to a new location, how you will expand capacity where needed, and how you will allocate charges.	Sets up network management plan.

4.1 Consider the Existing Network and Its Users

The Germans speak of designing "auf eine grüne Wiese"—on a green meadow. By this, they mean designing as if absolutely nothing had come before, as if the world were pure, flat, and pristine. We would all like to be able to design with no constraints other than those imposed by the underlying logic of our problem.

Occasionally, we are fortunate enough to be able to do so. More often, however, we have to deal with an existing network, with existing applications, and with existing internal or external customers. Each of these existing factors may impose maddening limitations, thwarting us from evolving the network in the direction in which we would think it should go. This can be particularly frustrating to those of us with an engineering temperament: Much of our satisfaction derives from clean and efficient design. The "legacy" infrastructure and installed base just gets in the way.

All I can counsel is *patience!* Those infernal customers probably represent the core business on which the new infrastructure must be cost-justified. Their needs for a graceful and painless migration are legitimate. Try to stay focused on your organization's business needs and to avoid getting carried away with love of technology for its own sake. Technophilia, the obsessive love of technology, is all too common a malady in our industry.

If you are working with an existing network, many of the steps in the model design process can be abbreviated or even eliminated. You may not have the need—or the ability—to change your backbone locations. You may want to add a transmission technology or two, but you will probably find it more difficult to eliminate any. Perhaps your addressing plan will require only minor enhancements, while your naming plan may be fine just as it is. You are likely to find the model sequence of tasks to be a useful checklist, just to make sure that you have considered everything that you need to, but you should not attempt to follow it slavishly.

In upgrading an existing internetwork, you should always bear in mind the old saw: *If it ain't broke, don't fix it.* Logic tells us that the contrapositive must also hold: *If it is broke, do fix it.* Dealing with an existing infrastructure *is* difficult. Do what you can to improve it without breaking it, and try to learn to relish that extra challenge!

4.2 Steps in the Preliminary Design Phase

The chapters that follow present the tasks of the preliminary design phase. The balance of this chapter introduces the topics on which those chapters will expand.

4.2.1   Select the Major Transmission Technologies

In the old days, if we chose to design an X.25 network, that choice carried an extraordinary amount of baggage with it. There were rippling implications into every nook and cranny of the network, from the security framework to the network management infrastructure. Today, we have a wide array of transmission media and protocols to choose from, including leased lines, Frame Relay, SMDS, and ATM. Moreover, internetworking enables us to mix and match! Our choice of technologies still drives many aspects of the design, but it is not nearly so one-dimensional as in former times. Chapter 5 provides necessary background on network cost elements and cost optimization techniques.

Chapter 6 then discusses a broad range of transmission technologies at a level of detail suitable for high-level design, explains the technical and business considerations associated with each, and identifies the modes of use that are best for each technology.

4.2.2   Determine the Levels of Hierarchy

The human mind can keep track of only so much complexity at once. Analogously, routers work best when they are in close interaction with only a limited number of their peers. For both of these reasons, most internetworks are designed in a compartmentalized fashion, generally in a hierarchy. This provides a useful element of *layering,* or information hiding, so that we (and our routers) can understand the internetwork in bite-sized chunks.

Industry experience is unambiguous: Large, amorphous collections of routers just don't work very well. A hallmark of good internetwork architectural design today is a crisply articulated hierarchical design.

Choosing a suitable number of levels of hierarchy, and assigning meaning to them in terms of the technologies and bandwidth ranges they will encompass, is one of the most profound and far-reaching decisions that we will make. At the same time, it is a very abstract process, one that is difficult to grasp. Chapter 7 lays out the main issues.

4.2.3   Identify Possible Backbone Locations

For many forms of life, if we know the shape of the skeleton, we have already largely defined the characteristics of the organism—its shape, its dimensions, and its carrying capacity. It is not for naught that the core of the network is called the *backbone!* Once we have identified the backbone locations—based on traffic patterns, availability of space to house the equipment, and circuit mileage characteristics—we have largely defined the characteristics of the network. In addition, we have laid much of the groundwork for homing access locations to the network. Where we have multiple levels of hierarchy, this process may itself progress in stages, from innermost core to outermost edge. Chapter 8 lays out the main issues in choosing backbone locations.

4.2.4 Create a Preliminary Access Design

The access design determines the means by which your end users will access the lowest (outermost) hierarchical layer of your internetwork. Most designers have a tendency to pay insufficient attention to the access design. At first blush, it seems straightforward and technically trivial. In fact, however, access homings play an inordinately great role in the overall economics of many internetworks, and more design options are available than many designers realize. Chapter 9 provides specific guidance about the access design.

4.2.5 Create Access Homing Designs

For an internetwork with more than two hierarchical layers, one or more intermediate layers will exist whose access service locations must be connected, or *homed,* to service locations at a higher hierarchical layer. Chapter 10 explains the techniques that are available and the trade-offs that must be made between cost and reliability.

4.2.6 Create a Preliminary Backbone Topological Design

Backbone topological design is perhaps the most romantic and exciting aspect of the internetwork design process. For that reason, it is also the one for which most tools are designed. Nonetheless, topological design continues to be performed by human beings. Automated tools serve mainly to validate the performance characteristics of a design that has already been created.

Chapter 11 provides a brief overview of the topological design process.

4.2.7 Create a Preliminary Technical Design

At this point, the basic shape and characteristics of the internetwork have been established. We proceed to a more detailed level of design, considering routing, as well as addressing and naming, security, the Internet, and network management.

- **Routing.** Routing within your organization is generally accomplished by using Interior Gateway Protocols (IGPs); routing to other organizations is accomplished by using Exterior Gateway Protocols (EGPs). Chapter 12 provides a brief overview of the characteristics of routing protocols.

- **Addressing and naming.** In recent years, IP addresses have become a scarce commodity and must be managed with care. Moreover, the naming and addressing plans that an organization develops significantly influence your ability to evolve the infrastructure and your ability to do adds, deletes, and changes of new workstations. Naming and addressing are implemented by people (possibly aided by automated tools); consequently, the naming and addressing plans need to consider the degree of centralization or decentralization of the administrative staff. If you intend to delegate responsibility for assigning addresses, the delegation for names must break along the same administrative lines; otherwise, you will have confusion every time you add a new workstation to your network. Chapter 12 lays this out in more detail.

- **Security.** In many cases, the security model for the network will have far-reaching implications. In general, a large or complex internetwork will need a variety of security services and products to cover the full range of security requirements. Chapter 13 discusses the options, and their interactions, in general terms.

- **The Public Internet.** If you are designing a network for an ISP, or a service based on public Internet services, you are likely to need to understand the structure of the Internet, particularly as it relates to network interconnection. Chapter 14 provides useful background.

- **Network management.** Last but by no means least, we consider network management. In the TCP/IP world, the enormous popularity of SNMPv1 has resulted in a preoccupation with fault management of very unreliable systems, to the exclusion of all else. In Chapter 15, we attempt to take a more inclusive and holistic view of network management.

4.2.8   Demonstrate That Your Design Meets the Requirements

When the design is complete, how do we assure ourselves that it does what we want it to do? This is by no means a rhetorical question. Once we have fully specified a large internetwork, it is by no means obvious that it will achieve the desired performance in terms of overall availability, end-to-end delay, throughput, or packet drops.

Chapter 16 discusses the mathematical and statistical techniques that can be used to evaluate the performance characteristics of a design. The emphasis is on practical, nuts-and-bolts applied techniques, not on theory. We present the rudiments of queuing theory and discrete event simulation and explain the use of conditional probabilities to compute overall availability. Even if you have automated tools to assist you, you should understand the underlying methodologies so that you properly interpret the results and can understand the conditions under which those results can be trusted.

What do you do if your design fails to meet requirements? Generally, you will revise the design, iterating until all requirements are satisfied. In some cases, you will soon discover that your requirements were unrealistic in the first place and that they need to be revisited.

4.2.9 Analyze Your Costs

At this point, your design should be fully specified and validated. This is the point at which you will want to roll up your final, overall costs.

What if you are over budget at this point? This is more often than not the case. An experienced network designer typically has his or her eye on costs throughout every stage of the design process, not just at the end, so we are rarely surprised but usually are not satisfied with the numbers we get the first time through.

At this point, we frequently begin an iterative "polishing" process. The major elements go something like this.

- Categorize the major cost elements; determine the portion of one-time and recurring costs associated with each.
- Starting with the categories that make the largest contribution to overall cost, review the design to identify possible design modifications—still consistent with meeting the stated requirements—that would result in savings.
- Iterate until the incremental savings with each successive change seem too small to matter much.
- If the costs are still too high, consider whether a relaxation in any of the underlying requirements might enable you to meet your budgetary targets without jeopardizing the mission of the internetwork. If so, consider renegotiating your requirements.
- If it is fundamentally impossible to build and operate an internetwork that can achieve its mission within budget, the overall business model is in doubt. You need to renegotiate your mission, your budget, or both with your management; alternatively, you need to acknowledge that the project is not feasible and to take whatever steps are appropriate.

5 Circuit Costs and Cost Optimization Techniques

Every network design is, in some sense, unique. Each comes with its own opportunities and pitfalls. At the same time, various tricks of the trade can be used to improve the economics of a network design. Many of these have broad applicability. It is useful to take the time to understand them at this point, because they will be coming up again and again as we discuss the network design process in detail.

We will begin with a brief discussion of the elements of internetwork cost and will explain the importance of optimizing circuit cost. We will then explain the elements of circuit cost. With that groundwork established, we will discuss several techniques that experienced network designers use to drive down unit costs while maintaining the quality of an internetwork.

This material provides necessary background for Chapter 6, where we choose transmission technologies for the network.

5.1   Elements of Internetwork Costs

In general, it is useful to think of the cost structure of an internetwork as comprising three main elements: equipment, circuits, and labor. For the circuits, it is often convenient to distinguish between local and long-distance circuits. We tend to pay particular attention to circuit costs because they are a significant fraction of total cost and are amenable to optimization.

The relative balance among these costs can vary greatly from network to network. We frequently find that labor, equipment, and local and remote circuits each represent about a fourth of the total cost. There is, however, no "right" balance among these cost elements; it all depends on what the job of the network is.

In some cases, the circuits can play quite a dominant role. For a large dialup internetwork, it would not be unusual to find the relative proportions shown in Figure 5-1. In this particular case, local and long-distance circuit charges represent 25% + 35% = 60% of the total recurring cost of operating the network. Circuit costs will not always represent this high a proportion of the total, but they will usually be substantial. The fundamental reason we strive to minimize circuit costs is the same reason the gangster John Dillinger robbed banks: That's where the money is.

5.2   Elements of Circuit Costs

It is helpful to understand how telephone companies (also called carriers, or sometimes telcos; overseas, they are usually referred to as *PTTs,* for *post, telephone, and telegraph* administration) price circuits. The examples in this book are based on the United States, although similar principles apply elsewhere. Even restricting ourselves to the United States, this is an extraordinarily intricate and complex subject, so we'll try to cover only the basics that you're most likely to need.

We'll start by describing the familiar tariff structure for voice telephone calls and then explain how this relates to the dedicated circuits ("leased lines") that are often used for data communications. Most of us place many phone calls each day. We tend to take the process for granted. It's useful to keep in mind that a great deal of sophisticated technology supports every phone call that we make. It is also important to bear in mind that the underlying structure of the telephone companies, in the United States and around

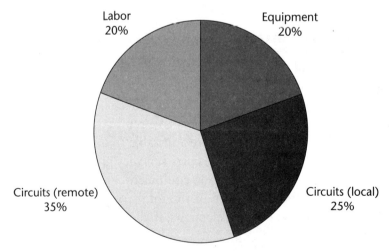

Figure 5-1: Cost elements of an internetwork in which
circuit costs dominate.

the world, is in the process of rapid evolution in terms of both technology and regulatory status.

The United States has been divided into *LATAs,* or *local access and transport areas.* The LATAs have been drawn in such a way that most phone calls are local: They never need to leave the LATA. Local telephone calls are typically handled entirely by the *local exchange carriers (LECs).* The LECs include familiar companies, such as GTE, U.S. West, Ameritech, and BellSouth, as well as some companies formed by recent mergers between Bell Atlantic and NYNEX, and SBC and PacTel. As a result of progressive deregulation of the telecommunications industry in the United States, we are also witnessing the emergence of newer competitive carriers, so-called *competitive access providers (CAPs)* and *competitive local exchange carriers (CLECs).*

If you need to talk to someone who is not located in the same LATA, you dial a phone number that includes an area code—sometimes called an *NPA*—and an exchange—called an *NXX*—for a different part of the country or a different part of North America. (You need not concern yourself with the derivation of the terms NPA and NXX.) If you were to dial someone in Boston at (617)-123-4567, 617 would be the NPA, and 123 would be the NXX. The LEC responds to your request by connecting your call through to the *point of presence (POP)* of an *interexchange carrier,* or *IXC.* The IXC provides long-distance connectivity and in turn connects you to a LEC in the LATA where the called party is located, based on the NPA/NXX you have dialed. That LEC completes the call and rings the phone of the party you are trying to reach. Figure 5-2 shows the steps in this process.

Large internetworks are sometimes built by using the switched or dialed telephone network, but they more often make use of "leased," or dedicated, circuits for high-speed router-to-router trunk connections. These circuits do not need to be dialed; they are always available. We permanently establish the desired connectivity at the time the circuit is deployed.

If a circuit is local to a single LATA, the LEC can do the entire job of establishing and maintaining it. The local circuit generally includes the so-called *local loop,* which connects the end locations to the LEC's *central office (CO),* as shown in Figure 5-3. In most cases, the two ends of the circuit will be connected to different COs, in which case interoffice charges, generally based on the mileage between the two COs, will also apply to the circuit.

The cost of the circuit depends on its speed, or capacity. Dedicated circuits in the United States are most commonly available in three speeds: DS-0, at 56Kbps; T-1 or DS-1, at 1.544Mbps; and T-3 or DS-3, at 45Mbps. In addition, we are beginning to see the availability of circuits based on new fiber-optic

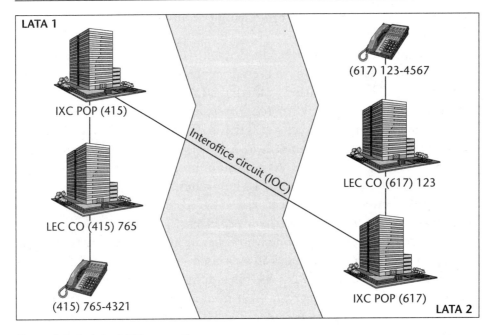

Figure 5-2: An inter-LATA connection.

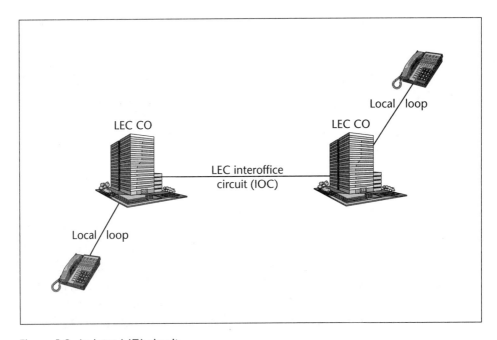

Figure 5-3: An intra-LATA circuit.

SONET facilities, beginning with SONET OC-3 at speeds of 155Mbps. In the future, carriers may offer SONET-based circuits at OC-12 (622Mbps) and OC-48 (2.5Gbps) speeds and beyond.

In many cases, a dedicated circuit needs to connect locations in different LATAs. In this case, the circuit will generally have a long-distance component provided by an IXC, as well as local circuits on both ends, much as we saw in Figure 5-2. It is often the case that separate LECs serve the LATAs on opposite ends of the same long-distance circuit. It is usually simplest to ask the IXC to order—or *provision,* in telephony parlance—the LEC portions of the circuit on our behalf and to coordinate and maintain all components of the circuit, LEC and IXC, as if it were a single circuit. The IXC assesses fees for these services. More sophisticated organizations may prefer to order the pieces separately, providing sufficient direction to the carriers on how to lash them together, in order to attempt to save money in various ways.

In general, LECs and IXCs charge an initial installation fee and a monthly recurring fee for their circuits. Federal taxes are usually included in their price, but state and local taxes, which can form a bewilderingly complex tapestry for a large network, are additional.

5.3   Cheaper by the Dozen

In some senses, telecommunications services can be viewed as a commodity, just like milk or eggs or dishwasher detergent. Many of the same basic economic rules apply. If you were raised in a capitalistic society, you already know a lot of what you need to know in order to understand the economics of network design, but you may not have organized this knowledge to the point that you can apply it to the network design process.

To illustrate this point, I took some notes in my local supermarket. Table 5-1 shows the prices I found for three brands of homogenized milk. A few

Table 5-1: Milk Prices

Price	Brand A	Brand B	Brand C
Half-pint			$0.39
Pint			$0.69
Quart	$0.69	$0.95	$0.95
Half-gallon	$1.29	$1.45	$1.49
Gallon	$2.39	$2.85	$2.89

trends are immediately apparent. First, brand A, the store brand, is cheaper within each size category than are the two other brands, while brand B is slightly cheaper than brand C. Is this sufficient reason to prefer brand A over its competitors? It might be: As far as I am concerned, milk is milk. There could, however, be qualitative differences among the three brands that fully justify the difference in price.

Second, larger quantities of milk sell at higher prices. Beyond this, it is difficult to infer more information from these numbers.

When we *normalize* the costs, the information becomes much more interesting. To compute the price per gallon, we multiply the price by the number of units in a gallon, as shown in Table 5-2. This enables us to perform more meaningful comparisons. If we look down any column, we can instantly recognize that the price per gallon declines as we purchase in larger volumes. Figure 5-4 graphs these relationships.

Table 5-2: Price per Gallon

Price per Gallon	Brand A	Brand B	Brand C
Half-pint			$6.24
Pint			$5.52
Quart	$2.76	$3.80	$3.80
Half-gallon	$2.58	$2.90	$2.98
Gallon	$2.39	$2.85	$2.89

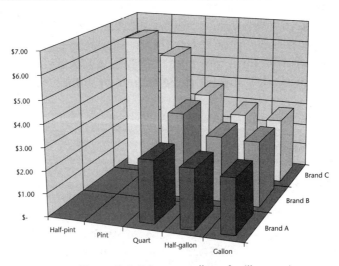

Figure 5-4: Price per gallon of milk.

The great industrial engineer F. Gilbreth said it best: Things tend to be cheaper by the dozen. "But I already knew that," you say? Just so! There is no magic to network design. It is mostly a matter of common sense, coupled with a knowledge of a few specific, arcane topics.

In Figure 5-4, we can also see that within each brand, the slope of the curve flattens as we move toward higher volumes. We can get a better look at this on a two-dimensional graph (Figure 5-5) that shows just one brand. What does this flattening of the curve tell us? If we are purchasing milk in small quantities, we can get a large relative improvement in our unit costs by increasing the quantity in which we place our orders. If we are already purchasing milk in larger quantities, the gain that we could potentially realize, expressed in percentage terms, is much less. Why should this be?

The *price* to the consumer is generally going to be closely tied to the *cost* to the store. For a half-pint of milk, the cost of the packaging is substantial in comparison with the cost of the milk. The supermarket also has fixed costs associated with tracking an extra item of inventory and with ringing it through the register at checkout time. For a half-gallon, the cost is already dominated by the cost of the milk, so the incremental savings in percentage terms in stepping up to a full gallon is modest.

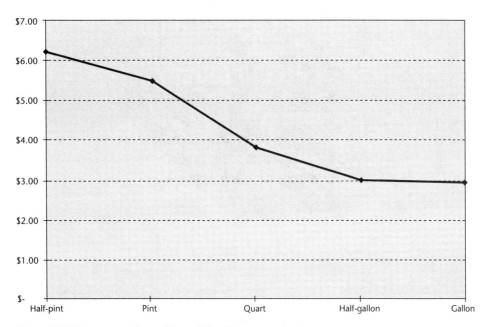

Figure 5-5: Price per gallon of brand C milk as quantity increases.

As it is with the price of milk, so it is with the price of circuits. If we look at the tariff prices of common circuit types in North America, T-1 (1.5Mbps) and T-3 (45Mbps), normalized to represent cost per month for 1Mbps of capacity, we see the trends shown in Table 5-3.

The prices in Table 5-3 assume that the circuit runs for 100 miles, that no local circuit is required, and that the circuit is procured on a month-to-month basis, that is, no term discounts.[1] Graphically, we have circuit prices as shown in Figure 5-6. Again, we see that unit prices decline when we order in larger volumes.

Table 5-3: IXC Circuit Prices in the United States

$ per Mbps	Carrier A	Carrier B	Carrier C
T-1	$3,960.14	$3,219.24	$4,278.02
T-3	$ 937.33	$ 831.11	$1,028.04

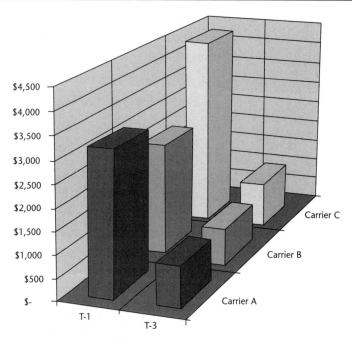

Figure 5-6: Circuit prices for several U.S. IXCs.

1. Except where otherwise noted, all tariff prices mentioned in this text are based on U.S. carrier prices and were correct to the best of my knowledge as of the date on which they were written. Please recognize that they are provided solely for purposes of illustration and that carrier tariffs are continually changing.

In real estate, it has been said, there are only three things that matter: (1) location, (2) location, and (3) location. In procuring telecommunications circuits, analogously, all that matters is (1) volume, (2) volume, and (3) volume. If you want to drive down your unit costs, you need to operate your network at sufficiently high volume. It is a simple point, but it bears repeating.

5.4 Concentration and Aggregation

We have seen the importance of volume. Does this necessarily mean that the only way to get a cost-effective network is to grow your business until it reaches mammoth proportions?

Most network designs seek to enhance their price/performance by means of various forms of *concentration*. Lower-bandwidth communication paths are funneled together (multiplexed) wherever possible to create a smaller number of higher-bandwidth paths in order to operate cost-effective high-capacity circuits wherever practical, as shown in Figure 5-7. For this reason, many private networks consist of a high-capacity *backbone* and a lower-capacity *access network,* as shown in Figure 5-8. Typically, the access at the periphery of the network might take place at modest speeds, such as 56Kbps, whereas the core of the network operates at higher speeds and at better economies of scale.

Very large private networks might use more than one level of concentration. These networks can be viewed as *concentrating* access lines before presenting them to the backbone, as shown in Figure 5-9. In effect, this kind of network has three levels of hierarchy: access, concentration, and backbone. Alternatively, one can view these networks as having a hierarchically

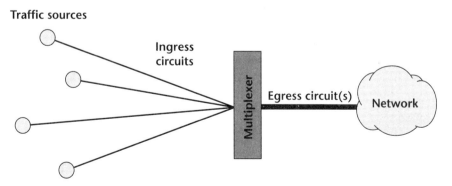

Figure 5-7: Funneling together (multiplexing) circuits to gain economies of scale.

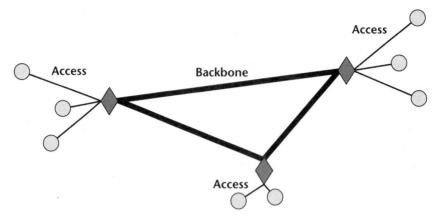

Figure 5-8: Backbone and access networks.

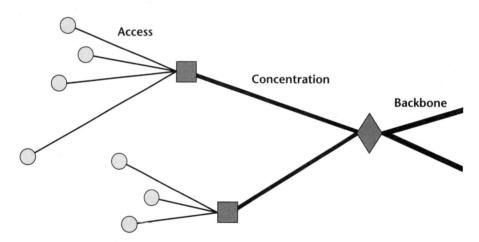

Figure 5-9: Hierarchical concentration into the backbone.

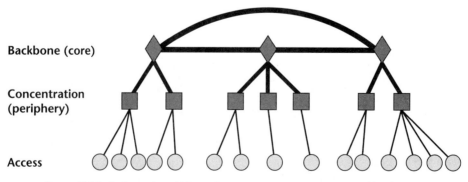

Figure 5-10: A three-tiered hierarchy: access, concentration, and backbone.

structured backbone, with a very high-bandwidth inner core and a less high-bandwidth periphery, as shown in Figure 5-10.

In short, concentration and aggregation can be used in various ways to enable our networks to achieve the economics associated with high volumes.

5.5 Statistical Multiplexing

We have seen that line concentration enables us to operate at greater economies of scale. In many cases, concentration provides a second, even greater benefit. When they multiplex circuits together, the telephone companies generally do so using simple time division multiplexing (TDM) equipment. For instance, when they aggregate 24 channels, each with 56Kbps of nominal data bandwidth, onto a T-1 circuit, the telcos have to allocate dedicated bandwidth to each channel, as shown in Figure 5-11. Ignoring overhead bandwidth used to manage the circuits, it takes $24 \times 56Kbps = 1,344Kbps$ of bandwidth to carry the traffic, which entirely consumes the T-1.

Routers and data switches do not operate in this way. When we use a router or a data switch to concentrate traffic, we capitalize on the inherently bursty nature of data communications traffic to gain substantial additional advantage. For example, Figure 5-12 shows a router concentrating multiple ingress (input, or entry) 56Kbps circuits onto a single T-1 egress (exit) circuit. Whenever the router sees a datagram—an independently addressed and transmitted unit of data, the atomic unit of data with which a router deals—on any of the ingress lines, the router inspects the datagram to see whether it

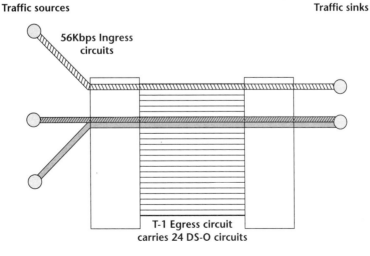

Figure 5-11: Time division multiplexing (TDM).

is addressed to a device on one of the other ingress lines. If so, the datagram is forwarded over the appropriate ingress line; otherwise, it is consolidated onto the egress circuit.

At this point, the router enjoys two benefits that the TDM multiplexer does not. First, if the egress circuit is momentarily available, the router can send the datagram over it, using the *full available bandwidth of the circuit,* not just a proportional fraction. Queuing theory, the mathematical discipline that deals with waiting lines, tells us that twice as fast is generally better than twice as many—this is a win.

Second, if the egress circuit is momentarily unavailable—that is, if it's already busy transmitting another datagram—the router has the option of placing the outbound datagram on an output queue, or waiting line, until the circuit frees up. It is permissible for the router to queue up the data, because a layered data communications protocol, such as TCP/IP, cannot depend on fixed and deterministic delay through the network. The router must assume that delay is limited only in a statistical sense. In other words, delay can be predicted to fall in a given range with a defined probability, but there is no fixed upper bound on delay for a given datagram. Since the services running on an internetwork are already obliged to cope with the lack of determinism in delay, the routers can take advantage of this fact by queuing data whenever they need to. (This explains why it is straightforward to use an internetwork to carry electronic mail, which is insensitive to delay, but difficult to use an internetwork to carry realtime voice, which requires consistent or predictable delay through the network.)

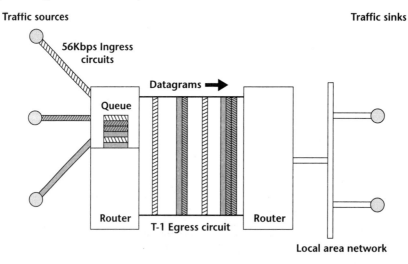

Figure 5-12: Statistical multiplexing as a superposition of Poisson processes.

Because of these properties, it turns out that a router can support ingress lines that collectively have far more bandwidth capacity than its egress circuit. *We capitalize on the knowledge that it is highly unlikely that every ingress circuit will be carrying the maximum possible load at exactly the same moment.* This is the essence of statistical multiplexing: We are placing a bet, knowing that the odds are highly in our favor and that the consequences of losing are small.

Statistical multiplexing works. For example, it has been common in the public Internet services in recent years for an Internet service provider (ISP) to support 8, 12, or even 20 customers, each connected over a T-1 ingress circuit, using a router with a single T-1 egress circuit. If the design is properly sized and configured, this configuration can deliver good performance to those customers. A circuit cost reduction of 8:1 or more represents a very substantial economic savings.

How much concentration can you hope to achieve in a given case? This is largely a function of the amount of traffic that the ingress circuits are throwing at your router.

The mean (average) traffic intensity on the egress line is simply the sum of the means of the traffic intensity on the ingress lines. Suppose, for instance, that circuit A in Figure 5-12 is carrying mean traffic of 10Kbps while circuit B is carrying mean traffic of 20Kbps. The egress circuit will then have mean traffic intensity of 10 + 20 = 30Kbps.

Note that the egress line *must* have at least enough capacity to carry its mean traffic; otherwise, queuing theory tells us that delay will grow without bound. Internetworking applications are forgiving with regard to large or variable delay, but they cannot accommodate *infinite* delay!

The egress line must, in fact, have significantly *more* capacity than the sum of the mean traffic *carried* by the ingress lines, although it will often have a smaller maximum capacity than the sum of the capacities of the ingress circuits. Determining how much more is not trivial. Queuing theory tells us that the more excess capacity we provide, the lower the delay we should expect. We know that there are more or less random deviations in the volume of traffic, and we know that there are certain predictable deviations as well. (For instance, traffic might be much higher at 2:00 P.M. local time than at 2:00 A.M.) We also know that as we aggregate more and more data sources, we get more and more benefit from the law of large numbers in that the variability of the aggregated traffic flow is *less* than the variability in the individual component data flows.

These deviations are important. The mean represents a sort of a steady-state average over the long run. Economist John Maynard Keynes best stated the limitations inherent in overreliance on mean statistics: "In the long run, we're all dead." We cannot ignore the short run. We need to deal with short-term variations, and, in particular, we need to provide our networks with sufficient capacity to carry traffic at busy periods without incurring delay that is unacceptable to our users.

Taking all of these factors into account, the total amount of excess capacity we will want to use for the egress circuit is less than the sum of those that we would choose on the ingress circuits. Why should this be? The discussion that follows draws on both queuing theory and statistics. (If you are not much interested in the math, you can skip to the end of this section without loss of continuity. Alternatively, you might choose to come back to this section after you have read the introductory queuing theory material that appears in Chapter 16.) Consider just the random factors in each ingress data flow, and assume for the moment that each of the ingress flows A and B can be regarded as a totally random process; in formal terms, we call each of them a stochastic Poisson process with a Markovian arrival pattern. As such, the egress traffic is called a *superposition* of Poisson processes. This superposition is itself a Poisson process, with a mean traffic intensity equal to the sum of the means of traffic intensity of the processes from which it is composed, as we have already noted. We know, however, that traffic intensity is not likely to be constant; it can vary from minute to minute over the course of the day, and we can measure that traffic intensity at intervals of our choosing. The variance—a statistical measure of variability—of traffic intensity—expressed as the number of datagrams that will arrive within a specified period of time, such as an hour—for a superposition of Poisson processes is equal to the sum of the variances of traffic intensity for the processes of which it consists.

In statistics, we tend to be more interested in the *standard deviation* than in the variance. The standard deviation enables us to develop *confidence intervals,* statements that there is a certain probability that a given random variable is, for instance, no greater than a particular value. The variance of a distribution of a random variable is simply the square of its standard deviation.

Let S_A be the standard deviation of A, and $S_A{}^2$ be the variance of A. We know, in this case, that

$$S_A{}^2 + S_B{}^2 = S_C{}^2$$

It is clear that

$$\text{sqrt}\,(S_A{}^2 + S_B{}^2) = S_C$$

This formulation tells us that the standard deviation of C is less than the sum of the standard deviations of the processes of which it is composed. To visualize this, consider the Pythagorean formula, which states that the length of the hypotenuse of a right triangle is equal to the square root of the sum of the squares of the lengths of the other two sides. Thus, the standard deviations of the number of datagrams arriving on two ingress circuits, as shown in Figure 5-12, bear the same relationship to the standard deviation of the number of datagrams departing on the egress circuit as do the lengths of two legs of a right triangle to the length of the hypotenuse. If the standard deviations associated with the traffic intensity on circuits A and B are represented by lengths of lines A and B in Figure 5-13, the length of line C corresponds to the standard deviation of the traffic intensity on circuit C. Variability can be thought of as adding up like a *vector* sum rather than a simple arithmetic sum.

In general, once we know the mean and the standard deviation of a distribution, we know enough to assert the probability that an observation drawn from that distribution falls within a given range of values. In particular, we can generally say that there is a 95 percent probability that any given observation is not greater than the mean by more than 1.96 times the standard deviation. You can think of this value as an estimate of the ninety-fifth percentile of the distribution. As shown in Figure 5-14, we generally expect 95 percent of the probability mass to be associated with observations that are not more than 1.96 standard deviations greater than the mean.

A smaller standard deviation thus translates very directly into a smaller expected value of the ninety-fifth percentile of the distribution. If you think of the ninety-fifth percentile of traffic intensity as a measure of traffic at a

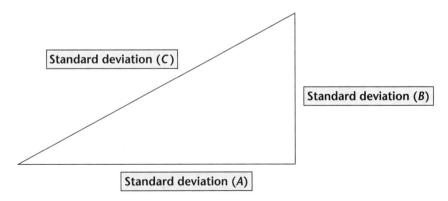

Figure 5-13: Variability of a superposition of Poisson processes.

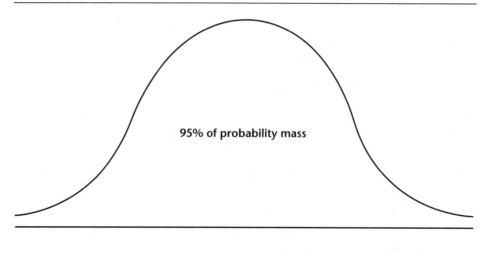

95% of probability mass

Mean   Mean (1 × s + dv)   Mean + (2 × s ÷ dv)

Figure 5-14: The mean and the standard deviation of the normal distribution.

period that is busy but not extreme, you begin to understand why it is a useful measure of the required capacity for a link.

At this point, you've seen an illustration that the ninety-fifth percentile of a superposition of Poisson processes will generally be less than the sum of the ninety-fifth percentiles of the individual processes. This is true, in general, but you should not interpret the result too literally.

First, you need to keep in mind that nonrandom effects usually dominate the random ones by a very wide margin. Everybody goes to lunch at roughly the same local time, for instance. The statistical approximations that we have discussed up to this point don't attempt to deal with any of that.

Second, an emerging body of research strongly suggests that traffic patterns in an internetwork violate some of the key assumptions associated with a Poisson process. The traffic patterns are extremely bursty, and, perhaps even more significantly, there is a sort of inertia or momentum in the observations: If one period is bursty, it's likely that the next will be, too. This finding, known as *self-similarity,* violates the Markovian, or "memoryless," property of the Poisson distribution and potentially invalidates the model.

What does self-similarity mean in practice? It does *not* invalidate statistical multiplexing. An enormous body of operational experience says that statistical multiplexing is effective. In the 1970s, queuing theory stood in a somewhat similarly paradoxical position: Everyone knew that arrival patterns were not in fact Markovian, yet classical queuing formulas generated useful and accurate results nonetheless. Eventually, that anomaly was resolved when the queuing theorists derived the classical formulas of queuing theory in new ways, showing that the same results would hold under more relaxed assumptions.

Self-similarity tells us that traffic patterns are a bit burstier than the traditional formulas would lead us to expect. It turns out that the traffic-arrival distribution has a "heavier tail" than was previously assumed. This is an important finding. Network performance, as perceived by the user, can be strongly and adversely influenced by ragged, irregular performance.

In practice, we respond to self-similarity by allocating capacity a bit more conservatively than we otherwise might have, much as we would have responded to higher than anticipated variability in service times. Further, self-similar burstiness of traffic will tend to have much less impact on user-perceived performance of big pipes than on that of small ones. Once you have your network in place, you should proactively monitor it not only for average use but also for variability in use, so that you can provide sufficient capacity to deal with the busy periods that your network is experiencing.

It is not necessary to totally disregard queuing theory, as some have advocated. Queuing theory continues to be one of the best ways to develop an understanding of the way in which data networks function under load.

5.6 Distance-Sensitive Tariffs

As we have seen, most telephone company tariffs—price lists and associated service descriptions—for dedicated inter-LATA circuits are based on a fixed charge per circuit, plus an incremental cost per mile. We can express the mathematical relationship as a simple linear equation:

Monthly charge = Fixed charge + (Miles * Mileage charge)

As an example, let's consider MCI WorldCom, the second-largest interexchange carrier (IXC) in the United States. Its standard tariffed price for a dedicated T-1 circuit (1.5Mbps) had at one time a fixed charge of $2,085, plus a mileage charge of $3.26 per mile. This corresponds to the graph in Figure 5-15. Because a graph of the X and Y values falls in a straight line, we call the corresponding equation linear.

These charges are likely to be an important component of your overall network connectivity costs; however, it is important to remember that they are not your only network connectivity costs, and they may not even represent the dominant component of those costs. Other major components include

- Local access circuits from the local exchange carriers (LECs)
- Various forms of cross-connection charges among IXC and LEC circuits

The highly carrier-specific cross-connection charges are complex, and they can be quite significant. It is surprising how often they are overlooked, even by otherwise astute designers. They go under such names as access connection, access coordination, central office coordination, cross-connection, and entrance facility fees.

You may find yourself dealing at some point with a long-distance carrier, an IXC, that prices dedicated circuits based on city pairs rather than mileage. In other words, its tariff may list one price from New York to Chicago and a different price from New York to Atlanta. An IXC ostensibly might not price based explicitly on mileage.

In general, mileage plays a very strong role in the pricing structure of dedicated inter-LATA private lines (leased lines) in every instance I am aware of in the United States. Understanding the underlying relationship will greatly facilitate your ability to analyze the tariff. It is quite possible that the carrier personnel you are dealing with do not have the information you want; however, it is fairly straightforward for you to derive the relationship between mileage and price yourself, in general.

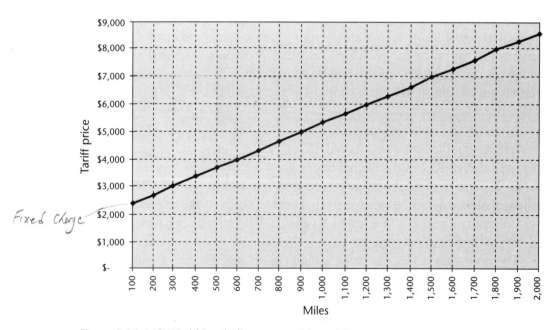

Figure 5-15: MCI WorldCom's distance-sensitive pricing.

Assume that you have obtained a number of list prices for the specific city pairs shown in Table 5-4. If you're trying to understand the relationships

Table 5-4: T-1 Pricing Based on City Pairs

From	To	Miles	T-1 Price
Baltimore, MD	Silver Springs, MD	31	$ 3,208
Arlington, VA	Baltimore, MD	40	$ 3,241
Charlottesville, VA	Washington, DC	99	$ 3,458
Mobile, AL	New Orleans, LA	132	$ 3,580
Atlanta, GA	Birmingham, AL	141	$ 3,613
Charlottesville, VA	Norfolk, VA	145	$ 3,628
Norfolk, VA	Washington, DC	146	$ 3,632
Atlanta, GA	Knoxville, TN	155	$ 3,665
Jacksonville, FL	Tallahassee, FL	157	$ 3,672
Morgantown, WV	Silver Springs, MD	159	$ 3,679
Knoxville, TN	Nashville, TN	160	$ 3,683
Jackson, MS	New Orleans, LA	162	$ 3,691
Morgantown, WV	Washington, DC	162	$ 3,691
Miami, FL	Tampa, FL	180	$ 3,757
Memphis, TN	Nashville, TN	197	$ 3,820
Birmingham, AL	Jackson, MS	214	$ 3,882
Birmingham, AL	Memphis, TN	216	$ 3,890
Mobile, AL	Tallahassee, FL	226	$ 3,927
Tallahassee, FL	Tampa, FL	227	$ 3,930
Atlanta, GA	Tallahassee, FL	228	$ 3,934
Lexington, KY	Morgantown, WV	269	$ 4,085
Atlanta, GA	Jacksonville, FL	284	$ 4,140
Atlanta, GA	Lexington, KY	297	$ 4,188
Jacksonville, FL	Miami, FL	325	$ 4,292
Los Angeles, CA	San Francisco, CA	351	$ 4,387
Atlanta, GA	Jackson, MS	352	$ 4,391
Atlanta, GA	Dallas, TX	720	$ 5,748
Dallas, TX	Los Angeles, CA	1,241	$ 7,669
Atlanta, GA	Greenville, SC	137	$ 3,721
Charlottesville, VA	Greenville, SC	311	$ 4,384
Total:		7,464	$120,586
Average:		249	$ 4,020

among data elements, it's always a good idea to graph them. By doing so, you will find that the mileage and the list price data fall on a nearly straight line.

At this point, you have a pretty good idea that the prices are basically a linear function of the mileage; however, it is possible to be much more precise. A statistical technique known as *linear regression* can be used to determine the equation of the straight line that best approximates data like this. For regression, "best" is usually interpreted as meaning that the sum of the squares of the differences between each point and the estimated line is minimized. (Any good statistics text will explain the underlying mathematics. For now we will simply apply the method. Linear regression software is widely available and is included at no extra charge with some spreadsheeting programs. If you have a copy of Microsoft Excel, you may wish to work through the example for this book.[2])

The regression output tells us that the Y intercept is 3,103.01807 and that the coefficient of X is 3.683743. In the context of this example, the tariffed fixed cost (fixed charge) of a T-1 circuit from this carrier is $3,103, and the charge per mile (mileage charge) is $3.68. If we compare this to the graph in Figure 5-16, we find that this result fits the data well. The cost of a T-1 never seems to dip below roughly $3,100.

Whenever you do a regression analysis, you should remember to do two things.

- Verify that the results are statistically significant.
- Analyze your residuals.

In testing for statistical significance, we are trying to determine that the goodness of fit is better than might have been expected as a result of random chance. If we look at the graph generated by this particular regression (Figure 5-16) there can be no doubt: The predicted Y values track the actual values so closely that we can scarcely even see the outliers!

The regression analysis generates a value referred to as r^2. This r^2 value provides a rigorous means of verifying statistical significance. The closer that r^2 is to 1.0, the greater the degree to which the result is statistically significant; conversely, the closer it is to 0, the less likely that the result is meaningful or trustworthy. In this case, the computed r^2 is equal to 0.99827345. Looking

---

2. This example can be found at the Web site for this book: http://www.awl.com/cseng/titles/0-201-69584-7.

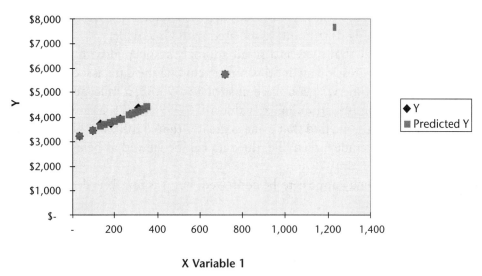

Figure 5-16: Predicted and actual circuit prices as a function of mileage.

this r^2 value up in a table in a statistics text, we find that it is statistically significant at the 99 percent level and is quite adequate to serve as a basis for analysis for most purposes.

A task often overlooked in regression analysis is the analysis of residuals. When you have completed the regression computation, the residuals are the "leftovers." They are the portion of each Y value that cannot be completely explained by the regression equation. If we examine the residuals in the T-1 example, we find that most track very closely to the regression line but that two stick out like sore thumbs, as shown in Figure 5-17.

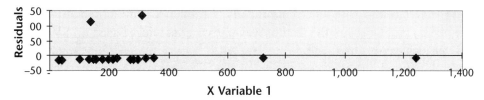

Figure 5-17: Regression residuals.

A detailed inspection of the residual values shows that most are low by approximately $9.00 but that two values are high by $113 and $135, respectively. It turns out that these two values are associated with Greenville, SC, and they are the only data points associated with Greenville.

We hypothesize that there is a small anomaly associated with Greenville and attempt the regression again, this time excluding the data associated with Greenville.[3] This time we get a fixed cost of $3,093.33, a mileage charge of $3,687, and a simply stunning r^2 value of 0.99999987! Examining our remaining residuals, we find that none is greater than $1.00. For all practical purposes, if we exclude Greenville, the data can be viewed as being perfectly linear.

This example may appear to be contrived, but it is not. It is derived from actual tariff prices.

5.7   Distance-Insensitive Tariffs

Classic network design was focused on the problems we have dealt with up to this point in the chapter: the optimization of costs for a network comprising leased lines. Many of the networks being built today, however, are based in part or in whole on new, fast packet carrier services, such as Frame Relay, SMDS, and ATM. *In most cases, interexchange carrier (IXC) tariffs for these services are completely independent of mileage within the continental United States. This radically alters the nature of the network design optimization problem.*

We'll start by considering IXC Frame Relay services. The pricing structure for these services is fairly stable by now; moreover, the Frame Relay pricing model tends to drive the pricing models for IXC SMDS and ATM, because all of these services are largely interchangeable. If you understand how to use IXC Frame Relay services, you will, for the most part, understand how to use their SMDS and ATM offerings as well. All of these services are discussed in greater detail in Chapter 6.

The discussion that follows is based on the use of permanent virtual circuits (PVCs). The protocol standards for Frame Relay also envision the use of virtual circuits that are dynamically established and taken down, or switched virtual circuits (SVCs); however, carrier services based on SVCs are not yet well established.

---

3. The detailed analysis can be found at the Web site for this book: http://www.awl.com.cseng/titles/0-201-69584-7.

5.7.1 Components of IXC Frame Relay Charges

IXC Frame Relay charges typically consist of three major components: a local access circuit from the LEC, a port speed on the IXC's Frame Relay switch, and a charge associated with the amount of bandwidth that the carrier is committing to deliver across any PVCs, as represented by a committed information rate (CIR).

5.7.1.1 The Access Circuit

The local access circuit is for a conventional intra-LATA LEC circuit. In many cases, an inter-LATA circuit will also be provided by the IXC. Prevailing practice in the industry is for the IXC to offer Frame Relay as if switches were available in every IXC point of presence (POP) in the continental United States; however, most IXCs have fewer switches than POPs. This requires each IXC to *back-haul* the traffic from the POP you have accessed to a POP that has a Frame Relay switch.

The cost of this back-haul is typically built into the IXC's overall pricing structure. It is not visible to you as a customer, and it has a minimal impact on the service that is delivered to you. (It increases propagation delay and may impact availability but not so much as to violate the IXC's service commitment to you.) This practice enables the IXC to offer Frame Relay service at a simple, completely uniform "postalized" price throughout the United States.

5.7.1.2 Port Speed

IXCs generally offer Frame Relay services at port speeds of 56Kbps and 1.544Mbps, and most also offer service at several fractional speeds between the two. Frame Relay services at T-3 speeds (45Mbps) are selectively available and are likely to become more common in the next few years. Note that it may be possible to obtain a port speed that is lower than the speed of your access circuit, thus incurring lower charges.

5.7.1.3 Committed Information Rate (CIR)

These port speeds represent an upper limit on the traffic you can hope to have the IXC deliver for you over these Frame Relay ports; however, they do not in and of themselves constitute a guarantee to you that the IXC has provided enough capacity to carry this much traffic to all of the locations you need. That assurance is provided by the committed information rate, or CIR, which is just what its name implies: a commitment that a given amount of information can be carried to the desired destination. When you set up a Frame Relay service at a given location with an IXC, you request a permanent virtual circuit from that location to each destination of interest and establish the CIR that you want to associate with that particular PVC.

The IXC is committing to deliver at least as many bits as specified by the CIR, with very high assurance. Bits beyond the CIR can, in principle, be either dropped or carried on a "best efforts" basis, with no assurance of delivery. In practice, it is customary for the IXC to attempt delivery on a best-efforts basis. The Frame Relay switch should notify the sender in the event that data is at risk of being lost due to congestion, using forward explicit congestion notification (FECN) and backward explicit congestion notification (BECN); however, there is no assurance that the equipment you have connected to the Frame Relay service will be able to do anything useful with those notifications.

Note that, in general, no explicit charge is associated with the distance that the traffic must be carried, as long as both ends of the PVC are located within the continental United States. Foreign PVCs tend, however, to carry substantial surcharges, reflecting not only the cost of transoceanic cables but also the regulatory environment in the source and destination countries.

Some IXCs permit you to pay for your total CIR on a simplex, or unidirectional, basis. This enables you to establish unequal CIRs in each direction for a given PVC, which gives you additional flexibility in tailoring your service to reflect your requirements. It is quite common, for instance, for residential users of online services and of the Internet to transmit far less data than they receive. If you use a Frame Relay infrastructure to carry data that ultimately originates with residential consumers, you may be able to take advantage of this asymmetry through the use of unequal CIR assignments.

5.7.2 Applications of Distance-Insensitive Tariffs

Our instincts about the design of wide area networks are grounded largely in a distance-sensitive world. To understand how to best and most cost-effectively use the services available today, we need to begin by thinking harder about what distance insensitivity means.

Let's start by thinking about a Frame Relay network interconnecting field offices in Chicago, Dallas, Atlanta, Washington, San Francisco, and Los Angeles to our corporate headquarters in New York City (see Figure 5-18). Each of the six field offices has average traffic of 32Kbps to and from headquarters during the busiest hour of the day. Traffic from one field office to another is negligible. Traffic never exceeds 56Kbps. We begin by assuming that each field office has a 56Kbps Frame Relay port with 32Kbps of CIR for a PVC to carry its traffic destined for New York. Let's say that New York

Figure 5-18: Service locations for a sample Frame Relay internetwork.

City will need something bigger than a 56Kbps port, since it has to accommodate up to six field offices times an average of 32Kbps during each peak hour. Let's plan on a T-1 local access circuit, a port speed somewhat less than T-1, and 192Kbps of combined CIR for New York. (We can assume for now that the CIR figures can simply be added together. That turns out to be a conservative assumption, but it's good enough for this exercise.)

It seems natural to consolidate the San Francisco and Los Angeles traffic in Chicago and the Dallas and Atlanta traffic in Washington. This yields the nice, hierarchical network depicted in Figure 5-19. In Chicago, we will need two 32Kbps CIR PVCs to Los Angeles and San Francisco. We will also need a 96Kbps CIR circuit to carry the combined Los Angeles–San Francisco–Chicago traffic to New York City. This, in turn, implies an aggregate traffic-handling capacity associated with a CIR of at least 160Kbps.

The traffic requirements in Chicago seem to call for a circuit larger than 56Kbps. This, in turn, is likely to necessitate a T-1 access circuit. By the same reasoning, Washington will also need a T-1 access circuit.

Hmm. All of these T-1 circuits are starting to get expensive. I thought that Frame Relay networks were supposed to save money! Did we go astray somewhere? What's wrong with this picture?

Dear reader, please bear with me. I have knowingly led you astray. I wanted to make sure that you fully grasped a key point. Look closely once again at the map in Figure 5-19 and ask yourself, What would the incremental cost be of

1st Design

Figure 5-19: A sample Frame Relay internetwork.

running the Los Angeles and San Francisco PVCs not to Chicago but all the way to New York City, as shown in Figure 5-20? In answering, consider only the service costs in Los Angeles and San Francisco, not the costs in New York or Chicago. The answer is clear, and it is independent of our choice of IXC Frame Relay carrier. So long as the tariff is truly distance insensitive, the incremental cost is *zero*.

2d Design

Beths

— Becorn FR.

Figure 5-20: An alternative realization of the sample Frame Relay internetwork.

The incremental cost for service at our headquarters in New York City is, under the assumptions previously stated, also zero. The combined CIR is still equal to the sum of the CIRs to each field office, to a first order, and the port speed is unchanged.

We have now established that concentrating traffic in Chicago and Washington did absolutely nothing to reduce the costs associated with Los Angeles and San Francisco and, by analogy, with Dallas and Atlanta. Did it improve the quality of the network?

Probably not. In Chapter 16, we will show that the expected end-to-end delay of this network is likely to be a bit better than that of the network with concentration in Chicago and Washington. The expected network availability should also be somewhat better with this design.

So what is different between the two designs? Mainly the cost. It's lower in the second design. A 56Kbps port with 32Kbps of CIR clearly suffices for both Washington and Chicago, which is far less than in the first design.

You should pause and take another look at Figures 5-19 and 5-20. Most people find this result to be very counterintuitive.

The sample network of this section might have a traffic matrix as shown in Table 5-5, with ninety-fifth percentile traffic requirements expressed in kilobits per second.

5.8   Distance-Sensitive versus Distance-Insensitive Tariffs

The existence of both distance-sensitive and distance-insensitive tariffs for services that are, in some sense, interchangeable inevitably gives you, the customer, numerous opportunities to optimize your network by trading one service off against another. Consider again Figure 5-20, in which all of the

Table 5-5: Traffic Matrix

From/To	New York City	Atlanta	Chicago	Dallas	Los Angeles	San Francisco
New York City	—	32	32	32	32	32
Atlanta	32	—	—	—	—	—
Chicago	32	—	—	—	—	—
Dallas	32	—	—	—	—	—
Los Angeles	32	—	—	—	—	—
San Francisco	32	—	—	—	—	—

Frame Relay services were carried all the way back to New York City. Suppose that we attempted to use dedicated circuits (leased lines) to carry the traffic all the way to New York instead of Frame Relay. Is that any better?

For the sake of this discussion, we'll use tariff pricing that was at one time standard for MCI, with no discounts. We'll allocate one sixth of the cost of the Frame Relay *port* in New York to each field office for a first cut at the analysis, but we need to keep in mind that the port is required if we choose to use Frame Relay for *any* of the field offices. With that groundwork established, we can proceed to figure out which field offices can cost-effectively be connected using leased lines.

At one time, MCI routinely charged $180 a month for a 56Kbps port and $57 a month for a simplex PVC. Since we would need a PVC in each direction, the incremental cost of connecting any of the six field office locations to New York by Frame Relay, once the New York Frame Relay port is in place, is $180 + (2 × $57) = $294 a month. Adding one sixth the cost of the T-1 port, we have $294 + ($1,470 / 6) = $539 a month. By contrast, a 56Kbps circuit costs $308 a month, plus $0.26 a mile.

If a circuit were 100 miles long, it would cost us $334 a month, which is cheaper overall than the Frame Relay solution. If the circuit were 1,000 miles long, it would cost us $568 a month, which is slightly more expensive than the Frame Relay solution. With a little arithmetic, we can demonstrate that the costs of the leased line and the Frame Relay are identical when the circuit is 888 miles long. For anything closer than 888 miles, leased lines are cheaper; for anything farther, Frame Relay is cheaper.

It is tempting to assume that we should serve closer locations, such as Washington, with leased lines and farther locations, such as San Francisco and Los Angeles, with Frame Relay. In most cases, that is indeed the best way to handle a design like this one. In this particular case, however, we need to remember that once we decide to use Frame Relay at all, the port in New York City becomes a "sunk" (already committed) cost. The incremental cost of $294 a month per additional 56Kbps costs less than the $308 a month we would pay for even a zero-mile 56Kbps circuit, so it might actually be best in this particular example to use Frame Relay for all locations.

What we have just demonstrated is that short distances tend to favor leased lines with distance-sensitive tariffs, whereas longer distances tend to favor fast packet services with distance-insensitive tariffs. On reflection, it should be easy to see that this is true in general, not just for the example we chose.

Recall that Frame Relay services include a back-haul component that is sufficient to carry data anywhere in the continental United States. When you order a Frame Relay port and PVC, you are paying for that back-haul, whether your data is traveling 2 miles or 2,000. If your data has to travel a great distance, the totally distance-insensitive Frame Relay tariff can be a good deal. If your data is traveling only a short distance, Frame Relay may be a bad deal.

Please keep in mind that this is a very simplistic analysis. Numerous factors, including the cost of local access circuits, were ignored. Also, in computing meaningful cross-over points for your organization, it is meaningless to use published tariff prices; you will tend to receive different discounting levels on different services, and these are likely to move your cross-over points either upward or downward. What you should take away from this discussion is not the figure 888 miles; rather, it is the notion that there will always be a cross-over point and that it is not difficult to figure out what it is.

5.9   The Bent Straw

Light normally travels in a straight line, or in what passes for a straight line in our universe of curved space time. Yet it is a well-known principle of optics that light, on passing from a less dense medium to a more dense one, bends toward the normal, where normal is defined as a line at right angles to the surface formed between the two media. This phenomenon enables us to create lenses. This phenomenon also causes a straw to appear bent when we look up at it through a glass of clear water, as shown in Figure 5-21.

Analogously, in some cases, the shortest (that is, lowest cost) line between two points is neither a straight line nor a Great Circle following the curvature of the earth. Consider an international boundary, such as the long, straight

Figure 5-21: A straw in a glass of water.

western boundary between the United States and Canada as shown in Figure 5-22. Here indeed are two media of different "density": The price per Mbps per line of a long-distance circuit through Canada is much greater than the similarly normalized cost of an equivalent circuit through the United States. This reflects the more advanced state of telecommunications deregulation in the United States.

Now consider the cost of a circuit from Seattle (point A) to Calgary (point Z). The shortest circuit would pass through point B; however, there are in practice, only a few border crossings for circuits, and point B is not one of them. The closest border crossing to point B is point C, which happens to be Blaine, Washington. Circuit ACZ may represent the lowest-mileage circuit between points A and Z, but it is not the least-expensive circuit. That honor goes to circuit ADZ. Running as much of the circuit as possible through the zone of lower "tariff density," the United States, results in lower overall cost, even though it results in a greater number of circuit miles.

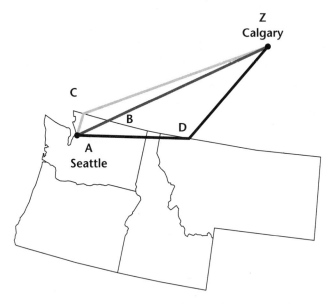

Figure 5-22: Alternative circuit routings between the
United States and Canada.

6 Selecting Transmission Technologies

One of your first tasks in phase 2, preliminary design, is to select from among a wide variety of candidate transmission technologies—primarily those operating at levels 1 and 2, the physical and data link layers, of the OSI Reference Model.[1] In the days before internetworking, this choice had a truly fundamental impact on your network design. It would percolate outward to every corner of the network and would color every other decision.

In a modern internetwork, the selection of transmission technologies is still important, but it no longer represents a black-and-white, global, and irrevocable commitment. The great distinction between a network and an internetwork is precisely that the internetwork offers media independence. An internetwork can consist of any transmission technology or of a mix of technologies. Internetworking can operate over practically anything that can move bits, whether it's a LAN, a private line, or a length of wet string. Internetworking thus offers the network designer a degree of flexibility that was heretofore unavailable.

Nonetheless, most networks are constructed from a limited mix of transmission technologies rather than from every technology that conceivably might be used. This is done primarily in order to keep the network comprehensible and manageable. Because of the need to limit choices to a manageably small number of transmission technologies, and because of the interaction between these choices and other aspects of the overall design, it is useful to select the primary transmission technologies early on.

This chapter begins by discussing the *roles* in which transmission technologies might be used and the roles for which each technology is most suitable. The variety of options available to the designer today can be bewilderingly rich;

---

1. H. Zimmerman, "The OSI Reference Model—The ISO Model of Architecture for Open Systems Interconnection," *IEEE Transaction on Communications,* April 1980.

consequently, it is helpful to start with a road map. We then proceed to discuss the technologies, one by one.

It is not my intent to explain any of these technologies in full detail. They are amply documented elsewhere, and if you are designing large-scale inter-networks, you probably already have a good understanding of how the lower-layer protocols work. Instead, I have attempted to present each trans-mission technology in terms of the most typical or most attractive modes of use and to explain the technical and business considerations associated with that use in practical, nuts-and-bolts terms that are relevant to the network designer. My aim in this chapter is to help you to understand *when and how to use* each of the transmission technologies that are available. For this, you will need to understand not only their functional and technical characteristics but also the typical structure of tariffs under which the carriers offer these services.

6.1   Roles for Each Transmission Technology

When we want to drive a nail, we do not reach for a screwdriver. When we want to drill a hole, we do not reach for a wrench. Each tool has its suitable domain of use. Analogously, each transmission technology has a domain of suitability, a range of applications for which it is technically and economi-cally well suited.

There is often a temptation to pick the most elegant or most technologi-cally advanced solution. Networking protocols are subject to cycles of fash-ionability, just like clothes and automobiles. It is clear that none of us would want to make a major investment in a technology that is on its way out; how-ever, predicting the next generation of winners is an exceptionally risky busi-ness. Even for the most knowledgeable among us, picking the up-and-coming technology winners is no easier than picking the winners in next year's Kentucky Derby or the stocks that will double over the next year. If you pick a solution solely because you think that everyone else will be using it soon, you may find yourself disappointed.

Table 6-1 is a summary of this chapter. This table is intended to provide a road map to what follows. Don't try to digest it all just yet. Instead, refer back to it fre-quently as you work your way through the chapter.

> In selecting technologies for your network, your choices should flow organically from your functional requirements. You should pick a set of tools that are appropriate to the task at hand.

Table 6-1: Roles for Various Transmission Technologies

Technology	Speed Range (Kbps)			Backbone Trunking	Access Concentration	Commercial Access	Residential Access
	Low	High	Future High				
Leased lines (copper)	56	45,000	45,000	X	X	X	
Leased lines (SONET)	51,000	2,480,000	9,920,000	X	X	Emerging	
Parallel circuits	2 × 56	n × leased	n × leased	X	X	X	
Channelization	56	620,000	2,480,000	X	X	X	
Circuit switching	56	2,480,000	2,480,000	X	X		
Frame Relay	56	1,544	45,000	X	X	X	
SMDS DXI	56	50,000	50,000		X	X	
SMDS SNI	1,544	45,000	155,000		X	X	
ATM UNI	1,544	2,480,000	9,920,000	X	X	X	
POTS telephony	N/A	56	56				X
ISDN BRI	64	2 × 64	2 × 64			X	X
ISDN PRI	64	23 × 64	23 × 64		X		
Cable	128/home share 2,000	2,000/home share 15,000	10,000/home share 60,000				
ADSL	128/256	600/6,000				X	X
VDSL	2,000/26,000	20,000/51,000	155,000/155,000		Not yet available	X	X
IP tunneling	56	1,544	45,000	X	X	X	X

In distinguishing among potential roles for each transmission technology, I have used the following major categories: mode of use, speed, and geographic expanse. Each category can be subdivided further.

Mode of use consists of the following categories:

- Backbone trunking: connections between core backbone infrastructure locations
- Access concentration: aggregation of remote connections into a smaller number of infrastructure locations or ports
- Commercial access: connections to business/organizational locations, including the connections that a corporation or any other organization of comparable scale would require for its business locations, be they remote sales offices or the corporate headquarters
- Residential access: connections to home locations—whether for entertainment use or for business telecommuting

6.2   Dedicated Circuits (Leased Lines)

Far and away the simplest means of connecting various locations over the wide area is with private (dedicated) lines, often referred to as leased lines. These circuits are available from the carriers; however, there is no need to establish a connection by dialing a phone number. The circuits are permanently in place.

Leased lines are used in many contexts in data communications. Here, we are concerned primarily with using leased lines as a direct connection medium between routers. The router drives the leased line directly, often through an external device known as a channel service unit/data service unit (CSU/DSU), as shown in Figure 6-1.

The interface between the router and the CSU/DSU typically follows any of a number of interface standards, such as RS-232/V.24, V.35, RS-422, or high speed serial interface (HSSI). We normally pay little attention to these interfaces, but they can, in some instances, have a significant impact on the performance and reliability of the system as a whole.

Leased lines are available with various speeds and specifications. In the United States, the most common types of leased lines are the DS-0 (56Kbps), the T-1 (1.544Mbps), and the T-3 (45Mbps).

The leased line represents the physical layer of transmission, but it is still necessary for the router to apply a protocol layer on top of this physical layer in order to provide the expected level of service to layer 3, the network layer.

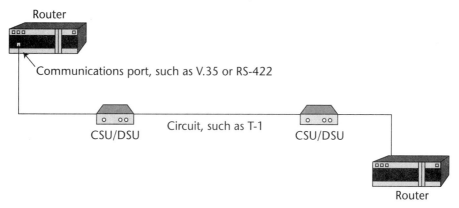

Figure 6-1: A pair of routers, CSU/DSUs, and a leased line.

Historically, it was commonly the case that an acknowledged data link layer protocol, such as high-level data link control (HDLC), would be used to provide a high level of assured delivery of data. More recently, it is often the case that the inherent reliability of the circuits is usually high, in which case it can be counterproductive to use an acknowledged protocol in an attempt to enhance an already adequate service. As a result, newer networks often support the leased line with a simple point-to-point protocol (PPP) interface, which provides HDLC framing—when used in conjunction with synchronous protocols, as would be the case on a high-speed leased line—and error detection but no error correction. With PPP, there is no retransmission at the data link layer.

6.3   Parallel Circuits and Inverse Multiplexing

In many cases, a design calls for an amount of bandwidth that is too large for one circuit size yet too small for the next larger size. For example, the design may call for 5.0Mbps of capacity on a particular path. This is far too much for a T-1 circuit, with its capacity of 1.5Mbps; however, it represents too little load to be cost-effective on the next larger circuit that you can obtain, a T-3, with a capacity of 45Mbps. You would be paying for far more capacity than you expect to use.

One way to deal with this situation is through the use of multiple, parallel leased lines between the same pair of locations (see Figure 6-2). Four leased T-1 circuits—with a capacity of 4 × 1.5 = 6.0Mbps—could accommodate 5.0Mbps of load and will generally cost far less than a T-3 circuit.

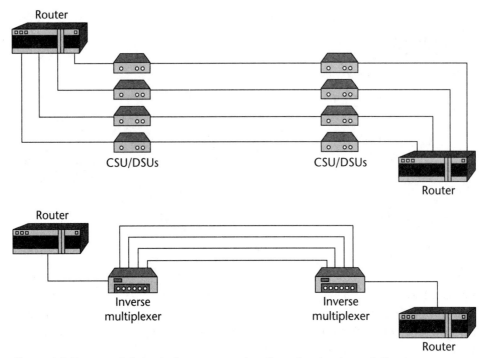

Figure 6-2: Four parallel circuits between two locations: two implementations.

In practice, one must compute the price/performance of each solution. It is sometimes prefcrable to order the next larger circuit, even though doing so may be an overkill relative to your requirements. A T-3 circuit, for instance, carries 28 times as much traffic as a T-1 circuit and will, in most cases, cost anywhere from 3 to 10 times as much as a T-1. When you look at the specific prices available to your organization and factor in the incremental cost of inverse multiplexing equipment, the multiple T-1 solution might prove to be more expensive than the single T-3 solution.

Queuing theory tells us that twice as fast is (almost) always better than twice as many. The effective throughput of parallel circuits is somewhat less than that of a single circuit with comparable aggregate bandwidth. Adding more circuits increases the effective aggregate bandwidth but at a slightly less than linear rate.

With careful design, parallel circuits can provide greater availability than a single circuit. If your carrier can provide you with circuit *diversity*—the assurance that the circuits take completely different paths through the carrier's network—you can regard the failure probabilities of each circuit as being statistically independent of the others. The probability that two truly diversely routed circuits will fail at the same time is much lower than the probability that either circuit alone will fail: In fact, it is the product of these probabilities. Thus, if each of the two circuits in the preceding example has an availability of 99.9 percent, this implies unavailability of $(1 - 0.999) = 0.001$. The unavailability of the two together is $0.001 * 0.001 = 0.000001$, which is to say that the availability is $(1 - 0.000001) = 0.999999$, or 99.9999 percent. There remains, of course, the risk that one of the two circuits fails, and this risk is still 0.001; however, a single circuit failure might result—again, with proper overall design—in gracefully degraded performance rather than a complete loss of service.

There are a number of ways to put parallel circuits to use.

- The routers can load balance a modest number of circuits directly, under a suitable interior routing protocol, such as open shortest path first (OSPF), interior gateway routing protocol (IGRP), or enhanced IGRP (E-IGRP), as shown in the upper portion of Figure 6-2.
- Many switches can load balance among parallel trunks.
- Special devices, called *inverse multiplexers,* can take two or more slower parallel circuits and can provide equipment at both ends with the appearance of a single fast circuit as shown in the lower portion of Figure 6-2. Inverse muxes usually incorporate the functionality of the CSU/DSUs.

The choice among these techniques can sometimes come down to a matter of taste. Letting the routers load balance among more than three or four circuits can be clumsy and cumbersome. Inverse multiplexers are in some senses the simplest and most elegant solution, yet they are felt by some to interfere with network management, since they make it difficult to tell what is going on with the underlying circuits. The inverse multiplexer might also represent a single point of failure for the collection of parallel circuits.

6.4 Channelized Circuits

In Chapter 5, we explained that nearly everything in this industry is cheaper by the dozen. Circuits are very much a case in point.

A T-1 circuit is designed to carry 24 DS-0 circuits; a T-3 circuit, 28 T-1 circuits. Yet the cost of a T-1 circuit is far less than that of 24 DS-0 circuits. It may correspond to as few as 4 DS-0s or to as many as 18, depending on your choice of carrier and on various characteristics of the circuits in question.

The T-1 circuit bandwidth is shared by means of *time division multiplexing (TDM)*. For a normal voice call, the amplitude of sound is sampled every 125 microseconds and an 8-bit value generated to reflect the amplitude of the sound waveform. When 24 of these octets have gone by, an additional bit is injected to provide for in-band control of the circuit. Similar techniques can be used to multiplex 28 logical T-1 circuits (sometimes called DS-1s) on a single T-3 circuit.

If you have a fair number of circuits that are all heading in the same direction, it may be cost-effective to combine them onto a single, higher-bandwidth circuit (see Figure 6-3). You may choose to do this yourself, with your own equipment, or you may choose to have your carrier do the multiplexing on your behalf.

Channelization provides no inherent statistical multiplexing advantage. Thus, you may prefer to aggregate circuits by using a router rather than TDM channelization, because the statistical multiplexing gain achieved by the router enables you to use fewer circuits than would be the case with a channelized solution. TDM channelization may nonetheless be advantageous in some circumstances. In particular, you may find it convenient to gain the advantages of a higher-bandwidth circuit in a location where it is either impractical or prohibitively expensive to deploy your own router or data switch: Your carrier can channelize on your behalf. Figures 6-4 and 6-5 show the relative merits of these two forms of aggregation.

Further, channelization is a very cost-effective means of achieving access concentration. You might have your LEC concentrate a dozen 56Kbps remote access circuits onto a single T-1 circuit, in order to provide a more concentrated "feed" to your hub location (see Figure 6-6). This is usually cheaper than

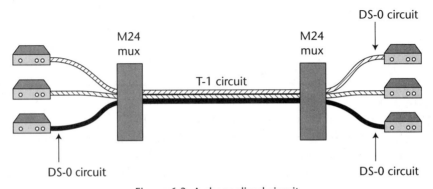

Figure 6-3: A channelized circuit.

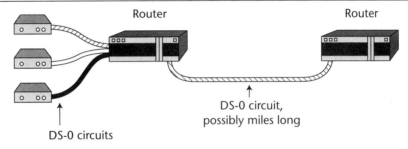

Figure 6-4: You achieve bandwidth savings by using a router to aggregate traf c.

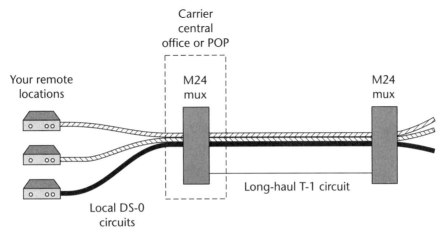

Figure 6-5: Your carrier can provide aggregation by channelizing on your behalf.

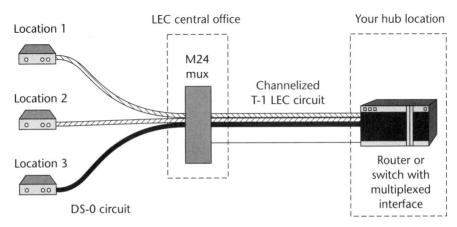

Figure 6-6: Channelization as a means of achieving access concentration.

bringing the corresponding number of individual circuits into your hub location. At the same time, you might find it advantageous to concatenate two or more of the adjacent DS-0 64Kbps circuits in order to obtain *fractional T-1* services at, for example, 128Kbps (2 × DS-0) or 256Kbps (4 × DS-0).

6.5   Circuit Switching

In some cases, it may be advantageous to take a simple circuit and to route it through one of your locations to reach another point on the network (see Figure 6-7). This is a standard technique in the telephony world. We sometimes speak of this as *drop and insert*. In the high-speed SONET world, this is accomplished with *add and drop multiplexers (ADMs)*.

Suppose that two channelized circuits are connected to one of your infrastructure locations. Some channels might be *dropped* off for use at the location. Viewed from the perspective of the channelized circuit, we would say that they are *inserted* into the channelized circuit as it passes through. Other channels might transparently be cross-connected from one of the channelized circuits to the other, as shown in Figure 6-7.

A positive aspect to these cross-connections is that they do not add switching or queuing delay. From that perspective, this can be a very attractive solution. Nonetheless, this style of networking is somewhat out of favor in the internetworking world today. The assignments are static, and changing them can be labor intensive. Operating a network in this way is stiff and inflexible in comparison with packet-switched techniques. Also, since circuit switching is just an application of circuit channelization, it does not inherently provide any statistical multiplexing advantage.

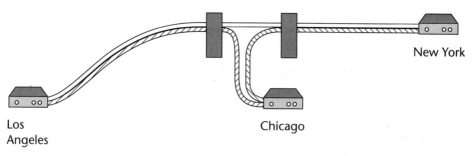

Figure 6-7: Circuit-switching techniques: dropping and insertion.

6.6   **Analog Dialup**

Most of us do not have leased lines of any shape or form to our homes. Neither can we access them from our hotel rooms when we travel. What options are available to us?

The one communications medium that is, in the United States at least, truly ubiquitous is the switched public telephone network: POTS, for plain old telephone service. We can make a telephone call from practically anywhere in the developed world.

With the aid of a *modulator/demodulator,* or *modem,* we can transmit data over these voice-grade telephone connections. At the current state of technology, speeds approaching 56Kbps in the favored direction (toward the residential consumer; the current generation of modems is optimized to provide consumers with more bandwidth for download than for upload) are routinely available.

The effective speed of transmission may in practice be significantly greater. Many of the dialup solutions available today include the use of *compression*. Various compression techniques exist, but they are all based on the principle that frequently encountered sequences of data should be encoded as compactly as possible, even if doing so means that infrequently encountered sequences must pay a penalty. On balance, compression can improve the effective speed of data transmission by as much as a factor of 2, and in some cases by more. Not every data stream benefits from compression—in some cases, compression could actually adversely impact the effective performance of the link; however, commercial implementations today commonly produce at least a 2:1 improvement for typical user data. Thus, the effective data rate of a 33.6Kbps modem might be in the range of 60–70 Kbps. That of a 56Kbps modem might be in the range of 100–120 Kbps (in the favored direction).

You are probably already familiar with a modem. You probably have one in your PC. Most often, a modem is a board or *Personal Computer Memory Card International Association* (PCMCIA) device that connects via a jack to a telephone line; alternatively, the modem might be an external device that connects to a serial port on your computer. Less familiar to most people are the devices used to concentrate data calls in a large-scale internetwork. In principle, one could use exactly the same devices that perform so well in your PC; however, the economics of doing so are prohibitive.

More often, an Internet service provider or other large-scale dialup provider uses large-scale devices that deal with incoming calls in bulk. Recall that a T-1 circuit contains 24 DS-0 circuits. This is true not only for leased lines but also for dialup lines. A typical device might support one or two channelized T-1 circuits and would contain enough modem chipsets to accommodate all of the 48 calls that this configuration could potentially support. The device would typically connect to the corporate or ISP internetwork across an Ethernet LAN (see Section 6.8) and would provide all of the network management, accounting, and user authentication/authorization services necessary for the provision of a commercial-grade service. Figure 6-8 depicts a typical dialup internetworking access solution. For large-scale applications, dialup terminal servers are now available that can deal with an entire T-3 circuit, thus accommodating up to 672 simultaneous calls in a single highly integrated device.

Dialup access to the Internet has been extremely popular in the United States in recent years; however, it has been problematic for the LECs. The LEC public switched telephone network was designed for calls with an average duration, or "hold time," of some 3 minutes. Data calls, however, tend to have hold times of 25 minutes or more. Consequently, data calls are tying up scarce resources within many voice switches, forcing the LECs to deploy additional, expensive equipment. Under current U.S. regulatory policy, the LECs are not permitted to pass these costs along to the customers who necessitate them.

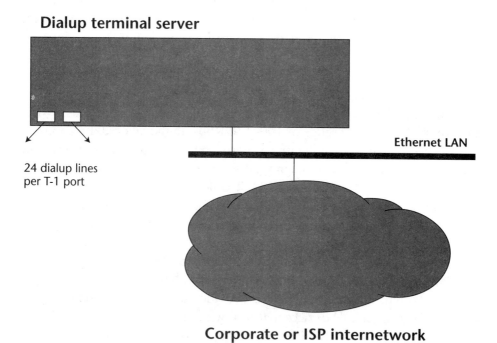

Figure 6-8: Concentration of data-bearing POTS calls.

The LECs have been increasingly unenthusiastic about providing the necessary network upgrades, since they typically lose money on them.

Some LECs will, as an alternative, offer to deploy terminal servers on behalf of an ISP, or service provider. This is, potentially, a win for all parties. The LEC can deploy the terminal servers in a way that minimizes their infrastructure costs—costs that are otherwise invisible to the ISP and that the ISP is not otherwise motivated to work to reduce.

6.7   ISDN

The telephone companies have been working for decades to devise a way of using the newer digital technologies rather than the analog techniques that were originally used to construct the telephone infrastructure. A major thrust in this regard has been the *Integrated Services Digital Network,* or *ISDN.* ISDN comes in several variants. A residential consumer would be most likely to use the ISDN Basic Rate Interface, or BRI. With ISDN BRI, the telephone company provides two data channels, each 64Kbps, over a single physical circuit. In addition, the line carries a 16Kbps channel for signaling and control of the circuit. The line is said to carry two *bearer* channels (of customer data) and one *data* channel, or 2B + D.

The other common form of ISDN is Primary Rate Interface, or PRI. In the United States, an ISDN PRI is physically provided across a normal T-1 line and carries 23 bearer channels, as well as a 64Kbps channel for control, or 23B + D. In Europe and elsewhere, the prevalent circuits are not T-1 but rather E-1. The E-1 is a 2.048Mbps circuit that carries not 24 but rather 32 DS-0 circuits. Since European ISDN PRI is based on the E-1 circuit, this implies that a European PRI has 31 bearer data channels, and 1 channel for control, or 31B + D.

Typical applications for ISDN include

- Residential consumer access, using ISDN BRI at speeds of 64Kbps or 128Kbps
- Concentration of many ISDN BRI consumers, POTS consumers, or a mix of the two, using an ISDN PRI interface at a service provider's point of presence
- Switched backup for leased line access

6.7.1   ISDN BRI for Residential Consumer Access

In recent years, the LECs have been deploying more ISDN capability in order to offer greater bandwidth to users of online services and Internet access. The two channels of an ISDN BRI can collectively transfer data at a speed of

128Kbps, which greatly exceeds the 56Kbps that currently represents the practical maximum on dialup communications.

Some LECs have priced an ISDN BRI line to be only slightly more expensive than a conventional POTS line. The customer must still pay for telephone calls placed on an ISDN line, just as with a voice line; moreover, these charges can, in the case of long-distance calls, be quite substantial. As with POTS, however, the desired destination may be within the "free" calling radius—the region within which no per minute charges apply—and those network providers that use ISDN generally design their networks to maximize the likelihood that this will be so. Thus, an ISDN BRI would seem at first blush to be a very attractive solution.

For a variety of reasons, however, ISDN BRI has not caught on to the degree that one might have expected.

- ISDN is complex to install and to configure.
- LECs have been slow to train their staffs to support ISDN.
- LECs have been slow to deploy ISDN, resulting in spotty and uneven availability throughout the United States.
- Use of both ISDN bearer channels of a BRI requires either inverse multiplexing or, more typically, multilink PPP,[2] but delays and incompatibilities in multilink PPP have inhibited the ability of consumers to achieve the 128Kbps that ISDN BRI claims to deliver.
- ISDN tends to be expensive to use and is expensive and cumbersome to set up, due partly to the need, in most cases, for a modemlike network termination device.

To these must be added an additional concern: PPP analog POTS solutions offer 56Kbps of bandwidth in the favored direction in conjunction with compression, at which point they may be roughly comparable in performance to ISDN BRI solutions that offer 128Kbps without compression. There is no fundamental reason why compression could not be offered over ISDN, but vendors have tended not to do so, in part because the limited market for ISDN has not warranted much expenditure on the part of the vendor community.

6.7.2 Concentration of Customers Who Use ISDN BRI or POTS

In Section 6.6, we showed how dialup service providers concentrate many dialup users of online services or of the Internet by using switched channelized

---

2. K. Sklower, B. Lloyd, G. McGregor, D. Carr, and T. Coradetti, "The PPP Multilink Protocol (MP)," *RIC 1990*, August 1996

T-1 circuits. In many cases, these service providers use an ISDN PRI, which serves as an intelligent switched channelized T-1 circuit, as an alternative to a conventional channelized switched T-1. LEC ISDN is not available everywhere, but where it is, it can be an interesting option.

Typically, a LEC ISDN PRI circuit costs slightly more than an equivalent switched channelized T1 circuit; however, the premium that one pays can differ greatly, depending on the LEC and, perhaps, also on the distance that the circuit must run to reach the LEC's ISDN switch. (Most LECs use a small number of ISDN-capable switches to serve a large number of their central offices. The customer may have to pay for the cost of back-hauling the data from the LEC CO to the switch.) Also, one occasionally finds that the LEC demands a very high installation charge.

Most LECs can flexibly intermix digital calls from other ISDN locations and conventional analog calls on a call-by-call basis. Thus, it is possible for a single ISDN PRI to simultaneously support consumers using P.OTS service and other consumers using ISDN BRI. The ability to deploy a single infrastructure to do both jobs can represent a substantial economic advantage; indeed, if you already have a requirement to support users over POTS, the incremental cost of also supporting ISDN BRI users may be very small.

Earlier in this chapter, we noted that LECs are increasingly reluctant to provide switched channelized T-1s as a means of concentrating voice customers. For the same reasons, they are reluctant to provide ISDN PRI connections. The connection still ties up valuable resources on their voice switches. In both cases, however, the LEC is usually obliged to provide the connection where their tariff lists it as an available service.

6.7.3 Switched Backup for Leased Line Access

In many cases, a leased line connection does not provide the availability—in the sense of reliability—that your application requires. It is usually possible to achieve greater availability by using a second circuit; however, doing so is generally expensive. You might need to acquire at least twice as much bandwidth as you would need in the absence of failures, in order to ensure that your solution still meets minimum requirements when one circuit is down. Further, you must work hard to ensure that your circuits provide for full *diversity*, which is to say that their failure probabilities must be *independent*: If one circuit fails, there should be no higher a probability of the other failing than you would expect based on random chance. The need for diversity can add cost and complexity to your solution.

ISDN and other services that offer *bandwidth on demand* can, in some cases, provide a simpler and cheaper way to provide high availability. Consider a remote site connected to your network infrastructure over a 56Kbps leased line. Assume that the availability of the leased line is 99 percent. To achieve an effective availability of 99.9 percent using only leased lines, you would typically need to at least double the cost of access lines to this location (see Figure 6-9).

Enhancing the availability using ISDN may be cheaper. Suppose that we were to establish centralized dialup servers at two locations that would provide backup only when the site's leased line was down (see Figure 6-10). As we have seen, an ISDN BRI might typically cost about $40 a month. This is more than a typical business telephone line but still quite affordable. The remote site would need to automatically dial an expensive long-distance call whenever the leased line is unavailable; however, if the leased line is available most of the time, the cost of these long-distance charges might be quite low. At the stated availability of 99 percent, the backup line would be used for about 7 hours—(24 hours a day) $\times$ (30 days a month) $\times$ (1.00 − 0.99)—in an average month. Thus, if the cost of the long-distance call is about $8/hour, the cost of redundancy for this location is the $40/month fixed charge for the ISDN BRI line, plus about 7 hours times $8/hour, for a total of $96/month. This is less, in general, than you would pay for the 56Kbps leased backup line assumed in the first scenario. Moreover, if you are supporting a large number of sites in this way, it will often be cheaper in terms of infrastructure expense to operate a couple of centralized inexpensive dialup servers than it would be to provide redundancy throughout your network.

The fly in the ointment is that ISDN is not available everywhere that you might need it. For most organizations, it's not practical for this to be the only

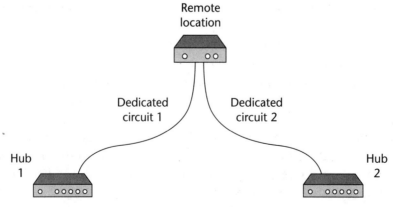

Figure 6-9: Achieving dual-homed redundancy with leased lines.

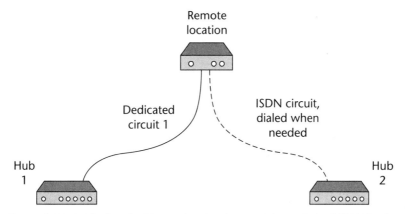

Figure 6-10: Achieving dual-homed redundancy with a switched ISDN backup.

mechanism you use to provide enhanced availability for an entire widespread network. Consequently, you might end up absorbing the cost of maintaining two distinct solutions.

6.8   Frame Relay

Frame Relay is one of the best and most cost-effective technologies available today for building internetworks. A clear understanding of its economic characteristics, and especially a clear understanding of how to intermix Frame Relay and conventional private lines, is essential to the design of cost-effective internetworks today.

In Chapter 5, we saw a number of examples of the use of Frame Relay. This section expands on that discussion, concentrating on presenting practical applications of Frame Relay services as a means of constructing public and private internetworks. First, we will consider the service definition for Frame Relay; next, we will discuss the protocol basis of the Frame Relay User Network Interface (UNI) definition but only to the level of detail necessary to enable you to understand how to design internetworks. We will then discuss the possible applications of private Frame Relay networks, followed by specific applications for LEC, IXC, and international public Frame Relay networks. Frame Relay tariffs, which were discussed in Chapter 5, are reviewed as necessary in the context of LEC and IXC applications.

6.8.1   Frame Relay Service Definition

Frame Relay moves bits from here to there. Like IP, it is a best-effort delivery service, not a guaranteed delivery service. It offers error detection but no error correction. (There is no retransmission mechanism.) In light of the lack of error correction, it is suitable for transmission circuits that have high inherent reliability and is less suitable for circuits with low inherent reliability. Frame Relay is typically supported at speeds of DS-0 (56Kbps), fractional T-1, and T-1. Frame Relay support at T-3 speeds (45Mbps) is becoming increasingly common.

Frame Relay services are based on the notion of a virtual circuit (much like X.25 networks). The virtual circuit is a logical path from one location in a Frame Relay network to another location. Frame Relay specifications envision *permanent virtual circuits (PVCs),* which are established through administrative procedures and may remain active indefinitely, and *switched virtual circuits (SVCs),* which are created dynamically when needed. A few commercial products support SVCs, but commercial services tend not to offer SVCs, and most carriers see little demand for such a service. In the interest of simplicity, we will limit our discussion to PVCs.

Data for many PVCs can coexist on a single point-to-point Frame Relay data link. Each PVC is identified by a *data link connection identifier (DLCI).* The DLCI is a numeric identifier, generally in the range from 0 to 4,095. Typically, the DLCI is assigned by the carrier, but some carriers will honor a customer's request for a particular DLCI number. The DLCI identifies a particular PVC to the Frame Relay devices at each end of the link. The DLCI has only local significance: Two ports in the same Frame Relay network could use the same DLCI number, either for the same PVC or for different PVCs, without confusion. There is no global identifier for a PVC.

Associated with each PVC is a *committed information rate (CIR).* Many carriers design their networks to carry at least as much traffic as specified by the CIR and to burst to higher data rates for limited periods of time, taking advantage of statistical multiplexing. Some carriers, however, simply capacitize their networks to carry the largest realistically expected volume of traffic and capacitize based on observed usage trends rather than on a level of demand asserted by the customer. Each approach has pros and cons. It is true that most customers have no idea of their real traffic demands; however, the absence of an explicit CIR means that the carrier's service commitment to the customer is vague, and possibly unenforceable.

The customer selects the port speed at each location and, for carriers that support CIR, selects the CIR associated with each PVC. The CIR of a single PVC should never exceed the port speed; however, the user may choose to order several PVCs whose combined CIR collectively exceeds the port speed. *Oversubscribing* the capacity of the port in this way can be perfectly reasonable to the extent that the user is confident that it is unlikely that all PVCs will be sending or receiving at their respective maximum rates simultaneously.

6.8.2 Frame Relay User Network Interface (UNI)

Frame Relay is a very simple protocol. It operates at level 2, the data link layer, of the OSI Reference Model. Each frame begins and ends with a flag octet (8 bits). Bit stuffing is used to ensure that the pattern used in the flag byte can never appear in the data within a frame, just as is the case with HDLC. (In fact, the framing is defined in the LAP-F core specification, where LAP stands for *link access protocol*. LAP-F is an expanded successor to the familiar LAP-B subset of HDLC, which is the usual data link layer for the familiar X.25 protocol family.) The protocol header normally consists of two octets, which primarily contain the DLCI number. The standards envision an optionally larger header with a larger DLCI, but in practice two octets are used. The *extended address (EA)* bits would be used to denote a longer address. The header format, as described in RFC 2427, is shown in Figure 6-11.[3]

The header also contains 2 bits that can be used to indicate network congestion: the *forward explicit congestion notification (FECN)* and *backward explicit congestion notification (BECN)* bits. The protocol designers of Frame Relay intended that these bits be used to indicate network congestion; however, the notification is of little value in an internetwork, because the

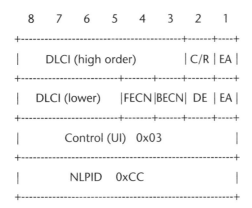

Figure 6-11: Frame Relay User Network Interface header format for encapsulation of IP data.

---

3. C. Brown and A. Malis, Request for Comments (RFC) 2427, "Multiprotocol Interconnect over Frame Relay," September 1998.

customer's routers are unlikely to respond in any useful way to FECN or BECN—and, indeed, it is not clear what they should do in that case.

The header also contains a *discard eligible (DE)* bit. The DE bit can be used to flag traffic that the network has accepted, even though that traffic exceeds the CIR for its PVC. The Frame Relay network is free to drop packets that have the DE bit set, if it needs to do so in order to reduce network congestion. In a properly engineered Frame Relay network, therefore, traffic up to the level of the CIR should always (or almost always) be accepted and carried by the network, whereas traffic in excess of the CIR can, optionally, be throttled back.

6.8.3 Typical Frame Relay Applications in Wide Area Internetworks

At the onset, it is helpful to consider Frame Relay's unique technical and commercial characteristics.

- Frame Relay is a statistically multiplexed transmission mechanism.
- Frame Relay operates at the data link layer of the OSI Reference Model.
- Frame Relay tariffs within a LATA are generally competitive with private lines.
- Frame Relay inter-LATA domestic tariffs are generally independent of distance.
- Frame Relay inter-LATA tariffs increase in proportion to bandwidth (typically, CIR).

We'll consider the applications of private Frame Relay networks, then of LEC Frame Relay, IXC Frame Relay, and international Frame Relay.

6.8.3.1 Applications of Private Frame Relay

In the mid-1990s, many large enterprises and Internet service providers felt that it was mandatory, on economic grounds, to use Frame Relay switching as the underpinnings for any large-scale wide area internetwork. The routers of that era offered insufficient port density: Too many were needed to serve a given number of customer locations. At one point, it was argued that Cascade (now Ascend and soon to be Lucent) switches offered a port density that was three times better than that of Cisco routers.

Today, these economics have largely reversed themselves. A pure router network offers better cost per port than a router/switch network and is generally more stable and more manageable. A switch/router internetwork may offer more sophisticated traffic management capabilities than a pure router-based internetwork, but this is not a strong enough driver to tilt the decision, in most cases.

An underlying private Frame Relay network can be attractive if a combination of the following considerations holds.

- You are a carrier or would otherwise like the ability to sell level 2 services.
- You need the ability to transport large volumes of nonroutable traffic, such as IBM SNA).
- You have a compelling need to run separable overlay networks on a shared infrastructure—for example, a test network and a production network.
- You have a strong business need for comprehensive traffic management.

6.8.3.2 Applications of LEC Frame Relay

LEC prices for Frame Relay are generally roughly competitive with their corresponding private line prices. Frame Relay pricing within a LATA, generally uniform and flat, includes the cost of the private line from the customer premise to the LEC Frame Relay switch; however, a large LATA may have a distance-sensitive pricing component, particularly where the distance exceeds about 30 miles. Most LECs implement aggregate CIR for all PVCs of either 0 or equal to the speed of the port; in neither case is there a meaningful charge associated with requesting either more or less CIR.

At the present state of deregulation in mid-1999 those U.S. LECs that were formerly part of the Bell system are not yet allowed to offer interstate Frame Relay services, although in a few instances, they can offer Frame Relay that is inter-LATA but intrastate. (Note, however, that non-Bell LECs such as GTE are able to offer interstate services today, and that Bell LECs (RBOCs) are likely to gain approval on a state-by-state basis shortly.) Today, therefore, LEC Frame Relay should be considered primarily as a concentration mechanism within the LATA rather than as an inter-LATA backbone transmission mechanism. Thus, it is not so common to see LEC Frame Relay used for an any-to-any mesh; instead, you might find it advantageous to use LEC Frame Relay to create small stars or dual stars within each LATA and to use other techniques to carry the traffic across LATA boundaries.

The inter-LATA transport could be effected by means of inter- or intra-LATA leased lines ("back-haul") or by IXC Frame Relay interconnected to the LEC Frame Relay, using the network-to-network interface (NNI). In the first scenario, you would order a LEC Frame Relay connection for the back-haul and would pay the LEC for the circuit to connect this Frame Relay port to (a) your own equipment within the LATA, or else (b) an IXC's POP, whence you would pay the IXC for an inter-LATA circuit to back-haul the

Frame Relay traffic out of the LATA to your network. In the former case, you would use whatever inter-LATA facilities were convenient to interconnect your equipment across LATA boundaries. In either case, the back-haul circuit ultimately terminates on your own equipment.

The circuit back-haul technique is simple, ubiquitously feasible, and does not necessarily oblige you to deploy your own concentration equipment to the LATA. It requires a moderate degree of sophistication on your part in terms of circuit provisioning if your equipment is outside the LATA, since it involves two carriers that may not be accustomed to interconnecting in this way. Moreover, if your traffic is very bursty, the leased back-haul circuit may represent something of an overkill for your needs.

The Frame Relay NNI is a potentially attractive solution; however, geographic availability remains spotty. Not all IXCs offer NNI interfaces to the LECs. Those that do typically offer NNI only in a small number of LATAs where demand is sufficiently high.

Curiously, Frame Relay concentration within the LATA is often implemented not to save on circuit costs within the LATA but rather to save on router port costs at your router concentration point. Consider, for example, Figure 6-12. Forty remote sites, each with an LEC Frame Relay connection at 56Kbps, are concentrated into a single "hub" Frame Relay port operating at the standard T-1 speed of 1.544Mbps. Note that this means that a single 1.544Mbps circuit is supporting up to $40 \times 56 = 2.24$Mbps of remote site traffic. How can this be? This sort of "oversubscription" is commonly done and works because we know that the 40 locations are unlikely to all be bursting at their maximum possible rates simultaneously; furthermore, no great harm will be done if the aggregate bandwidth utilization occasionally exceeds the capacity of the line, as long as the utilization does not remain at those levels for long enough for users to notice. This is an example of statistical multiplexing, which was discussed in Chapter 5.

For the "hub" part of the intra-LATA star, a single T-1 Frame Relay circuit will tend to be much cheaper than 40 DS-0s. Moreover, a single T-1 port on the router will tend to be vastly cheaper than 40 individual ports. To understand whether this is an advantageous solution, we need to compare it to the real competition: a multiplexed, channelized T-1.

In Section 6.4, we explained that it is often advantageous to let the LEC multiplex multiple DS-0 circuits onto a single T-1. This solution provides a hard maximum of 24 DS-0 circuits per channelized T-1, since the multiplexing is accomplished by means of straight TDM. The statistical multiplexing of Frame Relay will usually achieve at least a 2:1 advantage compared to

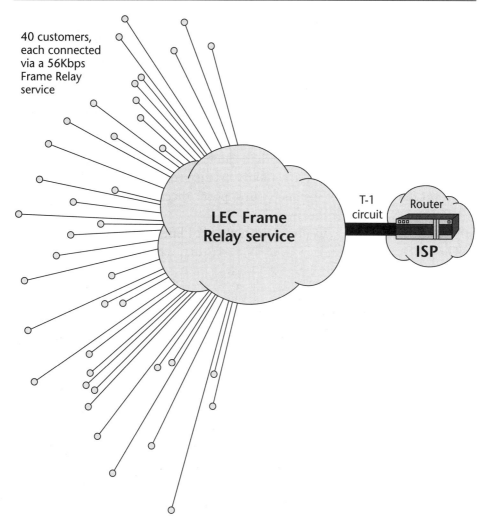

40 customers,
each connected
via a 56Kbps
Frame Relay
service

**LEC Frame
Relay service**

T-1
circuit

Router

ISP

Figure 6-12: Frame Relay concentration.

straight TDM, which can be advantageous *if you have a large number of DS-0s to work with*. The channelized solution also concentrates many DS-0s into a single T-1 and also uses a single router port, albeit a rather expensive one. In many cases, I have found the TDM solution to be more cost-effective overall. My advice would be to work this trade-off analysis with real numbers that correspond to your particular circumstances.

This assumes that most of your remote sites need connectivity at speeds of 56Kbps. If more than a handful of your remote sites instead need connectivity at speeds of T-1, Frame Relay is probably the wrong answer, because the LECs are unable to provide a "hub" port at speeds in excess of T-1. You are unable to get enough benefit from concentration. Furthermore, the T-1 Frame Relay price is likely to represent less of a break, in comparison to the price of a leased line, than does the DS-0 Frame Relay price.

Overall, the use of LEC Frame Relay is likely to be preferable to the use of LEC leased lines and channelization where some mix of the following applies.

- Most remote locations need access at speeds of 56Kbps or less, and few require access at speeds greater than can be achieved with fractional T-1.
- Most or all remote sites are relatively far from your "hub" location within the LATA—for instance, rural post offices are a better candidate than are urban movie theaters.
- You are looking to concentrate more than 24 lines per LATA.
- The LATA in question is in U.S. West territory, where Frame Relay is relatively cheap.

6.8.3.3 Applications of IXC Frame Relay

IXC inter-LATA Frame Relay is generally sold on a pricing basis that is completely insensitive to the distance that data must travel within the continental United States. In general, a base price reflects the speed of the Frame Relay port; to that is added a charge reflecting the associated CIRs. In general, CIR is charged based on data *sent* from a given location; receipt of data is "free," which is to say that it is assumed to have been paid by the sender. The cost of the LEC circuit—generally a leased line, not a Frame Relay connection—from a remote location to the IXC's point of presence is charged separately, usually at a rate based on the incumbent LEC's standard FCC tariff for the circuit; however, many IXCs take a markup on the LEC tariff.

There are significant differences among IXCs. Sprint has offered pricing plans for PVCs with 0CIR, with no explicit charge for CIR. (This does not necessarily imply that its prices are cheaper than those of its competitors.) Some IXCs offer pricing options that reflect the volume of data sent rather than the CIR subscribed to.

The costs of the port and of the CIR tend to increase almost linearly with bandwidth. There is rather little tendency for this service to be "cheaper by the dozen." As a result, IXC Frame Relay is more attractive for concentration of many low-bandwidth locations than for meshing of high-bandwidth locations.

This distance insensitivity is a very interesting property. As we saw in Chapter 5, it significantly alters the way that we might look at network economics and leads to a number of counterintuitive optimization strategies.

In conjunction with the nearly linear trend of cost per megabits per second, it argues for using IXC Frame Relay primarily to concentrate low-bandwidth sites that are in out-of-the-way places, that is, where we would otherwise need a leased line with a lot of mileage. Phrased differently, IXC Frame Relay can provide a convenient means to service remote parts of the country where it is not cost-effective to establish your own local presence.

Finally, since the IXCs generally charge for CIR on a simplex (unidirectional) basis, or at least support this charging mode, it may be particularly advantageous to use IXC Frame Relay if your data is inherently asymmetric. This is routinely the case for many online services and Internet access providers, since a "hit" on your Web browser typically might transmit only a small number of characters to the Web server yet might initiate the transfer of a large file or graphic image back to your browser. With a private line, you generally have no choice but to pay for equal bandwidth in both directions. With IXC Frame Relay, you may be able to tailor your PVC configuration so as to pay only for the CIR that you need.

As with LEC Frame Relay, it is usually advantageous to "hub" the data from a large number of low-bandwidth remote locations into one or two "hub" locations. The IXCs are capable of delivering a partial- or full-mesh logical network of PVCs; in most cases, however, a bushy mesh turns out to be impractical. The routers tend to be limited in the number of PVCs they can efficiently support over a single interface. Moreover, if you try to configure too many PVCs over a single port, you tend to slice the total CIR up to a level where things become unworkable. A partial mesh or a full mesh for a small core of routers can be perfectly satisfactory, but a full mesh for a network consisting of hundreds of routers is a bad idea. A great many IXC Frame Relay networks are consequently built as stars with one hub. My preference is to use two hub locations for IXC Frame Relay, with enough distance between them to reduce the risk that they will both be taken out by the same earthquake or hurricane. The two hubs need not be geographically close to each other; recall that distance, within the United States, is irrelevant to your price. These topological alternatives are discussed at length in Chapter 11.

In most cases, you are still limited to a maximum speed of T-1 at the hub locations, which tends to make it unattractive to connect remote locations operating at T-1 speeds. (Fractional T-1 port speeds may still be attractive.) Some IXCs, however, are able to provide T-3 Frame Relay access, generally as a special assembly rather than as a tariffed service. It does not hurt to ask. If so, it becomes very feasible to use Frame Relay to concentrate remote locations operating at T-1 speeds.

To recapitulate, IXC Frame Relay can be advantageous when some or all of the following factors are met.

- Most remote locations need access at speeds substantially less than T-1, and many need access at speeds of 56Kbps or less.
- Either most remote sites are widely dispersed, or some are far from areas where you have local presence.
- Demands for bandwidth are asymmetric.

6.8.3.4 Applications of International Frame Relay

International Frame Relay services vary greatly from provider to provider; nonetheless, we can extract a few general rules. First, the cost of transoceanic international Frame Relay is very high, as is the cost of international leased lines. One way or another, you need to obtain statistical multiplexing advantage in order to keep your costs down. If you feel that you need significant burst capacity but not a great deal of continuous sustained capacity, international Frame Relay may be attractive. Second, costs can be greatly influenced by the local circuit in the country where the connection lands. Deregulation is proceeding rapidly in Europe, but the local circuit in France or Germany can still be dreadfully expensive.

6.9   ATM

Asynchronous transfer mode (ATM), an emerging technology oriented toward high bandwidth, attempts to provide an integrated means of carrying voice, video, and data over a single modern network encompassing both the local area environment and the wide area. No single technology, not even ISDN, has generated as much hoopla and confusion in the industry as ATM has. It has followed the usual pattern of inflated claims, hype, and disappointment but on a grander scale than other technologies. In this section, we attempt to take a sober, dispassionate look at ATM and to understand what it can and cannot realistically achieve for us.

It is helpful to note at the outset that ATM and Frame Relay have more in common, from a network designer's point of view, than we might assume at first blush. Both technologies provide statistical multiplexing of the data link, and both have a virtual circuit model of data transmission. At the crossover points in terms of bandwidth, both have similar pricing structures; indeed, this must necessarily be the case! Both are offered by the same carriers. If the pricing were substantially more advantageous for one than for the other, the carriers would cannibalize their own installed base.

We will discuss ATM in roughly the same sequence in which we discussed Frame Relay. First, we will consider the service definition for ATM; next, we will consider the protocol basis of the ATM User Network Interface (UNI) definition but only to the level of detail necessary to enable you to understand how to use ATM to design internetworks. We will then discuss the possible applications of private ATM networks, followed by applications for LEC, IXC, and international public ATM networks. We will discuss ATM tariffs as necessary in the context of LEC and IXC applications.

6.9.1 ATM Service Definition and Protocol Interface

Like Frame Relay, ATM moves bits from here to there. Like both Frame Relay and IP, it is a best-effort delivery service, not a guaranteed delivery service. ATM offers error detection but no error correction. (ATM does not offer a retransmission mechanism; however, it may benefit from error-correction features offered to it transparently by the physical layer.) In light of the lack of error correction, ATM is suitable for transmission media that have high inherent reliability and is less suitable for media with low inherent reliability. ATM was designed with the high-speed fiber-based Synchronous Optical Network (SONET) in mind, although it can also operate at slower speeds that are consistent with traditional copper-based transmission systems. ATM is typically supported at speeds of T-1 (1.544Mbps), T-3 (45Mbps), and over SONET at speeds of OC-3 (155Mbps) and above.

ATM services are based on the notion of a virtual circuit, a logical path from one location in an ATM network to another location. ATM specifications envision *permanent virtual circuits (PVCs),* which are established through administrative procedures and may remain active for years, and *switched virtual circuits (SVCs),* which are created dynamically when needed. We noted earlier that most carriers have not implemented Frame Relay SVCs, claiming that there is no demand for such a service. It is natural to wonder whether ATM SVCs will suffer the same fate; however, there are potential applications for ATM SVCs, notably interactive video. We should view the jury as still being out as regards the market viability of ATM SVCs.

Connection-oriented protocols generally require signaling mechanisms, and ATM is no exception. The standard for ATM signaling is Q.2931.

Data for many VCs can coexist on a single point-to-point ATM data link. Each VC is identified by a *virtual path identifier (VPI)* and a *virtual channel identifier (VCI).*

Associated with each PVC is a *sustained cell rate (SCR).* The ATM SCR has essentially the same meaning as the Frame Relay CIR, representing a commitment on the part of the carrier to allocate sufficient network capacity to carry at least the committed level of traffic.

Also associated with each VC is a quality of service, or QoS. Voice and video require low delay and low variability of delay, while e-mail is relatively insensitive to delay. The QoS specification provides a means of expressing such application needs to the network.

ATM is a rather complex set of communication protocols. It can be viewed as operating at the data link layer of the OSI Reference Model, although some would assert that it functions more like a transport layer. For purposes of this text, we will treat it purely as a data link function.

Data link frames are broken up into cells, each with a single constant length. For historical reasons, this length was established as 53 octets. Five of these 53 octets are set aside for the ATM header. The remainder are available for data, a portion of which must be set aside for managing the *segmentation and reassembly (SAR)* function, which disassembles and reassembles cells into frames.

To date, five flavors of the SAR function have been defined, each associated with a different *ATM adaptation layer (AAL),* and each associated with a different kind of data stream. AAL 1 is associated with constant bit rate traffic, traffic that must be delivered with deterministic delay, typically because it corresponds to voice traffic. AAL 1, connection-oriented, has been used to provide T-1 emulation across an ATM backbone—in other words, transparently carrying a T-1 circuit across the network is the apparent service definition.

AAL 2 was intended for connection-oriented traffic requiring constant delay, such as realtime video. It has seen very limited use to date but might potentially see substantial use by carriers in the coming years. AAL 2 could potentially provide carriers with an efficient means of interconnecting conventional voice switches.

AAL 3 and 4 have largely been superseded by AAL 5, which is oriented toward data. AAL 5 has an *unspecified bit rate,* or *UBR,* and also supports the much more sophisticated *available bit rate,* or *ABR,* which is suitable for the transmission of IP data over ATM.

For the transmission of IP data, ATM is extremely wasteful of bandwidth. This overhead, sometimes referred to as the "ATM cell tax," is computed in Table 6-2. First, every ATM cell contains 5 octets of header for every 48 bytes of potential data, which corresponds to a waste of roughly 9.4 percent. Second, AAL 5 generally results in a partially empty last cell, since it does not support mixing multiple data link layer frames into a single cell (see Figure 6-13). This results in another 7.7 percent of wastage, assuming a typ-

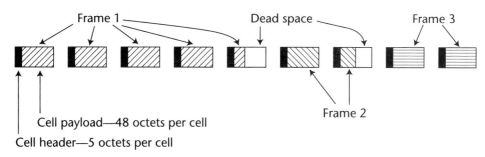

Figure 6-13: The last ATM cell for a frame is partially empty.

ical IP datagram length of about 280 octets, which is what we observe in the public Internet. Finally, the AAL 5 trailer itself is 8 octets long, representing an additional 2.6 percent overhead. Thus, when we use ATM to transmit IP datagrams, a total of nearly 20 percent of the data stream in ATM is wasted, compared to about 2 percent for IP over Frame Relay. Expressed differently, the capacity of the link needs to exceed the offered load by about 25 percent. This ignores ATM's physical encapsulation, which can introduce additional inefficiencies compared with other protocols.

For most purposes, this approximation is close enough. In reality, the

Table 6-2: ATM Cell Tax

Computation Element	Amount		Percent of Link
Cell size	53.0	bytes	100.0
ATM header	5.0	bytes	9.4
Payload per cell	48.0	bytes	90.6
Average bytes per IP datagram	280.0	bytes	
Average cells per IP datagram	6.0	cells	
Average waste in the last cell	24.0	bytes	7.7
On average, one cell per IP datagram will be half full			
AAL5 MTU trailer (one AAL 5 trailer required per datagram)	8.0	bytes	2.6
Average waste per cell: 24 + 8 = 32 bytes per IP datagram)	5.3	bytes	
Useful IP payload per cell (average)	42.7	bytes	
Utilization effectiveness	80.5%		80.3
Overhead (relative to useful payload)	24.2%		

overhead is slightly less. A significant fraction of TCP/IP traffic consists solely of TCP acknowledgments and of other datagrams that comprise exactly 40 bytes of TCP and IP data. These datagrams fit snugly within a single cell—assuming no use of what is known as *Sub Network Attachment Point (SNAP)* encapsulation—and thus represent a fairly efficient use of ATM. Taking this into account and using empirical datagram length distributions based on measurements of the public Internet, the most rigorous analysis that I have seen shows an expected ATM cell tax overhead of 17 percent rather than the 19.5 percent shown earlier.

6.9.2   Typical ATM Applications in Wide Area Internetworks

It is useful to consider ATM's unique characteristics, considering both public carrier services and enterprise network capabilities.

- ATM is a statistically multiplexed transmission mechanism.
- ATM could ideally provide an integrated transmission vehicle for audio, video, and data over a single transmission infrastructure.
- ATM can be viewed as operating at the data link layer of the OSI Reference Model.
- ATM inter-LATA tariffs are similar to those of Frame Relay at similar bandwidth and increase roughly in proportion to bandwidth utilized (SCR).
- ATM entails considerable overhead and complexity.
- ATM could potentially support very advanced traffic management.
- ATM can support very high bandwidth.
- ATM can—in conjunction with Frame Relay and service interworking— scale to support very large networks. It may be less suitable for small networks.

ATM services may be suitable for a number of applications. In order to understand how best to use ATM, it is necessary, at the outset, to consider the circumstances under which public or private ATM services are unlikely to be cost-effective.

ATM entails significant overhead, in comparison with lightweight protocols, such as Frame Relay or synchronous PPP. For typical IP data, we have seen that the overhead associated with ATM consumes nearly 20 percent of the capacity of the link. ATM equipment costs are equal to or greater than those of Frame Relay; indeed, in many cases, the equipment is largely the same. For ATM to be cost-effective, then, there must be some other technical or economic advantage that offsets this incremental cost.

We might reasonably expect that ATM will be unattractive for those tasks that are already admirably addressed by Frame Relay. Where the bandwidth requirements are low—T-1 or less at all locations—and where there is no need for functionality beyond that offered by Frame Relay, there is simply no business case to be made for ATM. Frame Relay will generally perform better and will generally cost less.

For ATM to be warranted, one or more of the following conditions have to hold.

- Bandwidth is required or desired for trunking beyond that readily available with other technologies.
- Concentration into hub ports at speeds of T-3 or above is warranted.
- You specifically need to run a level 2 network service anyway—for instance, you are a carrier or would otherwise like the ability to sell level 2 services.
- Realtime voice and/or video, or other traffic with deterministic delay requirements, must be intermixed with conventional internetworking data traffic.
- ATM's traffic management has to be so strongly advantageous as to outweigh its high costs and complexity.

We'll consider these five scenarios in turn.

6.9.2.1 Use of ATM to Support High Bandwidth

Today, the highest speeds available over copper-based telephony circuits are T-3, with a nominal bandwidth of some 45Mbps. Relatively few networks use links faster than T-3, but that number is growing rapidly.

A few years ago, many analysts and technologists felt that ATM would be the only practical way to drive data networks at speeds in excess of T-3. Today, alternatives exist, and the prospects for ATM in the core of high-speed networks must be judged in comparison to competing alternative solutions.

In the United States, the most common option at speeds beyond T-3, and thus the main competitor with ATM for high-speed networks, is the *Synchronous Optical Network (SONET)*. There is also an emerging tendency, as we shall see, to operate routers directly over the optical layer of a high-speed network, bypassing SONET entirely.

There are rather few options for driving data across SONET facilities today.

- You can use a SONET multiplexer, or mux, to break the SONET circuit down into multiple DS-3 channels, each equivalent to the data path over a T-3 circuit.

- You can use a direct serial interface, such as Cisco's *Packet over SONET Interface Processor (POSIP)*.
- You can use ATM switches.

The SONET mux approach can be straightforward (see Figure 6-14). The mux takes in a SONET OC-3, for example, and breaks down the 155Mbps data stream into three DS-3s, each with a nominal bandwidth of 45Mbps.

The SONET mux solution is workable but not ideal. SONET muxes are neither simple nor cheap. Moreover, this approach cannot capitalize on the full potential of the OC-3. First, there is some wastage of bandwidth in breaking up the OC-3: (3×45Mbps = 135Mbps, which is about 15 percent less than the nominal 155Mbps of the OC-3 channel). Second, the three DS-3 channels are not as good, in terms of expected delay, as a single 135Mbps data path. As we noted earlier, it is a general truism from queuing theory that twice as fast is almost always better than twice as many.

The direct packet over SONET serial connection, by contrast, is very workable. For Cisco equipment, an interface card in the Cisco 12000- or 7500- series router provides a direct SONET interface that does not depend on ATM. (We discuss this option later in this chapter.) In fact, in recent years, packet over SONET interfaces for Cisco routers have tended to stabilize and mature sooner than correspondingly high-speed interfaces for ATM.

Thus, there is no longer a compelling need to use ATM switches to drive IP traffic over underlying SONET or optical transmission facilities.

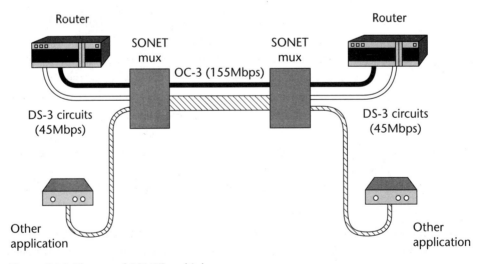

Figure 6-14: The use of SONET multiplexers.

IP directly over the optical layer is still an emerging area. Any solution will have to provide reliability in ways that do not depend on SONET failover mechanisms. This will likely be an important technology in the coming years, but it is still a bit early to predict how exactly things will settle out.

6.9.2.2 Concentration into Hub Ports at Speeds of T-3 or Above

We have seen that Frame Relay lends itself to concentration of large numbers of 56Kbps customers into a small number of "hub" ports, operating at speeds of T-1 (1.5Mbps) or greater. In much the same way, ATM can serve to concentrate large numbers of higher-speed customers onto a small number of circuits at T-3 (45Mbps) speeds or, conceivably, at even higher speeds (see Figure 6-15). This can result in significant savings in terms of hardware port costs and also, possibly, in terms of network management (fewer components to deal with).

At T-3 speeds, the cost of the ATM service should be contrasted with the cost of emerging carrier Frame Relay offerings operating at T-3 speeds and also with carrier switched multimegabit data service (SMDS) offerings, as described later in this chapter. The Frame Relay offerings will tend to have somewhat more favorable utilization of the transmission link, since they are not burdened with the ATM cell tax; conversely, the SMDS offerings will have slightly worse utilization, because they are burdened with not only the cell tax but also the overhead associated with large SMDS Network Interface (SNI) headers. You should take this into account in comparing services.

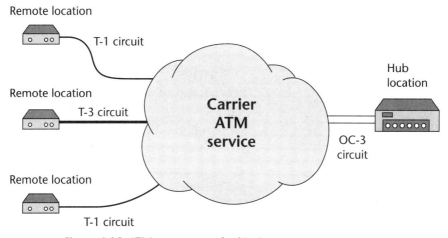

Figure 6-15: ATM as a means of achieving access concentration.

In the final analysis, the difference between these services is not qualitative. You can view it as a simple price/performance trade-off, based on the tariffs that are in effect or anticipated when you make the comparison.

A potentially interesting option is just becoming available: hybrid Frame Relay/ATM solutions, based on service interworking. In these hub-concentration scenarios, the use of ATM may be acceptable or necessary on the hub circuits, but it is inefficient or impractical on the numerous low-speed tail circuits to remote locations. We can use ATM/Frame Relay service interworking to transparently map between Frame Relay and ATM, thus achieving the best of both worlds (see Figure 6-16).

We use Frame Relay service to connect to the remote locations at speeds ranging from 56Kbps to T-1 (1.5Mbps). We use ATM services to connect to any remote locations that need T-3 access and also for the faster hub connections at speeds of T-3 (45Mbps) or above. This provides high bandwidth where we need it yet avoids the complexity and overhead of ATM on the numerous low-bandwidth remote connections.

6.9.2.3 Requirements for a Layer 2 Network

Some organizations have a specific business or organizational requirement to run a network that functions at level 2 of the OSI Reference Model. Typical reasons include

- The need to sell bandwidth to third parties, as a carrier does
- The need to transport large volumes of nonroutable traffic, such as IBM SNA

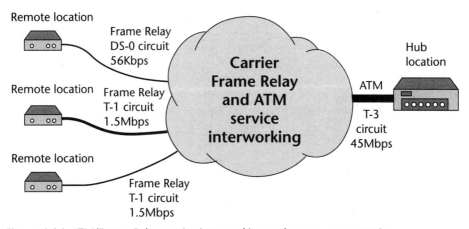

Figure 6-16: ATM/Frame Relay service interworking and access concentration.

■ A need to run separable overlay networks on a shared infrastructure, such as a test network and a production network

If your organization is a carrier, it is quite possible that all three reasons will pertain.

6.9.2.4 Integration of Realtime Voice or Video

ATM was designed from the ground up to carry voice, video, and data over a shared transmission infrastructure. It is not, however, the only solution to this problem. Other options include

■ Time division multiplexing (TDM) for voice and video, with an overlay network for data
■ Voice and video over IP

The TDM approach is essentially the one that the carriers have always provided: You would use conventional multiplexers to provide dedicated bandwidth for your voice and video applications. The voice and video traffic operates as it always has, over a dedicated circuit. If both voice and data volumes are substantial, it may, in some cases, be desirable to consolidate the traffic in order to gain economies of scale (see Figure 6-17).

This sort of network has tended to decline in popularity in recent years. Many organizations find that the operational cost and hassle of operating the muxes is not worth the possible cost savings.

Voice and video over the data internetwork is something else. The great advantage of voice and video over IP is that IP is available, or can be made available, to nearly any desktop system. This is in sharp contrast to ATM.

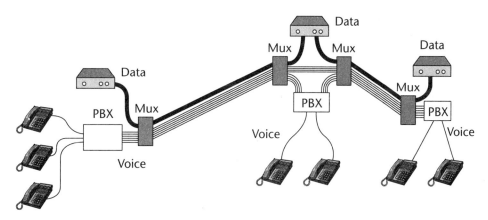

Figure 6-17: A TDM network with a data overlay.

A few years ago, ATM advocates expected that ATM would be ubiquitous—that it would be the dominant access technology in most WANs and LANs. Today, it is clear that this will not be the case. This implies that ATM can carry voice or video only up to the boundary of the ATM network and that some other solution must be found to carry voice or video to the user's telephone, desktop system, or whatever. It is conceivable that ATM usage to end systems might be accelerated as a result of deployment to set-top boxes, or via high-speed *digital subscriber line (DSL)* connections to the home (as described later in this chapter), or as a result of Sprint's ION system (which is intended to provide metered ATM access to the home); however, these initiatives, even if they succeed in the marketplace, will still not assure ATM of true ubiquity.

IP does not suffer from this limitation. IP has already achieved the ubiquity that ATM once sought. Tens of millions of end systems directly support IP today.

Many of us have experienced today's halting attempts at voice and video over the public Internet. The quality may be acceptable, or it may be scratchy and uneven. It does not necessarily offer the predictable voice quality that we have come to expect from the public telephone system. There are a variety of reasons for this.

- The Internet protocols are not designed to provide deterministic delay to users.
- Router products have fundamentally not been designed to support the kind of traffic engineering essential to delivery of traffic with bounded delay characteristics.
- Our access lines to the Internet may represent a bottleneck.
- Internet providers have, in some cases, undercapacitized their circuits and their interconnects with one another.

The Need for Deterministic Delivery. Internet protocols offer only best-efforts delivery, with no assurance that data will be delivered within a fixed time period, if it is delivered at all. This IP service is well suited for data applications such as e-mail; however, it poses a problem for realtime bidirectional voice traffic. Delay cannot be variable; voice must be delivered at a steady pace. We can reduce the variability of delay by adding some constant delay on the receiving side of a transmission but only up to a point; if delays get to be too great, the speakers at both ends of a call are likely to collide with each other from time to time, as those who have placed international calls over geosynchronous satellite links know all too well. The notion of intermixing voice with data over internetworks has enormous appeal; however, it is unlikely to achieve the popularity that it seems to merit until a technical solution is adopted that ensures suitably low variability of delay.

Over the past few years, the Internet Engineering Task Force (IETF), the standards group responsible for TCP/IP protocols, has produced a constellation of standards collectively known as the Integrated Services Architecture (ISA). The ISA includes RSVP, a protocol that provides a means by which an application can request a specified quality of service. The network then attempts to deliver traffic with the specified *Quality of Service (QoS)*, but with a degree of assurance that still falls short of a guarantee.

Products that nominally support the ISA are available, but commercial deployments are rare. Increasingly, the Internet community feels that the Integrated Services Architecture was overly ambitious. The RSVP approach requires that routers maintain too much state associated with each connection; consequently, the approach cannot scale to deal with anything remotely approaching the number of voice interactions that will ultimately be needed.

More recent efforts have focused not on QoS but rather on a more modest objective of achieving Differentiated Services (DiffServ). Traffic that needs deterministic delivery would be identified at the point of ingress to the network. Routers would use preferential queuing to ensure that such traffic got first crack at link bandwidth through the network and at processor bandwidth within the router. Routers capable of supporting DiffServ on a large scale should be widespread in 1999; however, commercial availability of DiffServ services may lag, perhaps for years. The business model under which DiffServ requests would be made, validated, and charged for are still largely undefined. The use of DiffServ across the public Internet is even more problematic, in that the business arrangements under which multiple ISPs might provide for DiffServ assurance across their interconnections is totally up in the air. It will take time for things to settle out.

Inadequate Access Line Capacity. The typical 28.8-, 33.6- or 56Kbps dialup access line to the Internet is likely to be quite adequate for realtime digital voice; however, it will be less than ideal for realtime video, which has greater bandwidth demands. Realtime voice traffic requires nominal bandwidth of 56Kbps, but can be compressed considerably, typically to about 8Kbps. Video, however, benefits from considerably greater transmission bandwidth. This places a much greater demand on the access line and on the underlying transmission infrastructure.

This tends to be less of an issue for desktop users connected over the corporate LAN. Over time, it will also tend to be less of an issue for home users, as such technologies as ISDN, IP over cable, and IP over digital subscriber line (DSL) become increasingly available.

Inadequate Internet Provider Capacity. Finally, we consider the existing Internet infrastructure. The backbone Internet service providers who place the greatest emphasis on reliability and quality work very hard to capacitize their networks so as to limit packet drops, typically to less than 1 percent of the total traffic. In recent years, they were not always successful. The backbone ISPs are doing a better job of keeping up with load today, but packet drops are still common at many shared interconnection points (see Chapter 14). Packet drops can cause gaps in the voice/video stream.

6.9.2.5 ATM and Traffic Management

An ATM network potentially enables the designer to place a PVC between any two locations desired and to associate any bandwidth or SCR desired with that PVC. With an IP network based on leased lines, by contrast, it can take more work to finesse IP traffic into taking the preferred paths through the network.

This is unquestionably an advantage for the IP-over-ATM network backbone. Some network designers ascribe great value to these traffic management capabilities, and there is no doubt that they provide operational convenience. For my part, I have never been persuaded that the traffic management advantages of ATM could justify the incremental cost, complexity, and overhead associated with an IP-over-ATM backbone, but this is perhaps a matter of taste.

6.9.3   Applications of ATM

ATM is suitable for different applications at the LEX, IXC, and international levels.

6.9.3.1 Applications of LEC ATM

LEC ATM pricing trends are still somewhat unsettled. In general, LEC ATM is priced to reflect the fact that the carrier never has to transport the data very far, since the service is constrained to operate within a LATA. This may change as telecommunication reform progresses in the United States and as LECs begin to offer in-region services that cross LATA boundaries.

It appears that the most promising application for LEC ATM will be for high-speed concentration as described earlier in this chapter and as shown in Figures 6-15 and 6-16.

6.9.3.2 Applications of IXC ATM

IXC inter-LATA ATM prices are still evolving, but there is a strong tendency for these prices to track Frame Relay prices, since the services can be viewed as largely interchangeable. If a carrier were to offer both services with a wide disparity in price between them, one service offering would cannibalize the customer base of the other. One carrier made this explicit by charging based on the port speed and CIR of the service, irrespective of whether it is Frame Relay or ATM.

Thus, ATM charges will tend to be distance-insensitive and to reflect a port charge and an SCR (similar to Frame Relay CIR) charge. The economics that we discussed for IXC Frame Relay will tend to apply to IXC ATM offerings as well. It is possible, however, that some IXCs will charge for back-hauling a high-bandwidth ATM service to the closest IXC point of presence (POP) at which they are able to offer the service, in distinction to their Frame Relay prices, in which back-haul is usually bundled into the basic price of the service.

For Frame Relay, we observed that the price of CIR increases almost linearly with bandwidth. Much the same is true for ATM. There is rather little tendency for this service to be "cheaper by the dozen." We have seen that Frame Relay is attractive for concentration of many low-bandwidth locations and less attractive for meshing of high-bandwidth locations. ATM makes sense only at high bandwidths and consequently has a smaller zone in which it is the optimal solution.

Recently, we have seen a surge in carrier ATM offerings that include service interworking, such that a Frame Relay PVC can be mapped transparently into an ATM PVC. This potentially enhances the attractiveness of a carrier's offerings. With service interworking, you could aggregate a large number of low-bandwidth remote Frame Relay locations into a small number of ATM ports at your major locations, such as the corporate data center.

IXC ATM may make sense in the following situations:

- To provide high-bandwidth service (T-3 or greater) to remote parts of the country, where it is not cost-effective to establish your own local presence, due to ATM's distance-insensitive tariffs
- In conjunction with service interworking, to provide lower-bandwidth service to remote parts of the country, where it is not cost-effective to establish your own local presence
- Where traffic is asymmetric or where you need a high-speed backup and can find a tariff for which you pay only for traffic that you ship

6.9.3.3 Applications of International ATM

A number of carriers are capable of offering international ATM services. These services tend to be dreadfully expensive, but the leased lines that they replace might be even more so. If you need high-speed connectivity to a large number of countries, it may be cost-effective to concentrate the traffic onto one or more high-speed ATM ports.

6.10 Switched Multimegabit Data Service (SMDS)

The *switched multimegabit data service (SMDS)* data transmission technology was championed for a time by a number of U.S. LECs and by MCI. SMDS is interesting in terms of its technology, but it entails high overhead and complexity. The market share of SMDS in the United States is declining relative to Frame Relay and ATM and is likely to continue to do so.

SMDS has always been viewed as a carrier service offering. It was never intended for private use, with large organizations deploying their own switches in enterprise networks. Unfortunately, carrier deployment has been spotty.

SMDS is capable of supporting very large logical frames, with frame sizes as great as 10,000 bytes. Each IP datagram is encapsulated within one of these frames. The frames are then sliced and diced into 53-byte ATM cells for transmission across the network.

SMDS grew out of earlier work with satellite-based data communications and out of the IEEE 802.6 standard for metropolitan area networks. The formal definition of SMDS reflects an *SMDS network interface,* or *SNI,* that operates over T-1 (1.5Mbps) and T-3 (45Mbps) circuits. On these link types, SMDS uses a physical format that conforms to ATM adaptation layer 3 (AAL 3).

Unlike Frame Relay and ATM, SMDS is connectionless. Each frame is independently addressed, using addresses based on the *North American numbering plan (NANP)* or, more recently, the E.164 standard of the International Telecommunications Union (ITU). The address is, in essence, a telephone number. SMDS can offer any-to-any connectivity, unlike its connection-oriented sister protocols. The service definition is similar to that of an Ethernet; however, in order to efficiently carry IP traffic over SMDS, the carriers routinely establish a *logical IP subnetwork (LIS)*[4] for a customer—sort of like a virtual LAN— to restrict traffic to a smaller community of interest and also to ensure that a

---

4. See D. Piscitello and J. Lawrence, Request for Comments (RFC) 1209, "The Transmission of IP Datagrams over the SMDS Service," March 1991.

carrier's entire customer base is not burdened with processing Address Resolution Protocol (ARP) requests that are of no interest to them.

As we have seen, Frame Relay bandwidth is managed by means of a PVC-based CIR; ATM bandwidth, by means of a PVC-based SCR. Since SMDS is connectionless, there are no PVCs. SMDS bandwidth is managed by means of a sustained information rate (SIR), which represents the maximum number of continuous bits per second that the provider is willing to accept over the interface as a whole. In comparison to a CIR, the SIR potentially makes traffic management simpler for the customer, at the expense of making it more difficult for the carrier. Carriers in the United States typically offer SIR rates of 1.17Mbps for T-1 ports and 4-, 10-, 16-, 25-, and 34Mbps for T-3 ports.

It takes a lot of bits to represent a phone number. SMDS uses a large header format and is further burdened with the ATM cell tax discussed earlier in this chapter. As a result, the maximum effective throughput for an SMDS T-1 circuit (with a nominal circuit capacity of 1.5Mbps) is only 1.17Mbps; the maximum effective throughput for an SMDS T-3 circuit (with a nominal circuit capacity of 45Mbps) is only 34Mbps.

When SMDS was first introduced, ATM cell formats were selected because ATM was expected to achieve extremely widespread deployment. Yet the routers of that era could not have processed ATM cells quickly enough to have kept up with a T-3 circuit. CSU/DSU manufacturers evolved products to fill the gap. An enhanced CSU/DSU, the *SMDS DSU (SDSU)* accepted frames from a router and performed all necessary "slicing and dicing" to turn data link layer frames into cells. An interchange format, the SMDS *Data Exchange Interface (DXI),* was developed to enable routers to communicate with SDSUs. In an unexpected turn of events, the SMDS DXI has evolved into a general-purpose interface specification. Some carriers now offer SMDS DXI-based services over the wide area at speeds ranging from 56Kbps through fractional T-1 to full T-1. These SMDS DXI services are not burdened with the ATM cell tax—at least not on the access circuit. SMDS may be attractive for concentrating a large number of T-1 (or possibly lower-speed) locations into a small number of T-3 hub locations, provided that you do not expect to need more than T-3 bandwidth at any one point.

Some U.S. LECs, notably Bell Atlantic and PacTel (now part of SBC), have invested significantly in SMDS. Others have no announced plans to ever offer it. Among IXCs, only MCI WorldCom has an inter-LATA SMDS offering.

6.11 Direct Use of SONET

As previously noted, Cisco offers direct packet-over-SONET interfaces for their 7500- and 12000-family routers, and other vendors offer similar facilities. Routers use these SONET interfaces as high-speed PPP point-to-point synchronous data links, thus avoiding the ATM cell tax. An emerging variant of this trend is to run IP directly over the optical layer, bypassing SONET altogether.

Packet-over-SONET solutions are very attractive. Current Cisco routers perform adequately at OC-12 speeds (622Mbps), and there is every reason to believe that routers from multiple suppliers will soon evolve to the point that they can efficiently support SONET links at speeds of OC-48 (2.5Gbps) and possibly higher. To do so, the routers have incorporated techniques that were commonly found in switches; they have "taken a page from the switch makers' book."

There are many indications of an industry convergence between routing and switching technology, including Ipsilon's *IP Switching*, Cisco's *Tag Switching*, Ascend's (Lucent's) *IP Navigator*, and the IETF's *Multi-Protocol Layer Switching*; however, it is a bit early to assess the degree of success that will greet these efforts and what the unanticipated side effects might be.

For now, direct use of SONET should be viewed as attractive if your immediate bandwidth requirements are in the OC-3 to OC-12 range and if your longer-term requirements are not likely to exceed OC-48 for some time.

6.12 IP Data over Cable TV Infrastructure

Earlier in this chapter, we noted that options for connectivity to residential consumers are somewhat constrained, with a normal telephone connection being the most widely available transmission medium. Most homes in the United States have two other wires entering: a power cable and a coaxial cable for cable television. Little work has been done to date with the use of the power transmission system to carry user data, due in large measure to the impracticality of getting data through a transformer. The cable TV infrastructure, however, represents a potentially attractive bypass to the telephone system as a means of reaching residential consumers.

The cable infrastructure was not originally designed to carry bidirectional traffic. Content was expected to be transmitted from a central location (generally associated with the "headend" of the cable) to the residential consumer. In recent years, many of the major cable TV providers have begun to upgrade their cable plants in anticipation of interactive video services, which would need modest "upstream" bandwidth (from the consumer toward the headend) and more substantial "downstream" bandwidth (toward the consumer). Interactive video applications have not materialized as viable commercial offerings; however, the modernized cable plant has characteristics that are highly suitable for the transmission of internetworking data to the home.

A number of firms offer *cable modems,* which use one or more 6MHz cable TV channels to provide Internet access to residential consumers. Some cable modems provide the user with the appearance of an Ethernet local area network (LAN). Personal computers and routers are already well equipped to deal with Ethernet; thus, services based on cable modems can be deployed quickly, without waiting for a new generation of personal computer hardware and software to support them. The emerging *Data-over-Cable Service Interface Specifications (DOCSIS)* standards,[5] which are expected to serve as the basis for the next generation of cable IP equipment, also envision the use of existing standard interfaces to the PC.

I had the good fortune to be one of the first alpha testers of Continental Cablevision's cable IP service (now MediaOne), and I am happy to report that the difference between cable and normal dialup, in terms of both speed and reliability, is quite extraordinary. The Ethernet interface supports transmission speeds of up to 10Mbps for combined input and output traffic. Compared to typical dialup speeds of 56Kbps, this results in an extraordinary performance gain: Cable is potentially faster by a factor of *200!*

The real speed advantage is quite a bit smaller than this maximum, but it is still significant. In practice, cable providers are unlikely to provide a full 10Mb of potential bandwidth to their customers. Further, a POTS line offers data compression, whereas a cable modem does not. Further complicating a meaningful comparison, the cable will tend to be shared among large numbers of users, whereas the phone line is dedicated. Taking all of this into account, a cable modem should still be able to deliver at least ten times as much bandwidth as a conventional modem, assuming that the cable operator provides sufficient underlying capacity.

Beyond raw speed, cable modems provide a degree of stability and reliability usually associated with a leased line, not with a dialed connection. Dialed connections typically take 10 seconds or more to establish, assuming

---

5. See, for instance, Cable Television Laboratories, "Cable Modem to Customer Premise Equipment Interface Specification," document SP-CMCI-I02-980317, available at http://www.cablelabs.com.

that the modems are able to sync up at all. (When V.34 modems first appeared, they failed to sync up about 5 percent of the time.) Dialed connections also fail from time to time after they are established, due to a variety of software and hardware maladies. With a cable modem, by contrast, connectivity is pretty much forever. Once you're up, you stay up. The value to the consumer of this enhanced reliability cannot be overemphasized.

A significant potential disadvantage to the use of cable for network access is also inherent in its use of a shared medium: All cable modems on the same cable channel physically see one another's traffic! More precisely, each cable modem physically sees all downstream traffic on its network segment and the upstream traffic of all systems that are physically downstream from it, that is, farther from the headend. It is common for the cable modem to filter out unicast messages unless specifically addressed to the end system to which they are attached; nonetheless, we should assume that any moderately determined hacker could easily gain access to the traffic physically present on the medium. Such a hacker could, potentially, see the traffic from hundreds of residential customers who are on the same cable, including any unencrypted passwords and financial transactions.

Cable modem vendors and *hybrid fiber coax (HFC)* cable plant providers are working to implement cryptographic security on their systems, based in many cases on DOCSIS standards. Some of these schemes protect primarily copyrighted program content, whereas others protect user data. Overall, the security of user data over cable is likely to improve over time. Today, however, the security exposures must still be viewed as significant.

The early-1999 going U.S. rate for cable-based Internet access appears to be about $40–$60 a month, with no explicit charge or limitation based on the amount of data sent or received. At this rate, cable should do very well in competition with POTS-based and ISDN-based Internet access offerings.

Some analysts and some articles in the trade press, however, have taken the cost comparison too far. They have suggested that at $50 a month, cable services will undercut the market for T-1 leased line access to the Internet. My belief is that this will not happen. Cable companies are able to charge $50 a month precisely because they know that the average residential consumer will not continuously send or receive traffic. If businesses begin to use cable services for high-volume traffic, you can rest assured that the cable providers will find a way to charge them market-based prices. The cost to the cable provider of moving large numbers of bits into or out of the global Internet is significant, and it is safe to predict that the cable companies will not sell Internet access indefinitely and in quantity at prices greatly below their cost.

For those of us who are fortunate enough to be able to obtain cable modem–based service, it is a dream come true. It is well suited to telecommuting and to general Internet access. Availability is still quite limited in geographic terms, however, and cable does not generally run to office buildings. Cable companies are eager to expand their coverage in support of internetworking access, but it will be a slow, gradual process. The lack of security and the performance impact associated with the use of a shared medium may further inhibit business use of IP over cable, until and unless the industry comes up with suitably bulletproof solutions.

6.13 ADSL and VDSL

The cable companies are not unique in their potential ability to deliver high bandwidth to the home. The local exchange carriers have long been interested in video services to the home. At one time, they had the naïve expectation that they would run fiber-optic cables to every home and would use them to deliver interactive video services to consumers. It subsequently became clear that the cost of running that much new fiber would be prohibitive. Consequently, the carriers have been paying a great deal of attention to techniques for squeezing more bandwidth out of the existing copper that runs to the home. The most promising and most immediate of these techniques is called *asymmetric digital subscriber line,* or *ADSL.*

ADSL was originally developed with interactive video services in mind. Various advanced techniques are used to increase the bandwidth that can be transmitted over a normal phone line (twisted pair). Large blocks of data are sent, in conjunction with *forward error correction (FEC).* It turns out that it is advantageous to support much higher transmission speeds in one direction than in the other; doing so reduces cross-talk between the inbound and outbound data paths. (Recall that a copper phone line also tends to act like a large antenna.) Current ADSL specifications are oriented toward a data rate of 6Mbps outbound toward the consumer and 600Kbps inbound from the consumer, although carrier services are usually implemented at lower speeds. These speeds are expected to be achievable over clean twisted pair at distances of up to 9,000 feet. The expectation is that LECs will use fiber to carry the data to a central office or other distribution point in the consumer's neighborhood and will use ADSL over a relatively short distance to the consumer's home or business. It is felt that a high proportion of residential customers in the United States could ultimately be served by using ADSL, perhaps 60 to 70 percent.

These characteristics are potentially very attractive for residential and small-business Internet access. The asymmetry mirrors the usage characteristics of the typical user, particularly as regards Web browsing. Most of us frequently download large files or images but only occasionally need to send or to upload large chunks of data. Most of the time, we are transmitting relatively small sequences of data to initiate transmission of the next Web page. The asymmetric bandwidth offered by ADSL tends to be somewhat less attractive for commercial sites, but it is nonetheless clearly superior to competing technologies, such as ISDN BRI.

For the incumbent LECs, ADSL is attractive. The LECs have an enormous investment in copper to the home. They would like to replace that copper with fiber, but it is not cost-effective to do so. ADSL effectively provides a "midlife kicker" to the LEC's copper plant, extending its useful lifetime into the twenty-first century.

We know that there is no such thing as a free lunch, so we should not be surprised to learn that ADSL does not represent a free lunch for the LECs. The existing public telephony infrastructure in the United States incorporates a number of features that interfere with the LECs' ability to deploy ADSL. Notable among these are *bridge taps* and *load coils*. In many instances, the LEC is able to tidy up an existing copper pair in order to make it suitable for use by ADSL; however, doing so inevitably adds cost.

When a customer orders ADSL, it is not necessary to replace or to eliminate the customer's existing phone service to that location. Traditional POTS telephone service can coexist with new ADSL data services in different frequency bands on a single set of copper wires. "Splitters" at each end separate out the voice traffic from the data.

As with many other technologies, standards wars have raged over details of how this should all be accomplished. A number of trade organizations have formed to try to maintain coherence in ADSL evolution. Among these are the *ADSL Forum* and, more recently, the *Universal ADSL Working Group (UAWG)*, which is seeking to promote a single interoperable worldwide ADSL standard, G.Lite, through contributions to the work of the International Telecommunications Union (ITU).

In addition, there has been interest in a longer-term migration to *very high-speed digital subscriber line,* or *VDSL,* at downstream speeds of 26- or 52Mbps. VDSL is particularly interesting in that it is capable of carrying not only voice and video but also high-definition TV over a single pair of copper wires; however, the maximum supportable distance at 52Mbps is only about 1,000 feet and thus much less than with ADSL. Consequently, wide-scale deployment of VDSL will depend, in most cases, on deployment of fiber to concentration points within a target neighborhood but closer than the nearest central office—an expensive proposition in comparison with ADSL.

Most LECs have initiated trials of ADSL, and some are delivering commercial ADSL services. Availability is nonetheless likely to be spotty for years to come. The experience with ISDN is instructive: The LECs have had a decade to roll out ISDN services, yet their coverage is still uneven. In the case of ADSL, this concern is exacerbated by current U.S. regulatory policy, which makes it difficult or impossible for LECs to recover their deployment costs, since they are obliged to make ADSL infrastructure available to their Internet service provider (ISP) competitors at prices the LECs regard as artificially depressed. Note that this is in sharp distinction to cable over IP services, where the cable provider is currently free under U.S. regulatory policy to offer access to the public Internet through a "captive" or internal ISP on a monopoly basis.

The business models and the back-end connectivity models associated with ADSL are still uncertain. A few years ago, many equipment vendors expected that independent ISPs would lease copper from the LECs and would deploy their own ADSL equipment to the LEC central office. In my opinion, this approach is prohibitively expensive for the ISP. My belief is that the only business model that ultimately makes sense is for the LEC (or perhaps some well-capitalized third party that can somehow achieve a high adoption rate in a specific geography) to provide the ADSL service and to provide ISPs and other bulk customers with a highly concentrated, statistically multiplexed "feed" to the service (see Figure 6-18).

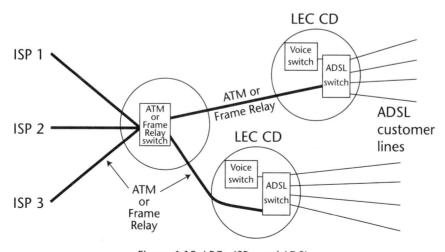

Figure 6-18: LECs, ISPs, and ADSL.

ADSL-based data services would appear to be attractive for Internet access and telecommuting on the part of residential consumers and small businesses. Such services are superior to ISDN in most respects and similar in overall capabilities to IP over cable. ADSL service is always on, like cable (and unlike ISDN, where a connection must be dynamically established). ADSL data services bypass carrier voice switches and thus avoid wasting expensive switch ports—a distinct advantage to the carrier in comparison with POTS or ISDN access to the Internet. Unlike cable, ADSL could potentially serve businesses as well, since a twisted pair already runs to office buildings; however, the asymmetry of bandwidth may pose a problem for business locations. Like cable services, ADSL is unsuitable for use by "road warriors," knowledge workers on the go, until and unless infrastructure is built out to hotels, airports, and other public places. Unlike cable, ADSL data transmission does not depend on the use of a shared medium, which implies that ADSL will not necessarily suffer from the same security exposures as cable.

ADSL and IP over cable are competing for roughly the same pool of prospective customers. Which is likely to win out? It is difficult to say at present. In the near term, the shared-bus IP-over-cable system would appear to offer somewhat lower unit costs—and thus lower prices to the consumer— than does ADSL, which requires special handling on both sides of each line; however, the scalability of bandwidth that ADSL offers—in conjunction with enhanced manageability and security—may prove to be crucial in the long run. If so, xDSL may do well in the long term, much as switched Ethernet solutions have competed effectively against older, shared-bus Ethernet solutions. For the foreseeable future, both ADSL and cable over IP are likely to coexist in the marketplace. At the same time, it is natural to speculate that ADSL and cable IP services collectively will ultimately put a huge dent in the market for ISDN BRI.

6.14 CDPD and Other Wireless Technologies

Wireless technologies offer the possibility of access that is not tethered to any particular physical location. This is potentially very attractive for any number of applications; however, wireless data has not yet found the large mass market that we might envision for it.

There are many ways to transmit data through the air. First, of course, it is possible to use a normal cellular telephone channel to transmit data, much as you would a normal POTS line. Special, tailored compression routines support this environment. Nonetheless, the throughput is severely limited in comparison to the data that you could send over a normal wireline (that is, a land line) POTS connection.

Cellular digital packet data (CDPD) represents an interesting attempt to make better use of the cellular infrastructure. Most of the major cellular carriers in the United States support this set of standards. CDPD takes normal analog cellular telephone channels and statistically multiplexes them in order to provide greater bandwidth to each end system (19.2Kbps), as well as significantly greater utilization of scarce bandwidth. The approach is reminiscent of that of the old ALOHA network, a wireless network whose principles of distributed control and statistical multiplexing were embodied in the technical design of the Ethernet local area network. CDPD incorporates a comprehensive model for mobility that transparently carries IP datagrams to wherever the user happens to be, even one who is attempting to maintain a TCP session while driving a truck from Maine to Florida! CDPD includes link layer encryption and standards for interchange of network management and accounting information. Despite all of its technical strengths, CDPD services are neither ubiquitous enough, nor anywhere near cheap enough, to foster truly widespread use.

For most organizations, if you need untethered access, a *public* wireless service is the only realistic option. Nonetheless, a number of firms offer solutions that enable an organization to build a *private* wireless network. These devices make sense for organizations with specialized requirements. A particular attraction of a private wireless network is that once the infrastructure is in place, there are no recurring charges from any telco for the use of the airwaves.

Wireless bridges and similar equipment are not particularly expensive, but they entail operational complexities that are not for the faint of heart. You will probably want to select gear that operates in frequency ranges not much impacted by precipitation. You need to erect antennae. For most technologies, you need to ensure that you have line-of-sight coverage of your intended service area, and you have to deal with Mother Nature; trees have a nasty habit of growing, and their leaves come out in spring, potentially blocking that line of sight you so carefully planned for. Finally, you need to consider how you will repair the gear or the antenna when problems arise.

6.15 Cryptographic Encapsulation over the Public Internet: The iVPN

Over the past year or so, there has been a great deal of interest in the idea of building corporate enterprise networks, or intranets, using the public Internet as if it were just a raw transmission medium (see Figure 6-19). Since enterprise

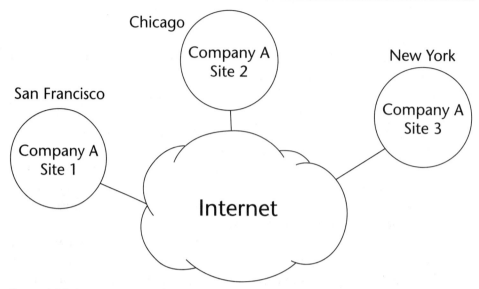

Figure 6-19: An Internet virtual private network (iVPN) operating across the public Internet.

networks sometimes carry sensitive data, the data that traverses the public network can be "tunneled," or cryptographically encapsulated, to conceal it from snooping (passive intrusions) or malicious modification (active intrusions). *Each IP tunnel should be viewed as the functional equivalent of a Frame Relay or an ATM PVC, and it is for this reason that I treat tunnels as a lower-layer transmission mechanism in this book.*

This whole idea is often referred to as a *virtual private network (VPN),* or more appropriately as an *Internet Virtual Private Network (iVPN).* This idea is intuitively appealing, and the trade press and analysts have been quick to fasten on it. For instance, a recent Forrester report claims that "five years from now, Internet VPNs will eclipse Frame Relay as the corporate WAN choice."[6]

Unfortunately, there is *less* to this notion than meets the eye. As we shall see in the remainder of this chapter, iVPNs are unlikely to compete effectively on economic grounds against domestic Frame Relay networks as a transmission vehicle for enterprise internetworks. Moreover, iVPNs are likely to be complex and problematic to administer in comparison with data link layer transmission mechanisms.

As with the rest of the transmission technologies we have discussed in this

---

6. M. Lopez, B. Hannigan, A. Davis, and M. Wakefield, "The New Public Network," Forrester, December 1998.

chapter, there are applications for which iVPNs are well suited and others for which they are ill suited. No single solution—not even the global Internet!—is likely to be ideal for all circumstances.

This is a very complex and confusing area, so it is perhaps useful to start by clarifying what we mean by an iVPN. Many of the same firewall and cryptographic technologies that could be used in support of iVPNs have great value in supporting electronic commerce and other sensitive applications among multiple organizations. If it is meaningful to speak of iVPNs at all, it makes sense only in the context of a logically or virtually private internetwork that interconnects multiple locations *that are under a common ownership or administration*. Where this is not the case, the tunneled environment should instead be thought of as an extranet, as described in Chapter 1.

> In this context, a tunnel is functionally equivalent to a data link layer transmission path, such as a Frame Relay PVC. Thus, iVPNs based on tunneling will succeed in the marketplace only if they are technically and economically competitive with other data link layer transmission technologies.

6.15.1 Security and Management Implications of iVPNs

Enterprise networks today can be viewed as providing *perimeter defense*: The good guys are inside the castle; the barbarians are outside the gates (see Figure 6-20). An implicit level of trust exists among the defenders who are within the castle. A good castle will

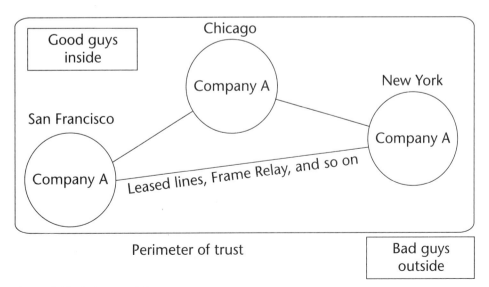

Figure 6-20: Perimeter defense.

have high walls and a moat. Nonetheless, some things have to get into the castle, and other things have to get out of it. That's why the drawbridge was invented. Analogously, most enterprise networks will have a small number of access points to the public Internet, often just one or two (see Figure 6-21).

Now, perimeter defense has its drawbacks. If the perimeter is breached at any point, everything within the perimeter is potentially exposed. Once they have crossed the moat and breached the walls of the castle, there is no stopping the barbarians. It is for this reason that network managers dread "back door," or undocumented and informal, access to the public Internet from locations behind the corporate firewall.

A significant problem with the iVPN, however, is that it potentially multiplies the points of exposure. Instead of one or two drawbridges, we would have tens or perhaps hundreds. If the barbarians can break through in force at any point—if the hackers infiltrate anywhere—we are in trouble.

This is a serious concern. With a large number of firewalls comes the need for a great deal of administration. The security policy must be consistent among all of them. Configuration changes could be frequent, if our enterprise internetwork is evolving rapidly. A configuration inconsistency at any point could open the gates to the barbarians.

This also implies a considerable burden in terms of network management. The number of points that require truly intense monitoring for security

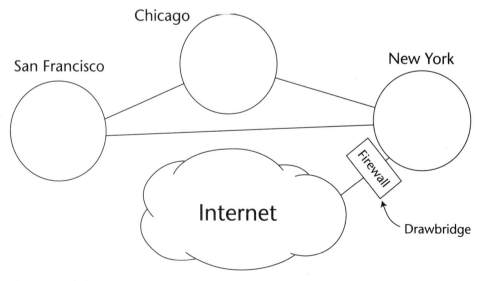

Figure 6-21: Access to the public Internet from a conventional enterprise internetwork.

incidents is much larger with this design than with a conventional enterprise internetwork.

Finally, there are technical and operational challenges in getting the data through the encrypting firewalls. The firewall's encryption hardware and software may impose bandwidth limitations. Non-IP data generally has to be manipulated or encapsulated to convert it to IP. If you add a new application—and thus one or more new TCP or UDP port numbers that the firewalls must permit—it may be necessary to reconfigure or perhaps even to modify the firewalls.

6.15.2 Economic Implications of the iVPN

With all of that said, let's go back to the top. Why did we want an iVPN in the first place? Ultimately, the only possible answer is price, or price/performance. The encrypted tunnel substitutes for a conventional link. Otherwise, an iVPN offers no meaningful functional advantage over a conventional link.

But Internet service providers use the same technologies to build their internetworks that large organizations use to build enterprise internetworks, layering additional services on top of the raw connectivity. And firewalls, including the labor to administer them, represent an additional cost. In general, ignoring market distortions, a secure Internet connection will tend to cost more than a domestic dedicated data link layer service offering similar bandwidth capabilities.

It is sometimes suggested that the combined cost of a private enterprise internetwork, in addition to the cost of Internet connections, would be greater than the cost of iVPN Internet connections alone. For an organization with a very small number of locations, this might conceivably be true; however, for a network of any significant size, the Internet connections represent a tiny fraction of the total network infrastructure cost.

In some instances, an iVPN might have economic advantages. These flow from the same aspects of distance insensitivity that we saw for Frame Relay. Internet providers do not charge a premium based on the distance over which data is carried. Therefore, if an enterprise internetwork consists of a small number of locations scattered over a great enough expanse, preferably a global expanse, there will tend to be significant net cost savings.

Even in this case, one has to question whether the game is worth the candle. In implementing the iVPN, you would be accepting a great deal of complexity and risk. And consider, too, that the current ISP global insensitivity of cost to distance is not cast in stone. The ISPs pay an enormous premium whenever they haul data across an ocean. It is difficult to imagine that they would not find it necessary at some point to impose surcharges to reflect those costs back to their customers.

6.15.3 Suitability of an iVPN

A number of circumstances favor the deployment of an iVPN. You should consider carefully what the overall financial and operational impact of an iVPN would be for your own organization if one or more of the following seem to apply:

- A small number of locations to be served
- Wide dispersion, or international dispersion, among locations
- Dialup requirements from a mobile workforce ("road warriors")
- Teams of knowledge workers who deploy on short notice to remote locations not under your control and who need prompt, high-speed, secure connectivity to your home network
- "Extranet" requirements, where you need to provide an additional level of trust to customers, distributors, or other stakeholders who are not your employees

The economic basis for the first two of these factors should be clear from the preceding discussion.

Dialup requirements are a good application for an iVPN because of the huge economic drivers that favor large dialup networks over small ones. A large carrier will generally be able to provide dialup capacity far more cost-effectively than your own organization can, unless your organization is exceedingly large and widespread. The complexity of the iVPN for a PC user need not be all that bad, as the administrative complexity is mostly in the network. And the network complexity can be confined to a small number of gateways between your network and the dialup provider's network.

Consulting organizations might be good candidates for the scenario involving remote teams of knowledge workers. If your remote team can piggyback on your client's existing dedicated Internet connection, the team can obtain high-quality connectivity without having to wait for a dedicated circuit to be installed by the LEC. The savings in time, productivity, and possibly customer satisfaction could be significant.

The extranet scenario is an obvious one, but perhaps the ramifications of the extranet are less obvious. You should also consider your requirements for application-level security. In many cases, the extranet is not in and of itself sufficient—you are likely to need additional end-to-end security at the application level. If so, you should weigh carefully whether the extra security offered by the extranet is worth the cost and management overhead associated with it; the application-level security might be sufficient for your needs. This is a complex trade-off: The emerging *IPSEC (IP security)* network layer security standard is in some ways less capable than application layer security, but it has the noteworthy advantage that all application traffic can enjoy at least rudimentary protection.

7
Determining the Levels of Hierarchy

Most internetworks today are constructed in a layered, hierarchical fashion. Traffic at the fringes of the internetwork is concentrated into successively denser aggregates as you proceed toward the center, gaining economies of scale at each step. This concentration enables the core of the network to take advantage of economies of scale on carrier circuits and services, even when the individual access connections are not big enough to benefit from them.

Hierarchy is primarily an abstraction, an aid to description. It helps us to understand the internetwork. In addition, hierarchy can result in a more manageable and more cost-effective network. There may be further benefit in propagating the hierarchical layering directly into the routing and addressing plan, although doing so is not a strict necessity.

7.1　The Concept of Hierarchy

Let's start with an extremely high-level conceptual view. The network can be viewed as being built up with successive layers, like the layers of an onion. The simplest kind of network might consist of a few workstations on a LAN. This one-layer network is flat: simple and monolithic (see Figure 7-1).

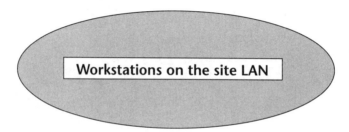

Workstations on the site LAN

Figure 7-1: A simple, "flat" network.

Most of us work for organizations that have a hierarchical organization structure: managers and subordinates. When we need to explain our organizational structure to others, we use an *organizational chart*. An org chart can serve as a convenient tool for showing the relationships in a hierarchical network. Figure 7-2 corresponds to the flat network hierarchy depicted in Figure 7-1.

Large-scale wide area internetworks almost invariably entail multiple layers of hierarchy—at least two or three levels. Consider, for example, the internetwork depicted in Figure 5-20, consisting of a few locations connected to corporate headquarters in New York. We now have a two-layer network: New York City is one, and the remote locations constitute the other. The conceptual view is shown in Figure 7-3, and the org chart view in Figure 7-4.

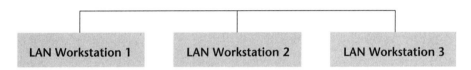

Figure 7-2: A flat, nonhierarchical network.

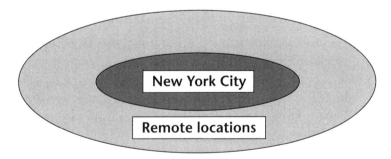

Figure 7-3: A two-layer, conceptual view of the internetwork.

Figure 7-4: An org chart view of the internetwork.

7.2   Partitioning the Internetwork

Why should a large internetwork be segmented or partitioned into a hierarchical structure? The reasons include

- Enhanced ability to understand and explain the network
- Reduced requirements for engineering design
- Improved routing performance
- Simplified network management
- Improved price/performance through concentration of traffic

We will consider each of these in turn.

- **Ease of comprehension.** If networks were amorphous and unstructured, it would be impossible to understand them fully without understanding every single structural detail. In a hierarchically structured internetwork, however, once we understand the layering structure, we know a great deal about that internetwork, without needing to understand the details of each individual location.

- **Reduced engineering design.** By partitioning the network into various *levels,* we standardize the design at each level, thus reducing the need to do individualized custom engineering for each location. Songwriters could choose to compose every note of a lengthy song, but few do; instead, they compose the notes of a single verse and then repeat each verse many times, sometimes with minor variations.

- **Improved routing performance.** Within a dynamic routing domain, the routers need to interchange topology and connectivity information with their peers. As the number of routers within an interior routing domain (an *autonomous system,* or *AS*) increases, the routers can consume too much time in exchanging routing updates and recomputing the topology. Some routing protocols are seriously impacted if the number of nodes in the routing domain is more than about 50. In a hierarchical internetwork, the levels of hierarchy can be mapped directly onto the routing plan and the associated addressing plan, thus simplifying the job that the routers have to do and improving performance.

- **Simplified network management.** If internetworks were constructed as amorphous globs, a problem at any point might impact performance or connectivity anywhere else in the internetwork. In partitioning the internetwork, we reduce its overall complexity, thus facilitating the isolation of faults. We also potentially enhance network administration by enabling delegation of responsibility for administration of names and addresses.

- **Improved price/performance.** We saw in Section 5.3 that it was economically advantageous to concentrate traffic in order to pay for a small number of circuits with high capacity and therefore with lower unit costs. Logically partitioning the design into backbone and access components facilitates this aggregation.

7.3   What Constitutes a Hierarchical Layer?

In a hierarchical internetwork, as we work our way from the bottom of the hierarchy to the top—from lower layers to higher ones—we generally find successively greater

- Concentrations of traffic
- Switching and trunk capacities
- Needs for reliability
- Geographic dispersion between a node (router or switch) and the lower-level nodes connected to it

We thus find it convenient to associate each hierarchical level with

- A limited range of circuit or service bandwidths
- A small set of transmission technologies or, if possible, a single technology
- A largely common equipment design for each service location
- A strategy for achieving the required availability, such as single or dual homing

In some cases, the bandwidth of a higher hierarchical level might be the same as that of the next lower level, but it should never be less than that of the next lower level. In mathematical terms, as you progress from lower to higher layers, the bandwidth should be monotonically nondecreasing.

7.4   How Many Layers?

How many levels of hierarchy should you use? As with many things, there is no single right answer. It's a little like asking how many stages are suitable for a multistage rocket: It depends a great deal on what you are trying to accomplish and on where you are planning to go! Different implementations have worked well with very different answers.

A hierarchical model can help you to think your internetwork through not only for the initial design phase but also later, when it's necessary to expand or to fix it. The ideal hierarchical framework would be simple and easily grasped and retained; however, large and complex internetworks tend to demand richer and more complex hierarchical models. As Einstein once remarked, "Things should be as simple as they can be, but no simpler."

The simple hierarchy shown in Figures 7-3 and 7-4 previously may be quite sufficient for your needs. These two layers may also be optimal in terms of price/performance. In general, however, large and complex networks with a wide range of access speeds can generally benefit from more layers of hierarchy.

In many cases, the structure of the telecommunications environment and of the circuits and services it provides will lead you to an obvious layering. The structure of the telephony industry in the United States is fundamentally hierarchical, with LECs representing a lower layer in the hierarchy and IXCs representing a higher layer. In many cases, you will find it convenient to define your layers so as to maintain a conceptual distinction between intra-LATA access connectivity, and inter-LATA trunk connectivity.

The wide disparity among the major categories of circuit capacity also lends itself to a hierarchical model. A T-1 circuit is equivalent to 24 DS-0 (56Kbps) circuits. A T-3 circuit is equivalent to 28 T-1 circuits. For some internetworks, for instance, it might be appropriate to regard them as comprising a lowest tier served by local access at speeds of 56Kbps, a second tier with regional distribution at T-1 speeds, and an upper, national tier built using T-3 circuits. Your need to support even higher-speed circuits might drive the need for more levels of design hierarchy. A single hierarchical layer might support a range of circuit speeds, not just a single speed; nonetheless, you will often find that major differences in the interface speeds you must support will tend to drive different trade-offs in your network design and that these design differences are appropriately reflected by defining distinct hierarchical layers.

As an example, consider Figure 7-5, the internetwork of internetMCI (a large backbone ISP, now a unit of Cable and Wireless PLC) as of early 1996: This internetwork can be viewed as hierarchical (Figure 7-6), with a top layer of core backbone locations connected using ATM switches operating at OC-3 speeds (155Mbps), a second layer operating over T-3 circuits (45Mbps) to provide concentration, and an access layer connecting customer routers to the concentration layer.

For now, I have chosen to ignore internetMCI's interconnections with its peers: the other large Internet backbone providers that collectively with internetMCI (now Cable and Wireless) comprise the public Internet. Those peering interconnections are discussed in Chapter 14.

It is convenient to think of each of the core backbone locations as also participating in access concentration. In other words, those locations partic-

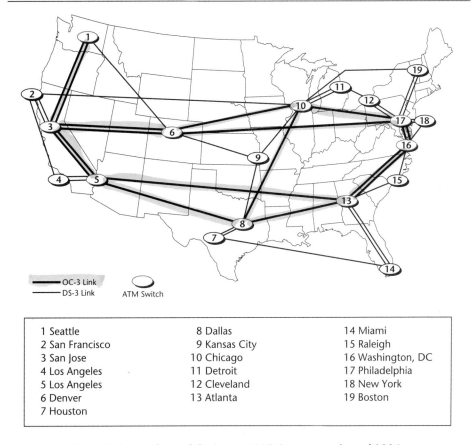

Legend:
- OC-3 Link
- DS-3 Link
- ATM Switch

1 Seattle	8 Dallas	14 Miami
2 San Francisco	9 Kansas City	15 Raleigh
3 San Jose	10 Chicago	16 Washington, DC
4 Los Angeles	11 Detroit	17 Philadelphia
5 Los Angeles	12 Cleveland	18 New York
6 Denver	13 Atlanta	19 Boston
7 Houston		

Figure 7-5: Topology of the internetMCI internetwork as of 1996.

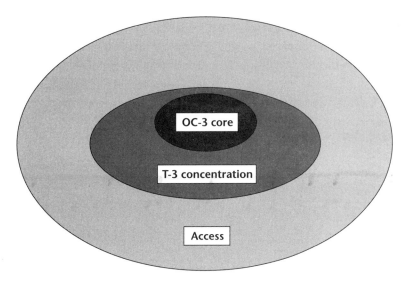

Figure 7-6: A conceptual view of the internetMCI internetwork.

ipate at two distinct levels of the hierarchy. It may be the same equipment or the same kind of equipment performing two different jobs; nonetheless, it is in two different roles in this internetwork and can thus best be viewed as operating at two distinct levels in the hierarchy.

With that in mind, an org chart view of a possible structure of the internetMCI internetwork might look like Figure 7-7.

7.5   Hierarchy and Network Topological Design

Once you have determined the appropriate hierarchical levels for your internetwork design, you are ready to proceed to the more detailed design phases dealing with network topological design. Recall that *topology* is a branch of mathematics that deals with the properties of geometric forms associated with their *connectivity*, irrespective of their *dimensionality* (length). In creating a topological design, we are going to use lines, or *links,* to connect the dots, or service locations. The next four chapters of this book provide detailed guidance on how to go about this.

I find it convenient to start by identifying candidate locations for the internetwork *backbone.* The backbone corresponds to the highest hierarchical level of the internetwork—the core, or spine, of the network. Chapter 8 contains guidelines on how to go about this.

We tend to approach most design tasks from the top down, consistent with the computer programming methodology known as *structured design.* For a number of reasons, I find it simpler and more straightforward to think of the balance of the network topological design task the other way around, in bottom-up terms. Thus, Chapter 9 deals with the access design, whereby end user locations are connected to the outermost tier of your internetwork. Chapter 10 provides access homing strategies, whereby access locations are connected to internetwork layers successively closer to the backbone. Finally, Chapter 11 deals with the topological design of the internetwork backbone itself.

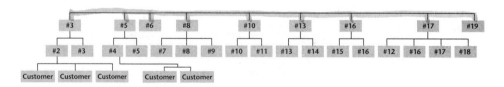

Figure 7-7: An org chart view of the internetMCI internetwork.

8 Identifying Backbone Locations

We have seen that many internetworks can most readily be constructed with a high-capacity backbone and with a lower-capacity access infrastructure. How can we determine which locations need to be on the backbone and which can most cost-effectively be served as part of the access infrastructure? It is tempting to think that this is a given, dictated from our traffic requirements. In reality, this determination is no less involved than any of the other aspects of network design with which we must deal.

Let's begin by reviewing the ways in which the backbone typically differs from the access portion of an internetwork. We'll then consider how each of these differences might motivate us to include or exclude a particular node from the backbone portion of the design.

The internetwork backbone comprises the service locations *(nodes)* and the transmission facilities that interconnect them *(links)* at the highest level of the internetwork design hierarchy. The backbone may correspond to a single service location or to many locations.

In Chapter 7, we saw that an internetwork may have multiple levels of hierarchy. For most purposes, you can pick any boundary between hierarchical levels in the internetwork and can view the levels above collectively as the internetwork backbone component and the levels below collectively as the internetwork access component. Thus, you can apply this methodology iteratively to successively lower layers of your internetwork hierarchy.

Many internetworks use a backbone that is distinct from the access infrastructure, doing so in order to achieve greater economies of scale in terms of transmission than could otherwise be justified solely on the basis of the individual circuit requirements. The backbone generally operates over higher-capacity circuits or services than do those that are cost-effective in the access portion of the internetwork. This is the first and most significant difference between the backbone and the access portions of the network.

Second, and precisely because of this concentration, a backbone failure is likely to cripple a far larger number of service locations than will an access failure. This means that backbone failures are expensive and are best avoided. Of course, if a particular service location is down, the users at that location may not care a great deal whether they have company; nonetheless, most organizations recognize that there are potentially very high costs associated with the failures that take down a great many users at once—the kinds of failures that are likely to get covered on the evening news. Therefore, backbones tend to be designed for higher levels of availability than are access networks.

Third, the backbone generally entails costs not present in the access infrastructure. The need to drive higher-capacity circuits may translate into additional hardware requirements. The need for high availability is likely to drive a need to multiply home the circuits and to provide redundancy in the hardware.

Finally, the backbone tends to operate over a smaller geographic expanse than does the access portion of the network. Speaking loosely, it tends to be deep, but not necessarily broad. It may well be that a backbone that is national or international in scope is served by many small access networks, each of them small; nonetheless, the access networks generally have a collective reach much greater than that of the backbone.

To summarize, we see that the backbone is characterized by higher-capacity circuits and services, greater requirements for high availability, additional costs over and above those that would be required to serve the same locations as access locations, and a smaller geographic expanse. In general, we do not have the luxury of simply adding every service location to the backbone, because we cannot afford the associated cost. We must make trade-offs. We must pick and choose.

8.1 Higher-Capacity Circuits and Services

There is no hard-and-fast requirement that all backbone circuits and services operate at the same speed; often, they operate over a range of speeds. It is usually the case, however, that the slowest backbone transmission media in an internetwork will be operating at a speed as great as or greater than that of the fastest access circuits or services that they serve.

These high-capacity circuits tend to be expensive. They are cost-effective only if they carry enough traffic to keep them reasonably full. You will generally want to select backbone locations that correspond to high-intensity traffic sources and/or sinks: locations that inherently produce or receive a large amount of your internetworking traffic.

The sites that are best suited to becoming backbone locations generally fulfill one or more of the following criteria.

- In a client/server environment, they are the location of high-volume servers, such as your Web "farm."
- A large number of low-volume access locations or some number of high-volume access locations are homed there.
- Traffic from multiple access locations can be concentrated there.
- The location is topologically adjacent to high-volume traffic interchange points with other internetworks.

For example, many internetworks are constructed in the form of a Frame Relay logical "star." Thus, in Figure 5-20, New York City was selected as the focus (and thus as the sole backbone location) of a Frame Relay internetwork. New York City was the corporate headquarters, and thus the largest source and sink of traffic, even though it was *not* at the geographic center of the network. That makes no difference in a network based on a technology with a distance-insensitive tariff structure from the carriers.

Again, the distinction between backbone and access is largely relative to your frame of reference. We might view the network in Figure 8-1 as having a backbone that consists of a single node, a single router, or a group of routers located in New York City. This is sometimes referred to as a collapsed

Figure 8-1: With distance-insensitive homing, traffic is the dominant consideration. New York can be viewed as representing a collapsed backbone in its entirety.

backbone. Alternatively, if this network provided an additional level of hierarchy—for example, if routers at Minneapolis and Indianapolis were connected by leased lines to the network service location in Chicago, we might view the routers connected over Frame Relay as collectively constituting the backbone. In this view, the backbone would comprise San Francisco, Los Angeles, Dallas, Chicago, Atlanta, Washington, and New York City.

8.2 Higher Availability

We generally provide higher availability to the backbone locations. For this reason, some critical locations lend themselves to being backbone locations even if their bandwidth requirements are modest. Suppose, for example, that an application were hosted at a single location. Perhaps that application does not require particularly high bandwidth but is essential to the overall ability of your internetwork to fulfill its mission. You might choose to serve this location as a backbone location, even though its traffic requirements do not otherwise warrant backbone service, in order to maximize the availability of your overall service.

In the Frame Relay star example in Figure 8-1, we might have chosen to serve New York City as a backbone location, even if it had not been a major source of traffic, for exactly this reason. In the context of the example, we know that the field offices need to talk to national headquarters but not to one another. If headquarters is down, the network is in effect down. Under these assumptions, we would want to ensure high availability to the hub of the network, and putting it on the backbone might well be the most cost-effective way to do so.

Let's look at this a different way. In the network shown, the loss of Frame Relay connectivity from any city to New York City would result in a loss of service for one city but not for all of the network. But suppose that the corporate headquarters were in Dallas. In that case, under the network design shown in Figure 8-1, a loss of connectivity from New York City to Dallas would cause *all* cities to lose connectivity to the corporate headquarters, which would typically constitute a much more severe outage.

8.3 Additional Costs

When we put a service location onto the backbone, we ensure that it has high bandwidth and high availability. Why would we not choose to put every network location onto the backbone?

In a word: *cost*. When we choose to put a location onto the backbone, we are generally saying that we will use higher-bandwidth circuits to serve it and that we will provide whatever level of circuit and equipment redundancy is necessary to achieve our target levels of availability. High-capacity circuits cost money. Equipment to drive fast circuits costs money. Extra circuits and equipment to provide redundancy cost money.

Not surprisingly, there is a trade-off. We will want to pick only the busiest or most critical sites for the backbone. Typically, we cannot afford to assign *every* site to the backbone.

8.4   Geographic Expanse

When Goldilocks experimented with the three chairs she found in the Three Bears' house, she found that they were, respectively, too large, too small, and just right. Analogously, the backbone of a network constructed using services with distance-sensitive tariffs, such as leased lines, can be too large, too small, or just right.

Consider, for example, the network in Figure 8-2. Let's suppose that there is clear justification for Washington, Atlanta, and Dallas to be on the backbone. Further suppose that West Palm Beach has more traffic than we like to see in an access network location but less traffic than other backbone locations. How might we feel about adding West Palm Beach to the backbone?

Figure 8-2: An internetwork backbone including Dallas, Atlanta, and Washington.

In a typical leased line design, adding West Palm Beach to the backbone would force us to absorb the cost of *two* expensive circuits (see Figure 8-3) in order to ensure redundancy. We might mitigate the cost impact by eliminating the circuit from Washington to Atlanta; nonetheless, we would be adding a lot of circuit-miles and a lot of cost! For this investment to be warranted, we would want West Palm Beach to handle a large volume of traffic or to require really critical redundancy. Failing this, we would say that the internetwork depicted in Figure 8-3 is *too big* to be cost-effective, and we might look for other ways to meet West Palm Beach's connectivity needs.

Alternatively, we might hope that expanding to West Palm Beach might reduce mileage charges to enough access locations to justify the high circuit cost. Suppose that our access locations in Florida include Miami, Ft. Lauderdale, West Palm Beach, and Tampa; further suppose that for technical, business, or policy reasons, we do not permit access locations to be concentrated into other access locations. Under these assumptions, a backbone location in any of the Florida locations would reduce mileage-based charges to the other access locations. A topology without any backbone locations in Florida (serving West Palm Beach as an access location rather than a backbone location) would look like Figure 8-4; a topology including a backbone location in West Palm Beach would look like Figure 8-5.

The access circuits to Ft. Lauderdale, Miami, and Tampa are roughly 650, 700, and 300 miles shorter, respectively, in Figure 8-5 than in Figure 8-4. Is that a good thing? It might be, depending on the amount of incremental

Figure 8-3: Addition of West Palm Beach to the same internetwork backbone.

Figure 8-4: West Palm Beach is not on the backbone.

Figure 8-5: West Palm Beach has been added to the backbone.

cost associated with handling two high-capacity circuits into West Palm Beach. If you've purchased a new car in the United States in recent years, you know what the sticker reads: "Your mileage may vary." The answer could depend on the relative speed of the circuits and the prices you pay for them, reflecting the discounts that your organization receives. The only way to know for sure is to sit down and work out the relative costs in your specific circumstances.

In determining the appropriate size of the backbone, the Goldilocks principle applies.

- An internetwork backbone is *too small* if it does not extend out aggressively enough—if it leaves too many Tampas and Miamis hanging around at the end of access circuits that are too long.
- The backbone is *too big* if it costs too much, without reducing the costs of access connections to the backbone by enough to compensate.
- An internetwork is *just right* to the extent that it optimally balances these trade-offs, keeping the circumference of the backbone as short as possible consistent with not necessitating a lot of long access circuits.

To the extent that your access locations are connected ("homed") to your backbone using services that have distance-insensitive tariffs, *your backbone cannot be too small.* If you are going to use a distance-insensitive service anyway, there is no advantage in expanding the circumference of your backbone to reduce the distance to access locations. Even experienced network designers seem to have a natural tendency to build out backbones in a vain attempt to reduce distances, and thus charges, for services that are already distance-insensitive, as we saw in Chapter 5. Doing so is, in my opinion, one of the most common and most costly blunders in internetwork design today.

— For Distance-insensitive tariffs,
  your backbone cannot be too small

9 Creating a Preliminary Access Design

At this point in phase 2, preliminary design, you should have established the primary transmission technologies that you intend to use, the hierarchical architecture of your network, and the locations that will constitute your internetwork backbone. You are now ready to proceed to preparing a detailed design for connecting your remote locations to the next-lowest hierarchical tier of your internetwork. This chapter explains the issues that you will need to consider.

You might wonder why we choose to design the lowest hierarchical tier first. The reason is that your traffic requirements ultimately drive the design process, and this traffic is fundamentally associated with your remote locations. You may have many options as to how you will connect ("home") this traffic to your backbone. How you choose to concentrate this traffic into successively higher hierarchical levels is thus an output from your design process, not an input into it. Consequently, it is best to work this portion of the design process from the bottom up rather than from the top down.

This chapter expands on the technology-oriented discussion of Chapter 6. In this chapter, we are applying specific technologies to provide remote access while concentrating the traffic as much as possible in the interest of economy.

Within the United States today, regulatory issues play a major role in defining what you can and cannot do at the access layer of the network. Historically, the LECs were not permitted to carry customer traffic across LATA boundaries. This restriction is gradually being eased by the Telecommunications Act of 1996, but this easing is a gradual process that will take many years to come to full fruition. Meanwhile, LATA boundaries will strongly influence your access design decisions.

9.1   Dedicated (Business or Organizational) Access

9.1.1   Access with Leased Lines

In the simplest access design, each remote location is connected to the backbone by a single leased line (see Figure 9-1). This is very simple and broadly applicable, but it can also be expensive, because it takes little or no advantage of economies of scale.

The circuits can be of different bandwidths. Circuits that are entirely within the LATA can be provided by the LECs or, alternatively, by *competitive access providers (CAPs)* operating in the LATA. Inter-LATA circuits will typically be provided by IXCs, in conjunction with LEC or CAP tail circuits to connect your locations at both ends of the circuit to the IXC's *point of presence (POP)*, a facility that houses the IXC's equipment, as shown in Figure 9-2.

9.1.2   Access with Multiplexing to Achieve Concentration

Chapter 6 discussed the merits of channelization to improve the price/performance of the access portion of the internetwork. When is it appropriate to use channelized facilities? Channelization generates savings in several distinct ways:

- Reduced unit costs for the circuit(s) to our equipment, due to bandwidth aggregation
- Possible circuit cost savings where voice and data traffic can share a higher-capacity channelized circuit

Remote Access Locations

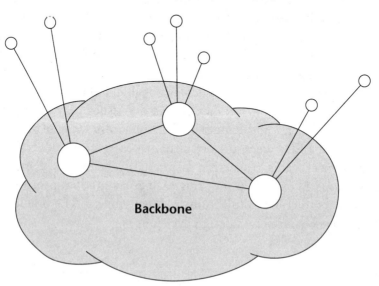

Figure 9-1: Single homing with leased lines.

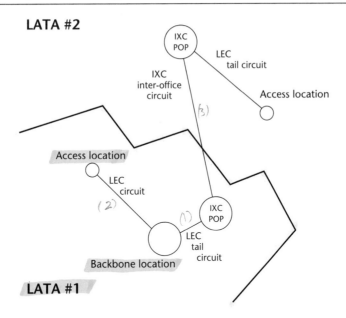

Figure 9-2: Homing by means of a single intra-LATA or inter-LATA leased line.

- Reduced number of router or switch ports
- Integration of the CSU/DSU function directly into the router or switch

To understand the circuit cost savings, we need to look more closely at the structure of the multiplexed service. In most cases, we ask the LEC or CAP to implement CO multiplexing *(CO muxing)* on our behalf. This may entail the use of M24 multiplexers, which multiplex up to 24 56/64Kbps and fractional T-1 services onto a T-1 circuit, or M1/3 multiplexers, which multiplex up to 28 T-1 circuits onto a T-3 circuit, or both. Many LECs have a tariffed offering for multiplexed services. In the absence of multiplexing, each circuit would be charged based on

- **Charge 1:** The distance from your network hub in the LATA to the nearest LEC wire center, *plus*

- **Charge 2:** The distance from your remote access location within the LATA to the nearest LEC wire center, *plus*

- **Charge 3:** A LEC inter-office circuit (IOC) charge reflecting the vertical and horizontal (V&H) mileage (where V&H mileage, as defined in Chapter 5, is based on the grid that carriers have historically used to compute billing) between the two wire centers, where they are not the same.

This scenario is depicted in Figure 9-3.

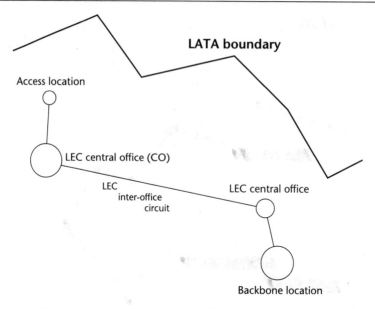

Figure 9-3: Cost elements in the absence of multiplexing.

If we were to instead use CO multiplexing, charges 2 and 3 would be essentially unchanged; however, unit costs associated with charge 1 could drop, perhaps dramatically, because they would be shared among multiple circuits.

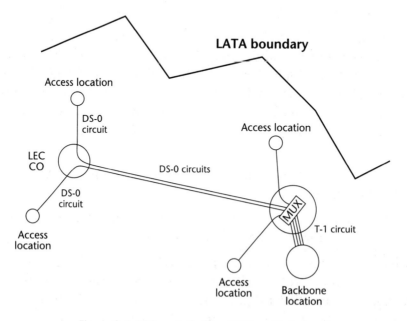

Figure 9-4: LEC central office (CO) multiplexing.

Instead of paying to connect up to 24 DS-0 circuits to our network hub, we would incur a lower charge to connect a single T-1 (see Figure 9-4). Our charge to the LEC or CAP would reflect an incremental charge to cover the cost of the multiplexer, but overall, in many cases, we would be paying less.

Whether this is beneficial depends on the number of channels that you are able to put to use. The T-1 will be more expensive than a DS-0, but it will not be 24 times more expensive. As a rule of thumb, if there are 8 DS-0s, it is a pretty good bet that CO muxing will save you money; however, you might hit breakeven with significantly less. In light of differences among LEC tariffs and among organizations, it is a good idea to compute these trade-offs yourself, taking your organization's unique circumstances into account.

If your organization has an integrated voice/data network, you probably have existing LEC circuits to connect your locations to IXC POPs at T-1 speeds or greater. These LEC circuits can be viewed as something of a sunk cost. In this case, the incremental cost to your organization of slicing off some number of channels for use by the data network may be little or nothing (see Figure 9-5).

9.1.3 Access with Fast Packet Services

In Chapter 6, we saw that Frame Relay, SMDS, and ATM all had potential application for access and for access concentration. It's time now to look more closely at the mechanics of how this is done.

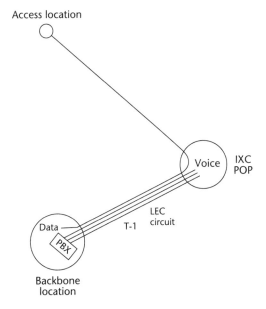

Figure 9-5: Taking advantage of an existing voice/data network.

It is important to keep in mind that in an internetworking environment, all services that can move bits from one point to another are, in some sense, equivalent. They all compete with one another. Thus, it is natural to think of fast packet services as competing with traditional leased lines. It makes sense to use fast packet services as an access mechanism only to the extent that they offer price/performance advantages over leased lines.

Similarly, fast packet services can be viewed for our purposes as being largely interchangeable. Our choice among Frame Relay, SMDS, and ATM is driven primarily by overall price/performance.

Following are three main reasons why a fast packet service might be attractive as an access technology for internetworking traffic:

1. Circuit cost savings, due to characteristics of the fast packet tariffs, including distance insensitivity

2. Equipment cost savings, due to port multiplexing

3. The ability to achieve aggregation, with statistical multiplexing, of multiple traffic sources onto a single circuit that is larger and, consequently, more cost-effective

9.1.3.1 Tariff Analysis of Fast Packet Services

The fast packet services that LECs and IXCs offer are, in technical terms, nearly identical. The economics of these services play out quite differently, however.

Within the United States, fast packet services are usually priced in a distance-insensitive manner. Because they know that they are not obliged to carry data outside of the LATA as a part of this service, LECs generally assess far lower charges than do IXCs for comparable fast packet bandwidth. An IXC Frame Relay service, for example, might be called on to carry Frame Relay data from Boston to Los Angeles; however, a LEC intra-LATA Frame Relay service cannot carry traffic outside of the LATA or the state (today; this may change as deregulation unfolds). IXC Frame Relay is more expensive because, on the average, the carrier must haul the data much farther. The IXC must absorb far higher circuit mileage infrastructure costs than does the LEC.

Let's continue this discussion in terms of Frame Relay, the most ubiquitous of these services, in order to keep things simple. For the most part, SMDS and ATM will follow the same economic patterns, but at higher bandwidth levels.

For LEC Frame Relay, the service cost is low, but the comparable leased line costs are also likely to be modest. Using LEC Frame Relay in lieu of a single leased line is, in many cases, not cost-effective. Hubbing many remote service locations to one or two concentration points within the LATA can, however, be economically attractive.

Within the LATA, there may not be a lot of opportunity for distance-insensitive tariffs to build up a significant cost advantage. Typically, your mileage from a concentration point—a "hub" location—to your various service locations within a LATA will be short. If you are evaluating access in a large LATA, however, or where many of your service locations are widely dispersed within the LATA, there may be more substantial net savings.

U.S. West Frame Relay tariff charges are unusually inexpensive. A U.S. West T-1 Frame Relay port, including access link and a PVC with a CIR of 1,544Kbps, currently costs about $260 a month, which is well below the rate of other LECs (typically in excess of $400). Moreover, many U.S. West LATAs are simply enormous. For both of these reasons, U.S. West Frame Relay service is often cost-effective in comparison with U.S. West leased lines.

To put all of this into perspective, one article quoted the average cost of IXC Frame Relay as $550 per port per month.[1] The same article lists the average cost of LEC Frame Relay as $188 per port and the cost of U.S. West Frame Relay as being less than $100 per port (see Figure 9-6). Any compari-

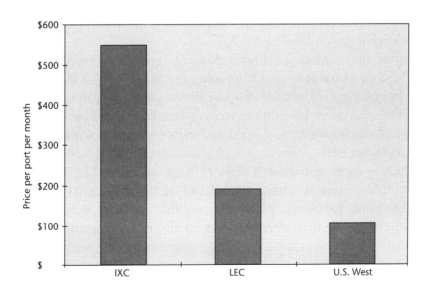

Figure 9-6: IXC, LEC, and U.S. West Frame Relay price per port per month.

---

1. Vertical Systems, a consultancy based in Dedham, Massachusetts, as quoted in *Communications Week* (November 18, 1996).

son of this sort must be taken with a grain of salt, for a variety of reasons. Most notably, the numbers appear to represent a blended average of cheap 56Kbps and more expensive T-1 ports. Nonetheless, the numbers are suggestive, and they appear to be in the right range.

So far, we have established that LEC Frame Relay

- May not be attractive in comparison with a single LEC dedicated circuit (leased line)
- May represent a significant savings over LEC leased lines where it is feasible to connect multiple locations to a small number of hubs
- Can be particularly attractive in large LATAs, such as those we find in U.S. West territory
- Is generally sold at lower unit prices than is IXC Frame Relay because it operates over shorter distances

The use of IXC Frame Relay across LATA boundaries has different properties from those of LEC Frame Relay. Suppose that we are trying to home remote location B to hub location A, as in Figure 9-7. We could, in principle, choose to do so with either an IXC leased line or an IXC Frame Relay connection. Which is preferable?

For this discussion, we will work with MCI tariffs.[2] The structure of the analysis would be much the same for any carrier, but details might differ. Also, we will assume that a single circuit or a single port and PVC provide adequate reliability.

Assume that remote location B normally sends and receives not more than 512Kbps of traffic to and from other locations via hub location A during its busiest hour. (Under non-usage-based charging, the traffic at other times of day has no impact on the analysis that follows.) This is a good case for a T-1 leased line or for a T-1 Frame Relay connection with a single PVC with a 512Kbps CIR.

Which is more cost-effective? In either case, a T-1 LEC tail circuit is required from remote location B to MCI's POP in the location B LATA. The cost is the same, for our purposes. Let's say that it's $400, which is a typical LEC T-1 cost. Note that all costs listed for this example represent monthly recurring costs and that we are ignoring one-time installation and termination charges, to keep things simple.

---

2. These prices, like all tariff prices that appear in this book, are included solely for purposes of illustration. In the interest of realism, I have attempted to use prices that were in effect when I wrote them; however, tariff prices are continually changing.

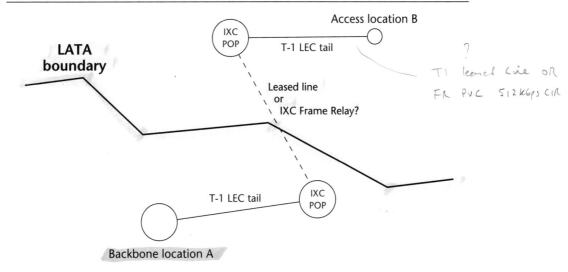

Figure 9-7: Connecting remote location B to hub location A.

For the leased line solution, the remaining cost comprises the following three elements:

1. A zero-mile (minimum, or base) charge of $2,696 for the leased T-1 line

2. A per mile charge of $3.86 for the leased T-1 line

3. A charge for a LEC circuit from location A to MCI's POP in the A LATA (assumed to be $400)

For the Frame Relay solution, we have instead the following four elements:

1. A port charge of $1,178 for a 1,024Kbps port on the remote location B side

2. PVC charges of two times $657 per month for 512Kbps of simplex bandwidth in each direction

3. A port charge of $1,470 for a 1,536Kbps port on the hub location A side

4. A charge for a LEC circuit from location A to MCI's POP in the A LATA (assumed to be $400)

Note that the Frame Relay charges cited here reflect MCI's fixed-price scheme, not its usage-based scheme. This was done in the interest of simplicity. Note, too, that the rationale for the particular port sizes chosen will be discussed later.

These charges yield an overall cost of $4,762 and a cost allocation of $3,204 for the Frame Relay solution, as shown in Table 9-1. For the moment, focus on the Cost column and ignore the Allocated Cost column. It is explained later.

Ignore, for a moment, the sharing of the hub side of the Frame Relay connection. Compared to the overall Frame Relay cost, then, the comparable fixed costs of the leased line—assuming, for reasons that will soon become clear, a distance of 328 miles—are simply those shown in Table 9-2.

At a circuit distance of 328 miles, the sum of all leased line circuit costs in this example works out to be $4,762, exactly the same as the equivalent Frame Relay cost. The $2,696 represents the base, or minimum, cost of a circuit; the $1,266 is the mileage charge, at $3.86 a mile.

Figure 9-8 depicts the relationship between V&H mileage (the distance metric that carriers use for billing) and the price for each of these services. The cost of Frame Relay service is constant irrespective of mileage, while the cost of a leased line steadily increases with distance. It is easy to compute that 328 miles represents a key crossover point for the economics of this circuit, under these assumptions. If the circuit length is greater than 328.0 V&H miles, the cost of this circuit will exceed the cost of the equivalent Frame Relay connection; if less, the leased line is less expensive.

Any time you do this kind of analysis, you can rest assured that there will be a crossover point. These are two linear equations. One has zero slope, and

Table 9-1: Cost Model for an IXC Frame Relay Access Line

Frame Relay	Cost	Allocated Cost
Location B		
LEC circuit	$ 400	$ 400
FR port (1,024Kbps)	$1,178	$1,178
Simplex PVC (512Kbps CIR)	$ 657	$ 657
Location A		
LEC circuit	$ 400	$ 67
FR port (1,536Kbps)	$1,470	$ 245
Simplex PVC (512Kbps CIR)	$ 657	$ 657
Total:	**$4,762**	**$3,204**

PAY   FR :   ccf
              Port   speed
              CIR

Table 9-2: Cost Model for an IXC Dedicated (Leased) Access Line

Leased Line	Cost
Location B	
LEC circuit	$ 400
Inter-office circuit (0-mile charge)	$2,696
Inter-office circuit (328 miles)	$1,266
Miles:	328.0
Location A	
LEC circuit	$ 400
Total:	**$4,762**

the other has positive nonzero slope, and so they cannot be parallel. They must intersect. However, the point of intersection may lie to the left of the Y-axis, which is to say that it corresponds to negative miles (which can never occur in reality); if so, you know that the fast packet service is more cost-effective irrespective of distance.

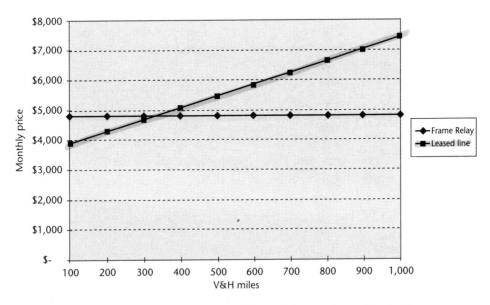

Figure 9-8: Crossover point for distance-sensitive and distance-insensitive tariffs.

This suggests a natural strategy for inter-LATA access: Use leased lines for short-distance access connections and Frame Relay for longer-distance access connections. This is, indeed, a sensible strategy.

You should understand that although this strategy is attractive to you as a consumer, it is potentially a nightmare for the provider. The Frame Relay provider has developed distance-insensitive pricing based on the assumption that people will procure a mix of shorter- and longer-distance services. If everyone were to order distance-insensitive services solely for long stretches, it would tend to increase unit costs for Frame Relay providers, thus cutting into their margins. You would be giving them only the least-profitable connections. What is optimal for you as a consumer is arguably "pessimal" (the opposite of optimal) for the providers. That is not necessarily your problem; however, you should understand that if arbitrage strategies such as this were to come into play on a truly widespread basis, it might well force the providers to rethink their pricing strategies.

Also, you should recognize that this approach entails some operational complexity. Consider what would have to happen each time that you were to add a new remote location to the network. You would need, in effect, to take a map, draw a dot to reflect the new service location, and then draw a circle with a radius of 328 miles (or whatever the right trade-off distance is in a model that reflects your own organization's unique parameters). If any of your "hub" locations happened to lie within that circle, you would use a leased line homing; if not, you would use Frame Relay. For a slowly expanding corporate network, this might be perfectly acceptable, but for an explosively expanding ISP environment, it might well turn out to be too labor intensive and too error prone.

Let's return to Table 9-1, which analyzes IXC Frame Relay pricing. We can assume that the fourth and fifth charges in the Frame Relay group—the port charge and the LEC circuit at location A—can be shared among multiple Frame Relay connections of this type. For reasons that will become clear later, it is reasonable to assume that six remote locations with capacity similar to that of remote location B could share the same hub Frame Relay connection to location A, so we have allocated only a sixth of the cost of the port charge and the LEC circuit cost, the fourth and fifth charges in Table 9-1, to this application.

The results of spreading and allocating the costs in this way appear in the Allocated Cost column of Table 9-1. If we allocate the costs in this way, however, there is no distance for which leased line costs are less expensive! This should not be viewed as a generally applicable result; it is unique to the particular parameters we are using in this example and also reflects the fact that we are computing this comparison using list (nondiscounted) prices. Moreover, it ignores the possibility that the leased line solution could also potentially achieve port-sharing economies of scale, for instance, by TDM multiplexing, which we consider in the next section.

9.1.3.2 Port Aggregation Advantages

We have seen that TDM multiplexing achieves savings by consolidating traffic from many remote locations onto a single access port. Fast packet services, such as Frame Relay (LEC or IXC), achieve much the same advantage, with the added benefits that statistical multiplexing confers. Indeed, we noted in Chapter 6 that port aggregation is often the primary motivation for using LEC Frame Relay.

A typical LEC Frame Relay deployment uses a T-1 hub Frame Relay port to concentrate a large number of slower connections, especially 56Kbps connections, as shown in Figure 9-9. This configuration is, in logical terms, a star network. Each remote location is homed to the hub, using a single PVC, typically with a CIR equal to one half of the port speed. In many Frame Relay implementations, this configuration enables the remote location to "burst" to use the entire port capacity on occasion.

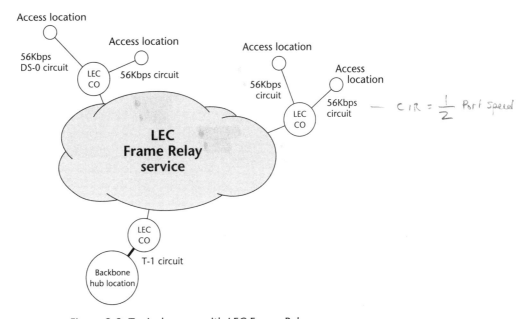

Figure 9-9: Typical access with LEC Frame Relay.

The hub port typically has the other end of each PVC, with equal CIRs in both directions, assuming that the traffic is symmetric. Where traffic is asymmetric, the hub could have either more or less egress CIR than the remote location.

It is possible to oversubscribe the CIRs on the hub port. This means that the sum of CIRs for the PVCs on the hub port can exceed the port speed of the hub port. We know that not all PVCs will need to burst to their respective maximum capacities at the same time. I routinely use an oversubscription factor of at least 2:1. Even larger oversubscription factors can work well in practice where traffic characteristics warrant. Figure 9-10 depicts the relationship between port speeds and aggregate CIRs in this example. Thus, a T-1 hub port used solely to concentrate 56Kbps remote-location tail circuits should be able to accommodate at least 48 of them, even though a simple TDM multiplexing would be able to accommodate only 24 56/64Kbps circuits.

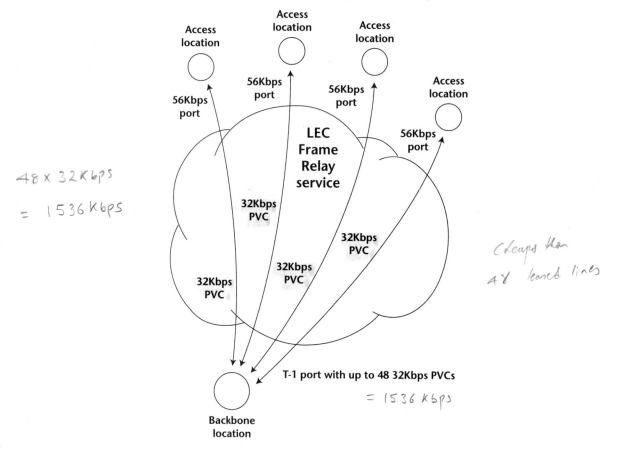

Figure 9-10: Typical port speeds and CIRs for port aggregation with LEC Frame Relay.

The combined effective cost of the entire configuration—including 48 access lines at 56Kbps, plus the T-1 hub line—will generally be less than the cost of 48 individual 56/64Kbps lines. This savings reflects at least the following factors:

- The LEC T-1 tail circuit from the hub location to the nearest LEC POP is usually much cheaper than 48 56/64Kbps circuits.
- A single multiplexed T-1 router port and CSU/DSU is *far* cheaper than 48 router ports and CSU/DSUs suitable for 56Kbps or 64Kbps each.

As previously noted, we could achieve nearly the same effect with conventional TDM multiplexing. To support 48 access circuits, each operating at 56/64Kbps, we would need *two* T-1 circuits. In terms of router equipment, a dual-port channelized T-1 interface, such as the Cisco MIP-2 Interface Processor board, could handle all 48 lines.

How do the economics of this solution compare to those of Frame Relay? It is difficult to say. The results of this comparison will tend to vary as a function of the specific characteristics of your particular network.

The LECs do not offer Frame Relay at speeds above T-1, except in a handful of locations. Thus, if you are interested in achieving similar port aggregation savings for multiple T-1 remote locations, you must look to other technologies, such as SMDS or ATM. The protocol details will differ, but the economic analysis follows much the same lines.

IXC Frame Relay can achieve the same port aggregation as LEC Frame Relay. However, the advantage is less significant when expressed in terms of the percentage of total cost, because the IXC Frame Relay service itself is more expensive to the point where it dominates any savings in equipment costs.

9.1.3.3 Traffic Aggregation Advantages

The final advantage of fast packet services—especially Frame Relay—as an access mechanism is their ability to achieve aggregation, with statistical multiplexing, of multiple remote-location traffic sources onto a single circuit or service that is larger and, consequently, more cost-effective. We have seen that LEC Frame Relay is significantly less expensive than IXC Frame Relay, when viewed in terms of price per port. It follows that if you are going to use Frame Relay for access in the first place, it is advantageous to look at concentrating traffic within a LATA. If you have multiple service locations within a LATA, this is often a good idea. Instead of providing one expensive IXC Frame Relay port for each service location, you use one higher-bandwidth IXC Frame Relay or IXC leased line connection per LATA and then home the service locations to the LEC's Frame Relay service, using less expensive LEC Frame Relay ports. For example, consider Figure 9-11.

Before we proceed, it may be useful to remind you once again that those incumbent LECs that were formerly part of the Bell System, or *Regional Bell Operating Companies (RBOCs)*, are not yet permitted to transport customer data across LATA boundaries. This may change as the RBOCs gradually achieve the regulatory relief envisioned by the Telecommunications Act of 1996, but it is likely that it will change with glacial slowness; furthermore, even if that happens, it is likely that intra-LATA Frame Relay will continue to be viewed as a separate product category from inter-LATA Frame Relay. The RBOCs sometimes speak as if their service offerings were a single, integrated service across their entire service area, but it is not so today. Today, with minor exceptions, each LEC Frame Relay, ATM, or SMDS service is an isolated island within its LATA. If you want an integrated service, you must either build bridges between the LATAs yourself or else work with someone else who has done so, such as an IXC Frame Relay provider with network-to-network interface (NNI) connections to multiple intra-LATA LEC Frame Relay networks.

The design shown in Figure 9-8 is similar, in some sense, to LEC CO multiplexing designs, in which you direct the LEC to use TDM multiplexers to

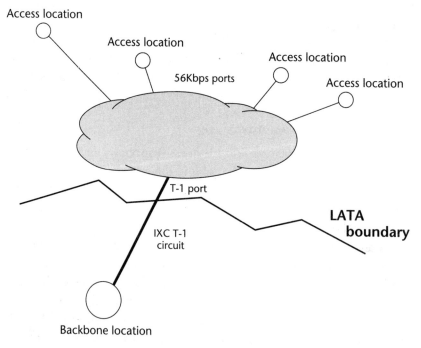

Figure 9-11: Using LEC Frame Relay to aggregate traffic.

consolidate many traffic sources onto a single higher-bandwidth circuit back to one of your hub locations. However, this design offers the added benefit that you can achieve statistical multiplexing advantage before the traffic enters your higher-bandwidth pipe. This can represent a very significant improvement in price/performance in comparison with a TDM solution.

Note that the design shown in Figure 9-8 does not require you to deploy or to maintain your own equipment at concentration points in each LATA in which you do business; the LEC has done that for you. The LEC's Frame Relay switching equipment achieves port aggregation and statistical multiplexing on your behalf, without requiring that you deploy additional equipment to the target LATA.

9.2 Switched (Residential) Access

We use a different set of technologies to access users at home, be they commercial users or residential consumers. The dominant technology today is plain old telephone service (POTS), with Integrated Services Digital Network (ISDN) placing a poor second. Newly emerging technologies, such as IP over cable TV and IP over ADSL, were touched on in Chapter 6.

In reality, there is little difference between the technologies we would use to concentrate POTS traffic and those we would use for ISDN today. In terms both of carrier infrastructure and of equipment, there is a great deal of commonality. To understand this, you should keep in mind that ISDN is placing what is, in essence, a digital telephone call. That call is routed through the same telco switches as are voice POTS calls, and it is typically charged in the same way as well.

ISDN can achieve higher bandwidth—128Kbps—if you use both B channels of an ISDN BRI (Basic Rate Interface), compared to 56Kbps as the current nominal maximum for voice—and it has some advantages in terms of manageability. Otherwise, they are much the same. The technical solutions for both were discussed in sufficient depth in Chapter 6.

When you concentrate switched calls across a large network, you generally have three options as to how you structure the service.

1. You can have the users place normal long-distance calls to your service location.

2. You can provide inbound 800 number (WATS) service to one or more central service locations.

3. You can provide local service close to the points to which you need to deliver service.

Many networks implement two of the three options or perhaps even all three. Yet there are profound operational and economic implications associated with the choices that you make at this level.

Toll calls are expensive. If you use the public telephone network, you know what a long-distance telephone call costs. Nationwide 800 services are also expensive: You are certain to pay several dollars an hour, no matter how great your volume of business with the carrier. Most designers have found that for large networks, it is most cost-effective to deploy service to each LATA, provided that the density of users you intend to serve in that LATA is sufficient. Indeed, it may be necessary to deploy service to more than one location per LATA, in order to keep toll charges down.

Now consider operational ease for users. The 800 number has the advantage that it is the same from all points covered by the North American Numbering Plan (NANP), which includes the entire United States and Canada. For roving users, there is no need to configure new telephone numbers into software on their laptops. And there is no need to enter credit card numbers or to otherwise arrange payment for the call.

Dialing a number or one of several numbers as a toll call, by contrast, places the burden of payment on the user. There are business models for which this may be appropriate; however, there is an increasing tendency for the service provider to assume these costs, whether the provider is a public service provider or a private corporate network.

If you choose to deploy local service to many LATAs, you will need distinct rotaries of phone numbers in each. You will need to somehow provide these phone numbers to your users. This can be particularly problematic for users who are constantly on the go. If such a user lived in California but was to call from the airport in Chicago, he or she would need to know the local access number for Chicago.

There are various ways to deal with this problem, including (1) an automated phone number look-up service, possibly hung off an 800 number, or (2) providing an 800 number as an alternative to the local access numbers, typically with some incentive to motivate users to prefer the cheaper, local-access numbers. Offering the 800 number as a supplement to the local number can have the added benefit that it also provides a comprehensive means of offering at least *some* service to those areas where it is not practical for you to maintain a local presence.

The exact placement of local-service facilities is black magic. It is a complex art in its own right. Large online providers, such as America Online, maintain whole departments of specialists who analyze the geographic distribution of their current and prospective customers and the available telco offerings in order to optimize the placement of facilities. The general principles, however, are the same in all cases: You want the maximum possible number of your users to be able to reach a telephone number associated with an area code and an exchange that is within their local calling area, that is, the radius within which they can place calls without paying a per minute toll charge, and you want to achieve this goal at minimum cost.

At this point, it is worth noting that there is considerable potential for regulatory "churn" in this area. Consider that your dialup network is, in practice, carrying customer data across LATA boundaries. The LECs have complained vociferously that current regulatory policy, which exempts this traffic from long-distance charges (the "ESP Exemption") should be changed. The LECs would like to collect per minute access charges for data calls, just as they do for voice long-distance calls that they deliver to the IXCs. There are additional regulatory anomalies relating to payments between LECs and CLECs ("reciprocal compensation"). It is quite possible that there will be significant changes in regulatory policy over the next few years, and these could alter the landscape considerably. You also need to keep in mind that if you choose to deploy service within multiple LATAs or to multiple locations within each LATA, you are splitting your user community into smaller subgroups. You pay a certain price for doing so—you sacrifice economies of scale.

The mathematics associated with the effectiveness of pools of dialed numbers is well understood. We will be discussing the use of *Erlangs* in Chapter 15. At this point, suffice it to say that large dialup pools are much more efficient than small ones. If your individual modem pools are too small, you will need a relatively large number of excess modems—beyond those required to serve your average usage—just to ensure that your blocking probability, the likelihood of a user's receiving a busy signal, stays acceptably low. This characteristic will tend to put an upper limit on how widely you disperse your deployment of modem pools. It also argues for doing whatever you can to achieve as large an effective user population as possible.

9.3 Bypassing the Carriers

In Chapter 6, we discussed various nontraditional approaches to access, including the use of private wireless solutions.

An organization that is not a carrier has no reason to procure a dime more of telco services than it absolutely must. The best telco access service is the one that you don't have to buy at all.

If your organization has assets that cross public thoroughfares, you may be able to employ more creative bypass solutions. For example, some electric utilities have found it cost-effective to build out their network infrastructure by wrapping fiber-optic cable around power lines. (This would have been impractical with older copper-based transmission media, but with fiber optics, there is no concern with induced current.) In this case, you might even consider selling surplus capacity back to the carriers. Some of the largest U.S. carriers got their start by capitalizing on rights of way that were originally obtained for railroads or gas pipelines.

Some organizations might also want to consider satellite communications as an alternative to land lines. There are two major scenarios to consider: geosynchronous satellites and low earth orbit (LEO).

Geosynchronous satellites have an orbital period of exactly 24 hours. Consequently, they appear to be stationary over a fixed point on the Earth. This greatly simplifies their use, but it has implicit drawbacks. They need to be stationed at an altitude of about 22,000 miles in order to maintain the correct orbital period (see Figure 9-12). At that altitude, they can cover a large portion of the globe; however, it takes signals a long time to reach them. The speed of light in a vacuum is roughly 186,000 miles per second. At that speed, it takes electromagnetic radiation about a fourth of a second to get from one part of the world to another by way of a geosynchronous satellite, or about a half a second of round-trip time. This is at least five times longer than a typical land line round-trip time across the United States. The geosynchronous satellite round-trip time is approximately constant, whether the data is traveling between locations that are 5 miles apart or 5,000. This extended propagation delay significantly impacts response time. Moreover, it can greatly reduce throughput over a TCP connection, which is sensitive to the bandwidth-delay product. It is possible to ameliorate this performance loss by using large TCP window sizes, but doing so implies a level of application tuning that can be unattractive to many organizations. Finally, there may be little that can be done to ease the impact on delay-sensitive UDP applications.

If your bandwidth and delay requirements are modest, this approach can nonetheless be cost-effective. Typically, you would deploy *very small aperture terminal (VSAT)* dishes to your remote service locations and would establish a contract with a satellite data carrier. You might avoid local circuit charges to the traditional carriers entirely. Some organizations with widely dispersed sites and low-bandwidth requirements have found this to be a good solution. At the same time, you need to be willing to make a significant investment in satellite dishes, and to tolerate the risk that they might become technically obsolete.

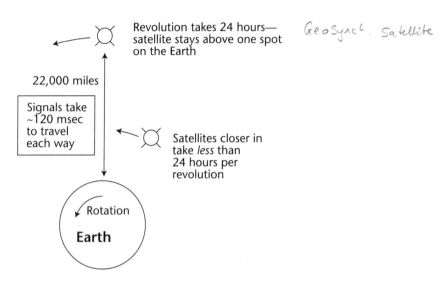

Satellites farther out take *more* than 24 hours per revolution

Revolution takes 24 hours—satellite stays above one spot on the Earth

Geosynch. Satellite

22,000 miles

Signals take ~120 msec to travel each way

Satellites closer in take *less* than 24 hours per revolution

Rotation

Earth

Figure 9-12: Geosynchronous satellites.

An emerging trend is toward the use of low earth orbit satellites, or LEOs. Proponents hope to deploy LEO data transmission systems within the next few years. These satellites will operate at altitudes just above the atmosphere, thus avoiding the propagation-delay problems of geosynchronous satellites (see Figure 9-12). LEOs offer greater technical challenges to their providers because the number of terrestrial miles that a given LEO can cover is necessarily more limited at these lower altitudes and because they are constantly moving relative to the Earth. In order to achieve global coverage, the Teledesic system expects to use more than 200 LEO satellites.

These satellites are capable of supporting high bandwidth and low delay; however, the associated services are not expected to be cheap! It is felt that it will be expensive to maintain such large numbers of satellites. Many analysts believe that LEO data transmission will cost more than land line transmission in countries that already have well-developed fiber-optic transmission infrastructure. It is thought that LEOs may be most attractive for transmitting information at high bandwidth to remote areas and to the developing world. There is still some question as to whether these market segments are sufficient to sustain a thriving LEO industry.

10 Developing Strategies for Access Homing

We have talked about strategies for connecting remote locations to your infrastructure. But how do you select among multiple candidate locations within your infrastructure? And how many connections will you want to provide for each remote location?

This chapter deals with strategies for connecting, or *homing,* remote access locations to your infrastructure. Historically, there was a tendency to view homing in the context of a two-tier network: an access tier and a backbone tier. Today, however, it makes more sense to view homing in terms of a multitier hierarchical network and to realize that there is always a need to home traffic from a lower hierarchical tier to a higher one. The homing process can be viewed as iterative, or perhaps as recursive.

This chapter discusses homing strategies. Chapter 11 discusses how to deal with traffic characterization in the context of hierarchical access homings.

10.1 Single Homing

Single homing is the simplest form of access homing. Single homing creates the equivalent of a star network topology, as shown in Figure 10-1, at the access level of the network hierarchy. (The star network topology is discussed in depth in Chapter 11.)

When homing an access location to one of several locations at the next hierarchical tier, which location should you prefer? Under most conditions, three guidelines suffice.

1. If there is a single suitable location of the next hierarchical tier within the same LATA as the remote location, home to it. If more than one, home to the closest.

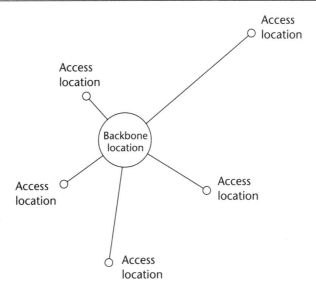

Figure 10-1: Single homing creates a star topology
at the access level of the network hierarchy.

2. In the absence of a homing target in the same LATA, for a distance-sensitive homing service, such as a leased line, choose the next tier location that is closest in terms of V&H miles, where *V&H* is the arcane vertical and horizontal grid that carriers use to compute mileage for pricing purposes.

3. In the absence of a homing target in the same LATA, for a distance-insensitive homing service, such as Frame Relay, choose the next tier location that minimizes your expected cost to carry the data within the next hierarchical tier.

Let's stop for a moment to consider these guidelines. All three are primarily cost considerations: You want to achieve adequate connectivity at minimum cost.

1. Guideline 1 reflects the simple reality that LEC circuits and services are generally much cheaper than are IXC circuits and service—due, in part, to the fact that IXC services almost invariably also include LEC services at both ends.

2. Guideline 2 also is a matter of cost optimization. Other things being equal, a shorter circuit will cost less and will tend to be slightly more

reliable: Many tariffs show circuit availability declining somewhat as circuit length increases.

3. Guideline 3 is perhaps less obvious. If you are using a distance-insensitive service, such as IXC Frame Relay, your homing cost is essentially constant, no matter which location you choose to home to. In this case, you do not need to have a large number of homing targets; one—or perhaps two for greater reliability—might suffice for the whole country.

In the last case, since the decision is not driven by the economics at the access level, you might as well select a homing target so as to minimize costs at the next hierarchical level up. Typically, this would mean that you would consider the traffic matrix associated with the remote location and would pick the homing target that obliged you to carry that traffic the shortest possible distance or that otherwise resulted in the lowest costs to haul the data where it would need to go.

Some organizations, notably Internet service providers, tend to use collocation space within carrier (telephone company) facilities to locate their gear. This somewhat complicates the homing decision, as it places a premium on using facilities from the same carrier on both ends of the circuit.

10.2 Dual Homing

Single homing is the least expensive way to home access locations to the next hierarchical tier; however, it obviously provides no recovery at all if the single access connection is down. For a typical T-1 leased line, expected availability is in the range of 99.8 percent to 99.9 percent, so single homing implies an exposure that the service will be down at least 0.1 percent to 0.2 percent of the time. For some applications, that is too much unavailability.

We can greatly reduce that exposure by running two connections to the access location. Assuming mutually independent failure probabilities, the risk drops from 0.002 (or 0.2 percent) to 0.002 * 0.002, which is 0.000004, or 0.0004 percent. Availability improves from 99.8 percent to 99.9996 percent, a huge improvement.

Unfortunately, assuring mutually independent failure probabilities is not as simple as one might imagine! It is quite possible for those two circuits to ride the same fiber-optic cable—and this can be true even if logic says that they should be running in different directions. That means that a single misdirected backhoe can sever both of your connections. Moreover, ordering circuits from two different carriers is not necessarily a good strategy for ensuring diversity; it is common for carriers to lease capacity from one another. You might have a single point of failure without knowing it. Your best assurance is to order from a single carrier and to specifically demand that the circuits be physically diverse from one another. Even then, there is a modest risk that your carrier will from time to time make errors in the course of routine "grooming" of its circuits. The only way that you will discover this is the hard way: Two circuits that should have been completely independent both fail simultaneously.

This situation may improve over time, as carriers deploy SONET rings with rapid, automatic failover in the event of a fiber cut. You should recognize, however, that not every SONET facility is a ring! Even if your access circuits are served by SONET, you will need to verify that they are served by a ring and not by a nonredundant spur. There is no panacea, no silver bullet. You will just have to work with your carriers on this and to do the best you can.

Figure 10-2 shows a typical scenario with two access circuits. Running the two homing circuits to distinct locations on the next higher hierarchical level is often referred to as *dual homing*. Dual homing provides the maximum gain in availability, as it protects against failures in access circuits, equipment, and connectivity at the next hierarchical layer, such as a partitioned backbone; however, it may also result in a large increase in cost. In many cases, one backbone

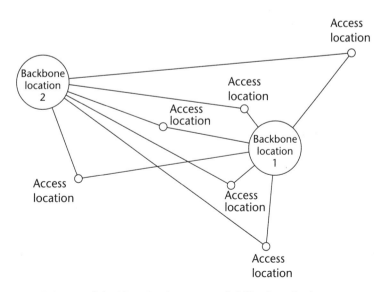

Figure 10-2: Use of dual homing increases reliability, but also increases cost.

location may be quite close to the access location, perhaps even within the same LATA, while the next closest may be hundreds of miles away. Thus, the backup circuit may cost vastly more than the primary circuit.

We need to draw an important distinction at this point: We are talking about running a second circuit to enhance *reliability*. If we were concerned solely with increasing *bandwidth* to the remote location, we could run parallel circuits both to the same backbone location, in which case the second circuit might cost no more than the first.

Note, however, that a second circuit to the same location as the first may also be appropriate as a means of enhancing reliability if the failure probabilities are associated primarily with access circuits or equipment and not with the connectivity at the next hierarchical level. This is often the case, particularly if the next-higher hierarchical tier of the network has high inherent availability. This yields the configuration shown in Figure 10-3.

In either design, the second circuit can either serve as a hot standby or else be used in a full load-sharing mode. In the former case, one circuit is used whenever possible; the other, only when the first is unavailable. Load sharing, or load balancing, means that traffic is somehow split over both access circuits. Load sharing makes more efficient use of the circuits, at the cost of increased complexity. It is easier to implement load sharing—and to do capacity planning for it—when both circuits land on the same router at the next hierarchical tier of the network.

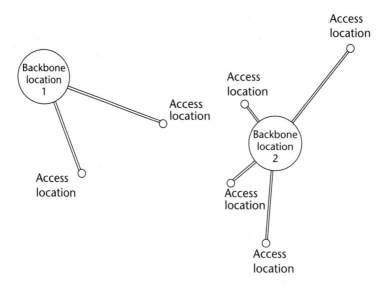

Figure 10-3: An alternative realization of dual homing.

Other strategies—each with its own advantages and disadvantages—exist for reducing the cost of the backup circuit. Some designs assign less capacity to the backup circuit than to the primary—for example, in order to cut costs. The reasoning is that in the event of a failure of the primary, some degradation is acceptable. Up to a point, this is reasonable; however, it is generally not a good idea to try to empty a bathtub with a teaspoon. The backup capacity must be at least marginally acceptable to your users.

Another possibility is to use a distance-sensitive primary connection, with a distance-insensitive backup. If you can find a distance-insensitive service with usage-based charging, it might be ideal for use as a hot standby; under normal conditions, you would pay very little for it, because you would have no usage at all. High per-bit charges might be quite acceptable if overall utilization is low, as should be the case here because the backup service comes into play less than 1 percent of the time.

10.3 The String of Pearls

As we have seen, it can be expensive to dual-home access locations to distinct locations at the next-higher hierarchical level. One design that can soften the blow a bit is sometimes referred to as the *string of pearls*. With this approach, each access location has a direct primary connection to the nearest service point for the next hierarchical level, such as the backbone. The backup connections, however, are from one access location to another. Thus, access locations serve to forward traffic from other access locations to the backbone in the event of a failure. If more than two access nodes are strung together in this way, the forwarding function is required even in the absence of a failure. The string of pearls is often economically advantageous because each of the expensive backup circuits serves two or more access locations in this design instead of serving only one access location, as in a typical dual-homing design. For a good example of how this is done, refer to Figure 10-4, which shows the internetMCI network (now operated by Cable & Wireless PLC), as it existed in 1996. In our previous discussion of levels of hierarchy, in Chapter 7, we noted that this internetwork could be viewed as comprising two tiers: an inner, backbone tier operating at OC-3 speeds (155Mbps) and an outer, concentration tier operating at DS-3/T-3 (45Mbps) speeds. The backbone links are thick; the concentration links are thin.

Look closely now at the loop from node 10 (the Chicago area) through nodes 11 and 12 (the Detroit and Cleveland areas) and then to node 17 (the Philadelphia area). Note that the connections from nodes 11 to 10 and from 12 to 17 are both primary paths, the paths that the data will normally traverse. Each of these paths consists of two T-3 circuits. The path from node 11 to 12, which exists primarily or exclusively for backup, consists of a single T-3.

In the event of a complete failure of the path from Detroit (node 11) to Chicago (node 10), Detroit would not be partitioned from the network. It would instead reroute traffic to the backbone node in Philadelphia (node 17), sending the data by way of Cleveland (node 12). The network might experience some degradation in dumping two T-3s worth of traffic onto the single backup T-3 between Detroit and Cleveland; however, some degree of performance degradation should be greatly preferable to a total loss of service. This can represent a reasonable engineering trade-off: A single backup T-3 provides a cost-effective failover capability for two primary paths of two T-3s each.

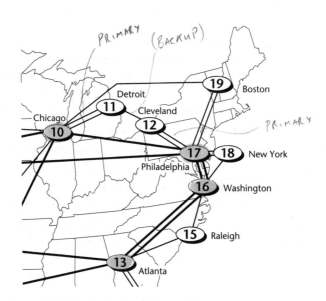

Figure 10-4: "String of Pearls" access homing: InternetMCI.

11 Creating a Preliminary Backbone Topological Design

This chapter explains how to develop a topological design for an internetwork backbone. Historically, most work in this area focused on cost optimization for partial-mesh leased line networks, the most complex class of networks. Although these networks continue to be significant, many internetworks today are constructed by using fast packet services, most notably Frame Relay, provided by the carriers. Over time, similar networks operating over carrier-provided ATM, or a mixture of Frame Relay and ATM, may enjoy comparable popularity. From an internetworking protocol perspective, classic partial-mesh leased line networks and Frame Relay/ATM–based networks are largely equivalent; however, they can differ significantly in cost, performance, and reliability. This chapter tries to present a balanced view of these two broad classes of designs.

At this point, your access design, as described in Chapter 9, should be complete. A great many networks can be constructed with just two levels of hierarchy: access and backbone. Larger networks may benefit from more levels of hierarchy. Chapter 10 described how to deal with access homings between the access level and successively higher levels of the hierarchy, up to and including the backbone.

This chapter comprises two major sections. The first describes the major topologies used in network design. The second walks you through the topological design process, starting with traffic characterization, particularly as it relates to a hierarchical view of your internetwork. The section then shows you how to construct and size a design for a simplified backbone based on a physical or logical star, a logical full mesh, or a partial mesh internetwork.

11.1 Fundamental Topologies

A network *topology* is the fundamental shape of the network. Topology, you will recall, is a branch of mathematics closely linked to geometry. Topology deals with the relationships among the nodes (points), lines, and faces of geometric figures but totally ignores the dimensions (sizes) of these elements. If in geometry, we often feel that we are constructing triangles and rectangles out of sticks, in topology, we are constructing them out of rubber bands.

The applicability to computer networking should be obvious: The points correspond to network service locations, or nodes; the lines correspond to network links, or circuits. The length of a link is largely irrelevant, except in terms of circuit cost and propagation delay. What we are really interested in expressing is the *connectivity* among the nodes and links.

Many designs are possible for the network backbone, the innermost core of the network. The designs have distinct properties in terms of cost, delay, bandwidth per link, routing complexity, and availability (reliability). The designer must make trade-offs. This section summarizes the pros and cons of the topologies commonly in use today.

11.1.1 Star

The *star* is the simplest network topology: A central "hub" location is connected to multiple remote locations, as depicted in Figure 11-1. The star generally has the lowest number of links of any network topology. There is one, and only one, connection from the hub to each remote location. You cannot

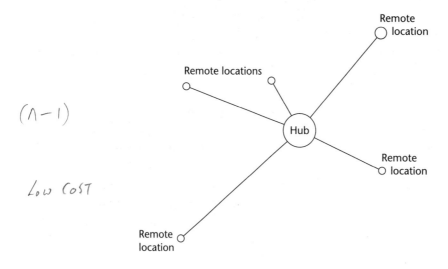

Figure 11-1: Star topology.

do better than that! The low number of links for this design will often be associated with low cost.

To understand the delay characteristics of a star network, we must consider the nature of traffic flows. If all of the traffic tends to flow from one remote location to another, the star network has an unappealing characteristic: All of the data must go through the hub location, which means that all of the data goes through two hops. In some cases, this could represent a significant disadvantage.

In many star networks, on the other hand, most or all of the end-to-end traffic goes from a remote location to the hub. If the remote locations have little or no need to communicate with one another, the potential cost of an extra hop is irrelevant. This is not a far-fetched case—it happens all the time. A great many networks connect, for instance, numerous remote sales offices to the corporate headquarters. Often, the sales offices are in frequent communication with headquarters but only rarely in contact with one another.

Once we understand the traffic flows, we can consider the capacity required for each link. Each link needs to have enough capacity to carry all of the traffic either to or from a remote location. Once again, it is better if the flows are primarily to and from the hub rather than among the remote locations. Other things being equal, a traffic flow between the hub and a remote location can be viewed as consuming only half as much aggregate network bandwidth as a traffic flow of comparable magnitude between two remote locations: The former consumes bandwidth on one link; the latter, on two.

The star is a very simple configuration from a routing perspective. The remote locations can use a default route to get to the hub location; that is, anything not specifically known to be local to the remote location is by default routed to the hub, which can use static routing to get to each remote location. There is no need for dynamic adaptive routing.

Now we come to the topic of availability. You should understand at the outset that according to one school of thought, star networks are inherently *evil* because they represent a single point of failure. If the hub location is down, the entire network is down. Moreover, if any circuit is down, a remote location is completely down.

That there is a single point of failure is indisputable. As with most things in this business, however, the reality is neither all black nor all white. There are a great many star networks in this world, and most of them look the way they do for good and valid reasons.

The statement that a single point of failure is a *bad thing* is a qualitative statement, a value judgment. People instinctively recognize that the likelihood that two components will fail for unrelated reasons at the same time is much lower than the probability that either one alone will fail.

But a system with a single point of failure does not necessarily have low overall availability; nor does a highly redundant system necessarily have high overall availability. If the single point of failure has sufficiently high innate availability, the system as a whole may be quite reliable.

Further, the notion that multiple components are more reliable tacitly assumes that the failure probabilities are mutually independent. If one component fails, there should still be no more than a random probability that the other one will, too. This is sometimes the case but not always. If two circuits share a common stretch of fiber-optic cable from the carrier, as happens all too often, their failure probabilities are *not* mutually independent. If two routers are running the same version of software or if they are both powered from the same power grid, their failure probabilities are *not* mutually independent. There is a significant probability that both will fail at the same time, with the same root cause.

Ultimately, you are trying to achieve high availability for your network. Avoidance of single points of failure can be a good way to enhance that availability, but it is not always necessary, and it is not always the best or the most cost-effective way to achieve the availability that you are looking for. Avoidance of single points of failure is one of several possible means to that end. It makes no sense to regard it as a goal in and of itself.

With all of that said, it is important to understand that a star *internetwork* may have characteristics that differ markedly from those of traditional star networks. A star internetwork exists at level 3, the network layer, and is based on a star topology that exists at level 2. In many cases, star internetworks are constructed using level 2 fast packet services, such as Frame Relay or ATM, as shown in Figure 11-2. This internetwork is a *logical* star, not a *physical* star. It is generally the case that the carrier's underlying physical topology, over which the Frame Relay or ATM service runs, is richly interconnected. The logical star may, depending on the carrier's implementation of fast packet services, be much less vulnerable than a physical star to single points of failure.

These logical star internetworks—a variant of a network design sometimes referred to as a *collapsed backbone*—are still vulnerable to failures of the hub router at the core. Also, the tail circuits connecting the service locations and the hub to the Frame Relay cloud can represent a point of vulnerability. There are ways to address both of these risks. In any case, the overall availability of a logical star network may be significantly better than that of a traditional, leased-line physical star network.

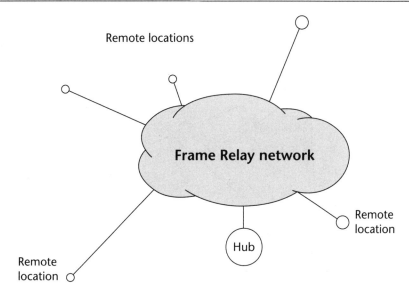

Figure 11-2: A logical star topology.

11.1.2 Full Mesh

At the opposite end of the design spectrum from the star network is the *full mesh* network. In a full mesh network, there is no central point, that is, no traffic cop to manage all of the traffic. Every remote location is directly connected to every other remote location, as shown in Figure 11-3.

From a cost perspective, a full mesh of dedicated circuits is usually the worst possible alternative, as it has the largest number of circuits. In fact, we can compute exactly how many circuits are necessary. Consider a full mesh of six nodes, as shown in Figure 11-3. Pick a node at random. It must have five connections to other nodes. Move to the next node. It also must have five connections to other nodes; however, we have already counted one of these, so there are four new connections. And so on. We see that the number of connections is 5+4+3+2+1, or 15. More generally, this sum represents the sum of an *arithmetic series*. A well-known formula shows the sum of such a series to be $(N * (N - 1)) / 2$, where N in this case is the number of nodes. Thus, for the six nodes in Figure 11-3, we have $(6 * 5)/2 = 15$ links, as we have seen.

Unfortunately, things get progressively worse. For 10 nodes, we would need 45 links. For 100 nodes, we would expect 4,450 links. And so it goes. For large N, the number of links is proportional to the *square* of the number of nodes.

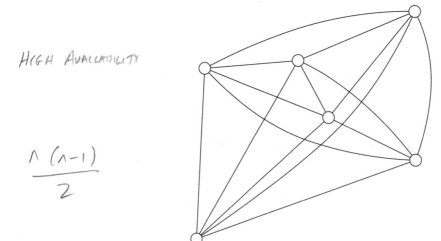

HIGH AVAILABILITY

$$\frac{\wedge (\wedge - 1)}{2}$$

Figure 11-3: Full mesh topology.

The required capacity for each link is simply equal to the volume of the end-to-end flows between the pair of remote locations that it interconnects. There is no forwarding of data, so there is no requirement for more bandwidth than that. In reality, however, we would tend to allocate additional capacity for recovery without performance degradation in the event that a link fails.

So much for cost. From a delay perspective, a full mesh is ideal. Every node is exactly one hop away from every other node.

In terms of routing, the full mesh is in some sense the most complex option, in that it must deal with the largest possible number of paths. Dynamic adaptive routing is required in order to permit failover in the event that a link goes down.

From an availability perspective, the full mesh is also ideal. Failure of a node affects only traffic to and from that node. Failure of a link causes traffic to be rerouted. Given that this is the most "bushy" possible network, rerouting should be easy, provided that we have allocated surplus capacity appropriately. Note, however, that this can be the most complex topology from a routing perspective.

As with other topologies, it is sometimes convenient to construct a full mesh network by using underlying fast packet services, such as Frame Relay, rather than conventional circuits. In this case, we avoid much of the cost associated with large numbers of individual leased lines. For a network of modest size or for a backbone of modest size in a larger network, this can be a fine design. For a network with a large number of nodes, however, the need to allocate CIR among a large number of PVCs can make this design impractical.

We saw earlier that the star network is inherently hierarchical, in that the hub location is fundamentally different from the remote locations. The full mesh network, by contrast, is inherently democratic, or egalitarian, in the sense that the nodes are inherently similar to one another in function. In hierarchical terms, a full mesh network is flat.

11.1.3 Ring

The *ring* network represents a somewhat different cut at topology. In a ring, every node is connected to exactly two other nodes, as shown in Figure 11-4. The ring offers low cost—in the sense of a low number of circuits—and better availability than the star; however, the ring sacrifices delay and has traffic characteristics that can be troublesome.

The number of circuits in the ring is exactly equal to the number of remote locations that must be connected. This is only one greater than in a star network—indeed, among fully redundant designs, this is the lowest link count possible. So this cost driver is low; however, as we shall see, other cost drivers must be considered as well.

The delay characteristics of a ring can potentially be a nightmare. Every bit of traffic has to go, on the average, one quarter of the way around the ring. (Recall that traffic can flow in either direction, following whichever route is topologically shortest.) Remember too that in the absence of failures, the

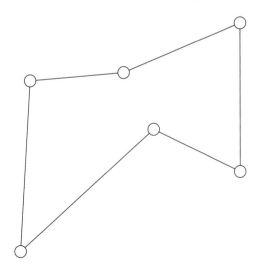

Figure 11-4: Ring topology.

worst case is halfway around, because routers should pick the shortest path; otherwise, delay would be twice as great. Thus, on the average, data will travel half of this maximum distance, which is half of half, or one quarter of the way around the ring. In a ring network of 101 nodes, data will travel 25 nodes on the average when the network is healthy, more when it is sick.

Is that a bad thing? It can be! If the network comprises heavily loaded circuits and routers, the queuing delays could add up to big numbers. On the other hand, in a lightly loaded network, they might be quite tolerable. And the delays could be ameliorated by using ATM, with its short cells and deterministic forwarding times through intermediate nodes.

From a link-traffic perspective, this design can be problematic. The high hop count corresponds to demands for high bandwidth. Indeed, each link must carry, on the average and in the absence of failures, one fourth of the entire traffic of the net. This might be tolerable for a LAN internetwork or a campus ATM network, where there is plenty of bandwidth and where there are no recurring payments to the carriers; however, it might be very unappetizing for a nationwide backbone network. It is largely for this reason that we rarely see a pure ring design in a wide area internetwork backbone.

Dynamic adaptive routing would typically be used to find the shortest path to a given node. This type of routing would permit automatic failover in the event that a link goes down.

From an availability perspective, the ring has some valuable properties. It has no single point of failure. If a single link fails, traffic routes around it transparently. If a single node fails, no other node is disrupted. This assumes, of course, that there is surplus capacity; a concern is that proper failover exactly doubles the already high bandwidth requirements associated with this network design. Again, it might be fine in a campus ATM network but might be problematic as a nationwide backbone.

Note, too, that any two concurrent failures will completely partition the ring. Like a full mesh network, a ring network is hierarchically flat.

11.1.4 Double Star

We have seen that the hub location at the center of a star represents a single point of failure. Is it possible to enhance the cost of the star network without altogether sacrificing its simplicity and low cost?

It is certainly possible to deploy a second hub location to the center of your network. Every remote location has two connections, one to hub 1, the other to hub 2, as shown in Figure 11-5.

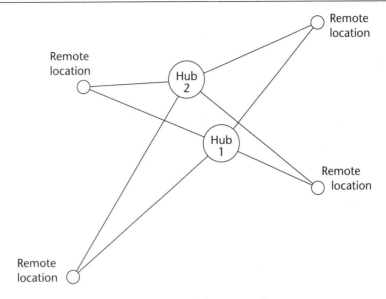

Figure 11-5: Double star topology.

In terms of cost, this design entails twice as many circuits as does a single star topology. For this reason, the double star is rarely seen in leased line networks. However, the design can be quite viable when deployed over a switched fast packet service such as Frame Relay. Instead of two connections to each remote location, we have two PVCs over a single Frame Relay port, as shown in Figure 11-6: a *logical* double star rather than a *physical* double star. Typically, this doubles the circuit cost for the network hubs, but has minimal cost impact on the remote locations. A relatively small increase in the total cost of the network can yield a large increase in overall network reliability.

Depending on the nature of your overall design and the application traffic you must carry, you might choose either to use one PVC as a hot standby to the other or to load share between them. Load sharing entails a risk that some packets will be delivered out of order. If you are carrying non-Internet protocols or applications that are sensitive to out-of-sequence packets, you may have to opt for the hot standby approach.

Delay characteristics are similar to those of the simple star. Traffic from any remote location to either hub requires one hop. Traffic from any remote location to any other remote location requires two hops.

Bandwidth requirements are also similar to those of a star, except that your hub traffic is divided between two locations.

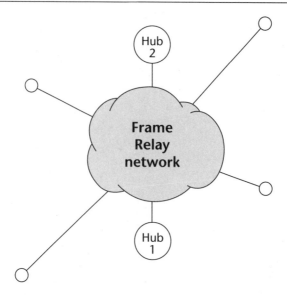

Figure 11-6: A logical double star network.

If you are using hot standby, you may be able to avoid dynamic adaptive routing by defining one PVC as a default link and the other as a backup. In all other cases, you will need to implement dynamic adaptive routing.

Finally, we come to availability. Note, first, that the reliability of the tail circuits and equipment at the remote locations is no better than in the simple star configuration. The improvements are all on the hub side. In a simple logical (single) star, a single failure of any of several components (see Figure 11-7) can result in a complete loss of service to all locations:

- The port associated with the hub location on the Frame Relay switch
- The CSU/DSU connected to that port, which might have been built into the switch
- The circuit connecting the Frame Relay switch to the hub location
- The CSU/DSU at the hub location
- The hub location router interface processor responsible for the Frame Relay port
- The router at the hub location

In a logical double star, however, a failure of one or more of these components usually results in a completely transparent recovery, with no loss of service, assuming that

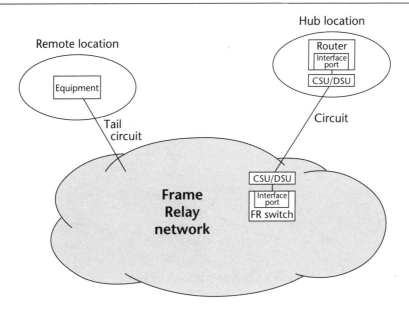

Figure 11-7: Potential failing components at the hub of a logical (single) star network.

- The failure probabilities are all mutually independent
- If more than one component fails, they are all associated with the same hub location
- The hub ports are configured with sufficient reserve bandwidth
- Routing protocols are correctly configured

This can be an excellent solution for environments where loss of a single remote location is acceptable but loss of the service as a whole is not.

11.1.5 Partial Mesh

We have seen that the full mesh network has excellent technical properties but suffers from high cost, due to the large number of circuits required. It is natural to think of taking a full mesh and pruning back the number of circuits in order to better balance cost against performance. Such a design is referred to as a partial mesh. Figure 11-8 depicts a possible partial mesh, but a wide range of designs can qualify for this name. Indeed, any design that does not clearly fall into some other category can be characterized as a partial mesh.

It is natural to view the partial mesh as an intermediate stage between the star and the full mesh topology. The number of links is greater than that of a star $(N - 1)$ but generally much less than that of a full mesh $((N * (N - 1)) / 2)$.

$> (n-1)$

$< \dfrac{n(n-1)}{2}$

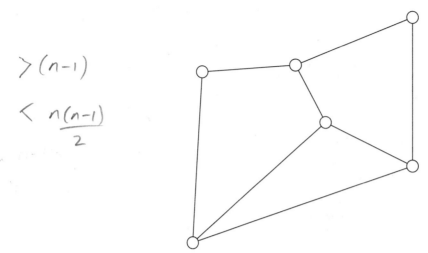

Figure 11-8: A partial mesh topology.

The average number of hops in a partial mesh will always be greater than that of a full mesh (1) and may also be greater than that of a star (2). This depends entirely on the design of the network.

Analogously, the average bandwidth required for each link will always be greater than that of a full mesh and may be greater than that of a star.

You will generally need to use dynamic adaptive routing for a partial mesh; however, the complexity will tend to be less than that of a full mesh, since the number of links can be much lower.

Availability is a more complex topic. We sometimes refer to a partial mesh as having *n*-connectivity, where *n* represents the minimum number of nodes to which any node is connected. We generally expect a partial mesh to have 2-connectivity or greater.

A partial mesh with *n*-connectivity will be less robust than a full mesh, but it can still be quite robust. If all failure probabilities are mutually independent, and if p represents the probability that any specific link and associated gear are available, we would expect that the probability that a given node has access to at least one of its neighbors is $1 - (1 - p)^n$. Now, $1 - p$ is a small number, generally 0.001 or less. So, as n increases beyond 2, $(1 - p)^n$ becomes *very* small indeed, and the overall expected availability becomes very nearly equal to unity.

The preceding formula is, of course, something of an oversimplification. Designing a partial mesh network so as to provide the desired level of availability, and providing sufficient capacity to enable it to perform properly in the face of failure of single components, is a complex task. We will return to this topic at the end of this chapter.

11.1.6 Hybrid Topologies

We have already seen that large networks are usually constructed in a hierarchical manner, and we know that an internetwork is a network of networks. It should therefore come as no surprise that many large internetworks are composed of more than one topology. In many cases, these topologies are associated with different levels within the hierarchical structure of the network.

It is quite common, for example, to see a network that combines a partial mesh backbone with a series of stars for remote access, as shown in Figure 11-9. This can represent a good trade-off between the need for high availability for the central core of the network, on the one hand, and the desire to economize on costs at the less critical periphery, on the other.

11.1.7 Summary of Network Topologies

The topologies we have discussed have the characteristics shown in Table 11-1. For leased line designs, a large number of links will tend to result in high cost.

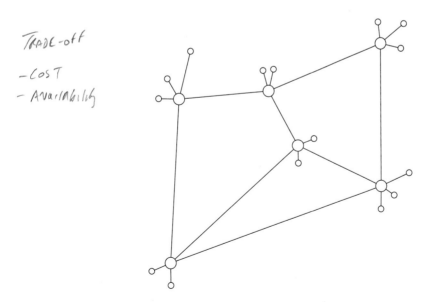

Figure 11-9: A hybrid topology: partial mesh core with stars at the periphery.

Table 11-1: Comparison of Alternative Network Topologies

Topology	Number of Links	Relative Number of Links	Max Hop Count	Complexity	Availability
Star	$N-1$	Lowest	2	Lowest	Lowest
Double Star (logical)	$2*(N-1)+1$	Low	2	Low	High at core, low at remote locations
Ring	N	Low	$(N-1)/2$	Low	Moderate
Partial mesh	Moderate	Moderate	$\log_n(N-1)$	High	Good
Full mesh	$(N*(N-1))/2$	Highest	1	Highest	Highest

Table 11-2: Partial Results of the Access Homing Phase of the Network Design

Kbps From/To	Backbone	Chicago	Detroit	Milwaukee	Minneapolis	Total
Backbone	—	230	25	5	10	**270**
Chicago	150	30	8	6	9	203
Detroit	10	7	2	1	2	22
Milwaukee	5	10	3	2	1	21
Minneapolis	5	8	2	2	1	18
Total:	**170**	**285**	**40**	**16**	**23**	

11.2 Creating the Backbone Design

Network design always flows from requirements. In order to understand how to design your network backbone, you need a thorough understanding of your traffic flows and your performance and reliability requirements. The performance and reliability requirements should have been captured in the first phase of the network design process (see Chapter 2). Your understanding of traffic flows, however, will need to be adjusted at this point to reflect the impact of access homings that you have already performed (see Chapters 9 and 10).

11.2.1 Traffic Characterization

In order to understand what capacity you need on a link-by-link basis, you first need to understand what capacity you need on an end-to-end basis. Recall, however, that we design large internetworks in hierarchical layers. When you design the innermost core of your backbone, you typically do not need to consider traffic flows down to the level of each individual workstation. End-to-end, in this context, can be viewed as a relative term: *You need to understand traffic flows only as they relate to the hierarchical layer you are designing at this moment.*

Suppose, for example, that you were designing a hierarchical network as depicted in Figure 11-10. In the previous design phase, you might have homed traffic from Minneapolis, Milwaukee, and Detroit into Chicago, with traffic characteristics as shown in Table 11-2. Your analysis shows an aggregate of 270Kbps flowing into the backbone at Chicago and an aggregate of 170Kbps leaving the backbone at Chicago (both highlighted in boldface type in Table 11-2). Now, you are ready to design the nationwide backbone to connect Chicago to Los Angeles, New York, and San Francisco. Do you still need to explicitly consider flows to Milwaukee?

You do not. Those flows have already been aggregated into Chicago's traffic. From the perspective of your end-to-end flows, you can deal with this aggregated flow to and from Chicago, ignoring the local traffic flows from Chicago to Milwaukee, Detroit, and Minneapolis. *We consciously do this in order to break the design problem down into bite-size chunks.*

Consider Figure 11-11. Several flows at a lower layer of hierarchy are folding together (in queuing theory, we call this *superposition*) to form a single, larger flow on the backbone, the innermost core of the network. When you aggregate multiple flows in this way, two things happen.

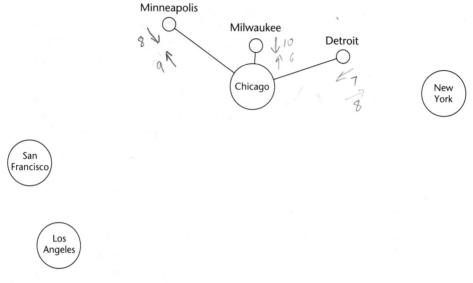

Figure 11-10: A hypothetical hierarchical network design.

1. The mean aggregate flow is equal to the sum of the means of the component input flows.

2. The aggregate flow has *less* variability than any of the component input flows.

If these flows were true *Poisson processes*—the random arrival pattern on which the mathematics of queues is based—queuing theory would tell us exactly what to expect in terms of their variability; however, viewed over the course of the day, it is generally inappropriate to view these data flows as simple Poisson processes. Bandwidth demands at 3:00 P.M. tend to be quite different from those at 3:00 A.M. We would say that the observations are drawn from different distributions. Further, data traffic tends to be bursty and to experience nonrandom variability. In many cases, therefore, it is impractical to predict the variability of these composite flows.

In light of these uncertainties, I generally prefer to use mean data rather than such measures as ninety-fifth percentile utilization for designing backbones. Means are simple and unambiguous.

At the same time, your design needs to take account of variability over the course of the day. It is generally impractical to design these networks for the largest traffic volume that they could *ever* carry: Nobody could afford it. Yet your network needs to comfortably carry the busiest traffic that will *routinely*

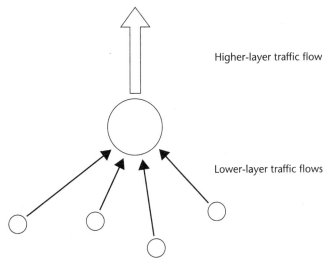

Higher-layer traffic flow

Lower-layer traffic flows

Figure 11-11: Superposition of network traffic flows.

appear. For these reasons, many designers work with traffic estimates for the *peak,* or *busiest,* hour.

Your primary task is to develop a *traffic matrix,* reflecting the end-to-end mean peak-hour flows among your backbone locations. For the example shown earlier, in Figure 11-10, the traffic matrix might look like Table 11-3. Note that the matrix in Table 11-3 happens to be *asymmetric* about the diagonal. The intensity of traffic from New York to Los Angeles is *not* the same as the traffic intensity from Los Angeles to New York.

Historically, many designers would, by default, assume traffic to be symmetric. Traffic was usually balanced in both directions. Today, however, we *often* find traffic to be asymmetric.

You need to understand the data that characterize your particular network. Traffic asymmetry has become fairly commonplace in internetworks in recent years, driven primarily by two phenomena:

1. The World Wide Web, which is the dominant application in many networks in terms of traffic, tends to be associated with small requests for data that generate large responses.

2. In the public Internet, the rules for traffic interchange among providers (shortest exit) tend to promote highly asymmetric flows.

Finally, you need to look at the probable evolution of your traffic patterns over time. Some designers tend to create a single design based on a single

PEAK BUSY HR TRAFFIC
Note Traffic in Asymetric eg. CHA→NY 100, NY→CHIc 200

192   *Creating a Preliminary Backbone Topological Design*

Table 11-3: A Sample Traffic Matrix

Kbps From/To	Chicago	Los Angeles	New York	San Francisco	Total
Chicago	—	50	100	20	170
Los Angeles	50	—	150	30	230
New York	200	300	—	140	640
San Francisco	20	30	70	—	120
Total:	**270**	**380**	**320**	**190**	**1,160**

FROM

To

traffic matrix, as if the traffic flows would last for all time. This is generally a bad idea, particularly if your business is evolving rapidly. If you understand where your network is likely to be in 6 months and in 24, it might influence how you would choose to do things today. It is usually good form to prepare a sequence of designs based on projected traffic matrices for several points in the future, in order to plan a migration path that avoids needless change and churn to the network design.

With that groundwork established, we can proceed to work through detailed network designs for each of the topologies described earlier in this chapter, starting with the physical star.

11.2.2 Physical Star Network

Select Hub based on • Dist

Designing a physical (leased line) star network is straightforward. You merely need to select the hub location from among your backbone locations. You simply connect the dots: Every remote location has a single link to the hub.

Your selection of a hub location is driven primarily by three factors:

1. geographic location

2. traffic intensity

3. reliability requirements

First and foremost, you want a hub location that will minimize the sum of all circuit lengths, in order to provide overall circuit costs that are as low as possible. This means, quite simply, that you want to pick a location at or near the geographic center of your network, corresponding roughly to the center of gravity of the locations that make up your network.

Second, if you have more than one reasonable candidate location for the hub, based on geography, you should prefer the one with greatest traffic intensity. The hub location can be accessed from any remote location in just one hop. By picking a busy location for your hub, you can improve overall average response time a bit and can also avoid the cost impact associated with needlessly sending transit traffic through the hub location.

On occasion, you may design a network where there is a strong requirement for reliability from one location to most or all of the others; typically, this location is one at which vital business functions are performed. This location will often, but not always, be a high traffic intensity location. You may want to give special consideration to making this location your hub, since the hub has fewer hops to the remote locations and thus greater reliability of access. You should bear in mind, however, that if reliability is your primary objective, the physical star is probably not your topology of choice in the first place.

If most of your traffic needs to flow to and from a location (such as the corporate data center) that is physically located at the *edge* of your network, alarm bells should start ringing at this point. The physical star is probably not the right design for such a network. You may instead want to look at logical star designs, in which the physical location of the hub within the United States has little economic impact.

For the sample network in Table 11-3, the clear choice for the hub location is Chicago. This yields the topology shown in Figure 11-12.

Figure 11-12: A realization of a physical star.

At this point, we need to determine the capacity for each link. To do so, we simply look at the totals on the rows and columns of our traffic matrix. Recall that the rows of the traffic matrix shown in Table 11-3 reflect the location that the traffic is coming *from,* and the columns reflect the location that it is going *to.* The total for each row thus reflects the total traffic intensity we must carry from that location to the hub. The total for each column reflects the total traffic intensity we must carry from the hub to that location. Note, incidentally, that we do not need to explicitly consider the hub's traffic at this point, because the hub's traffic is already factored into the requirements associated with the remote locations.

Leased lines are symmetric in their carrying capacity. That means that we need to obtain lines that can carry the greater of the two. Table 11-4 summarizes the required capacity. Looking at the totals in Table 11-4, we see that the smallest is 200Kbps and the largest is 800Kbps. It is clear that we need more than a 56Kbps line in all cases. Since no capacity exceeds that of a T-1 circuit (1,536 usable kilobits per second), we immediately suspect that T-1 lines are the right solution.

At this point, we need to briefly consider two related topics: overhead and reserve capacity. Many kinds of overhead exist in an internetwork. First, we have to consider the overhead imposed by the data link layer encapsulation. For the PPP or proprietary encapsulation protocols that we would normally use on a leased line, these are generally in the 1 percent or 2 percent range, small enough to ignore for most purposes. There are also SNMP network management messages, routing updates, and other aspects of router administrivia. In practice, we usually ignore these, too, but they could in some instances be significant.

[handwritten diagram: SF, Chicago, NY, LA, ATL connected in a star]

Table 11-4: Required Link Capacity for a Physical Star

	Egress	Ingress	Link Capacity
Atlanta	140	220	220
Los Angeles	260	410	410
New York	800	400	800
San Francisco	130	200	200
Total:	1,330	1,230	1,630

[handwritten notes: ignore overhead • Protocol • SNMP]

Now we come to reserve capacity. No network runs at 100 percent sustained utilization. Queuing theory tells us that queuing delays grow without bound as utilization approaches 100 percent. Our users would not be happy with a network with infinite delay.

Any network needs to have a portion of the capacity of each link set aside to keep the queuing delays within reasonable bounds. But what does "reasonable" mean? And how much reserve capacity is enough?

We use queuing theory to relate this reserve capacity to delay. The mathematical techniques are covered later, in Chapter 16. At this point, it is sufficient to work with some rule-of-thumb guidelines.

Many networks are designed with reserve capacity of 30 percent to 50 percent, which corresponds to peak-hour mean utilization of 50 percent to 70 percent. Your choice of where to draw the line largely reflects your business objectives: Is it more important to minimize costs or to provide the snappiest possible response to your user community? The material in Chapter 16 will help you to understand these trade-offs.

If you are dealing with circuits that are fast (T-3 or above) and long, you could consider working with less reserve capacity, because propagation delay for a widespread network will dominate any queuing delay, anyway. I find that a reserve of 20 percent above that required to carry peak-hour mean traffic can be quite adequate under these conditions. For slower circuits, you would tend to work with greater reserve capacity in order to maintain decent response time. In any event, you should take such rules of thumb with a grain of salt and interpret them in light of the expectations and the observed traffic variability of the user community you intend to serve.

For now, let's assume that we want to work with 40 percent reserve capacity in the peak hour, and that this is sufficiently generous that we can choose to ignore other overheads. Reserve capacity of 40 percent corresponds to mean peak-hour utilization of 60 percent. In the case of a T-1, 60 percent utilization corresponds to about 925 Kbps. Since the links to Atlanta, Los Angeles, and San Francisco in our example all require no more than 410Kbps, we see that T-1 circuits will work very nicely for them. The circuit to New York, at 800Kbps, is a bit "warm," but it is still within our guidelines, so a single T-1 suffices for this case, too; in practice, however, we might want to also factor in the anticipated rate of traffic growth over time to understand how soon we would need to upgrade and how we would do so.

In this design, we might consider using fractional T-1 circuits for the lower-bandwidth cities, such as San Francisco; in most cases, however, the dollar savings in doing so (if any) are simply not worth the added hassle.

USE T1 Links
Allow for 60% utilization

11.2.3   Logical Star Network

Select Hub based on Traffic Flow

We know that any of these topologies can be constructed by using carrier-provided fast packet services, such as Frame Relay. How might the star network of the preceding section look if it were constructed using a Frame Relay service offering rather than leased lines?

Well, a star is still a star. But the distance-insensitive character of IXC Frame Relay tariffs means that there is no longer any motivation to locate the hub at the geographic center of gravity of the network. Traffic intensity becomes the dominant consideration.

Consider Table 11-3 again. Figure 11-13 shows the traffic patterns. It is obvious that the traffic flowing outward from New York is dominant. Among the return flows, it is also clear that there is more traffic returning to New York than is flowing between any other pair of locations. Thus, New York is the natural hub location for the logical star network. This yields the topology of Figure 11-14.

A design like the one in Figure 11-14 bothers many people's esthetic sense. The design seems counterintuitive. You have to really force yourself to remember that distances are truly irrelevant when you use carrier services with distance-insensitive tariffs. Rather, they are *largely* irrelevant. There is

NY is dominant
Natural Hub for logical Star

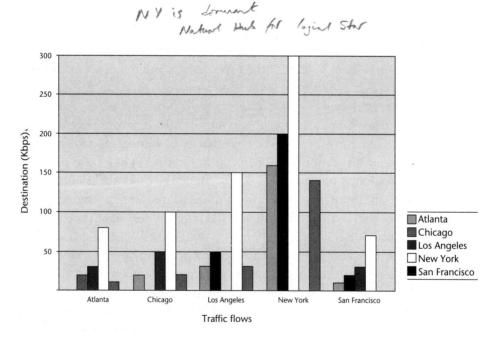

Figure 11-13: Relative magnitudes of traffic intensity in the sample network.

Latency = (Propogation Delay, CLK Delay, Hops)
Transport   f(Speed & PacketSize)
Q. delay

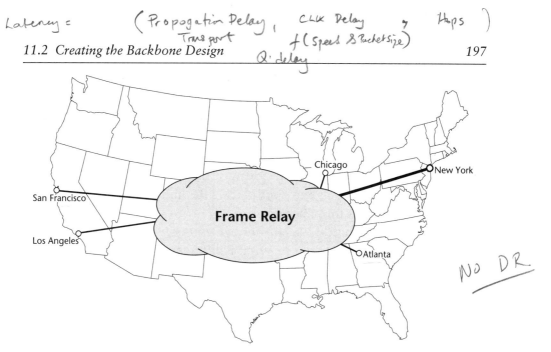

NO DR

Figure 11-14: A realization of a logical star.

one unavoidable consequence: The increase in overall mileage causes an increase in propagation delay. Does that matter? In terms of performance, there is a trade-off between the distances involved versus the time to clock a packet onto the line, which is a function of line speed, assuming a consistent average packet length. Assume that it takes about 70 milliseconds of round-trip time to send a packet across the United States and back. This design adds significant additional delay time to traffic that has to go to New York and then back out again (a small fraction of the total traffic in this example). A path from San Francisco to Atlanta by way of Chicago might typically entail about 70 milliseconds of round-trip propagation delay (distance roughly equivalent to that across the country); a path from San Francisco to Atlanta by way of New York might entail somewhat more, perhaps 100 milliseconds.

250 × 8
56 000
≃ 40 nS

Let's change our parameters a bit to make this point clear. Suppose that we were using a 56Kbps leased line to connect each location. If we assume a packet size of 250 bytes, it would take on the order of 40 milliseconds to clock each packet onto a 56Kbps line, which happens four times per round trip in this case, twice heading toward the hub and twice heading away from it. Typical queuing delays on the link would at least double that again, assuming average load on the link of 50 percent or so.

Thus, in this configuration, traffic headed from San Francisco to Atlanta might take (4 * 2 * 40) + 70 = 390 milliseconds of round-trip time with a

Logical Star   LS ○——→○ NY   Round Trip   Double RT time for Q delays.
Hub in NY   ↗ Hub NY   (4×2×40) +70
                4X   ↓○ AT

physical star hubbed in Chicago. By comparison, (4 * 2 * 40) + 100 = 420 milliseconds of round-trip time would be needed with a physical star hubbed in New York. This is, for most purposes, a very acceptable "hit." Moreover, it is largely offset—in this example and in many real networks—by the avoidance of the intermediate router hop in Chicago for traffic that is truly destined to New York, which is the recipient of the vast majority of the traffic. For the traffic matrix in this example, placing the hub in New York probably results in an overall performance *gain*.

Nonetheless, you need to keep your eye on this. With faster lines, especially at T-3 speeds or above, or with a different traffic matrix, it could become a significant factor. Where the speeds are greater or the traffic matrix less starlike, you might prefer a partial mesh design.

At this point, we need to determine the capacity requirements to each of the four cities in our example. For the remote locations—Chicago, Los Angeles, and San Francisco—the port speed requirements are exactly the same as for the physical star we analyzed in the previous section. New York, however, must accommodate the sum of all the traffic. This rolls up as shown in Table 11-5.

The numbers in Table 11-5 reflect the fact that the Frame Relay port in New York must accommodate not only New York's own traffic but also all of the transit traffic among the other remote locations. In some networks, that traffic might be negligible. For instance, Atlanta, Chicago, Los Angeles, and San Francisco might be sales offices with little need to communicate with one another. In this particular example, however, the transit traffic among those remote locations is significant.

CIR FROM NY

Table 11-5: Link Capacities for a Logical Star

	Egress	Ingress	Port Capacity
Atlanta	140	220	220
Chicago	190	290	290
Los Angeles	260	410	410
San Francisco	130	200	200
Total:	720	1,120	1,120
New York	1,120	720	1,120

The total traffic works out to 1,120Kbps. That should physically fit onto a single T-1 circuit, which has a nominal capacity of 1,536Kbps; however, it may not leave adequate reserve capacity. In our previous example, we established a nominal objective of loading the circuits not more than 60 percent, or 925Kbps, during the busy hour. Under that assumption, you would have to order up two T-1 circuits and to somehow split the load between them. (There are a number of options on how to do this. More along these lines appears in Chapter 12.)

For the CIRs, it is usually reasonable to set these at or just slightly above the expected peak-hour mean traffic, taking advantage of Frame Relay's capability to enable the user to "burst" above the CIR. It is, however, a good idea to make sure that you understand your Frame Relay provider's capacity management strategies, and what happens to traffic above the CIR. It may be advisable to add more surplus capacity to the CIR if your provider is aggressive in policing the CIR. Dropped packets are expensive in terms of their impact on perceived performance. Here we have yet another classic trade-off between cost and performance, but the details in this case must be worked out with your provider.

In this case, then, the PVCs from New York to Atlanta, Chicago, Los Angeles, and San Francisco should in general have their CIRs set to the first available size that exceeds 220Kbps, 290Kbps, 410Kbps, and 200Kbps, respectively. The PVCs from Atlanta, Chicago, Los Angeles, and San Francisco to New York should have their CIRs set to the first available size that exceeds 140Kbps, 190Kbps, 260Kbps, and 130Kbps, respectively. Note that many Frame Relay providers support asymmetric CIRs and provide pricing on a simplex (unidirectional) basis that makes it possible to get a price break that reflects this asymmetry.

Before we leave this example, we should note that this was not an ideal case for the logical star. We are about to discover that the logical full mesh is a better solution to this particular scenario because it avoids the cost impact of running transit traffic through New York. In general, the logical star is most suitable for access concentration, not for a backbone with "meshy" flows. It is most useful where bandwidth demands are low, especially where bandwidth demands are for 56Kbps or less; where traffic flows for the most part converge on just one or two locations; and where geographic dispersion is great.

11.2.4 Logical Full Mesh Network

In a full mesh network, every location has direct connectivity to every other location. A full mesh network design for the network described in Table 11-3 would look like Figure 11-15. A physical (leased line) full mesh network usually results in more circuits, and thus more cost, than anyone is willing to accept. Logical full mesh networks based on fast packet services are sometimes warranted. The logical equivalent to the network in Figure 11-15 might look like Figure 11-16. In this case, computing the requisite port speeds and bandwidths is child's play. Each pair of distinct destinations corresponds to a Frame Relay PVC. Each of the nonzero cells in Table 11-3 corresponds to a simplex Frame Relay CIR. (We obtain the next-highest available CIR, in practice.)

The port speed requirements are driven by the sum of all ingress traffic or the sum of all egress traffic for that location, whichever is greater. The port speed requirement in this case for each location is given in Table 11-6. This level of capacity is consistent with a single T-1 to each location. Note that this is a lower-cost choice than the logical star network that we evaluated previously; the former required two T-1 circuits to New York. The total CIR is also lower. Why is that? In this network, every location is exactly one router hop away from every other location. There is no transit traffic at all (when the network is healthy).

This illustrates once again a key, but counterintuitive, aspect of distance-insensitive tariffs: In a distance-insensitive world, it is best to carry the traffic as close as possible to the ultimate destination in a single hop—sometimes referred to as a "home run." Why should you want to pay the carrier to haul your data twice, if you have the option of paying the carrier just once to get the data exactly where it needs to go?

Figure 11-15: A realization of a full mesh network.

Table 11-6 represents sufficient capacity to operate the network under normal conditions. What happens if something fails? Do you need more capacity?

In general, a full or partial mesh should be capacitized to permit the network to recover with, at worst, graceful degradation in the event of a single component failure. This failover capability is, after all, part of the reason why you selected this design in the first place. Computing reasonable levels of backup capacity is easy enough in a tiny network like this one, but in a large network, it can be quite complex. In this particular example, however, we need to consider carefully the failure scenarios against which we wish to defend. It may be useful to risk digressing a bit at this point, because it helps illustrate the considerations that come into play in real networks.

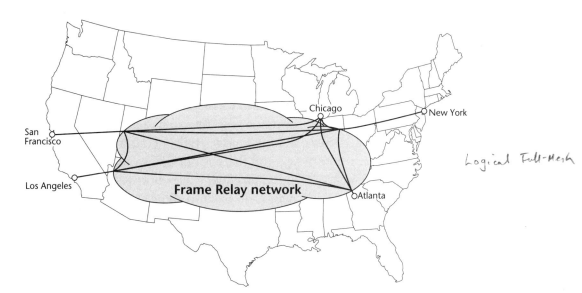

Figure 11-16: A realization of a logical full mesh network.

Table 11-6: Port Capacity for a Logical Full Mesh Network

	Egress	Ingress	Port Capacity
Atlanta	140	220	220
Chicago	190	290	290
Los Angeles	260	410	410
New York	800	400	800
San Francisco	130	200	200

Assume that we have one router, one router port, one CSU/DSU, and one LEC circuit connecting us to the Frame Relay service at each location. Further assume that the carrier's Frame Relay network will automatically and transparently recover from backbone link outages, if other paths exist. With these assumptions, under what circumstances would we want to route through an intermediate location to recover from a failure?

The short answer is that there appear to be no circumstances under which such a failover is beneficial for this example and under these assumptions. There are two failure scenarios.

First, if a router, router port, CSU/DSU, or LEC tail circuit fails—or, in most cases, if the single port or (if distinct from the port) the CSU/DSU for the Frame Relay service itself fails—all connectivity to that location is lost. At the same time, this is a full mesh; thus, no traffic between any other pair of locations was going through the failed location at the time of the failure. Thus, there is no possibility of recovering connectivity to the failed location until the fault is repaired, but there is also no impact on any other locations. There is no need to arrange for rerouting of traffic, because there is no benefit.

The second potential failure scenario involves the Frame Relay provider's infrastructure. In the event of a failure, there are two possibilities: Either a switch adjacent to one of our locations fails, or a nonadjacent switch or link fails. If a switch adjacent to one of our nodes fails, or becomes isolated, we have once again lost connectivity, and there is nothing to be done for it. If a switch or a link elsewhere fails, the provider's network will, in most cases, automatically recover; again, there is no need to route traffic through intermediate nodes at level 3.

If the provider's network is *not* set up to recover automatically from a failed PVC, we might want to establish backup PVCs. In that case, however, there is still no obvious advantage in rerouting traffic at level 3. The backup PVCs might as well connect the same pair of nodes that otherwise communicate over the default PVCs.

There are plenty of network designs in which it is necessary and appropriate to build in excess capacity in support of failover operation. This happens not to be one of them.

11.2.5 Partial Mesh Network

Perhaps the most common design for the network described in Table 11-3 is the partial mesh. A partial mesh of dedicated circuits (leased lines) can provide good performance and robust recovery from failures at moderate cost.

Computing the topological design and the bandwidth requirements for a tiny network like the one in our example is not difficult; however, as the number of nodes and links in the network increases, the complexity rapidly exceeds that which can be comfortably dealt with using back-of-the-envelope computational techniques. For this reason, most designers use commercial tools to evaluate networks in this class. A commercial tool is not a substitute for a basic understanding of how to construct a network, but it can greatly simplify the computation.

Why is it so complex? There are many reasons. First, the number of potential paths between nodes is, as we have seen, $(N * (N - 1)) / 2$. Second, you have to deal with transit traffic through intermediate nodes, and you need to sum multihop traffic up in order to get total utilizations on the links. Third, the multihop characteristics are themselves dependent on the routing table. And fourth, you generally want to evaluate capacity and robustness in the face of various failures, which require that you permute the routing matrix. And so on.

It is perfectly possible to map these characteristics, using nothing more sophisticated than a spreadsheet. To do so, you generally need to be fanatical about accuracy, persistent, perverse, or masochistic. I happen to be all four. I routinely use spreadsheets to model partial-mesh networks with traffic matrices as large as 20×20. I do not recommend this practice. Let me explain the kind of computations you would have to do, to help you to understand why you do not want to do them.

1. First, you need to characterize the nodes in the network and how they are interconnected to form the links.

2. Then you need to establish the next-hop routing matrix between them. I generally specify this by hand.

3. Then you need to enter the traffic matrix. You might imagine that that's the easy part, but in practice it can be the most difficult part of the job.

4. Now comes the interesting part. You have to figure out where the traffic would go on its first router hop, based on the routing matrix, and sum that traffic for each link.

5. At that point, you look at the traffic. If it all got to its end destination, you're done; if not, you need to compute a residual traffic matrix—a traffic matrix reflecting where traffic got to after *n* hops—and repeat steps 4 and 5.

6. When you're through with that, you can finally compute the capacities you need for each link and can also estimate the cost.

7. Now that you know both the load and the capacity on each link, you can use queuing theory to compute individual link delays.

8. At this point, you can use your knowledge of link delays and the routing matrix to estimate end-to-end delays between any two points in the network.

9. You need to sanity-check your work. A model is only as good as your ability to validate it against some objective reality.

10. Finally, if you've gotten this far without having made egregious errors, you typically want to perform a range of what-if analyses to see how the design would change if you modified your assumptions, your connectivity, or your routing matrix. Doing this with a spreadsheet model tends to be demanding.

None of this is rocket science, but it is complex and error-prone. You must keep track of a lot of detail. If you are designing nontrivial partial mesh networks, a commercially available design tool is a wise investment. Some of the commercial design tools that you might want to consider are, in alphabetical order, Autonet (NDA), NetMaker (Make Systems), Netsys (Cisco), WANDL, and WinMind (NAC).

With all of that said, let's return to the network described in Table 11-3. Assume that we want to construct a partial mesh with 2-connectivity—in other words, every location has at least two connections to somewhere else.

Typically, we begin by constructing a ring around the periphery of the nodes. In this case, the ring will connect all of the nodes. In larger network, however, some nodes might be left in the interior. At this point, the design looks like Figure 11-17.

Next, we selectively add "crossings" to the partial mesh, for three main reasons:

1. We may need to pick up interior nodes (but not in this example).

2. We want to increase reliability and redundancy.

3. We want to reduce the "diameter" of the network, in terms of hops, in order to improve performance.

For this simple example network, the traffic flow between Los Angeles and New York is quite large, with 300Kbps away from New York and 150Kbps toward it. It is therefore an excellent candidate for a crossing. There is very little traffic among Chicago, Los Angeles, and Atlanta—no flow with

Figure 11-17: First step in the design of a partial mesh network.

more than 50Kbps—so these are poor candidates for direct crossings. It is better to forward their traffic through intermediate nodes. New York to San Francisco is a moderately good candidate, with traffic of 140Kbps from New York and 70Kbps toward it, but that is probably not good enough; instead, we can forward traffic through Los Angeles. At this point, we have considered every possible link in this trivial network.

Let's say that we decide to proceed with the network topology shown in Figure 11-18.

Computing link traffic requirements takes some thought, even in this trivial network. Consider, for example, the link from Chicago to New York. In addition to carrying the traffic from the Chicago–New York cell in the traffic matrix, it might also carry traffic from San Francisco to New York, and vice versa. (Or does that traffic instead flow by way of Los Angeles?) Furthermore, it may need some surplus capacity for failover in the event that the link from Los Angeles to New York fails. (Or does that traffic instead flow by way of Atlanta?) Even in this trivial case, you need to think through your traffic matrix and your failover strategies in order to understand how traffic will flow. Tools can help you in this analysis, but there is no substitute for gray matter.

We just went through a greatly simplified partial mesh design. A considerable body of theoretical work has gone into network design algorithms. Many of

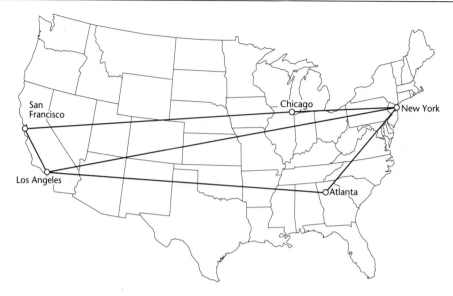

Figure 11-18: A partial mesh network topology.

the commercial network analysis tools are geared primarily toward *evaluating* network designs rather than *creating* them. If you are looking to design a large and complex partial mesh network from scratch, you might want to take a look at design algorithms in a reference text such as Mischa Schwartz's.[1]

Look @ Design Tools

Autonet   (NDA)
NetMaker   (Make Systems)
Netsys   (csc.)
WinMind   (NAC)

---

1. M. Schwartz, *Telecommunication Networks: Protocols, Modeling, and Analysis* (Reading, Mass.: Addison-Wesley, 1987).

12 — Naming, Addressing, and Routing

This chapter provides an overview of three interrelated aspects of your detailed network design: naming, addressing, and routing.

- A *name* is what we call something, generally something that is accessible from the network. A name is usually designed to be intelligible to human beings and easy to remember.
- An *address* is a way to identify something that is accessible from the network. An address is not necessarily designed to be intelligible to human beings or memorable. It may encode information—and in the IP world specifically *does* encode information—that helps the network to figure out how to most efficiently reach this network location.
- *Routing* is the process whereby we compute the most efficient path to reach a specific network location. In the case of IP, we use the IP address to determine the most appropriate path to the specified network location.

Human-intelligible names are mapped to IP addresses and vice versa by means of the *domain name service (DNS)*. Thus, the two topics are intimately tied to each other. Routing is heavily dependent on network and subnetwork addresses; thus, again, the topics interact in complex ways.

In this chapter, we will discuss names, addresses, and routing, in that order. A great deal has been written on these subjects; indeed, whole books have been written on the DNS alone. My intent in this chapter is to try to distill enough of the essentials to enable you to quickly make sense of the detailed specifications that appear in the associated RFCs.

12.1 Naming and the Domain Name System (DNS)

In the TCP/IP world, names are generally of the form <zzz. <yyy.>> xxx.hld, where left and right angle brackets (< or >) denote an optional element; hld denotes a *high-level domain,* such as .com (for commercial organizations), .net (for networks), .edu (for educational institutions), and .org (for other governmental or nonprofit organizations). If xxx is the domain name, yyy can then be viewed as an optional subdomain name, which may in turn be further subdivided. In all cases, the most-significant identifier is at the right, and successively less-significant identifiers appear as you work your way to the left. The leftmost identifier is a host name, typically identifying a single (host) computer system, such as the PC on your desk. For a more exhaustive description of the syntax and semantics of domain names, consult RFC 1034.[1]

12.1.1 Origin of Domain Names

As this is being written, domain names with the hlds just described are being assigned by the interNIC (Network Information Center). The name-assignment function of the interNIC is operated by a single private corporation, Network Solutions, Incorporated (NSI), under contract to the National Science Foundation (NSF) of the United States.

At the same time, other hlds associated with various countries are administered by national authorities within those countries. Thus, there are hlds for France (fr), Australia (au), and Germany (de). Within each of these hlds, the national authority determines how to assign domain names.

This system is in a remarkable state of flux. The contract between NSI and the NSF is winding down. The *Internet Corporation for Assigned Names and Numbers (ICANN)* was formed to take overall responsibility for IP address space allocation, protocol parameter assignment, domain name system management, and system management of DNS root servers. This process is still in its formative stages.

In the modern Internet, domain names have potential value, even though they are not "sold" in the normal sense. For example, a number of individuals have obtained domain names that largely overlap company names or other registered trademarks, in anticipation that the companies that own those trademarks would eventually want to use those names badly enough to pay for the privilege. Thus, the assignment of domain names, which was long viewed as a purely technical function, is now deeply intertwined with the law of trademarks and of intellectual property in general.

---

1. P. Mockapetris, Request for Comments (RFC) 1034, "Domain Names—Concepts and Facilities," November 1987.

12.1.2 Servers and Resolvers

The DNS is fundamentally a client/server system. The DNS client is referred to in the relevant RFCs as a *resolver.* See Figure 12-1. The resolver resides in a host system and issues DNS queries as necessary. For example, if you asked the browser on your PC Windows system to connect you to a URL located on www.gte.com, the resolver on your PC would be invoked, unless it had already saved, or *cached,* the required answer in response to a previous request. The resolver would issue a DNS query to one or more preconfigured DNS servers. The server would respond, ideally with the IP address of www.gte.com, which happens as of this date to be 207.121.186.191. Your browser would then be able to use the IP address 207.121.186.191 to open a TCP session with the target host, www.gte.com.

The DNS *server* can be viewed as a kind of distributed database; however, it has some unique characteristics, many of which flow from work done by Oppen and Dalal at Xerox PARC.[2]

- The design capitalizes on the fact that data will be *accessed* far more often than it will be *updated.*
- It is better, in general, to use slightly out-of-date information than none at all. (Similarly, if you use the postal system to mail a letter to the old address of a friend who has just moved, the letter will most likely either be returned to you or else will be forwarded to your friend.)
- There is thus no hard-and-fast requirement for absolute realtime consistency of the distributed, replicated database.

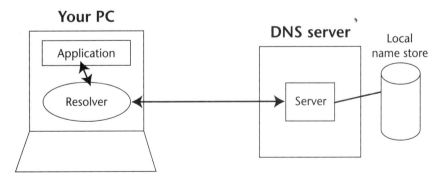

Figure 12-1: The DNS as a client/server system.

2. D. Oppen and Y. Dalal, "The Clearinghouse: A Decentralized Agent for Locating Named Objects in a Distributed Environment," OPD-T8103, Xerox Office Products Division, Palo Alto, Calif., October 1981.

The totality of the name space is partitioned into *zones* among a great many DNS servers. Any particular zone usually has at least two DNS servers that are *authoritative;* they have complete information about that domain and have been configured to regard themselves as being definitive for that domain. (Two, rather than one, are used in order to ensure sufficient reliability of the DNS service.) Other DNS servers may be capable of responding to a particular query about a domain for which they are not authoritative; however, a responder that receives responses from more than one DNS server should always prefer an authoritative response to a nonauthoritative one.

If a particular DNS server does not have the information necessary to respond to a DNS request, it could

- Invoke another DNS server on the client's behalf (*recursion*) and return the response to the client as if the information had been locally available (Figure 12-2)
- Refer the client to another DNS server (*iteration*) (Figure 12-3)
- Report back to the client that it is unable to provide the requested information

All DNS servers are required to be able to refer the client to another DNS server (iteration).

12.1.3 DNS Name Space

As previously noted, DNS names can be viewed as having the format <zzz.<yyy.>> xxx.hld. Names thus consist of several *labels,* each of which is delimited with a period at the end. Labels can contain letters, numbers, and hyphens but not spaces. These names can be thought of as a tree structure, where the leftmost (and thus most specific) labels constitute the leaves. As we

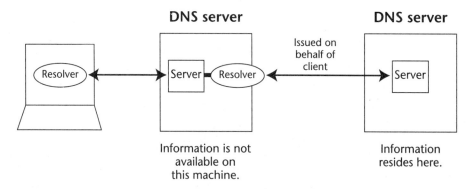

Figure 12-2: Invocation of another server on the client's behalf (recursion).

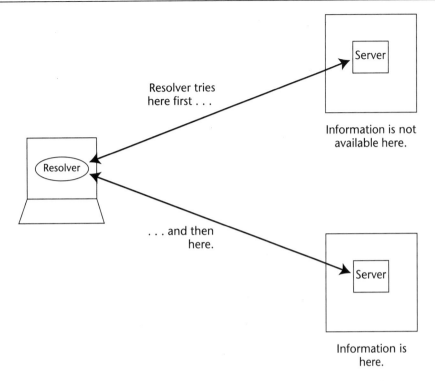

Figure 12-3: Referral of the client to another DNS server (iteration).

move to the right, we progress through branches, getting successively closer to the root.

Formally, a complete, or absolute, domain name must end in a period, where the trailing period denotes the root of the DNS tree. (The root itself does not need to be named, since there can be no ambiguity as to which root we mean—there is only one.) We often omit the trailing period when we speak informally, but it can be important to low-level software.

12.1.4 DNS Records

Each domain name represents a *node* in the domain name system. Each node can, in turn, be associated with zero, one, or more *resource records (RRs)*. Among the several distinct kinds of resource records, the most common are

A   the address record, which is used to map from names to 32-bit addresses

NS   used to delimit zones and to name the authoritative server for a zone

PTR   a pointer to another part of the name space, used most
            commonly for mapping addresses to names

MX   the mail server for a domain

CNAME   an alias for a host

SOA   the authority and management parameters associated
            with a zone or a group, or subtree, of zones; a single
            SOA is associated with the top-level zone and identifies
            an authoritative server for the zone

In addition, a new RR has been defined in support of the future IP protocol,
IPv6:

- AAAA   an IPv6 address record, which is used to map from names to
            128-bit addresses

The use of aliases (CNAME records) can be confusing. It is thus a good
idea to avoid needless use of CNAMEs. At the same time, they can be useful
on occasion, particularly as a means of mapping from a functionally oriented
generic domain name, such as www.gte.com, to a specific, canonical name
such as aurelius.gte.com. Perhaps there would always be a www.gte.com, but
whether that role is assigned to aurelius.gte.com or to augustus.gte.com at a
particular point in time might be controlled by a CNAME record in the DNS.

12.1.5 Primary and Secondary DNS

As previously noted, you would generally arrange to have at least two
authoritative servers for any zone. This is an important reliability consideration. As a practical matter, if the DNS service is down, your access to the
Internet is down. A single DNS server could become unusable for any of a
number of reasons, including configuration errors, software or hardware failures, or a network partition. You do not want to put all of your eggs in one
basket. You would arrange to have two DNS servers and would want to do
your best to ensure that it is unlikely that any single failure could bring both
to their knees.

The primary DNS is generally administered by editing a master file or,
possibly, a database and periodically installing that file into the primary DNS
server. Secondary DNS servers periodically check the primary DNS server
and download the updated configuration if it has changed.

Most organizations derive some level of DNS support from their Internet
provider. If yours is a small organization just starting out on the Internet, you

might choose to have your provider perform both primary and secondary DNS administration.

Many organizations find that as they grow and as the frequency of updates to the primary DNS increases, it becomes impractical to have a third party maintain the DNS. At that point, your organization would most likely assume the responsibility; however, it is still quite workable in general to have your Internet service provider operate the secondary DNS service on your behalf.

12.1.6 Zones and Delegation

One design decision you will need to make early on is the allocation of zones within your organizational domain. This seemingly simple decision entails complex trade-offs. For example, consider the hypothetical Oddball Corporation. Oddball decides to connect to the Internet. With the assistance of its ISP, Oddball secures the domain name oddball.com. You have just been hired as the network administrator of Oddball Corp. How are you going to manage the assignment of domain names to the various hosts within the oddball.com domain?

Suppose that oddball.com is a small, centralized enterprise with 20 employees and no expectation of rapid growth. Everyone is located at a single facility, and everyone is connected to a single LAN, with a single LAN administrator. It might be perfectly reasonable for you to assign host names of the form platinum.oddball.com, titanium.oddball.com, and so on. This is a simple scheme, easy to explain and remember; after all, there are more elements than employees! All you would need to do is to keep a list—a master file—to help you remember to whom you had assigned each domain name and associated IP address. You would also need to assign e-mail addresses to each of your users. Again, a simple solution might suffice. For instance, the e-mail addresses for John Smith and Roberta Jones might be jsmith@oddball.com and rjones@oddball.com, respectively.

Now, consider the same facts but with a company with 10,000 employees. The naming problem becomes more complex, because you are not allowed to have any duplicates. You might choose to have the employees choose their own host names; however, you might implement a centralized system to ensure that any new name does not conflict with any of the existing names. E-mail addresses would also require care, since it is quite likely that there would be many Smiths and Joneses at oddball.com. This system would be a bit more difficult to administer, but not out of the question.

Now, suppose that oddball.com has operations in Atlanta and Los Angeles. Each city has its own network administrator, and the administrators report to different managers and are not used to working together. In this situation, you might prefer to create two zones within oddball.com: east.oddball.com and west.oddball.com. The former would be used for Atlanta; the latter, for Los Angeles. Responsibility for maintenance of each zone would be delegated to the network administrator responsible for the city in question.

This slightly simplifies the problem of selecting host names and user names, since each name would need to be unique only within its zone. In this example, that might not make much of a difference; with 10,000 users and two zones—5,000 user names per zone—it would still take a fair bit of work to make sure that no new name was a duplicate of an old one. Nonetheless, the partitioning could be helpful.

Another consequence of the use of zones is that names would become somewhat longer and thus more cumbersome. Instead of sending an e-mail to jsmith@oddball.com, we might now send an e-mail to jsmith@east.oddball.com; indeed, we might need to do so to avoid ambiguity with that other Smith, jsmith@west.oddball.com. Some users might be unhappy about this state of affairs. Others, perhaps those who routinely use aliases for e-mail addresses, might think nothing of it.

Some organizations choose to implement a flat name space for e-mail, even though they delegate administrative responsibility for multiple zones. For this to work correctly, it is necessary to deal with the possibility of duplicate names. As an example of what can happen if you fail to do so, I once mistakenly received an e-mail intended for Scott McNealy, the president of Sun Microsystems, Inc., because scottm@sun.com resolved to scottm@east.sun.com (my e-mail address several years ago) instead of the intended scottm@west.sun.com (McNealy).

Administrative zones could reflect geographic, functional, or organizational boundaries. The important considerations are that (1) zones should be defined in a way that makes sense in terms of the manner in which administration will be delegated; and (2) delegation of DNS zones should follow the same administrative boundaries as IP addresses, because the two must necessarily be administered in lockstep.

12.1.7   The IN-ADDR.ARPA Domain

It is frequently useful to map not from a name to an IP address but rather from an IP address to a name. The design of the DNS system includes inverse translation functions; however, these are optional in the DNS specification and are not universally implemented. The standard technique is to instead use conventional DNS lookups in conjunction with a special domain called, for historical reasons, IN-ADDR.ARPA.

The mapping from host name to IP address is *one to many* because a host may have more than one IP address; however, the mapping from IP address to host name is always *one to one*. This implies, incidentally, that the associated DNS lookup operations are not necessarily invertible—if you start with an IP address, look up the associated host name, and then look up an IP address associated with that host, you might retrieve an IP address *different* from the one you started with.

When IP addresses are displayed for readability, they are displayed in *dotted decimal* notation, where each successive 8 bits of the 32-bit IP address are represented as a decimal number from 0 to 255. The four decimal values are displayed from left to right, most significant first (leftmost), with each 0–255 number separated by a period (decimal point).

In the DNS, however, the most significant information is displayed last (rightmost). Because the order is the opposite of that of IP dotted decimal notation, we find an odd inversion in the way that IN-ADDR.ARPA is structured. The four numbers, each in the range 0–255, appear in the *opposite order* in IN-ADDR.ARPA from that in which we normally read them!

Thus, my personal computer happens to be 171.78.112.213. (More precisely, that is the IP address of its Ethernet adapter.) Its name is aurelius. I might expect that, somewhere in the DNS server for GTE, there would be a record of the form

213.112.78.171.IN-ADDR.ARPA   PTR   aurelius.gte.com

Note that this is a PTR record rather than an A record, because the data that it contains—the information to the right of the characters PTR, which denote the RR type—is a domain name rather than an IP address.

The reversed dotted decimal notation is unquestionably awkward; however, other aspects of the structure of IN-ADDR.ARPA are convenient, even elegant. Notable among these aspects is the ease of delegation of authority, provided that delegation is effective at an octet boundary within the IP address. Delegation for IN-ADDR.ARPA follows exactly the same rules as for other domain names. Thus, to assign the Class B address block 171.78.0.0/16 to GTE, one would need to delegate responsibility for 78.171.IN-ADDR.ARPA to GTE.

This is yet another reason why control over DNS zones should be delegated along the same organizational lines as control over IP addresses. In general, whenever a new permanent IP address is assigned, a new DNS A record and a new IN-ADDR.ARPA DNS PTR record will be required.

12.1.8 More Exotic Uses of the Domain Name System

In recent years, a number of unanticipated modes of use for the DNS have become commonplace. Noteworthy among these is the use of the DNS in support of load-balancing World Wide Web servers. Suppose that your firm had a large Web presence, too big to maintain on a single server. You might implement a half-dozen servers, each with identical content and capabilities. If every Web client browser were to "hit" the same server, however, you would not have accomplished any useful balancing of your load.

Sometimes, intelligence is added to the DNS server itself, although some purists would frown on doing so. Instead of always returning the same IP address for a particular domain name, the DNS would instead make an intelligent selection of a preferred Web server. In the simplest case, the DNS might implement a round-robin among your six servers in order to achieve a workable balancing of load. Alternatively, it might periodically check the health of the Web servers and round-robin only among those that were fully operational. As yet another alternative, the intelligent DNS might favor Web servers that were topologically close to their browser client—a difficult thing to determine with certainty, but not intractable—or those that were on the highest-performance servers. The possibilities are endless.

Another interesting application is known as the "split-brained" DNS. Viewed from outside, only a handful of hosts are visible: precisely those that offer services that are intended to be externally accessible. From inside, the full range of hosts might be visible. This approach is often used in conjunction with private (RFC 1918[3]) address space, as we shall see later in this chapter.

12.2 Addressing

We begin this discussion by providing a general overview of IP addressing principles and by explaining at some length why public IP addresses must be assigned sparingly. The IP address for the current version of IP, IP version 4, is 32 bits long. IP addresses consist of two main portions: a *network* portion and a *host* portion. Each communicating device on a network—be it a PC, a workstation, a server, a router, whatever—is associated with at least one distinct IP *host* address. More precisely, the host address corresponds to a specific interface connected to the host; thus, a host with multiple interfaces will have multiple distinct IP addresses, each associated, in the usual case, with a single interface. Host interfaces that are on the same network—which might be a dialup connection, a local area network (LAN) such as an Ethernet, a

---

3. Y. Rekhter et al., Request for Comments (RFC) 1918, "Address Allocation for Private Internets," February 1996.

dedicated serial wide area link, whatever—have a common IP *network* address. Figure 12-4 gives an example.

The IP address is thus associated with the network topology. This has some important and perhaps counterintuitive consequences.

- The IP address is not a permanent attribute of a particular host interface. If you change the topology of your network such that a given host is reached through a different network, you will generally need to change the IP address of that host.
- If an IP host is reachable through more than one network—that is, if it is *dual homed*—as will usually be the case for a router, it will generally use different IP addresses on each network.

See Figure 12-5 for an example.

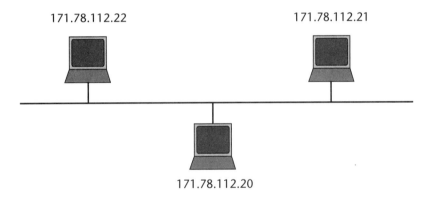

Figure 12-4: An example of IP addressing.

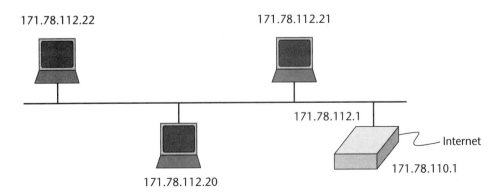

Figure 12-5: IP numbering for a dual-homed device.

12.2.1 Networks and Subnetworks

This section describes the classical structure of IP network addresses, as modified by subnetworking. We look at IP addressing constraints and subnetwork addressing. The newer system of *Classless Inter-Domain Routing (CIDR),* which has largely supplanted the original IP addressing scheme, is discussed in Section 12.2.2.

12.2.1.1 IP Addressing Constraints

As previously noted, IP addresses are 32 bits long, potentially providing addressability to more than four billion end systems. When IP was developed, this was felt to be more than ample; however, thanks to the explosive growth of computer networking and the poor allocative efficiency with which these addresses were historically provided (less than 1 percent efficiency[4]), these 32 bits could conceivably be exhausted within a few years.

To understand why this is so, we must first understand the use of address classes. In RFC 791,[5] the fundamental definition of IP, addresses were defined to fall in one of three classes: A, B, or C, corresponding roughly to huge, large, and small networks, respectively. (The additional D and E network types have since been defined.) For each of these address types, the first (left-hand) portion of the address represents a network number, while the right-hand bits represent a host interface: a classic hierarchical addressing scheme. The IP address is encoded so as to make it simple to algorithmically determine which type of network (A, B, or C) is associated with a particular IP address.

In practice, these network classes are very much like the Three Bears in the children's fable. Class A, C, and B networks, respectively, are too big, too small, and just right. Class A addresses are of limited utility: There are too few of them, and they support far more end systems (sixteen million) than are needed in most networks. Conversely, Class C networks are too small (some 250 end systems) for many environments. Class B networks tend to be the most useful, but less than a fourth of the available IP address space is allocated to them. Class B address space is all but exhausted, thanks to the explosive growth of the Internet.

---

4. C. Huitema, "Address Assignment Efficiency," in *IPng: Internet Protocol Next Generation,* ed. Scott O. Bradner and Allison Mankin (Reading, Mass.: Addison-Wesley), 1996.

5. J. Postel, Request for Comments (RFC) 791, "Internet Protocol," September 1981.

12.2.1.2 Subnetwork Addressing

The original ABC design of IP addresses did not foresee the rapidity with which LANs would proliferate. In the original concept, each LAN was to be assigned a distinct network address. This would have rapidly exhausted the address space for the Internet and would also have required routers to implement inconveniently large routing tables. In order to stretch the address space and reduce the address table size, a procedure called *subnetting* was developed.[6, 7] Subnetting defines mechanisms for routing data within an IP network, transparent to other IP networks. It thus eliminates the need to assign a network number to each LAN. Also, by creating an implicitly hierarchical routing structure, subnetting ameliorates the explosion in routing table size that would have been required if every router on the Internet had to know how to route to every LAN.

Subnetworks have been used for many other purposes as well, including point-to-point links between pairs of routers, where each link constitutes a subnetwork connecting exactly two hosts.

The subnetwork number was carved out of the host portion of the IP address. This number could comprise any number of the host bits but, historically, usually represented a fixed number of bits within a given IP network. The initial specification of subnets in RFC 950 had not explicitly required routers to support subnet masks of different lengths within a single IP network *(variable-length subnet masks)*; consequently, routing protocols (notably RIP, which is described later in this chapter) were designed without the ability to support subnets of different sizes within a single IP network. This fixed-length restriction was eased only with the advent of the OSPF routing protocol (also described later in this chapter), which also made variable-length subnets viable.

Historically, the subnet was identified with a *subnet mask,* expressed in the same dotted decimal notation used for IP addresses, where each 1 bit represented a portion of the network or subnet number, and each 0 bit represented a portion of the host number. The subnet mask potentially offered enormous flexibility; in practice, however, subnet masks have generally been used to identify a contiguous string of bits starting from the left. Since the advent of CIDR, therefore, there has been a tendency to speak of the network

6. J. Mogul and J. Postel, Request for Comments (RFC) 950, "Internet Standard Subnetting Procedure," August 1985.

7. J. Mogul "Subnetting: A Brief Guide," *Connexions* 3, no. 1 (January 1989).

prefix as the number of contiguous bits used by exterior routing protocols and the extended network prefix as the number of contiguous bits used by interior routing protocols. Thus, a subnet mask of 255.255.255.0 corresponds to an extended network prefix of /24.

Subnetworks were meant to be invisible outside of the network that contains them.[8] This implied that all subnetworks of a given network must be reachable from all other subnetworks without the need to route traffic outside of the IP network. A more general way to think of this in the new CIDR world is to observe that the existence of subnets is transparent to exterior routing because they all fall within the same network prefix. This provides a useful hiding of information: Your interior routing might be complex, but the complexity is transparent to networks external to your own.

12.2.2 Classless Inter-Domain Routing (CIDR)

In recognition of address exhaustion, especially of Class B addresses, and of the explosion in the number of external routes that default-route-free Internet routers must maintain, the Internet Engineering Task Force (IETF) explored a number of tactics and strategies and made a number of concrete recommendations. Perhaps the most important near- and intermediate-term strategy was *Classless Inter-Domain Routing (CIDR)*.[9]

This approach can eliminate the traditional concept of the IP Class A, B, and C networks altogether. Any IP network can simply be represented as an IP address and a mask, where the mask specifies the number of bits that make up the network portion of the address. Indeed, the normal tendency today is to refer to a network based on the number of contiguous bits that comprise the network portion of the IPv4 address; thus, a /19 is a network address consisting of the first 19 contiguous bits of the 32-bit address. Note that a /19 is equivalent to 32 Class C addresses, or to 8,192 host addresses.

CIDR effectively formalizes the transition that began with OSPF's use of the more generalized area in place of the old concept of the subnetwork and extends it to the realm of Exterior Gateway Protocols. This facilitates subnetting and supernetting, the logical aggregation of multiple networks. This in turn enables routers to treat a collection of, say, Class C networks as a single target, for routing purposes.

---

8. Ibid.

9. V. Fuller, T. Li, J. Yu, and K. Varadhan, Request for Comments (RFC) 1519, "Classless Inter-Domain Routing (CIDR): An Address Assignment and Aggregation Strategy," September 1993.

CIDR has been brilliantly successful both in fostering use of address space based on aggregates of Class C addresses that would otherwise have been of only limited utility and in preventing an explosion in size of the Internet routing tables. Prior to deployment of CIDR, the Internet routing tables had grown dramatically,[10] as shown in Table 12-1. This represents exponential growth, with the number of routes roughly doubling every year.

CIDR was specified late in 1993 but took several years to come into widespread deployment. Figure 12-6 shows that the rate of growth slowed to a more modest linear growth after January 1994.

CIDR has been very important, but it was not the only factor in this slowing of growth in the number of IP addresses. Two additional technology trends also helped: (1) the assignment of dynamic IP addresses, especially to dialup users, and (2) the deployment of application layer gateway (ALG) firewalls that could make an entire network appear externally to be a single Class C network.

The migration of the IP Internet to the use of CIDR has taken considerable time and energy. For a time, the newer concepts of areas and classless routing overlapped and coexisted with the older concepts of networks and subnetworks. The result was a crazy patchwork quilt of complex interrelationships. Even today, router configuration is usually expressed in terms of the extended network prefix, while host configuration often expresses essentially the same concept in terms of the subnet mask.

12.2.3 Developing the Address Plan

It is helpful to keep the following criteria firmly in mind in allocating IP addresses to network end systems.

Table 12-1: Growth of the Internet Routing Tables Prior to CIDR Deployment

End of	Routes
1990	2,190
1992	8,500
1995	More than 30,000

10. C. Semeria, "Understanding IP Addressing: Everything You Ever Wanted to Know," 3Com Corporation, February 1999, http://www.3com.com/nsc/501302.html.

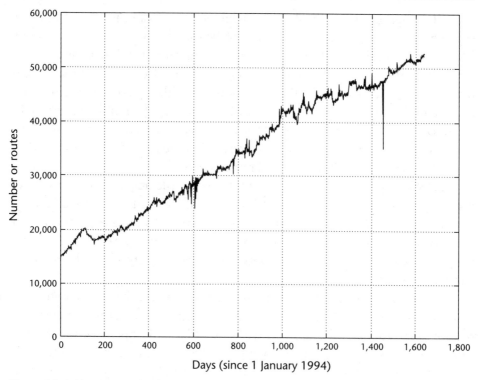

Figure 12-6: Linear growth of Internet routes from January 1, 1994, to July 18, 1998. (Courtesy of Tony Bates, July 18, 1998, http://www.employees.org/~tbates/ cidr.hist.plot.html.)

- **Simplicity:** The design should be as simple as it can be (but no simpler).
- **Efficiency of routing and filtering:** The address plan should permit the routers to route and, if appropriate, filter efficiently.
- **Effective exploitation of natural structures:** The design must capitalize on the inherent physical and logical topology of the network.
- **Efficient use of public IP address space:** Public IP address space is scarce, so you must use it effectively.
- **Support for fault tolerance and for security:** The addressing structure can influence the ability of the network to recover from outages of components or groups of components and interacts with the security framework of your internetwork.

We now turn to strategies for optimizing address assignments in the network design, in order to help you to navigate the numerous challenges and trade-offs associated with IP address plans.

12.2.3.1 Use of Private (RFC 1918) Address Space

In developing your address plan, one of the most fundamental choices you must make is whether to use private address space and, if so, where. Private address space is defined in RFC 1918.[11] RFC 1918 notes that Internet hosts can be thought of as falling into one of three categories:

1. Those that require comprehensive IP access to the global Internet

2. Those that need access only to a limited set of outside services (such as e-mail or FTP)

3. Those that have no need at all to access other systems outside of the enterprise internetwork

RFC 1918 advocates the use of private IP addresses for hosts that fall into the third category. These IP addresses must be allocated within one or more of a small group of permanently assigned IP network prefixes that are never supported or even visible for exterior routing. An unlimited number of organizations can reuse these same addresses.

For those in the second category, private addresses are still appropriate, but address translation to IP addresses that are valid in the global Internet must take place in order for access to outside applications to work. Two classes of products exist to accomplish this: network address translation (NAT) devices (or NAT functionality within your firewalls or routers) and application layer gateways (ALGs). Translation of IP addresses would appear, on the surface, to be clean and straightforward, but it is not—the NAT cannot function as a pure network layer device, because it must modify not only the IP checksum but also the TCP checksum (due to the inclusion of the so-called IP pseudoheader in the TCP checksum), as well as any IP addresses that may be embedded in the application's data stream.[12] The NAT can mechanically pass a full range of applications, but it may stumble over IP addresses embedded into the data stream; conversely, the ALG will do the right thing with any embedded IP addresses but may not handle the full range of applications. On balance, the ALG is often the better choice.

Those hosts that require extensive interaction with the global Internet should use conventional public IP addresses, just as would be the case in the absence of RFC 1918. Nonetheless, RFC 1918 can be beneficial overall. For

---

11. Y. Rekhter et al., RFC 1918, op cit.

12. K. Egevang and P. Francis, Request for Comments (RFC) 1631, "The IP Network Address Translator (NAT)," May 1994.

many organizations, only a small fraction of the hosts in the network require public IP addresses.

Use of RFC 1918 can greatly reduce the amount of public IP address space that the organization must obtain. Its use can simplify your addressing plan by providing you with, for instance, an entire Class A address, with no external approvals required. It reduces the risk that hosts might have to be renumbered at a future date, due, for instance, to your changing your ISP and thus losing your address block. Use of RFC 1918 may benefit the Internet as a whole by reducing the size and the complexity of routing tables. And it can enhance the security of the organization because it is difficult for outsiders to hack a privately addressed system they cannot even see, a point we return to later in this chapter.

Against these benefits must be weighed the additional operational complexity of the network and the possibly greater difficulty of doing end-to-end troubleshooting when a user has problems accessing an external service. Incremental equipment costs are usually modest enough to play only a minor role in your decision.

Perhaps the biggest risk inherent in the use of private RFC 1918 address space is easily overlooked. Supposing that two organizations, each of which independently chose to use private IP addresses in Class A network 10.x.x.x subsequently decide to merge. It is likely that one of them will either have to undergo a massive renumbering or else implement another solution that is just as unpleasant.

12.2.3.2 Methodology for Developing the Address Plan

It is helpful to take a top-down approach to specifying the address plan. We begin with the most significant bits of the IP address and proceed into successively less significant bits.

1. In general, the Autonomous System, or AS, can be viewed as the first level of the addressing hierarchy. We begin by determining whether to use a single autonomous system for the network or multiple autonomous systems.

2. We continue by assigning network prefixes, taking into account the number of hosts to be supported, the physical topology of the network, traffic patterns, routing efficiency, and security requirements.

3. We then determine the extended network prefixes and the associated subnetwork masks to be used.

4. Next, we consider host-specific aspects of the addressing plan.

5. Finally, we iteratively refine the design until it is balanced and workable.

Determining the Number of Autonomous Systems. An *autonomous system (AS)* is a routing domain that is under the administrative control of a single organization. An AS exchanges routing information with other ASes by means of an *Exterior Gateway Protocol (EGP)*. An AS may comprise one IP network or many.

In defining your routing and addressing plan, one of your most fundamental decisions is whether to work with one autonomous system, none, or many. It is usually a good idea to keep things as simple as possible.

The AS is used primarily to enable other organizations to route to your organization over the public Internet. *Unless your network is large in scope, if you have a single connection to a single Internet service provider (ISP), you probably do not need to have your own AS at all.* Other organizations can treat you as part of your ISP's AS for exterior routing purposes. Your ISP can route to your organization, using static routing over the single connection, and you can specify the connection to your ISP as a default route for anything that is not within your own network. (There is no benefit in using dynamic adaptive routing, because there is no possibility of recovery in the event that your single link fails, anyway.)

If you have two or more connections to a single ISP (more precisely, to a single AS), you still have no need for an AS of your own, in general. You could still operate as part of your ISP's AS but would use interior routing protocols in order to efficiently direct traffic to and from the most appropriate connection to your ISP—and also in order to provide automatic recovery in the event that one of your connections to your ISP goes down.

If you are connected to two ISPs or, equivalently, if you are connected into distinct autonomous systems of a single ISP, you will in general need your own AS, and you will probably need to run an exterior routing protocol (usually BGP-4) to each of your ISPs. In this case, you would need to have an AS number assigned to your organization. Within North America, you would generally obtain an AS number from the *American Registry of Internet Numbers (ARIN).*[13]

If you have a very large network, you might consider a different approach. You might intentionally break your network up into multiple autonomous systems. The primary advantage is fault isolation—if routing gets fouled up in one AS, it will not necessarily cause problems in the others.

In this design, you would typically use one AS as a *transit* AS. It would serve as a backbone, interconnecting all of the other ASes, which would be

---

13. Information is available at www.arin.net.

"stubbed" off of this AS. As we shall see later, this transit AS is similar in function to the backbone area of an OSPF routing domain, and its relationship to the stub ASes parallels that of the OSPF backbone area to other areas in the OSPF routing domain.

As a variant of this scheme, you might consider defining your autonomous systems as a *confederation*. External ASes would connect only to your transit AS. In a confederation design, they would regard your entire network as if it were a single AS, the transit AS; they would not need to know about your stub ASes. This reduces your exterior routing complexity and reduces the complexity of routing in the Internet as a whole.

Again, the use of multiple ASes adds significant overall complexity to the network design. Further, it will tend, in many instances, to slow recovery time in the event of a failure; BGP-4 is much slower to reconverge than is OSPF. You should entertain this option only if your network is very large or very complex.

Network Prefixes. The IP prefix is the atomic unit of addressability for IP exterior routing protocols. The assignment of prefixes should reflect not only the topology of your internetwork but also the anticipated traffic patterns and security requirements. Consequently, systems that are closely related organizationally should, where practical, be part of the same IP prefix. In addition, the assignment of public IP addresses must take into account economy of use of address space, as well as allow for room to grow, without necessitating continual churn and rework to the address plan. The addressing plan needs to balance these mutually contradictory objectives.

Your network address allocations may represent a single CIDRized IP address block—a single network prefix (represented as a /xx)—or multiple address blocks. In either case, however, you must ultimately parcel out individual IP addresses to your routers and hosts. The second case differs from the first in that each noncontiguous address block will result in distinct routes that external systems will need to keep track of in order to route traffic to your internetworks.

Typically, you would receive your first address allocation from your ISP, and the allocation would consist of a single contiguous address block. However, if your organization requires an address block that is a /19 or larger, you may wish instead to apply directly to the ARIN for your own address block, preferably with the assistance of your ISP.

Allocating Address Blocks. In developing the address plan, I often find it simplest to start with an allocation of IP addresses to the core of the network—which may correspond to the OSPF backbone area, if you are using the OSPF routing protocol—and to work my way out from there. This "area of areas" is the one to which all other areas must attach. It is often convenient to use a distinct Class C address (that is, a /24 address block) for the backbone area.

Every OSPF routing area requires physical or logical connectivity to the backbone area. In practice, other OSPF areas are generally "stubbed" off of the backbone. Each should have a distinct and contiguous block of addresses, in order to keep the routing of traffic as simple as possible. Figure 12-7 shows an example of a network numbered along these lines.

You will generally want the IP addresses for the next-lower hierarchical level of your network to fall within each of the blocks you have already assigned to the OSPF stub areas. The idea is simple: Within the core, or backbone area, of your network, you would like each IP address to simply and unambiguously indicate in which direction the data should be sent, with as little analysis on the part of the router as possible. This yields an IP numbering plan as depicted in Figure 12-8.

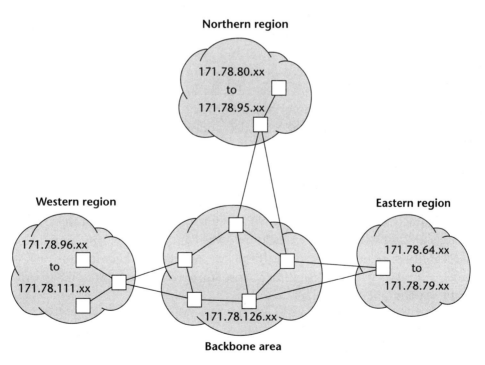

Figure 12-7: A simple IP numbering plan.

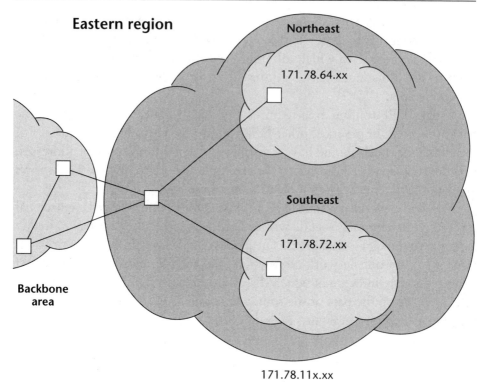

Figure 12-8: A more complex IP numbering plan.

You should proceed to allocate addresses in this manner until you reach the level of individual transmission media, for instance, individual serial links or Ethernet LANs. At that point, the number of address bits specified, starting from the left, constitute the extended address prefix. The remaining bits are the host address field.

Determining the Size of the Host Address Field. The host portion of the IP address field represents the bits left over after you have assigned your extended network prefixes, as shown in Figure 12-9. Selection of the appropriate size for the host address field involves complex trade-offs, in light of the scarcity of IP addresses today. If the host address field is too large or too small, addresses will be wasted. In a sense, this problem relates to the granularity of your addressing plan.

The size of the host field must be large enough to accommodate the maximum number of hosts that can be supported by the extended network prefix. The maximum number of host addresses is equal to 2^n, where n is the number of bits in the host address field. If the number of hosts in an extended prefix does not map well to a power of 2, potential address space will be wasted. Furthermore, a realistic address plan cannot hope to allocate every potential address; it must leave some room for expansion, or the address plan will have a short life.

At least two host addresses should be set aside within each extended network prefix: the all-0s and all-1s historically served as broadcast addresses. In addition, any addresses used by routers or monitoring systems are not available for hosts. If the number of bits allocated to the prefix is too great, and thus the size of the host field is too small, these lost addresses can represent a significant fraction of the total address space.

For point-to-point links, such as serial leased lines between routers, the leased line constitutes a tiny subnetwork. We would typically assign an extended network prefix of /30, corresponding to just 2 bits of host address for the two routers, as shown in Figure 12-10. These two bits correspond to only two host addresses, because host addresses 0 and 3 represent broadcast addresses. Alternatively, it is permissible to use *unnumbered* links in this case, so as to avoid assigning any IP address at all; however, in doing so, you would lose the ability to independently address these particular router ports. It would thus be impossible to ping the ports in question to determine whether they were reachable and working correctly. It is usually preferable to assign addresses.

Modern routing protocols, such as OSPF, can support variable-length subnet masks, where the size of the host field for various subnetworks within a single network prefix could be different. A few years ago, this tended to be problematic but today is becoming increasingly commonplace. If you use the Routing Information Protocol (RIP), version 1, however, you are restricted to

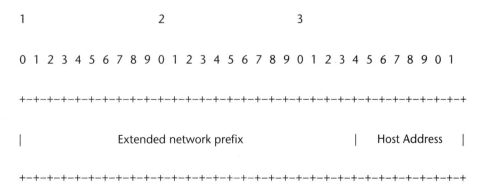

Figure 12-9: The host address field with a /24 extended network prefix.

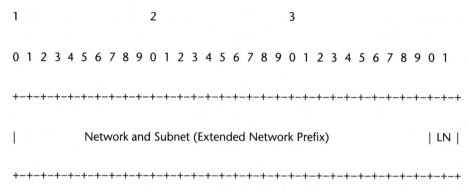

Figure 12-10: An addressing scheme for a serial line. **LN** addresses the two ends of the serial line.

using fixed-length subnets, because RIP makes no provision for incorporating subnet masks into its exchanges of routing information.

Host Addresses. Each host within an extended network prefix must be configured to an agreed-on subnet mask. The mask indicates the length of the extended network prefix. If an IP datagram is destined for a system on the same subnet (prefix) as the sending host, the sender knows exactly where to send it. If not, the sending host must instead forward it to a router that will forward it on appropriately.

One approach to allocating addresses for hosts involves the definition of certain well-known addresses. This technique is already an established standard in the case of the all-0s and all-1s host addresses within each subnetwork, which have been used to implement multicast services. Similarly, you could define other addresses to have special significance and to be well known within your internetwork. An example of this, suitable for use with a /24 extended network prefix, is shown in Table 12-2. The well-known IP addresses listed in the table can be easily masked. This simplifies the application of packet filtering techniques.

For the assignment of subnet numbers and host numbers, you should consider the use of "mirror image" numbering, as described in RFC 1219.[14] In effect, this RFC advocates assigning host numbers in increasing order starting from the right of the IP address and assigning subnet numbers in

---

14. P. Francis (was Tsuchiya), Request for Comments (RFC) 1219, "On the Assignment of Subnet Numbers," April 1991.

Table 12-2: A Typical Definition of Well-Known Host IP Addresses

Host Address	Usage
0	Subnetwork broadcast
1	Default router for the subnetwork
2–10	Servers
11–254	Hosts
255	Subnetwork broadcast

increasing order *starting from the left,* thus leaving the middle of the address space uncommitted for as long as possible. In doing so, mirror image numbering can improve the efficiency of use of the address space and can reduce the likelihood of needing to renumber hosts at a future date. The main cost associated with mirror image numbering is that some people will find your numbering plan to be counterintuitive and difficult to grasp.

Dynamic Allocation of Host Addresses. Historically, it was necessary to permanently assign an IP address to a host by manually configuring the host. Today, it is increasingly common to dynamically assign IP addresses by means of the Dynamic Host Configuration Protocol (DHCP), as described in RFC 2131.[15]

DHCP interacts closely with the Bootstrap Protocol (BOOTP), which is used to download initial configuration information. DHCP can be used to initialize not only a host's IP address and subnet mask but also the IP addresses of its DNS servers and its next-hop router. Thus, DHCP can establish all necessary aspects of a host's IP identity.

For permanent users on your corporate LAN, you might have IP address assignments that are stable over time (in order to permit the DNS to point to them correctly) but would use DHCP in order to gain flexibility. With DHCP, you are able to easily renumber your hosts. Without DHCP, renumbering is a significant chore.

For dialup users, you would tend to allocate addresses dynamically out of a pool, in order to conserve IP address space. (Only a small fraction of the potential users are likely to be dialed in at any particular moment.) You would not need DHCP in this case—PPP can dynamically assign IP addresses.

---

15. R. Droms, Request for Comments (RFC) 2131, "Dynamic Host Configuration Protocol," March 1997.

Iterative Refinement. It is rarely the case that a designer sits down and finds that every aspect of the routing plan fits perfectly, with just enough headroom. Inevitably, you will find that the host field is too small here, or that too many addresses are wasted there. It usually is necessary to polish the design—to progressively refine it until all aspects make sense.

12.2.4   Security and the Addressing Plan

Two security mechanisms interact significantly with the addressing plan: *filtering* and *address translation*. When you *filter* packets, you pass them selectively. Typically, you would use a router to perform filtering, in order to restrict traffic flow among the various portions of your internetwork and also between your internetwork and the outside world.

Filtering is used for a number of reasons. First, broadcast storms can be localized by filtering. Second, filtering provides a first, but admittedly primitive, line of defense for your internetwork. Access to the global Internet could potentially open your door to hackers. It is particularly important that the routers representing your gateway to the world be suitably selective in what they allow into the network. Typically, you would filter on the basis of destination and a source address, and you would, for example, want to ensure that no packets arriving from *outside* your network contain source addresses that would be valid *inside* your network. Since many of the popular applications in the TCP/IP suite are associated with globally unique permanent port numbers, router filtering can also have the effect of selectively permitting or prohibiting access to the network for specific applications.

In the interest of efficiency, you generally will want to filter as much as possible at the *edge* of your internetwork, at the point of traffic ingress. The routers in the core of your internetwork will be busy forwarding datagrams just as quickly as they can; you do not want to bog them down by burdening them with the task of filtering the datagrams as they fly by.

Address translation achieves a similar objective but in a more extreme way. As we have seen, the use of private IP address space, as described in RFC 1918, has many advantages. From a security perspective, the use of private IP address space can make it more difficult for an external hacker to gain a foothold into your network. The public Internet discards packets addressed to your "real" private IP addresses. The only way in is through the network address translation (NAT) or application layer gateway (ALG) services.

At first, this approach might appear to be foolproof, but it is not idiotproof. You still need to contain the always-significant risk of internal subversion, and you are still potentially exposed to an external hacker if you have been so foolish as to provide a clandestine physical "back door" into your internetwork. Also, for those systems that are permitted to reach outside of the network by means of address translation, you need to watch out for possible infiltration; any of them could potentially serve as a beachhead for an external hacker.

If you choose to use the RFC 1918 approach, you would typically create a DNS for internal users and another one for the rest of the world. This is sometimes referred to as a "split-brained" use of the DNS. The external DNS would contain entries only for those services that you wish to advertise to the public. Typically, these services would be placed outside of your security perimeter, in a demilitarized zone (DMZ) that uses conventional, non–RFC 1918 address space. This is shown in Figure 12-11.

12.2.5 Internet Protocol Version 6 (IPv6)

Between 1991 and 1994, the Internet Engineering Task Force (IETF) endeavored to develop a long-term response to the potential exhaustion of IP addresses—as distinct from CIDR, which was a necessary and valuable short-term expedient—particularly Class B IP addresses, by developing an entirely

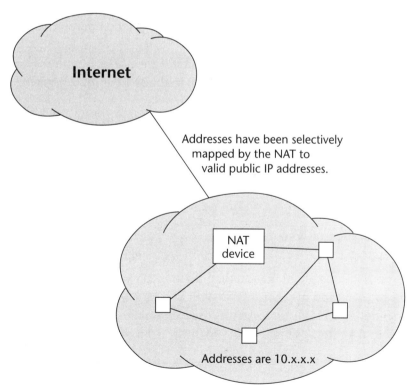

Figure 12-11: A typical application of RFC 1918 private address space.

new addressing scheme, accompanied by changes to the IP protocol. This was a wrenching change, for two reasons:

1. Among protocols in the TCP/IP protocol suite, IP is the *one* protocol that is used by practically everything.

2. Changing IP necessitates changes to much surrounding infrastructure, notably including the DNS. It has ripple effects on the *Internet Control Message Protocol (ICMP)*, accounting, security, and network management.

A number of potential solutions were proposed. What followed might euphemistically be called a spirited debate. Ultimately, the IETF settled on a variant of the protocol known as *Simple Internet Protocol Plus (SIPP)*. This became the primary basis for the next-generation IP, *IPng*.[16] It has been officially designated IP version 6, or *IPv6*.

By its choices for IPng, the IETF opted for the proposal that diverged as little as possible from the current Internet Protocol, IPv4. IPv6 preserves all of the significant semantics of the service offered by IPv4, but it offers a number of additional features and services, including

- Hierarchical addresses with a length of 128 bits, compared to 32 bits for IPv4.
- An improved header format that facilitates the use of IP options and simplifies the mandatory header in comparison to IPv4 by relegating infrequently used fields to options.
- Optional support for flows, in support of quality of service, as might be required for sending realtime voice over IP.
- Security extensions in support of authentication, data integrity, and privacy. Use of these features is optional, but all implementations are required to support them.

12.2.5.1 Adoption of IPv6 to Date

To date, IPv6 has seen scant acceptance by users. This should come as no surprise—it is the same phenomenon that the industry observed earlier in regard to OSI protocols and in regard to SNMPv2. If an existing standard is widely implemented and highly successful, it is extraordinarily difficult for a new standard to take hold. This is a simple illustration of the enormous role that

---

16. R. M. Hinden and S. E. Deering, "IPv6 Technical Overview," in *IPng: Internet Protocol Next Generation,* op. cit.

externalities (a phrase borrowed from the economists) play in networks: The
value of a network to the user is largely a function of who else is reachable
on that network. If an existing network infrastructure already offers connectivity to a huge number of people, it becomes difficult for anything else to
compete.

The case of IPv6 is not quite so simple, in that it was intended to represent
an evolutionary upgrade to the existing IPv4, which would not detract from
connectivity to existing IPv4 users. But in their initial comments to RFC
1550—an IETF document that solicited input from the community regarding
functional requirements for an IPng—many experts noted that the transition to
any IPng would necessarily be complex and costly and would initially offer no
benefits to individual Internet users, even if the transition were ultimately necessary to the survival of the system as a whole. John Curran put it this way:

> From the perspective of an existing IPv4 site, IPng provides little tangible
> benefit until IPv4 address depletion occurs and organizations reachable only
> via IPng appear. Given the absence of benefits for migrating, it is uncertain
> whether a significant base of IPng sites will occur prior to IPv4 address
> depletion. . . . it is not clear that IPng will secure sufficient following to
> attain market viability. In the past, we have seen internetworking protocols
> fail in the marketplace despite vendor promotion. IPng will not succeed if it
> is not actively deployed. As currently envisioned, IPng may not be ambitious
> enough in the delivery of new services to compete against IPv4 and the
> inevitable arrival of NAT devices.[17]

Indeed, if we return to the four advantages noted earlier, we find that

- The expanded address space offers no near-term benefits to the individ-
  ual user except, perhaps, after address depletion is in full swing.
- The simplified header, in conjunction with the longer and more complex
  addresses of IPv6, is unlikely to generate tangible savings (in equipment
  costs, for example) for the user.
- The flow mechanisms are no more likely to be available in IPv6 than in
  IPv4, thanks to the work of the IETF's *Multi-Protocol Label Switching
  (MPLS)* Working Group (WG).
- The security mechanisms are no more likely to be available in IPv6 than
  in IPv4, thanks to the work of the IETF's *IP Security (IPSEC)* Working
  Group (WG).

---

17. John Curran, "Market Viability as an IPng Criteria" [sic], in *IPng: Internet Protocol Next
Generation,* op. cit.

The *costs* associated with transition to IPv6 are substantial. Despite the very significant investment that was made in developing clean transition mechanisms for IPv6, you should reasonably expect to invest a significant amount of high-priced engineering labor into this migration. Early adopters are likely to encounter bugs in software for routers, hosts, and DNS servers. And finally, there is a nonnegligible risk that at the end of the day, the industry will pick some other approach. (Organizations that attempted a premature migration to OSI protocols, thinking that they would inevitably triumph, presumably wasted a great deal of time and money when the OSI protocols failed to achieve critical mass in the marketplace. It is conceivable that IPv6 might, in similar fashion, be superseded before it is fully deployed.)

Meanwhile, address depletion has proceeded far more slowly than was initially anticipated in 1991. Factors that have ameliorated address depletion include

- The brilliant success of CIDR, which has enabled the allocation of blocks of relatively plentiful Class C (/24) addresses instead of scarce Class B (/16) addresses while avoiding a concomitant explosion in the size of routing tables
- Increasingly common use of dynamic IP address allocation for switched or occasional access
- Increasingly common use of private IP address space (and ALGs) pursuant to RFC 1918

These last two points merit some expansion. If you dial up your Internet provider, it is unlikely that you will use a permanently assigned IP address. As we have seen, it is far more likely that your provider will assign you a free address that happens to be associated with the terminal server port to which you connected and will do so in real time. This means that dynamic addresses can be allocated from very compact address pools. It also means that the provider does not need as many addresses as customers; rather, the number of addresses is driven by the maximum number of customers who are simultaneously connected. Ideally, this reduces by an order of magnitude the number of IP addresses required.

A second, related factor is the use of RFC 1918 addresses. In assigning private IP addresses that are unreachable from the public Internet—and that have no impact on the global pool of IP addresses—you are assuming that many of your users have at most limited needs for access to the global, public Internet: sufficiently limited that they can be met by, for instance, mediating their external requests with the aid of application layer gateways (ALGs).

Your users can send and receive e-mail without having externally visible IP addresses at all. (It is your Simple Mail Transfer Protocol [SMTP] *server* that must have an externally visible IP address.) Your World Wide Web (WWW) server must be externally visible, but it requires just a handful of IP addresses, or perhaps just one (and this may be your Web hosting provider's address in any case, if you choose to use an external Web hosting service). Your users probably need to occasionally browse external Web sites; however, they can do so by using a NAT and/or firewall to translate their addresses to public IP addresses, solely for the duration of the Web TCP session. Once again, this implies the need for far fewer IP addresses than users.

In sum, address depletion is not forcing a quick migration to IPv6.

In responding to RFC 1550, Eric Fleischman (Boeing Computer Services) summed up his concerns as follows:

> Fortune 100 corporations which have invested heavily in TCP/IP technology in order to achieve their (non-computer-related) business goals do not generally view the coming of IPng with excitement. . . . There is a natural tendency to continue to use the current IP protocol, IPv4, regardless of the state of the Internet's address space. Motivations supporting inertia include the following: existing application dependencies (including Application Programming Interface (API) dependencies); opposition to additional protocol complexity; budgetary constraints limiting additional hardware/software expenses; additional address management and naming service costs; transition costs; support costs. . . . The significance of this inertia is that unless there are significant business benefits to justify an IPng deployment, economics will oppose such a deployment.[18]

Taking this argument to its logical conclusion, we have seen that most users have no motivation to transition to IPv6 (and many reasons to delay transition) until address depletion is well advanced and that address depletion has slowed dramatically. *Taken together, these factors tell us that migration to IPv6 will take place very slowly, if it happens at all. Our plans should reflect this reality.*

Please note that not everyone in the industry will agree with this assessment, and some may be offended. I would hasten to add that it is my sense that IPv6, or something like it, will prove to be necessary to the long-term evolution of the industry. Nonetheless, I would advise you to proceed cautiously with IPv6

---

18. Eric Fleischman, "IPng and Corporate Resistance to Change," in *IPng: Internet Protocol Next Generation,* op. cit.

deployment. The following sections attempt to outline a pragmatic, conservative approach that supports eventual accommodation of IPv6 if appropriate.

12.2.5.2 Migration Capabilities of IPv6

The full range of IPv6 transition capabilities appears in a number of publications, most notably in an article by Ross Callon and Bob Gilligan.[19] In this section, I will discuss only those IPv6 transition capabilities that you need to understand to follow the migration path I am suggesting. The three mechanisms that are particularly relevant to this discussion are selection of the types of IPv6 addresses to use, DNS mechanisms, and tunneling of IPv6 traffic within IPv4. IPv6 supports several kinds of IP addresses, all with a length of 128 bits.

Address Mechanisms. The three types of IPv6 addresses relevant to our discussion are provider-assigned unique IP addresses, link-local IP addresses, and addresses that encapsulate IPv4 addresses.

- Provider-assigned IPv6 addresses, similar to CIDRized IPv4 addresses, are assigned from a block associated with an organization's ISP and are globally unique.
- Link-local IPv6 addresses, unique within the domain (e.g., organization) to which they are relevant, are intended for use by organizations that do not (yet) connect to the public Internet. These addresses offer the possibility that the subnet address for this link could serve as a prefix to the MAC address, such as the 48-bit Ethernet/IEEE 802..3 address, of each attached device. This introduces the possibility of automatic address configuration, which would appear on the surface to be a very attractive characteristic.
- Addresses that encapsulate IPv4 addresses are intended as a compatibility feature. They make it possible to route to an IPv6-only host, for instance, across an IPv4-only routing infrastructure. Such an address is referred to as an *IPv4-compatible IPv6 address.*

You have considerable latitude as to which of these address forms you will use, and for what.

DNS Mechanisms. The DNS is used to map between domain names and IP addresses. The transition plan to IPv6 envisions a new format of the DNS

---

19. R. Callon and R. Gilligan, "IPv6 Transition Mechanisms Overview," in *IPng: Internet Protocol Next Generation,* op. cit.

record. Where the A record references an IPv4 32-bit address, the AAAA record—so-called because the address is four times as long as that stored in an A record—references an IPv6 128-bit address.

Note that there is no requirement that a DNS request for an IPv6 address be *transmitted* using IPv6. You need not have IPv6 connectivity to an IPv6-capable DNS server.

If the DNS contains both an A and an AAAA record for a given host, nothing in the IPv6 specifications indicates which it must return. This, and a number of relevant policy decisions, are presumably left as options to the implementer of the relevant software. In most cases, the software implementers are likely to leave these choices as configuration options for the end user. Thus, you will most probably have considerable opportunity to influence the selection of whether to use IPv4 or IPv6 through suitable manipulation of the DNS, and of the software that uses the DNS.

Tunneling of IPv6 within IPv4. The IPv6 specification envisions the ability to tunnel IPv6 datagrams within IPv4 datagrams. In essence, an IPv4 header is prepended to the IPv6 datagram, and the entire thing is shipped off to the next hop, according to the contents of the IPv4 header. The process is then reversed by the tunnel end point, which is not necessarily the end system.

Tunnels could be used router to router, router to host, host to router, or host to host. In all cases, you need to carefully consider how to administer the decisions as to what gets sent where, according to which version of IP.

12.2.5.3 Impact of IPv6 on Your IPv4 Address Plan

As previously noted, I advocate a cautious "wait and see" attitude toward your preparations for IPv6 protocol transition. A number of assumptions underlie the recommendations that follow.

- Address depletion will occur slowly and gradually over a period of many years.
- Transition of users to IPv6, if it happens at all, is unlikely to begin in earnest until IPv4 addresses (of some kind, at least) are nearly gone.
- IPv6-capable products are unlikely to achieve true production quality until there is a significant production deployment of IPv6.
- Non-address-space benefits commonly attributed to IPv6, such as flow-based QoS support and packet-level authentication, will in fact be available under both IPv4 and IPv6.
- Products that support *only* IPv6 are not likely to appear to any significant degree until IPv4 usage has become rare.

- Internet service providers are unlikely to drop support for IPv4 until it becomes exceedingly rare.
- Most organizations will do whatever they can to ensure that important systems that need to be accessible from the public Internet retain an IPv4 address for as long as possible.

Note, too, that the following recommendations are geared toward end-user organizations, not toward Internet service providers. With that said, we can consider transition in terms of your hosts, your router infrastructure, and your DNS servers.

Hosts. Once organizations begin to convert in earnest to IPv6—*if*, indeed, this happens—it is probably a good idea to deploy dual-stack hosts, supporting both IPv4 and IPv6, if you have the opportunity to do so. My inclination would be to deal with this gradually and opportunistically, whenever it is technically and economically convenient.

There is no need to *use* IPv6 in your end systems until there are end systems with which you need to communicate and that are reachable only by means of IPv6. Even then, you may wish to achieve connectivity to such sites by means of an IPv4/IPv6 address translation device, or equivalently by means of a router with address translation capability, as long as there are only a few such destinations. Assuming that you already have a reasonable allocation of IPv4 addresses, you can afford to adjust gradually to the water in the pool. You don't have to dive in all at once.

If you are not already using RFC 1918 (i.e., private IPv4) address allocations, you should consider doing so. Your use of RFC 1918 address space prolongs your ability to operate under IPv4 and also reduces address demands on the global Internet.

To the extent that you find it necessary to begin to use IPv6 addresses to communicate to external systems that do not have IPv4 addresses, my inclination would be to use IPv4-compatible IPv6 host addresses when feasible. To the extent that you already have IPv4 addresses for your current equipment, you can automatically translate these into equivalent IPv4-compatible IPv6 addresses; just prepend 80 bits of hexadecimal X'00' and 16 bits of hex X'FF' to the 32 bits of IPv4 address. This avoids the need for complex address translation in the near term.

I would suggest that you steer clear of the new IPv6 automatic address assignment, based on MAC address, until all or nearly all of your hosts are routinely using IPv6. Until then, an address-assignment regime based, for *client-only* hosts, on the *Dynamic Host Configuration Protocol (DHCP)* will tend to be much simpler, as it avoids the need to use different address-assignment mechanisms for IPv4 and IPv6. For *servers,* you will want to use stable IP addresses, since you will not want these IP addresses to be continually changing; however, it is still a good practice to administer these addresses using DHCP. The use of DHCP simplifies any IP address changes that you might have to implement in the future.

Routers. As with the hosts, it would be prudent to ensure that your routers have IPv6 *capability* long before you need to use it; however, I would tend to leave the internal routers using IPv4 rather than IPv6 for as long as possible.

You should pay special attention to the routers at the edge of your network that connect you to your Internet service provider (or providers). These routers could play a unique role in your migration. If it were necessary to tunnel a relatively small amount of traffic over IPv4, you would probably want these routers, or perhaps a router adjacent to them, to implement the tunnel. That same router might implement any necessary network address translation between IPv4 and IPv6 addresses. The idea is that you would operate, for as long as possible, exclusively with IPv4 addresses within your organization's network. You would translate any IPv6 addresses into IPv4 addresses on entry to your network, and IPv4 addresses to IPv6 if necessary at the point of egress from your network. An example appears in Figure 12-12.

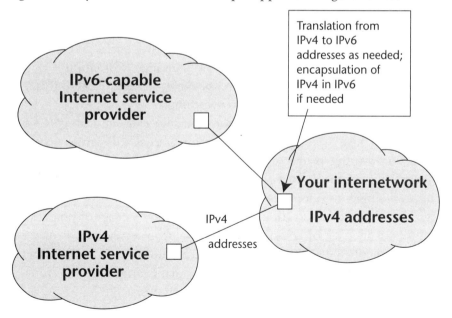

Figure 12-12: Translation of IPv6 addresses on entry to and exit from your network.

If IPv6 traffic grows to be a significant fraction of the external traffic, you will, at some point, want to begin to use IPv6 as a native protocol in your network. I find it most natural to first ensure that all of your internal routers correctly support IPv6 and that your Internet service provider supports IPv6 and only then to permit your host systems to use native IPv6. This minimizes complexity for your host systems.

DNS Servers. You guessed it: You should ensure that your DNS servers are capable of supporting type AAAA records long before you need to use them. My inclination would be to return only type A records (with IPv4 addresses) from the DNS until you are forced to allocate IPv6 addresses to one or more of your hosts. If your DNS server has both a type A and a type AAAA record for the same host, return the type A record. If any of your hosts ever map a domain name to both an IPv4 address and an IPv6 address, configure them to use IPv4 to reach the host in question.

12.3 Routing

This section provides general background on routing protocols. The choice of routing protocol is closely interrelated with the addressing plan.

Routing and *forwarding* are not the same thing. A router's primary job is to *forward* IP datagrams: to move them from an input transmission medium to an output transmission medium. To do this, the router must have some means of knowing in which direction it should forward a given chunk of data. The router gains this knowledge by exchanging information with other routers, using routing protocols. Strictly speaking, routing refers to this information interchange, not to the act of forwarding.

Routing protocols come in two flavors: interior routing protocols—often referred to, for historical reasons, as *Interior Gateway Protocols (IGPs)*— and exterior routing protocols, or *Exterior Gateway Protocols (EGPs)*. Interior routing protocols coordinate routing among multiple routers that all belong to a single autonomous system (AS), which is to say that they are under a common administration, implement a common set of policies, and belong to a defined set of IP networks. Cisco's proprietary Interior Gateway Routing Protocol (IGRP), the Routing Information Protocol (RIP), and the Open Shortest Path First (OSPF) are well-known examples of interior routing protocols that are suitable for use with the IP protocol.

Exterior routing protocols, by contrast, operate between routers in different *autonomous systems (ASes)*, generally between routers that form the border between distinct ASes. Exterior routing protocols may thus be required if your network must route to a network under someone else's administration; however, it is also quite possible that your network will not need to explicitly support exterior routing protocols at all. The Border Gateway Protocol (BGP) is the primary exterior routing protocol that is relevant to TCP/IP.

This section touches briefly on support for host redundancy, a topic that is related to IGPs.

12.3.1 Interior Routing

In this section, we quickly review some of the IP interior routing protocols (IGPs). We begin with the simplest of these, RIP and RIPv2, then progress through the Cisco proprietary IGRP and E-IGRP protocols to the nonproprietary OSPF routing protocol.

Other things being equal, you will want to use the simplest interior routing mechanism that meets your needs. If you need a full-featured IGP for your network backbone, you should still consider simpler mechanisms at the edges.

Whether you would want to employ a proprietary IGP depends largely on your relationship with your router vendor. You should consider this carefully and cautiously.

12.3.1.1 Static/Default Routing

Network designers tend to forget that the best routing protocol may be no routing protocol at all! In most networks, a great many routers at the edges are singly homed to the core of the network. This is driven by basic economics: Dual homing those locations would provide redundancy and thus enhance availability; however, the second circuit may not be affordable. For these singly homed sites, which make up the majority of locations in most networks, no alternate routing is possible. There is no need to run a routing protocol to make decisions that do not need to be made. Instead, *static routing* is typically used to route traffic from the core to the correct edge router, and *default routing* is used to route traffic from the edge to the core.

For each of these locations, you would generally configure the edge router to forward any traffic addressed to locations that it itself does not recognize to the adjacent core router. This constitutes a *default route*. Very little routing intelligence is needed at the edge of the network.

Getting traffic from the backbone to the edge is only slightly more complex. One would typically configure static routing into the routers in the core of the network. You would design your addressing plan such that traffic destined for a particular location, and perhaps for other locations with address blocks contiguous to that location, all wound up at the correct router at the edge of your network backbone. That router would then be explicitly configured to send that network's traffic down the appropriate single transmission path to the desired edge router.

Many organizations use a variant of this model for their connection to their Internet service providers in order to achieve connectivity to the global Internet. If you have a single connection to a single ISP, you do not need to use routing protocols to get to your ISP. Traffic destined for locations outside your firm can be default routed to your ISP, and your ISP can use static routing to get traffic to you. Typically, you would receive IP address allocations from your provider's CIDR blocks and would operate as part of your provider's AS. In this case, you would have no need to implement exterior routing protocols on your own—your provider has to do the heavy lifting for you. This approach markedly simplifies the work that you have to do to maintain an Internet presence; however, it may increase your dependence on your provider, since the IP address allocations from your provider's CIDR block are likely to remain with your provider if you choose to go elsewhere at a future date.

12.3.1.2 Routing Information Protocol (RIP)

RIP is a so-called distance-vector algorithm, often referred to as a Bellman-Ford or Ford-Fulkerson algorithm. Protocols of this type were used in the ARPANET, the predecessor to the modern Internet, from its inception in 1969; however, RIP itself is based on work done at Xerox PARC for the XNS protocols.

RIP was distributed with the popular Berkeley UNIX system in the early 1980s and played an important role in the evolution of the Internet. RIP has been documented in RFC 1058[20] but has long since been relegated to "historic" status. Perhaps the best one can say about RIP is that it is simple and easy to deploy: It is essentially plug and play, requiring minimal configuration. On the down side, RIP is inappropriate for large networks, for numerous reasons, and it cannot deal with more than 15 hops. It is suitable only for networks of modest size and with relatively homogeneous transmission media.

---

20. C. Hedrick, Request for Comments (RFC) 1058, "Routing Information Protocol," June 1988.

As previously noted, RIP uses a distance-vector algorithm. Distance-vector algorithms require each router to independently compute the best next hop to get to each group of destinations. Doing so can be time-consuming and also entails the risk that different routers will reach different and possibly incompatible conclusions about how traffic should best be routed. Thus, after the failure of a router or a link, it can take a long time for the network to reconverge to a new, stable equilibrium.

The original RIP lacked support for variable-length subnets, for CIDR, and for many other critical features of the modern Internet. RIPv2 (RFC 1723)[21] was developed to deal with these issues; however, it does not attempt to address the scalability restrictions. RIPv2 also provides a modest improvement over the original RIP in security, supporting the use of simple passwords as a primitive means of authenticating routing protocol exchanges.

Despite its shortcomings, RIPv2 is likely to continue to be used extensively for some time to come for simple networks that do not require the functions and attendant complexity of a more full-featured routing protocol. Also, it will continue to be useful at the *edge* of large networks, even when the core requires a more complex and comprehensive routing protocol.

12.3.1.3 Interior Gateway Routing Protocol (IGRP)

Cisco defined IGRP[22] for routing in an autonomous system containing arbitrarily complex topology and media with diverse bandwidth and delay characteristics. It is far more general and robust than RIP.

Unlike RIP, which essentially uses a simple hop count, the IGRP routing metric reflects the sum of segment delays and the lowest-segment bandwidth for each route, as well as reliability and any maximum transmission unit (MTU) restrictions. Further, IGRP supports path load balancing. An additional IGRP advantage in comparison with more sophisticated routing protocols is that it is very simple to configure.

The most noteworthy disadvantage of IGRP is that it is proprietary. It does not support the interchange of routing information with other vendors' routers. Cisco's decision to maintain IGRP as a proprietary protocol is not without advantages. Cisco should be quick to point out that it is able to adapt IGRP

---

21. G. Malkin, Request for Comments (RFC) 1723, "RIP Version 2: Carrying Additional Information," November 1994.

22. C. L. Hedrick, "Fast IGRP," memorandum on Cisco mailing list, June 16, 1990; also "An Introduction to IGRP," Rutgers University, Center for Computers and Information Services, Laboratory for Computer Science Research, August 22, 1991.

and its successors rapidly to meet changing market requirements, without being obliged to wait for the IETF standardization process to catch up.

As with RIP, IGRP is slow to converge in the event of a failure, because it, too, uses a distance-vector algorithm.

Enhanced IGRP (E-IGRP) is an enhanced multiprotocol version of IGRP. The distance-vector technology used, as well as the distance information, remains basically the same as for IGRP; however, the convergence properties and the operating efficiency of this protocol have improved significantly. This allows for an improved architecture, while maintaining Cisco's existing investment in IGRP. IGRP has been extended in E-IGRP to be network layer protocol independent, allowing it to work for the AppleTalk, IP, and Novell/IPX protocol suites. Like IGRP, E-IGRP is proprietary and is thus not directly interoperable with other vendors' routing products.

12.3.1.4 OSPF Routing Protocol, Areas, and IP Address Masks

The Open Shortest Path First (OSPF) protocol, as described in RFC 2328,[23] is an open, nonproprietary IGP that offers significant advantages over RIP and IGRP, including

- Rapid routing convergence time (on the order of 2 or 3 seconds, compared with minutes for RIP or IGRP)
- Low protocol overhead
- Numerous operationally useful features, such as stub areas and virtual links
- Support for variable-length subnetworks
- The potential to support routing based on *type of service (ToS)*
- In comparison with IGRP, multivendor interoperability

The main disadvantage of OSPF is that it is somewhat more complex to configure than RIP or IGRP.

It was long recognized that the IP network address structure, even when enhanced by subnetting, was inflexible, and moreover that it was exceptionally wasteful of address space. With the OSPF routing protocol, the IETF adopted a generalization of subnetting that offered far greater flexibility. The IETF adopted a concept of *areas*, routing domains defined by a simple list of IP address ranges. A routing area may thus include noncontiguous blocks of IP addresses, although a single IP address prefix per area is the ideal case.

---

23. J. Moy, Request for Comments (RFC) 2328, "OSPF Version 2," April 1998.

Areas are defined through the specification of address masks that define the portion of the IP address that uniquely identifies a given address as falling in this area. These masks are simply bit patterns, typically expressed in hexadecimal notation. Significantly, there is no requirement that the masks all be of a constant size within a given IP network or AS.

An OSPF AS comprises one or more of these areas. Every OSPF AS must contain a backbone area, an area to which all other areas must be physically or logically attached. Additional areas are typically implemented as stubs off of the backbone area; however, it is possible to "heal" a loss of connectivity to the backbone through an adjacent nonbackbone area, if desired, using a feature known as the "virtual link."

OSPF implements a centralized routing computation, based on an algorithm developed by Edsger Dijkstra in 1959. Each router runs the full computation for the area or areas in which it participates; however, all routers should have consistent information, so all should reach the same results. This process is computationally efficient and should, under most circumstances, enable routers to recover in seconds from the loss of a link or a router.

As a practical matter, it is not possible to support an arbitrarily large number of routers in an OSPF area. For Cisco products, common practice is to refrain from having more than 30 to 50 routers—but excluding static/default edge routers, as these add little complexity—actively participating in an OSPF area; however, these numbers are heavily dependent on how those routers are configured, how much routing they are doing, and the specifics of the routing software implementation. It is always prudent to verify your network design with your router vendor.

OSPF is an open, nonproprietary protocol. Routers from most vendors are interoperable. Nonetheless, you should be cautious about intermixing products from different vendors. If you choose to intermix products, it may be a good idea to maintain only limited boundaries where the products of two vendors must interoperate at an OSPF level.

12.3.2 Host Support for Redundancy

We have talked about the use of routing protocols to achieve redundancy in the core of the network. Sometimes, however, hosts need the ability to use either of two (or more) LANs to access either of two (or more) routers, in order to achieve a suitable level of reliability.

Several techniques exist for determining that a router is reachable and for automatically recovering if it is not. Historically, the more common techniques have been the use of Cisco's *Hot Standby Router Protocol (HSRP)*[24] and the use of RIP within the host system. Running a routing protocol within the host system is problematic at best, as it adds complexity. In the future, the likely preferred vendor-independent solution will be the IETF standards track Virtual Router Redundancy Protocol (VRRP).[25]

12.3.3 Exterior Routing

A number of protocols have been used to provide exterior routing among IP autonomous systems. As a practical matter, the only protocol that merits serious consideration today in an IP environment is the *Border Gateway Protocol Version 4 (BGP-4)*, described in RFC 1771.[26]

BGP routes among ASes, not among networks or systems. That is what makes it an exterior routing protocol. However, BGP interacts with interior routing protocols, such as OSPF, and can be used for distributing routes within an AS.

Systems that participate in BGP—known as *peers*—communicate with one another by means of TCP/IP connections. Thus, they need not be adjacent, from a level 3 perspective. Each BGP speaker sends its neighbors the shortest path that it knows of—in terms of the number of AS hops, which might be quite different from the number of IP hops—to every other AS of interest. The recipient typically adds its own AS to this path and compares the length of the path to the shortest path of which it was otherwise aware. If the new path is preferable (shorter), it becomes the preferred path. For each destination AS, BGP determines *one* preferred AS path. There is no concept of load balancing in BGP-4.

Two interesting bits of filigree, or fine detail, have been added to some BGP-4 implementations in recent years. One of these is the *multiexit discriminator (MED)*. Another is the concept of *confederations*.

The MED is specifically relevant to physically contiguous ASes. In many cases, there will be more than one point of interconnection between these ASes, particularly if both of them are global backbone Internet providers. By

---

24. T. Li, B. Cole, P. Morton, and D. Li, Request for Comments (RFC) 2281, "Cisco Hot Standby Router Protocol (HSRP)," March 1998

25. S. Knight et al., Request for Comments (RFC) 2338, "Virtual Router Redundancy Protocol," April 1998.

26. Y. Rekhter and T. Li, Request for Comments (RFC) 1771, "A Border Gateway Protocol 4 (BGP-4)," March 1995.

default, each AS will route to the other by using *shortest exit,* which essentially means that each AS will independently *send* traffic so as to minimize its internal cost, as defined by its IGP. There is no concept of global optimization: The sending network does not even know the topological distance that the traffic must go within the receiving network.

The MED attempts to correct for this. It represents a directive from the receiving network to the sending network, establishing an order of preference, a "pecking order," among the multiple interconnections between the two ASes, for each range of IP addresses. Thus, the receiving network might direct the sending network to prefer a California interconnection point for traffic to West Coast locations and a New York interconnection point for its East Coast locations. The MED tends to impose cost on the sending network; consequently, the sending network is unlikely to honor it unless there is some specific business reason to do so, such as a customer/provider relationship between the two networks.

Confederations meet a very different need. In an effort to enhance scalability and fault tolerance, some organizations have constructed very large enterprise networks as a collection of ASes, rather than a single AS, as noted earlier in this chapter. In general, a single core AS fulfills the same function that an OSPF backbone AS otherwise would. Other ASes are connected to the core AS as stubs. The structure is analogous to that of OSPF but is implemented by using BGP-4 instead of OSPF.

In this scenario, there are many reasons why you might not want to expose your internal AS structure to the outside world. With a confederation, your ASes collectively appear to the outside world as if they were a single AS. In the most common case, all of your external AS connections would interconnect to your backbone AS, none to your stubs. The stub ASes would be invisible to the outside, and their existence would thus be a purely internal matter.

13 Security

This chapter attempts to deal with perhaps the most complex and difficult topic in the network design. Many designers tend to leave security as an afterthought, to leave it for last, or to view it as something distinct from the overall network design. It may indeed be appropriate to tackle security late in the design process, because you need to know what the network is that you are securing; however, it is a bad idea to shortchange this part of the design process.

Why is security so difficult?

- Networks are complex! Attempting to keep abreast of the constant evolution of equipment, communication protocols, and threats is a daunting task.
- Today's hackers can be determined and ingenious. If your network contains information assets that are valuable in terms of money, military value, or whatever, you should expect that hackers will be especially highly motivated to attempt to break in.
- The technologies used to address network security vulnerabilities are inherently complex.
- There is no single solution to all of your network security problems; you will need to combine elements from several solutions.
- Network security is not a mere matter of securing the bits and bytes. You need to deal with the totality of the network. Physical security and personnel security are just as critical as the logical security of the network.

We begin the chapter by considering typical security threats. We then briefly review the security services that your network may provide and proceed to discuss the technologies available to deal with security threats. Finally, we consider the limitations of perimeter security.

13.1 Threats to Network Security

In its early days, the Internet was open to exploitation to a remarkable degree. Nonetheless, serious incidents of hacking were relatively rare prior to the well-known Morris "worm" program of 1988.[1] Most of the thousands of Internet users were professionals, and a climate of trust and cooperation prevailed.

Today, the Internet is used by tens of millions of people, not by thousands. Nearly all major corporations have a presence on the Internet. Increasingly, business is conducted over the Internet: stock trades, book purchases, travel arrangements.

These trends have increased the potential value of improperly exploiting the Internet. The risks are further compounded by the relative anonymity the Internet provides and by the immaturity of the legal and judicial systems in dealing with improper or criminal use of the Internet. The attractiveness of hacking, viewed purely in economic terms, is far greater than it was just a few years ago.

In recent years, a *subculture* of hacking has emerged that makes it fashionable to infiltrate commercial and government networks. Infiltration might be effected to realize personal gain, but it is also done for the sheer joy of demonstrating that it is possible. This is, perhaps, a bit analogous to teenagers taking a joy ride in a stolen car. This is incomprehensible to most of us, but it is real. Hackers are far better organized than you might imagine; indeed, they have their own Web sites, through which they exchange information and tools.

We normally attempt to guard against malefactors by securing the external entry points to our network, usually by means of security devices known as *firewalls*. We sometimes forget that not all malefactors are external! In assessing threats, you must also consider the possibility of infiltration of your own staff. Indeed, if your data has high intrinsic worth, and if you have established excellent security against external infiltration, you have made it nearly inevitable that you will be attacked from inside, because you have made it worth an attacker's while to infiltrate someone onto your payroll!

Numerous specific types of attacks are possible today.

■ A common type of attack is *impersonation*: someone *masquerades* electronically as someone who has legitimate access to systems on your network. Perhaps the hacker has found routers or servers for which the

1. J. Reynolds, Request for Comments (RFC) 1135, "The Helminthiasis of the Internet," December 1989. http://info.internet.isi.edu:80/in-notes/rfc/files/rfc1135.txt.

initial administrative password was never disabled. Perhaps the hacker guessed a password and user ID combination. (These threats represent a strong argument for good operational controls on the selection of user IDs and of any multiple-use passwords on your systems!) Perhaps the hacker infiltrated one system in your network and used it as a base of operations to "snoop" on traffic on your LANs in order to view many additional user passwords.

At the IP level, it is trivial to forge any source IP address that the sender wishes. Thus, at one level, masquerading at the IP level is easy. However, the global Internet routing system will not generally route traffic to a system that is pretending to have an IP address that is inconsistent with the subnetwork on which it finds itself. Thus, it is trivial to send a single UDP datagram with a forged IP address but much more difficult to obtain a response in order to establish real interchange of data using a forged IP address. Moreover, the exposure to forged addresses can be further mitigated by suitable configuration of router filters or a firewall at the point of entry to your network.

■ *Snooping* poses the threat of loss of privacy of your communications. Your traffic might be passively monitored, with no obvious, immediate damage. This is the data communications equivalent of a wiretap. If your data has high intrinsic value, this form of passive attack might be far more costly to you than an active, intrusive attack, which is likely to be identified and corrected more quickly.

A malefactor who is able to snoop may also be able to inject messages or to substitute modified messages for legitimate ones. Normal TCP/IP integrity mechanisms make this difficult, but it is not impossible. Of increasing concern in recent years have been *man-in-the-middle* attacks, where a third party interposes itself into an otherwise legitimate network interaction between two systems. In the case of a TCP/IP session, this implies the ability of the attacking system to "hijack" a TCP session on the fly by injecting messages with appropriate TCP sequence numbers.

The malefactor could, alternatively, retransmit (or *replay*) the same presumably valid messages that you have already transmitted. Even though unable to decrypt your messages, the malefactor might still be able to replay them. This is a serious threat to financial institutions: the effect of recording the same bank deposit five times in response to replayed messages can be radically different from the intended effect of recording that deposit just once.

■ *Denial of service (DoS),* an increasingly common threat, can be difficult to guard against. Someone may intentionally or inadvertently place service demands on your servers or network, reducing their availability to legitimate users. The Morris "worm" is one example of a DoS attack. An ISP recently experienced another, as its mail server received vast numbers of requests to open TCP sessions but never received the TCP messages required either to fully open the session or else to subsequently close it. The resulting rapid growth in the number of sessions soon crippled the ISP's mail server.

■ *Traffic analysis,* by contrast, is a threat that many organizations could safely choose to ignore. The concern is that a malefactor might be quite interested in detecting with whom you are communicating. This tends to be a significant concern to the military but not necessarily to commercial users.

13.2 Fundamentals of Network Security

The uses to which we intend to put the network drive the security requirements for our network, and these strongly influence the security solutions we will choose and our degree of willingness to invest in network security solutions. Some networks require relatively little security; others may require a great deal. Web sites that provide only publicly available advertising material might fall in the former category, whereas networks that support national defense or that provide electronic funds transfers will tend to be in the latter category. You should bear in mind, however, that a successful break-in may result in significant intangible costs to an organization's reputation, even though there may have been little tangible damage, as, for instance, when hackers replaced the home page of the WWW presence of the U.S. Central Intelligence Agency.

13.2.1 Security Services

It is useful to review from Section 3.5 the typical security services that a network could offer, in order to understand how they relate to network design.

13.2.1.1 Authentication

Authentication consists of unambiguously determining who a party (e.g., a user of the network) is. It is a fundamental prerequisite to most other network security services—if you don't reliably know who someone is, how can you possibly know how you should be dealing with them?

However, not every network service requires authentication. Authentication is often based on something a user *knows,* such as a password; *has,* such as a smart card; or *is*, such as a fingerprint or a retinal print. Where possible, it is best to base authentication on *two* of these: Passwords can be guessed, smart cards can be stolen, but it can be significantly harder for a malefactor to compromise two of these at once. Banks use the same principle with the cards for their automatic teller machines; a pickpocket who steals your ATM card must still guess your personal identification number (PIN) in order to derive benefit from it.

Passwords represent the most basic form of authentication. Today, many organizations perceive a need for stronger authentication than a multiple-use password can offer. It is just too easy for a malefactor to "snoop" the password and to use it to impersonate an authorized individual. Suitable techniques include "smart cards" with single-use passwords, and certificates incorporating cryptographic signatures.

13.2.1.2 Authorization

Authorization, the security service that determines whether a given party has the right to do something specific, may be implemented together with authentication through a single mechanism. For example, when you log in to a UNIX host, you establish your userid (authentication) and also obtain certain rights, such as the right to read or update files (authorization). Again, authorization is largely meaningless in the absence of authentication.

13.2.1.3 Integrity

Integrity is the network service that ensures that the data received is the same as that sent. It determines whether the data has been corrupted, either maliciously or inadvertently, while en route.

As an example, a software downloading service might utilize a cryptographic checksum to reduce the risk of "Trojan Horse" modifications to its programs.

13.2.1.4 Privacy

Privacy, or *confidentiality,* prevents others from knowing what was sent. Privacy is generally implemented using bulk encryption, preferably based on strong cryptography.

13.2.1.5 Nonrepudiation

Non-repudiation, particularly important for financial transactions, is the security technique of establishing an electronic "signature" that the user cannot repudiate, or disclaim. If I, as a customer, order an item of merchandise over the network from an electronic catalog, and you, as an electronic merchant, ship the goods to me, you need to be able to bill me for the item. You cannot afford to have me claim that I never ordered the item.

13.3 Security Solutions

This section briefly reviews a number of security solutions, most of which depend on cryptography in one way or another. We start from the lowest levels of the OSI Reference Model, progressing from dialup encryption to link layer encryption, network layer encryption, session layer encryption, and application layer security. We conclude by discussing firewalls.

13.3.1 Encryption

Some people devote their entire careers to network cryptography. Here, my intent is merely to introduce some key concepts and issues.

Most of us encountered some form of basic cryptography as children. We may have played a game or read an activities book where we were perhaps asked to substitute a number from 1 to 26 for each letter in some sentence or phrase. Our friends might have found it difficult, but not impossible, to derive the original sentence or phrase from the sequence of numbers.

Computer cryptography flows from the same principles, but is infinitely more complex. In general, our intent is to make it prohibitively expensive for a malefactor to derive the encrypted information. Phrased differently, we want to ensure that the cost of breaking our encrypted code—measured in terms of the economic cost of the equipment needed, the time for which that equipment is needed, and the cost of associated labor—is greater than the value of the information that could be retrieved.

Most encryption today is *private key,* or *symmetric,* encryption. The data to be secured is transformed, generally using a *key* that is known to both the sender and the recipient of the data. The key thus constitutes a *shared secret.* The recipient applies an inverse transformation to the same data on receipt, utilizing the shared key and thus restoring the data to its original form.

It is important that the algorithm used to apply the transformation be thoroughly analyzed and secure. A malefactor may have access to many encrypted messages; it is important that the malefactor not be able, at reasonable expense, to derive either the key or the messages from the encrypted text. Note, however, that the algorithm itself is likely to be well known and public.

How is the shared secret made available to both parties? Presumably by some means external to the immediate exchange of encrypted data. Key distribution using private key cryptography alone can be tricky, because it is difficult to bootstrap the process. You would like to distribute keys securely over the network, but to do so you need to have already distributed a shared secret.

An alternative form of encryption is *public key,* or *asymmetric,* encryption. In public key cryptography, encryption and decryption are implemented using two different keys, which collectively represent a matched set of keys. One of the keys can be made publicly available, but the other must be kept private. Thus, when I send information to you, I encrypt it using your public key, which everyone knows. You decrypt the information using your private key, which is known to you alone.

The same technology can be used to implement digital signatures. If you encrypt some well-known bit of text using your private key, anyone can decrypt it using your public key, which can be known to all. But only you should have been able to create a message that would decrypt correctly, since your private key is known to you alone.

The security of public key cryptography depends on certain trap-door algorithms, which can be computed far more efficiently in one direction than in another. Thus, it may not be difficult to compute a pair of keys from a given starting point, but it is essential that knowledge of the public key not enable a malefactor to compute the private key.

It is increasingly common to build working systems that attempt to draw on the best features of both private and public key cryptography. Private key tends to be much faster and more efficient than public key cryptography, but does not lend itself to key distribution. Some modern systems use public key cryptography to establish a shared-secret private key that is active only for a short period of time—a *session key*. The bulk interchange of data then takes place using efficient private key encryption. This has the additional virtue that it tends to limit your exposure; in the event that a single session key has somehow been compromised, that exposure has not in general made it any easier for a malefactor to decrypt information in other sessions. This property is known as *perfect forward secrecy*.

13.3.2   Authentication of Dialup Users (PAP, CHAP, and RADIUS)

If your network is connected to a host computer system over a private (leased) line or over a LAN, you usually know whom you are talking to. For systems that connect to the network using switched facilities, such as a dialup line, you generally have no *a priori* notion as to who is at the other end of the phone line. We generally address this need using data link layer authentication and authorization.

Authentication and authorization can and do take place at more than one level in a network. IPSEC can play a very useful role in end-to-end authentication at the network layer, but it does not obviate the need for authentication at the data link layer, level 2 of the OSI Reference Model.

Most systems that connect using IP over dialup lines today use the *Point-to-Point Protocol, PPP*.[2] (Older systems may use the *Serial Line Interface Protocol, or SLIP*.[3]) When a PPP connection is initiated, the two communicating systems exchange options whereby the link will be managed using PPP's *Link Control Protocol (LCP)*. In the course of this *link-establishment* exchange, the communicating systems determine how authentication will take place: usually, by means either of the *Password Authentication Protocol (PAP)*[4] or of the *Challenge Handshake Authentication Protocol (CHAP)*.[5] They may also choose to bypass authentication, which is optional in PPP.

If the systems elect to use PAP, the system that is dialing in—typically, a personal computer—sends a user ID and password to the terminal server at the other end of the dialup connection. With PAP, the multiple-use password is sent in the clear; thus, anyone able to eavesdrop on the dialup connection would subsequently be able to impersonate the dialup user. This clearly represents a significant exposure, but many organizations choose to live with it.

CHAP can provide much stronger authentication. The terminal server responds to the user ID by sending a challenge to the user's computer. Typically, a human user sees the challenge and uses a smart card to respond, either by encrypting the challenge or by providing a response that reflects the time of day. In either case, the user's response will be different each time he or she logs in; thus, little or no damage is done if the user's response is snooped by a third party.

Figures 13-1 and 13-2 show PAP and CHAP authentication protocol exchanges, respectively. The use of either protocol implies the existence, somewhere in the network, of a database that lists the user ID and password or equivalent information for every authenticable user. The obvious solution,

---

2. W. Simpson, Request for Comments (RFC) 1331, "The Point-to-Point Protocol (PPP)," May 1992.

3. J. L. Romkey, Request for Comments (RFC) 1055, "Nonstandard for Transmission of IP Datagrams over Serial Lines: SLIP," June 1, 1988.

4. B. Lloyd and W. Simpson, Request for Comments (RFC) 1334, "PPP Authentication Protocols," October 1992.

5. W. Simpson, Request for Comments (RFC) 1994, "PPP Challenge Handshake Authentication Protocol (CHAP)," August 1996.

and indeed the first one that the equipment vendors attempted, was to build suitable configuration options into each terminal server. If you have a very small network and a very small number of users, this is a perfectly legitimate solution; however, it quickly becomes unmanageable for a large network with a large number of users. It is not *scalable*.

Consider the scaling problem. Suppose that you had 100 terminal servers and 10,000 users. How often would your user ID/password table need to change? Would you want to download new versions of the table to each of your 100 servers every time your organization hired or fired someone? How great would the risk be that a disgruntled employee who had just been fired might attempt to log in and do damage during the several hours it might take to update all of your tables?

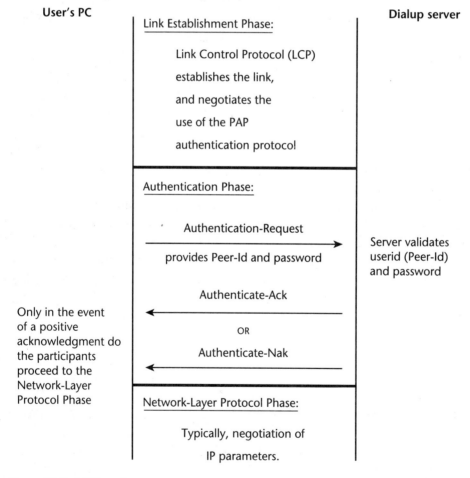

Figure 13-1: A PAP exchange.

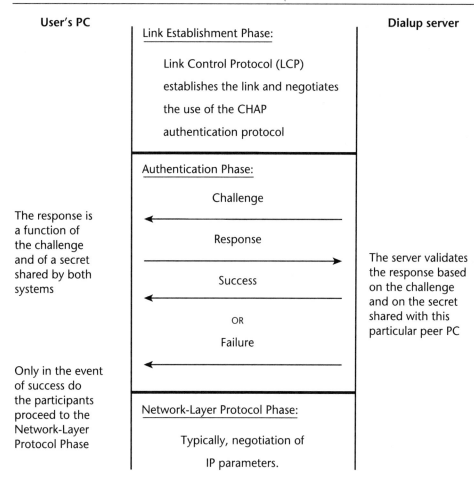

Figure 13-2: A CHAP exchange.

There is a better way! The *Remote Authentication Dial In User Service (RADIUS)*[6] authentication protocol provides a means by which the terminal servers can query a central database of user ID/password information. Centralizing such information greatly simplifies the administration of the system as a whole and also potentially enhances overall security, because there are far fewer places that hackers can profitably attack. Typically, you would provide at least two RADIUS servers in order to ensure sufficient fault-tolerance; most terminal servers can be configured to use a backup RADIUS server in the event that their primary RADIUS server fails to respond.

6. C. Rigney, A. Rubens, W. Simpson, and S. Willens, Request for Comments (RFC) 2138, "Remote Authentication Dial In User Service (RADIUS)," April 1997.

The RADIUS protocol interchange is, for the most part, conceptually independent of the authentication exchange that takes place over the link, but it must obviously be different for challenge response than it is for a simple password-based authentication. Thus, a RADIUS exchange in support of PAP would be as shown in Figure 13-3; a RADIUS exchange in support of CHAP would be as shown in Figure 13-4.

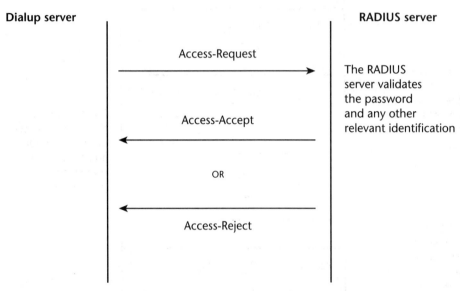

Figure 13-3: A RADIUS password validation exchange in support of PAP.

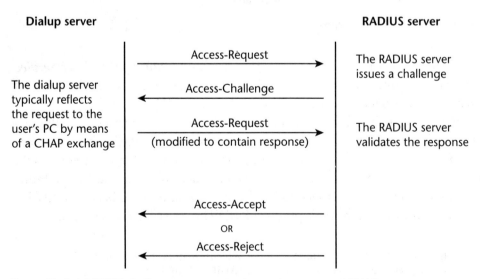

Figure 13-4: A RADIUS challenge-response exchange in support of CHAP.

RADIUS protocol exchanges are checksummed cryptographically, using the MD-5 encryption algorithm,[7] using symmetric encryption based on a secret that is shared by the RADIUS server and client and that is typically configured manually into each. This provides integrity but not confidentiality. In other words, it is possible to identify and discard messages that have been maliciously tampered with, but there is no explicit protection against eavesdropping. These choices were made in order to facilitate exportability of RADIUS-based solutions under current U.S. law and guidelines, but they have the unfortunate consequence of increasing the vulnerability of RADIUS to certain attacks.

Service providers sometimes find it convenient to use RADIUS in a *proxy* mode. For example, a service provider might be managing dialup servers for several commercial organizations, each with thousands of users. Under these circumstances, it might make good operational sense for each of those organizations to maintain its own table of user IDs and passwords rather than having the service provider maintain a table for all of them. The service provider could accomplish this by maintaining a proxy RADIUS server that would determine which of the commercial organizations was responsible for a given user and would then act as a RADIUS client to query that organization's RADIUS servers. This process is transparent to the organization's RADIUS servers: All RADIUS requests appear to come from the service provider's RADIUS server, as if the service provider's server were a huge terminal server. This process is depicted in Figure 13-5.

RADIUS is used primarily for authentication. However, it has some applicability to authorization as well. For example, you might simply fail the authorization attempt of a customer who has not paid his or her bill. You could also consider other information about the user, such as the port address or speed.

Some organizations find it convenient to use extensions to the RADIUS protocol in support of user accounting. RADIUS inherently generates a message to the RADIUS server whenever a user connects to a terminal server and thus establishes the user's identity unambiguously. If your usage accounting depends primarily on knowing how long a user was connected, that already gets you more than halfway to where you need to be. Some RADIUS-capable terminal servers provide an additional, optional RADIUS message that denotes the end of a connection. By storing the information contained in these session termination messages and sorting and matching those records with the information contained in the session establishment records, it is possible to compute the duration of any connection.

---

7. R. Rivest and S. Dusse, Request for Comments (RFC) 1321, "The MD5 Message-Digest Algorithm," MIT Laboratory for Computer Science, RSA Data Security Inc., April 1992.

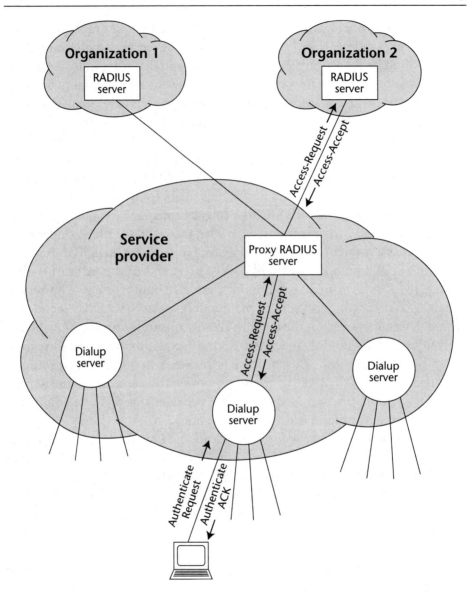

Figure 13-5: A proxy RADIUS server.

13.3.3   Link Layer Encryption

One of the oldest and simplest forms of security consists of link encryption. Encryption devices are placed between two communicating systems, instead of CSU/DSUs, as shown in Figure 13-6.

Link layer encryption can be relatively straightforward. Systems of this type can be particularly difficult to infiltrate, because the cryptography is typically performed in a distinct external cryptography box that provides no

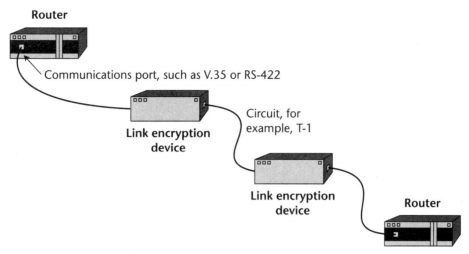

Figure 13-6: Link layer encryption.

easy access to a hacker. Bulk encryption provides not only confidentiality and integrity as the data travels between adjacent systems but also excellent protection against traffic analysis.

At the same time, the weakness of this system is precisely that it operates at the link layer, not at the network layer or above. Link layer encryption does not, in and of itself, protect the data while it is in a router or a server; that is the province of the security features of the router or server itself. It does not inherently provide authentication or authorization, at least not on an end-to-end basis. It tends to lead to a lack of uniformity in the network design, because each type of link may require a distinct type of link encryption device. Finally, the integrity and confidentiality that are offered are only point to point, not end to end.

13.3.4 Network Layer Security (IPSEC)

In recent years, the IETF has been hard at work on a new constellation of security protocols intended to provide a general-purpose means of protecting all traffic at the IP network layer. These protocols are known as *IPSEC*, the *IP security* protocols.

IPSEC comprises two basic mechanisms: the *authentication header (AH)* and the *encapsulating security payload (ESP)*. AH provides connectionless integrity, data source authentication, and optional protection against replays, but it does *not* provide confidentiality. ESP provides confidentiality, and optionally provides connectionless integrity, data source authentication, and protection against replays. Note that ESP provides functionality that is, for the most part, a superset of that of AH; consequently, there has been some sentiment within the IETF that AH is superfluous.

Both AH and ESP are designed to support either IPv4 or IPv6. Both support two modes: *transport mode* and *tunnel mode*. Transport mode primarily protects the layers above IP, while tunnel mode encapsulates the entire IP datagram, thus providing protection for IP and for the layers above it.

IPSEC is expected to be used in several different configurations. It could be employed directly between IPSEC-capable host systems (see Figure 13-7). Alternatively, a *security protocol gateway (SPG)* could implement IPSEC on behalf of other host systems (see Figure 13-8). The SPG could be an intermediate system whose identity has been configured into the associated hosts; in many cases, however, the router that connects your corporate or enterprise network to the Internet will have IPSEC capability and will function as an SPG. Note that transport mode is expected to be used only between hosts, not by SPGs.

Each IPSEC-capable system, whether a host or an SPG, is expected to contain a *security policy database (SPD)* or to provide equivalent functionality. The SPD determines whether a given IP datagram will be dropped, transmitted using IPSEC, or transmitted bypassing IPSEC. The SPD contains *selectors* that identify traffic flows of interest, typically based on characteristics of the IP datagrams, such as the IP source and destination address ranges, and possibly on source and destination TCP or UDP port addresses. *Note that an IPSEC SPG can perform IPSEC on behalf of a host or a group of*

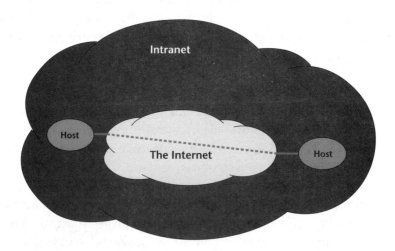

Figure 13-7: IPSEC between host systems.

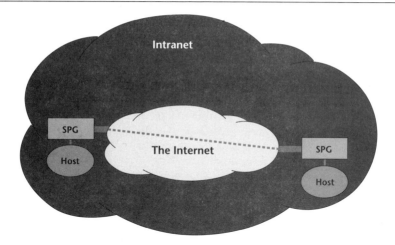

Figure 13-8: IPSEC between security protocol gateways (SPGs).

hosts, whether or not the hosts are IPSEC-capable, with no reconfiguration required to the hosts.

Figure 13-8 depicts a configuration that may well become commonplace, and that is likely to be the initial configuration for IPSEC usage in most of the environments where IPSEC is deployed. SPGs can be used to implement a VPN (or rather, an iVPN in the parlance introduced in Chapter 1). Market forces are driving IPSEC into routers and terminal servers. Designers are likely to use SPG IPSEC on behalf of hosts long before host IPSEC implementations are widespread. If IPSEC succeeds in the marketplace, we should expect to see a later proliferation of host IPSEC support and a gradual migration of deployed networks from SPG IPSEC to host IPSEC.

IPSEC cryptography requires the use of a shared key between the sending and receiving system. Shared keys can be manually configured or can be generated using the *Internet Key Exchange (IKE)*, another protocol within the IPSEC family.

13.3.5 Session Layer Security: The Secure Socket Layer (SSL)

The *Secure Socket Layer (SSL)* represents one approach to securing applications. SSL operates above TCP but below such applications as HTTP, Telnet, and FTP, as shown in Figure 13-9. Thus, SSL can be used to secure data sent across the World Wide Web and is, indeed, integral to modern browsers.

The application needs to be aware of SSL; however, SSL deals with many of the complexities of key generation and negotiation in an application-independent way, thus freeing the application developer from many messy

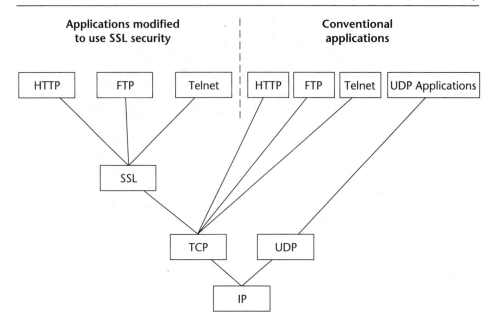

Figure 13-9: The role of the Secure Socket Layer (SSL) in the TCP/IP stack.

details. SSL support is available in suitable versions of Winsock (the transport layer application program interface, or API, for Microsoft Windows) and of UNIX sockets.

SSL services are usually fully transparent to the end user. Internet luminary Vint Cerf has impishly observed that SSL is the only security service that works today, and that it works solely because the user scarcely knows that it is there.

SSL provides the application with a *secure communications channel,* authenticating the server to the client and optionally also authenticating the client to the server. SSL encrypts the data being transmitted, thus ensuring both confidentiality and privacy; however, it cannot protect data at the TCP or IP layers. It also contains protection against replay attacks.

SSL requires a connection-oriented transport service. It is not suitable for UDP applications. Public key cryptographic exchanges are used to establish unique session keys for traffic flowing in each direction, thus reducing the exposure of the master key to cryptographic attacks. Once the symmetric session keys have been established, however, the bulk encryption of session data is accomplished using private (symmetric) key cryptography, which is faster and more efficient than public key encryption.

The SSL client and server will generally negotiate the strongest encryption that they both support. SSL implementations produced in the United States for export abroad commonly operate using short keys, in order to comply with U.S. export restrictions, even though this results in a cryptographically weak solution.

13.3.6 Application Layer Security (PGP, Kerberos, and X.509 Certificates)

There are numerous advantages to providing security directly at the application layer, because the application understands its own security needs better than any general solution can. It is this very tailoring to the application, however, that implies that an application layer solution cannot apply to all applications. Nonetheless, a number of building blocks for application layer security are available.

One of these is *Pretty Good Privacy (PGP)*, which was developed by Phil Zimmerman in 1991. A number of civil libertarians hoped to gain widespread acceptance of strong encryption; consequently, they distributed PGP as freeware. The U.S. government attempted for several years to prosecute Zimmerman but finally gave up in 1996. Freeware versions of PGP continue to be available, as well as commercial implementations from Network Associates, Inc.

PGP can be used to encrypt files, generally in order to send them across a network. PGP incorporates strong cryptography, with key lengths of 128 bits or better. It can be integrated into a number of commercial e-mail packages, including QualComm's Eudora and Microsoft's Outlook.

Kerberos is an authentication technology that was developed at the Massachusetts Institute of Technology (MIT), based on work done at Xerox PARC by Needham and Schroeder.[8] Kerberos generally uses an initial exchange based on symmetric keys in order to establish session keys and to authenticate the Kerberos clients to one another. The applications must be Kerberos-aware.

Certificates constitute an important building block for many applications, including S/MIME (Secure Multipurpose Internet Mail Extensions), PGP, and SSL. The primary function of the certificate is to authenticate the identity of its owner, but it also provides a means of distributing the owner's public key.

The most commonly used format for certificates is specified in an international standard known as X.509,[9] which is part of the family of ITU (International Telecommunications Union) specifications related to directory

---

8. R. Needham and M. Schroeder, "Using Encryption for Authentication in Large Networks of Computers," *Communications of the ACM,* December 1978.

9. Telecommunication Standardization Sector of the International Telecommunications Union (ITU), *The Discovery–Authentication Framework,* Recommendation X.509, 1997.

services. X.509 describes, among other things, a certificate that authenticates a user and also, optionally, establishes the user's authorization levels. X.509 is based on public key cryptography, which explains in part why it appears as part of the X.500 family of specifications, which deal primarily with directory services. The certificate can reside in a public directory, since knowledge of the certificate does not divulge the private key.

Each certificate is digitally signed by a trusted third party in order to provide reliable authentication. In the case of X.509, those third parties are known as certificate authorities (CAs). CAs are organized into a hierarchy of trust, where the top of the hierarchy necessarily corresponds to authorities whom we trust axiomatically. That trust is then delegated downward.

X.509 also contains mechanisms for exchanging certificate "black lists"—lists of certificates that are no longer valid.

The X.509 certificate should be viewed as a building block. Applications that depend on authentication and authorization, including electronic commerce applications, can be constructed using X.509 certificates as a well-understood and standardized component.

13.3.7 Intrusion Detection

According to one school of thought, no matter how good your security measures may be, hackers will test your perimeters and will sooner or later break through. If that is the case, it is natural to think that it may be more important to detect the probing and to respond aggressively than it is to anticipate and to protect against every possible threat in advance.

This principle is familiar in other contexts. The human body is designed to make it difficult for microorganisms to get in, but it also relies on active defenses, such as the white corpuscles, to detect and to actively engage those intruders that get past the first line of defense. Analogously, most of us have watched movies in which soldiers stood guard behind the crenellated crests of a medieval castle; no matter how well designed the castle, it would have been vulnerable to innumerable threats in the absence of active surveillance and defense.

In recent years, a number of *intrusion detection systems (IDSs)* have come on the market as standard commercial offerings. Among these are Net Ranger (ISS) and Network Flight Recorder (Ranum). Some organizations prefer to customize a workstation or a PC to perform this function; however, my recommendation would be to use a commercial product unless your organization has unusually strong network security expertise. In either case, an IDS typically might passively monitor LAN traffic and might otherwise look for telltale "footprints" that suggest that hackers have been active.

13.3.8 Decoys

The *decoy* is motivated by much the same logic as the IDS. If you assume that hackers are likely to break in sooner or later, you would like to channel them away from your most sensitive targets. Some organizations find it expedient to implement decoy systems—systems that exist for no other purpose than to get hacked.

One of the things that your IDS should be watching for is hacker activity on your decoy systems.

13.3.9 Firewalls

In a building, a firewall is intended to help limit the spread of fires, not to prevent them. Analogously, network firewalls are intended to establish a control point at which security policies can be enforced and to make it possible to limit damage in the event of a break-in.

The term *firewall* encompasses a number of technical solutions, with somewhat different strengths and weaknesses. Perhaps the simplest form of firewall functionality consists of nothing more sophisticated than packet filtering, based on such characteristics as the source and destination IP address and the source and destination TCP or UDP port number. A firewall of this type does not need to be customized to support various applications; however, it provides a very coarse-grained, primitive level of security.

A more interesting solution is to use the firewall as an application layer gateway. Firewalls of this type typically terminate an inbound or outbound application by serving as a proxy on its behalf, as shown in Figure 13-10. A firewall that actively participates in the application layer interactions can be far more intelligent about preventing malicious behavior; however, by its very nature, it must understand every application for which it serves as a proxy. Consequently, the firewall vendor has a significant software maintenance task in keeping the unit current as application layer protocols evolve.

Why is the firewall necessary? In an ideal world, each application would already be adequately secured within your organization, and the firewall would be superfluous. Unfortunately, we do not live in an ideal world. To a significant degree, the firewall exists to help you to guard against configuration errors and poor security practices within your own organization. That is a key part of its mission.

Firewalls often also serve as the point at which cryptographic encapsulation occurs in support of Internet VPNs (iVPNs). This is a natural role for the firewall, because it needs to support efficient cryptography anyway and because a lot of your external traffic flows through it. In many cases, the firewall is sitting

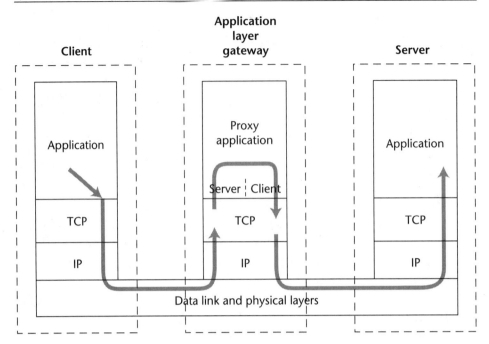

Figure 13-10: A firewall serving as an application layer gateway.

at the boundary between your internal network and the public Internet, which is exactly the point at which you need cryptographic encapsulation.

Firewalls can be useful not only as a means of guarding against certain kinds of attacks but also as a control point at which you might apply countermeasures if you are under threat, since all applications pass through the firewall.

Firewalls can be a very useful component of your overall security program; however, you should not assume that the firewall is all the security that you will ever need. Think of your network security as being a bit like oral hygiene. If you want healthy teeth, you should have a good diet, floss and brush regularly, and see your dentist periodically. Brushing your teeth does not in and of itself guarantee good teeth, no matter how conscientious you are about brushing; however, *neglecting* to brush pretty much guarantees that you will have problems sooner or later.

13.4 Perimeter Security

As we have seen, computer networks are under vigorous attack today. They are subject to numerous, continuously evolving threats. Most of the known threats can be addressed by using one security technique or another; however, no single cure addresses every security malady. Moreover, the guys in the black hats are developing new threats just as quickly as the guys in the white hats are developing countermeasures to the known exposures. New feature-rich software systems create new vulnerabilities for the hackers to exploit. *There is no panacea. There is no silver bullet.* Most organizations need to carefully consider their security needs, the sensitivity and value of their data, and their organizational culture in crafting an overall security solution that draws on a number of security components.

We can once again learn from those medieval network security architects who designed castles. In general, a castle of any sophistication did not consist of a single defensive wall but instead was more likely to include a moat, a drawbridge, and possibly outer and inner rings of fortifications. If a castle had only a single defense, no matter how well crafted that defense was, it might be highly vulnerable to an attack specifically aimed at that single defense. By having multiple defenses, complementary but largely independent, the overall security of the system was enhanced because a successful attacker had to independently thwart many different defensive mechanisms.

13.4.1 Limitations of Perimeter Security

Many organizations attempt to achieve security by erecting the highest possible barriers against external intruders. That is a natural thing to do, and it is not necessarily a bad thing. It is *excessive reliance* on perimeter security that can be detrimental. There are a number of reasons why this is so.

First, *not all of the barbarians are outside the gates.* As we noted earlier, if your data has high intrinsic worth and if you have successfully erected good barriers against subversion from the outside, you have practically ensured that someone will find it worthwhile to infiltrate a compatriot *inside* your organization.

Second, perimeter security can be compromised if it runs counter to your organizational culture and in the absence of training and policing. As an example, many of your employees may have their own dial-up accounts for accessing the Internet. What happens if one of those users dials his or her Internet provider while connected to your corporate LAN? That user has just punched a nice little hole through your security perimeter fortifications, as shown in Figure 13-11.

"Why," you might ask yourself, "would a user even want to do such a thing?" It is important to keep in mind that most security systems tend to constrain or hamper user behavior. The user cannot do certain things that he or she used to be able to do. Thus, there is a natural tendency to want to bypass security systems. The more onerous your security system, the greater

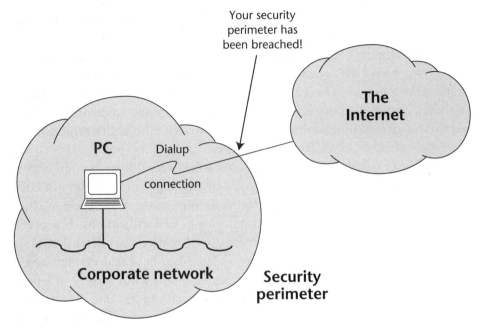

Figure 13-11: A user inadvertently compromises perimeter security.

the risk that your own users will undermine it. For this particular hazard—and for many others—it is important to establish clear security policies and to educate your user community.

It is also important to keep in mind that most organizations need to compartmentalize information, even among employees. No matter how much you trust your sales force, you generally will not want to expose your payroll information to them. No matter how much confidence you have in your engineers, you will want to keep them away from personnel information unless they have a legitimate need to know. Trust is not a simple yes-or-no kind of thing.

13.4.2   A Castle with Inner and Outer Walls

Some organizations find it expedient to complement external security with internal compartmentalization of information, as shown in Figure 13-12. In the figure, the organization has supplemented perimeter security with internal perimeters that segregate functional areas—personnel, marketing, and engineering. These internal partitions potentially reduce the cost of a break-in to the organization, because an intruder might be unlikely to compromise more than one of these areas. That might turn out to be a major advantage for your organization.

At the same time, you do not want to get carried away: If these security measures were so intrusive as to make it difficult for people to do their work, they might introduce security exposures of their own by tempting people to violate the organization's security policies. Excessive fragmentation and compartmentalization of the network could make it difficult to maintain and enhance, and fragile in the face of failures. As with most things, balance and sound engineering judgment are necessary.

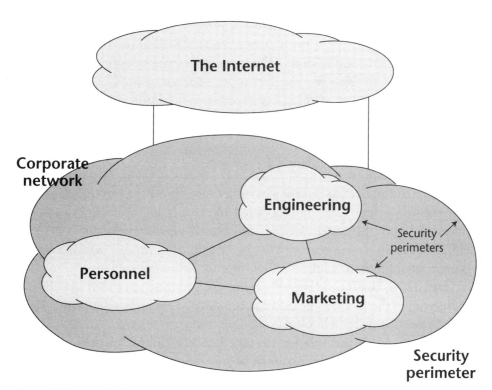

Figure 3-12: A castle (or security system) with inner and outer walls.

14

The Public Internet: Unique Design Considerations

Much of our discussion up to this point has focused on design for private intranets and enterprise internetworks. How do things change when we design for the global, public Internet? How might the design of the public Internet interact with design considerations for enterprise internetworks?

The first six sections of this chapter deal with the overall design of the Internet, explaining how that system has evolved over time. They will be of particular interest to anyone designing for an *Internet service provider,* particularly for anyone designing a network for a *backbone ISP,* but they have other applications as well. For instance, understanding the structure of the Internet helps a business to order the most appropriate Internet access service and to position its Web servers and other sources of high traffic volume. Thus, the final section of this chapter contains helpful hints for ordering Internet access from an ISP.

14.1 Evolution of Today's Internet

Today, there is no overall central planning function for the Internet. Changes set in motion a few years ago have led to the present system. In order to understand how the system works, and how it was intended to work, it is helpful to return to the year 1993—the last point in time at which a grand vision existed for the evolution of the Internet as a whole.

Until 1995, the U.S. National Science Foundation provided the core of the Internet in the form of the NSFnet, a publicly funded backbone network. The NSFnet was restricted to carrying only traffic associated with research or education. By 1993, the NSF felt that the Internet had sufficient commercial viability to stand on its own two feet. Moreover, the NSF understood that as long as the government provided the backbone of the Internet at no cost, there could never be a broad private Internet industry. Private industry could not compete with a service provided at zero cost. In order to permit an industry to spring into being, the National Science Foundation would have to step aside.

The NSF initiated this transition through a public solicitation document, Solicitation 93-52, in which the NSF described a future Internet structure comprising

- *National service providers (NSPs)*, providers of Internet access operating on a national scale
- Internet service providers (ISPs), operating on a smaller scale than NSPs
- Public shared interconnection points called *network access points*, or *NAPs*
- A transit service to interconnect the regional ISPs formerly funded by the NSF
- A *very high speed backbone network service (vBNS)* to interconnect a handful of research laboratories and to serve as a testbed for new high-speed Internet services
- A *router arbiter* service, both to rationalize routing in the global Internet and to provide a central anchor point for routing research and statistics

Figure 14-1 shows a notional view of what the NSF had in mind.

On balance, the NSF was very successful in taking itself out of the innards of the global Internet without massive disruption. However, some aspects of its plan were more successful than others. It is instructive to look at the results of each element of the plan.

14.1.1 National Service Providers and Internet Service Providers

A number of NSPs and a far larger number of ISPs were already in operation at the time of Solicitation 93-52. Today, there are at least five major backbone ISPs and somewhere between six and perhaps thirty smaller backbone ISPs that could be described as NSPs. We will discuss the distinguishing hallmarks of a backbone ISP later in this chapter.

By all accounts, there are several thousand ISPs today. *Boardwatch Magazine* currently lists some 4,855 ISPs in North America.[1]

The NSF did not attempt to create NSPs and ISPs; rather, in exiting the public Internet space itself, it created the market forces that would foster the formation of NSPs and ISPs.

---

1. *Boardwatch Magazine,* http://boardwatch.internet.com/isp/spring99/introduction.html, June 1999.

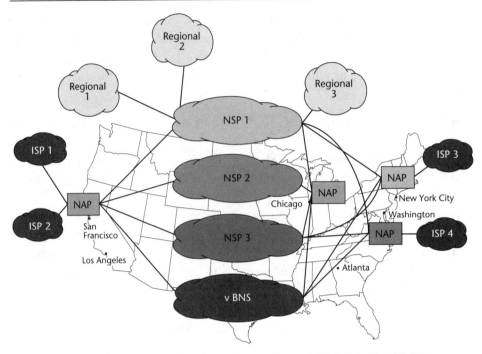

Figure 14-1: The architecture of the Internet, according to NSF Solicitation 93-52.

14.1.2 Network Access Points

Solicitation 93-52 sought to create at least three network access points, or NAPs, located in the San Francisco Bay area, the Chicago area, and the New York City area, as well as additional NAPs to the extent that funding might permit. The NAPs were expected to operate at the data link layer of the OSI Reference Model; they might be implemented as a shared high-speed LAN or as an SMDS or ATM service providing shared interconnection among NSPs/ISPs.

Each NAP would provide interconnection among NSPs and ISPs for purposes of traffic interchange—known in the trade as *shared interconnection,* and sometimes referred to as *public peering.* In an *interconnection,* or *peering,* relationship, Internet providers agree to accept traffic destined for one another's respective customers but not necessarily for other third parties. In a *customer,* or *transit,* relationship between Internet providers, by contrast, the transit provider typically agrees to accept traffic destined for any point in the global Internet.

The solicitation resulted in the NSF's supporting four NAPs. Those NAPs, along with their sponsoring firms, are shown in Table 14-1.

Table 14-1: Network Access Points and Sponsoring Firms

NAP	Sponsoring Firms
Chicago	Ameritech/BellCore
New York[1]	Sprint/San Diego Supercomputer Center
San Francisco	PacTel/BellCore
Washington, D.C.	Metropolitan Fiber Systems (MFS), in a facility called MAE East

1. New York is something of a misnomer: Sprint responded to the NSF's request with a proposal to locate its NAP in a facility situated some 90 miles southwest of New York, across the Delaware River from Philadelphia.

In the flurry of acquisitions that followed the Telecommunications Act of 1996, the identity of a number of these organizations is changing or has changed. BellCore has been acquired by SAIC; PacTel has been acquired by SBC; Ameritech is in the process of being acquired by SBC; and MFS was acquired by WorldCom, which subsequently became MCI WorldCom as a result of its acquisition of MCI.

The NSF's program was basically successful, even though things did not work out exactly as initially envisioned. The Washington NAP, better known as MAE East, and the Sprint NAP evolved into full-fledged national and global traffic interchange points; the Chicago and San Francisco NAPs, however, have been problematic since their inception. Initially, they suffered from technical problems associated with attempting to drive large volumes of IP traffic over still immature ATM switching products; subsequently, these NAPs have lacked a critical mass of large national backbone ISPs. As a result, they function, in practice, in the role of regional traffic concentration points. Quite a few additional regional public interchange points have come into existence in the United States in recent years, although they do not appear to play a strong role in the overall traffic flows of the Internet.

Meanwhile, the lack of a stable public peering point on the West Coast of the United States was, briefly, problematic for the NSP/ISP community. In practice, the large national backbone ISPs soon converged on a facility called MAE West, operated jointly by MFS and NASA.

As a result, the work originally envisioned for the NAPs can be viewed, for most purposes, as being performed by MAE East, MAE West, and the Sprint NAP. All three of these were based in the recent past on Fiber Distributed Data Interface (FDDI) LAN technology, and all three augmented the FDDI with high-speed LAN switches (gigaswitches). The gigaswitches support full-duplex FDDI, thus offering, in theory, 100Mbps of input and output simultaneously between each pair of routers.

By 1996, all of these facilities were suffering from inadequate capacity. In 1998, MCI WorldCom upgraded its MAE facilities in Washington (MAE East), San Jose (MAE West), and Dallas to offer modern ATM switches as a high-capacity alternative to the FDDI/gigaswitch architecture.

As we shall soon see, a largely unanticipated consequence of the evolution of the Internet away from the pure NSF 93-52 model has been a migration of interconnection traffic away from these three locations and into private arrangements among the NSPs. These *direct interconnections* are sometimes referred to as *private peering*.

14.1.3 Transit Service among Regional ISPs

Eight large regional ISPs went through a competitive bidding process, which resulted in a series of contracts for *transit* service—where transit represents carrying of data to other ISPs—being awarded to MCI. MCI connected the NSF-sponsored regional ISPs to one another and carried their traffic to other NSPs and to the NAPs. The arrangement worked well, in general, but it has largely been phased out today. The original regional ISPs have outgrown their need for transit services; however, most backbone ISPs now offer transit services, which continue to play a huge role in the public Internet today.

14.1.4 The Very High Speed Backbone Network Service (vBNS)

The NSF also awarded the vBNS to MCI. MCI runs routers over an infrastructure of ATM switches to interconnect a number of NSF-sponsored research institutions, including the supercomputer centers at Cornell University, Pittsburgh, San Diego, NCAR, and NCSA. The vBNS was initially operated at OC-3 speeds (155Mbps) and was subsequently upgraded to OC-12 (622Mbps).

The program has generally worked as intended; nonetheless, there are issues. First, it serves only a portion of the institutions to which connectivity is offered. (Thus, it is not available to all of Cornell University). Second, the original intent of using the vBNS as a testbed for research into high-speed internetworking may be inappropriate for a production network used to accomplish real work.

More recently, some of the functions of the vBNS have been subsumed by two newer initiatives: the *Next-Generation Internet (NGI),* and the *Abilene* project of *Internet 2.* The NGI is a U.S. government–sponsored initiative to provide a high-speed private internetwork among a number of major U.S.

agencies. Abilene is a high-speed private internetwork interconnecting members of UCAID, a consortium of research universities and private industry. Abilene has benefited from significant "in-kind" contributions of circuits and equipment from Qwest, Cisco, and Nortel.

Meanwhile, the original vBNS contract will soon expire. MCI WorldCom intends to replace it with a privatized next-generation vBNS network based on packet-over-SONET at OC-48 speeds.

14.1.5 The Router Arbiter (RA) Project

The Router Arbiter project was intended to conduct research into routing and to provide a database of Internet topology and policies, in order to enhance the stability, robustness, and manageability of the Internet. The Router Arbiter project also produced statistics about the Internet as a whole (see Section 14.6).

14.2 Structure of the Internet Today

Traffic interchange among backbone ISPs is fundamental to the operation of this system. As previously noted, in an *interconnection* relationship, Internet providers agree to accept traffic destined for one another's respective customers but not necessarily for other third parties. This is different from a *customer,* or *transit,* relationship between Internet providers, where the transit provider typically agrees to accept traffic destined for any point in the global Internet.

Historically, interconnection was called *peering,* in order to imply that traffic was interchanged among providers that were similar in size and capability. Over time, it came to be recognized that peers need not be similar in size; rather, what was important was that there be comparable value in the *traffic interchanged.*

I find it convenient to think of today's Internet as comprising two kinds of ISP: backbone ISPs and all others. The backbone ISPs interconnect with all other significant ISPs by means of a full set of interconnection relationships. Other ISPs may have some interconnection relationships, or they may not, but they have a significant dependency on a customer or transit relationship to one or more backbone ISPs. (Thus, the ability to reach all Internet destinations without the need for a transit relationship—sometimes called, somewhat inexactly, *default-free* status—is a strong indicator that an ISP should be viewed as a backbone ISP.) This yields the complex, Medusa-like structure shown in Figure 14-2.

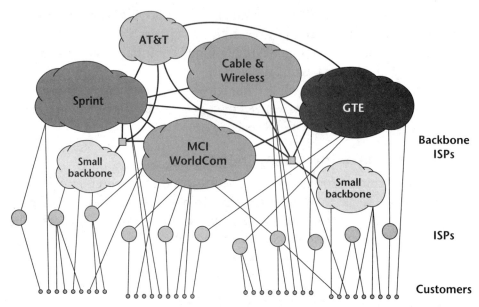

Figure 14-2: Present-day Internet structure: Backbone ISPs and other ISPs.

By these criteria, Cable & Wireless (formerly internetMCI), MCI World-Com (including UUnet, ANS, and other previously independent ISPs), Sprint, AT&T, and GTE (including the former BBN and Genuity) should clearly be viewed today as backbone ISPs. Somewhere between six and perhaps thirty other ISPs could also be viewed as backbone ISPs. The vast remainder are dependent on the backbone ISPs for global interconnectivity.

14.3 Direct and Shared Interconnections (Public and Private Peering)

Over the past few years, there has been a marked trend away from the use of the shared interconnection points on the part of the large backbone ISPs. In absolute terms, there is still significant traffic growth at MAE East, MAE West, and the Sprint NAP; however, the growth is not commensurate with the growth in overall traffic in the Internet. Thus, these facilities are losing "market share" in terms of the number of bits that flow through them.

The trade press has been perplexed by this trend and has occasionally presented it as if it were a predatory tactic on the part of the large backbone ISPs. In fact, simple economic and technical considerations drive the move to direct interconnections (private peering). For that matter, the migration to private peering is, for the most part, neutral in its impact on smaller ISPs—which indeed have severe problems with the affordability of interconnections but not because of the upsurge in direct interconnections among large backbone ISPs.

Even our way of thinking about shared interconnection has evolved. Historically, we referred to the NAPs and MAEs as *public peering points*. This was something of a misnomer, as, in almost all instances, peering was not public! Interconnection (peering) at a shared interconnection point would be established as a bilateral business relationship between two backbone ISPs, often at no direct cost to either party, based on the shared perception that both parties benefited from that interconnection.

In 1993, it might have seemed that the NAP-based architecture shown in Figure 14-1 could be expanded indefinitely. As each component was outgrown, it would simply be upgraded. When the NAP shoe started to chafe, the NAP provider might simply buy a shoe of larger size.

Things have not played out quite the way that they were expected to. First, LAN technology did not keep pace with the growth in Internet traffic levels. As traffic at the three major interconnects grew, the shared-medium FDDI (with 100Mbps of bandwidth to *all* ISPs present) was upgraded several times but never seemed to be able to keep pace with traffic. More recently, the largest MAE facilities have migrated to ATM; nonetheless, the main reason that the Internet as a whole has not long since collapsed under its own weight is that the major backbone ISPs have diverted most of their traffic away from the shared interconnection points.

The second main factor in this migration is that the economics of interconnection work differently as the bandwidth ramps up. Under the original concept of a NAP, a single T-3 connection from each NSP would carry all of the peering traffic for that NSP for a major portion of the United States. The NAPs made economic sense because they allowed multiple peers to share resources. They also provided economies of scale, because operating a single shared T-3 circuit was far more cost-effective than operating one or more T-1 circuits to each of several peers.

Today, if a given backbone ISP has enough traffic to another backbone ISP to fill a T-3 circuit, there is no incentive to use a shared interconnect for that traffic. Indeed, in light of current Internet traffic levels, use of a public interconnect

- Would introduce the risk of overloading the shared interconnect, to the detriment of both backbone ISPs and possibly also of third parties

- Offers no additional economic incentives in the form of economies of scale
- Potentially complicates future upgrades, in that three parties are involved (two backbone ISPs and the shared interconnect facility manager) instead of two (just the two backbone ISPs)

For a large backbone ISP, the natural tendency is to use

- Private interconnects to those backbone ISPs with which one has a lot of traffic to interchange
- Shared interconnects to interchange traffic with smaller backbone ISPs and, possibly, with small ISPs

This yields a system that looks like Figure 14-3. The majority of interconnections among providers may continue to take place at shared interconnection points; however, the preponderance of traffic already flows across private peering interfaces, and this tendency is sure to accelerate in the coming years.

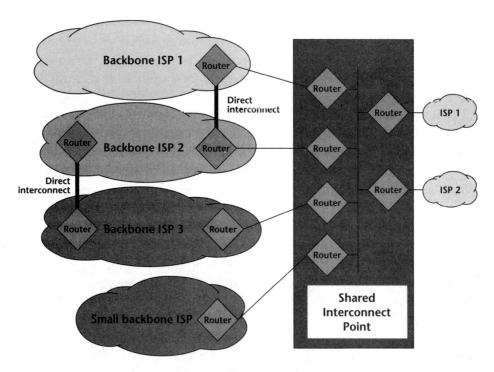

Figure 14-3: Direct and shared interconnections (private and public peering).

14.4 Traffic Characterization in Light of Shortest-Exit Routing

Whether the peering connection is implemented at a shared interconnection (public peering) point or through direct interconnection (private peering), the prevailing pattern in the Internet today is to perform routing between peers on the basis of *shortest exit,* sometimes called *hot-potato routing.*

Shortest exit is, from a routing technology point of view, fairly simple. If a pair of ISPs or NSPs peer in more than one location, the *sender* determines the interface over which to send the data. The sender will generally choose to send the data at the earliest possible opportunity, in order to minimize cost to itself (while maximizing cost to the provider with which it peers).

This resulting system is, overall, fair to both parties under most circumstances; however, the economic implications of shortest-exit routing may not be immediately obvious to the casual observer. For that matter, the trade press has been exceptionally confused when it comes to shortest exit.

Suppose, for example, that a Massachusetts GTE customer chooses to access a Web page maintained by a Los Angeles customer of, say, Sprint. What happens? As we work through this example, pay close attention to Figure 14-4. The GTE customer selects the URL that he or she wants, and presses Enter. The customer's PC system will determine the IP address of the destination and will then start to open a TCP connection by sending what is

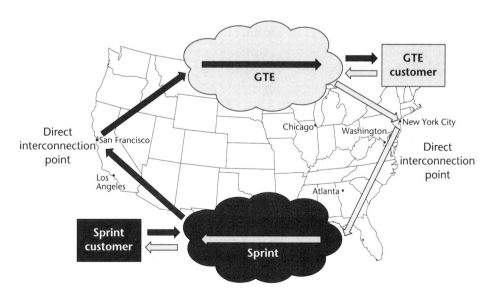

Figure 14-4: An example of shortest-exit routing.

called a SYN packet to the destination host. Routers within the user's company will recognize that this IP address is external to the company and will route it to their Internet provider, GTE (following the light gray lines). GTE's routers will, in turn, recognize that the IP address was assigned by Sprint and will route the datagram to the nearest interconnection point with Sprint. Let's suppose that the interconnection point is located near New York City.

At this point, Sprint has the obligation of carrying the datagram across the country using its own infrastructure. When it arrives at a Sprint router in Los Angeles, the datagram is sent to the customer's router, which in turn routes it to the Sprint customer's Web server.

The Web server generates a TCP acknowledgment of the SYN packet. Routers within the customer's internal network send this datagram to Sprint (the dark gray line). Sprint routers recognize that this datagram is destined for a GTE customer, so Sprint routes it to the nearest interconnect point with GTE, which, for our example, might be at Palo Alto, California. The traffic is handed off to GTE at that point and then carried on GTE's network back to Massachusetts, where it is finally handed off to the GTE customer who originated the request.

This somewhat arcane system has some subtle implications.

- Traffic flows are generally asymmetric.
- The system tends to be fair as long as data volumes are roughly balanced between transmit and receive, with no systematic bias toward or away from any particular geographic location, and as long as both providers are hauling data comparable distances.
- It is indeed more blessed to give than to receive: better to transmit data than to receive it. The recipient of traffic is burdened with the cost of hauling it for long distances. Shortest exit thus tends to favor providers with Web hosting traffic (asymmetric flows favoring transmission) and to put dialup providers (asymmetric flows favoring reception) at an economic disadvantage.
- There are innumerable ways to "game" the system—to so structure your business as to artificially reduce your costs, at the expense of other providers.

In light of shortest exit, large backbone ISPs tend to offer peering privileges at no cost only to other backbone ISPs that can peer in locations on both coasts and that can provide sufficient bandwidth between the coasts, subject to various other technical and business considerations. These represent necessary, but not sufficient, conditions for shortest-exit peering to be reasonably equitable. And it is for these same reasons that backbone ISPs either do not offer peering or else insist on charging for peering for small ISPs who can peer in only one location—the small ISP cannot meaningfully reciprocate the service that the large backbone ISP provides, because the distances over which it operates are not comparable.

14.5 International Internet Traffic Flows

Not surprisingly, the NSF's view of the evolution of the Internet was focused primarily on its evolution within the United States. What about the rest of the world?

For historical reasons, the Internet evolved in a U.S.-centric way. It started in the United States, which today still represents the vast majority of the traffic on the Internet, although the rate of growth in other parts of the world may be even higher than that in the United States.

The prevailing tendency until quite recently has been for each foreign ISP to maintain a connection to a U.S.-based backbone ISP, at the foreign provider's expense. Thus, connectivity to the rest of the world was provided by the United States—a system sometimes called "hub and spokes." This is depicted in Figure 14-5. From the perspective of foreign providers, the system could be quite irritating; it implied that traffic to any other provider's customers would generally go to and from the United States, even if both customers in question are located in, say, Europe.

Moreover, the foreign provider would pay for the circuit to connect to the U.S. NSP. Those circuits are expensive! A T-1 or an E-1 circuit across the Atlantic can cost almost as much as a T-3 across the entire continental United States. It is not surprising that foreign ISPs have been unhappy with this system.

It has been suggested that U.S. backbone ISPs should pay for half of the cost of circuits to foreign providers; this, however, is clearly a wrongheaded notion. The distribution of market forces does not support this distribution of cost; were the situation otherwise, it would already be in effect.

NAP-like public interconnects have appeared in a number of European locations and in Kobe, Japan. These interconnects can provide local concentration of traffic. During 1998, traffic interchange in Europe increased markedly, and it became increasingly common for traffic between European providers to be exchanged within Europe.

Today, the vast majority of Internet content is based in the United States. This reflects the reality that, in many parts of the world, circuits between two adjacent countries may cost nearly as much as a circuit from either country

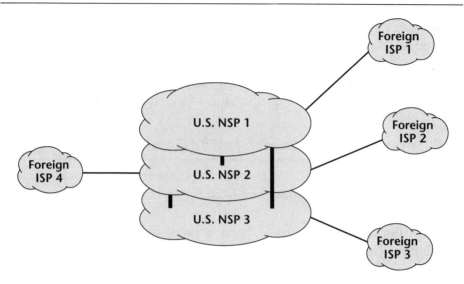

Figure 14-5: The "hub and spokes" system whereby foreign ISPs connect to a U.S. NSP.

to the United States. As a result, if a foreign firm wishes to place its content in a single location that will provide optimal international visibility at minimum costs, that location will usually be in the United States, *even if the target audience is primarily foreign.* Circuit prices in Europe have begun to plummet even faster than transoceanic circuit prices over the past year as a result of deregulation. As a result, these economics have begun to reverse, and the system is visibly starting to right itself.

In 1999, backbone providers began to offer global Internet access to foreign ISPs from POPs in major overseas markets. The price of these wholesale services is considerably less than that of a comparable transoceanic circuit. These services are likely to lessen the cost disparity between U.S. and foreign ISPs.

14.6 Traffic Statistics

It is natural to want to model traffic flows through the Internet as a whole, particularly when we find that we are not getting the performance that we would like. Unfortunately, at present, very little global data is being captured, and the quality of what exists is uncertain.

The Router Arbiter project developed a number of statistics about the Internet as a whole. Of particular interest were measurements based on a tool called NetNow, which attempted to characterize delay and packet loss through the backbones of various backbone ISPs. The definition of the associated metrics has since been taken up by the *IP performance metrics (IPPM)* activity of the IETF.

A number of other statistics-gathering initiatives are in the pipe. It is not clear that *any* of the existing or emerging studies will generate statistical data that is both valid and useful. Partly, the technical problems are daunting; partly, the decentralized nature of the Internet, as well as the legitimate desire of ISPs to protect their proprietary data, make it difficult to capture useful and meaningful overall statistics.

For the foreseeable future, we will all be working largely in the blind as regards the characteristics of the Internet as a whole. Individual backbone ISPs will, in some instances, have good data about their own networks, and may in some cases be able to draw valid inferences about the Internet as a whole. Nobody, however, will have good, comprehensive data about the system as a whole.

14.7 Internet Access

The typical access to the Internet happens in one of two ways: either dialup access, including ISDN access, as is commonly used by residential consumers, or dedicated access by means of leased lines or Frame Relay. Dialup access is implemented by using terminal servers. For dedicated access, a few additional considerations are worth noting.

The most common dedicated access is implemented over a leased line, as shown in Figure 14-6, using a CSU/DSU and a router or, equivalently, a router with an integrated CSU/DSU.

As a customer, you should carefully consider the placement of this Internet connection. In general, you will want to minimize the cost of access (for instance, a leased line from the LEC) to the provider's facilities. But if you are operating a large Web hosting operation, for example, it is likely to be important to situate the Web servers at a point where your provider has good connectivity to other providers, bearing in mind that most of the traffic is probably destined for customers of other ISPs, since no single ISP has a majority of the market as a whole.

In fact, it is for this reason that you may wish to consider *Web hosting* services, where the provider houses the Web server at the provider's own premises. This enables the Web server to gain very direct access to the ISP's infrastructure, which can be highly advantageous; however, it may also imply more distance from the server to the rest of the customer's facilities. Whether

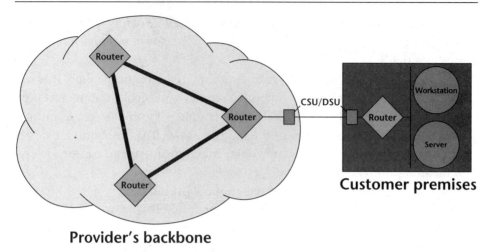

Figure 14-6: A typical dedicated Internet connection.

this is a good thing or not needs to be evaluated carefully in light of the design of the customer's underlying applications.

A single line from the ISP's router to your router can represent a single point of failure. Depending on the nature of your applications, this may or may not be acceptable. There are various alternatives for connecting to your ISP over multiple links or at multiple locations. These may differ from ISP to ISP. Some of these provide good throughput but limited failover capability; others provide good failover but do not provide maximum effective capacity. This is a choice that you would need to make in careful consultation with your ISP.

You may also wish to consider maintaining connections to multiple ISPs. In general, doing so will necessitate that you run BGP-4 exterior routing protocols, a major increase in complexity.

BGP-4 is a very powerful and flexible protocol, but you are nonetheless likely to find that some things become more difficult as a result of using it. Load sharing across multiple links, in particular, can require significant fiddling to get right. Relatively few people in the industry have experience with advanced applications of BGP-4, and many of them already work for ISPs. In general, then, you are likely to want connections to multiple ISPs only after careful consideration of the pros and cons, and only if your organization has a strong skill base in IP routing.

For residential consumers and *Small Office—Home Office (SOHO)* use, dialup Internet access is usually much more cost-effective than leased line access. Many dialup providers offer service at a fixed monthly rate, irrespective of the amount of traffic you generate or the number of hours for which you are connected. There has been a trend over the past few years for some providers to charge for hours beyond some fairly large fixed threshold, largely as a means of discouraging customers from staying continuously connected for the entire month; for those users who never reach the threshold, these services are still effectively flat rate. In the United States, it is often possible to find an ISP that provides service that is within your local calling radius and that is, therefore, free of per minute charges from the LEC under current regulatory policy.

In all cases, when you select a dialup ISP, you should consider how many hours a month you are likely to use the service and whether it provides local access with no per minute charges from the LEC. You would also want to consider the quality of the services provided; however, this will be largely subjective or anecdotal, since there are, in my opinion, no sound, objective publicly available comparative measures of dialup ISP quality. The various surveys of various ISPs are at best suggestive, not definitive.

You should also consider high-speed access alternatives available in the consumer space, particularly if you are a "power user," someone who makes heavy use of the Internet. These high-speed services include ISDN, ADSL, and IP over cable. Make inquiries to determine the actual throughput capacity of each service. For the service to provide several megabits per second of access speed to your home means nothing to you if the service provider's access to the Internet constrains you to a few kilobits per second of actual throughput, as is often the case. Considerations for ISDN are very similar to those for dialup: Local calling radius is important. In all three cases, you would have to contact your cable provider, LEC, or ISP to determine whether service is available to your home or office; even if ADSL coverage is available in your area, your particular line might not be suitable. If the service is available, with ISDN or ADSL, you will generally be free to choose from among several ISPs; with IP over cable, however, you may, under current regulatory policy and cable industry business practice, typically be constrained to use the cable provider's "captive" ISP (RoadRunner for Time Warner, @Home for TCI). Several municipalities and state governments have challenged the cable providers' right to impose these exclusive arrangements, but there is as yet no consumer protection at the national level to ensure freedom of choice of ISP for cable IP customers.

15 Network Management

In designing a network, it is important to keep the operational aspects of the network in mind. The network should be as manageable as possible. Although some people view manageability as something distinct from design, it is more fruitful to think of the manageability aspects of the network as an integral part of the design. A complex and convoluted network architecture will tend to lead to a network that is difficult to manage; conversely, a simple and easily grasped network architecture will tend to lead to a more manageable network. Moreover, specific manageability requirements may preclude some candidate network designs and favor others. For all of these reasons, it is prudent to treat network management as an integral part of the design.

This chapter begins by discussing the protocols and methodologies used to implement network management. We then proceed to explore management requirements, using the TMN model as a framework for analysis. In TMN, we consider operational and management requirements in terms of the following *layers:* business management, service management, network management, and element management. Finally, we consider ways to address specific requirements. The requirements are categorized according to a shorthand developed as part of the OSI standards effort: FCAPS, for fault management, configuration management, accounting, performance management, and security management.

Most wide area internetworks today are managed primarily *in-band;* that is, management requests are carried over the same network as user or customer data. Among carrier and Internet service provider networks, however, there is a growing tendency to deploy a logically or physically distinct *out-of-band* network for management purposes, and this is beginning to spill over into enterprise internetworks as well. In either case, you may wish to augment in-band capabilities with out-of-band access (for instance, via dialup) to at least the most important network devices.

15.1 Network Management versus System Management

Powerful microprocessors are at the heart of most modern communications devices. One might imagine, then, that managing a communications device is not much different from managing any other general-purpose computer system.

For a variety of both practical and historical reasons, the management of networks has evolved somewhat distinctly from that of computer systems. Network devices tend to be implemented with simpler and more limited software support than are general-purpose computer systems. Carriers deploy them in vast quantities; consequently, vendors place great emphasis on standardization of interfaces and on scalability of management capabilities. General-purpose computers tend to offer richer interfaces but, in many cases, provide less standardized means of access. Here, we will first consider the protocols used to interface to network devices, and we will then consider the management of general-purpose computer systems.

15.1.1 Network Management Protocols

One way or another, network management generally entails communication between one or more network management stations *(managers)* and a large number of managed entities, represented by management *agents* that process management requests on their behalf. The managers must report that information to human users, typically through a *graphical user interface (GUI),* a *command line interface,* or both. The information is usually highly structured according to a *structure of management information (SMI),* which helps to regularize the form of the data, much as a schema helps to render the data in a database more useful and intelligible. The collected data will typically be stored in a file or a database for postprocessing, trend analysis, and the like. This flow of information is depicted in Figure 15-1.

In the recent past, all of the associated information flows were handled using vendor-specific or product-specific protocols and techniques. One of the significant advances of the past decade has been the emergence and widespread acceptance and availability of standardized, open protocols and methodologies for these functions. The state of network management today still leaves much to be desired, as we shall see, but it nonetheless represents a vast improvement over what was available just a few years ago.

We will consider, in turn, the major communication protocols used in the network management of internetworks:

- Simple Network Management Protocol (SNMP)
- The OSI network management framework, including CMIS-E and CMIP

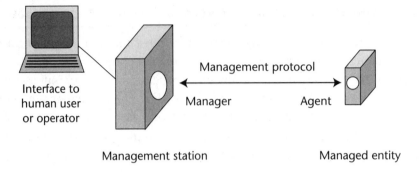

Figure 15-1: Information flows in a network management environment.

■ The Telecommunications Management Network (TMN) framework
■ Conventional networking protocols that can be applied to network management, including TELNET, TFTP, and HTTP.

15.1.1.1 Simple Network Management Protocol (SNMP)

Among standardized network management protocols, perhaps the best known is the *Simple Network Management Protocol (SNMP)*. SNMPv1 is almost universally available among router and terminal server products and is widely available among WAN and LAN switches, CSU/DSUs, and most other components typically used in an internetwork.

SNMP is specified in a series of documents from the Internet Engineering Task Force (IETF). These documents are known as Requests for Comments (RFCs). Many RFCs have the status of standards; however, it is important to remember that not every RFC represents a standard. Some are merely informative. The current standardization status of RFCs is itself available as an RFC.

SNMPv1 is specified primarily in RFC 1157.[1] SNMP's structure of information has evolved over the years, with the latest specifications appearing in RFCS 2578, 2579, and 2580.[2] These documents are also available on the Internet.

---

1. J. Case, M. Fedor, M. Schoffstall, and J. Davin, "A Simple Network Management Protocol (SNMP)," RFC 1157, May 1990.

2. K. McCloghrie, D. Perkins, J. Schoenwalder, J. Case, M. Rose, and S. Waldbusser, "Structure of Management Information Version 2 (SMIv2)," RFC 2578, April 1999; Ibid., "Textual Conventions for SMIv2," RFC 2579, April 1999; and Ibid., "Conformance Statements for SMIv2," RFC 2580, April 1999.

The SNMP SMI establishes a logical tree of object identifiers, or OIDs, a characteristic it shares with the OSI SMI. Groups of interrelated data elements are collected into a *management information base,* or *MIB.*

With SNMP, the manager polls the agent to determine its status. The manager requests one or more elements of information from one or more MIBs in each such *Get* request. The SNMP protocol is, in principle, independent of the underlying data transport mechanism; however, the protocol was designed to operate over the UDP, a connectionless datagram protocol.[3] SNMP does not depend on a reliable, connection-oriented transport, nor would the protocol as designed benefit significantly from running on top of a reliable transport service.

SNMP provides only limited support for the use of unsolicited alarms. In SNMPv1, the only mechanism is an unsolicited and unacknowledged *Trap* from agent to manager. SNMP version 2.0 (SNMPv2) expands marginally on this to include an acknowledged, data-bearing *InformRequest,* but only from manager to agent. Since SNMP typically uses unacknowledged UDP, there is always the possibility that a *Trap* will be lost; consequently, standard industry practice is to depend on the polling mechanism rather than on the unsolicited *Trap* mechanism. The unsolicited alarms are viewed as being at best a "helpful hint" that it's time to poll the device.

The use of UDP provides some scaling advantages, in terms of the number of devices that a single manager can manage; however, it also implies numerous limitations. The largest response to a Get that an agent can safely make is 484 octets of UDP data; thus, for an SNMP 1 agent to return a large table, the manager must make a great many requests. It is, for the most part, a "stop and wait" protocol. This has numerous performance implications. Moreover, there is no way to ensure time synchronization among the various requests and responses, so the manager has no way of knowing whether the table is in a consistent state. (It may have changed between the first response and the second.)

These design choices made sense, from the perspective of the original SNMP design goals. The protocol is optimized to deal with networks that are operating on the ragged edge of catastrophic failure. That was a useful characteristic and is arguably still a useful capability; however, one might hope that we might eventually see a migration toward more flexible and capable

---

3. SNMPv2 Working Group, J. Case, K. McCloghrie, M. Rose, and S. Waldbusser, "Transport Mappings for Version 2 of the Simple Network Management Protocol (SNMPv2)," RFC 1906, January 1996.

management protocols that also function efficiently when the network is working correctly.

SNMPv1 suffers from extremely limited security capabilities. The only authentication and authorization mechanism is associated with a *community name string*—in essence, a clear-text password associated with each SNMP request. Regrettably, in today's Internet, the network designer has to start from the assumption that any transmission can potentially be "sniffed," or intercepted by third parties. Thus, a multiple-use password provides no meaningful protection.

A few years ago, the Network Management Working Group (WG) of the IETF attempted to revise SNMP to produce a secure SNMPv2. For reasons too numerous to catalog here, the effort bogged down. The WG ultimately produced an SNMPv2 with security features that were watered down to the point where it offered no compelling advantages in comparison with the popular SNMPv1. Consequently, SNMPv2 has seen little deployment, particularly in managers, and the widely deployed SNMPv1 continues to suffer from an abysmal lack of security.

More recently, the IETF has published a series of RFCs that collectively represent SNMP Version 3 (SNMPv3). RFC 2570[4] provides an introduction to SNMPv3, and also contains pointers to the remaining SNMPv3 documents. SNMPv3 offers the protocol and SMI enhancements of SNMPv2, including 64-bit counters, GetBulk and Inform, and augments these capabilities with a security framework that provides source authentication, data integrity, protection against replay attacks, and optional data confidentiality.

SNMPv3 appears to represent a significant step forward for the industry, and vendor acceptance is promising. Hopefully, enough users will deploy SNMPv3 to provide critical mass in the marketplace.

SNMP supports the *Set* request in addition to the Get request. One might imagine that SNMP could be used to control network devices, not just to monitor them; however, in light of the absence of meaningful security in SNMPv1, very few organizations have been willing to make significant use of the Set request. If SNMPv3 achieves widespread acceptance, we might see greater use of the SNMP Set.

Compared to all that came before, SNMPv1 has been an enormous success, providing a simple and standardized means of monitoring network devices for faults. Unfortunately, SNMPv1 has been of limited utility for most

4. J. Case, R. Mundy, D. Partain, and B. Stewart, "Introduction to Version 3 of the Internet-standard Network Management Framework," RFC 2570, April 1999.

other network management functions. SNMPv3 significantly expands on the capabilities of SNMPv1, and may possibly take on a somewhat broader network management role over time.

15.1.1.2 OSI Network Management Framework

Over a period of many years, the *International Standards Organization (ISO)* and the *International Telecommunications Union (ITU)*, the preeminent bodies associated with telecommunications standards, jointly developed a series of standard, open protocols for communications known as *Open Systems Interconnection,* or *OSI.* Many aspects of their work are now passé, but others live on or have been assimilated into the products and services that now dominate the internetworking marketplace.

OSI includes a comprehensive model for network management, much of which was assimilated in simplified form into the SNMP model of network management. Indeed, SNMP was initially envisioned, by some at least, as a kind of "pidgin OSI" network management protocol that would serve as an interim network management solution until OSI management was sufficiently mature to replace it.

OSI includes a management protocol, the *Common Management Information Protocol (CMIP),* which is somewhat more complex than SNMP, as well as a service definition (almost a programmatic interface definition), the *Common Management Information Services (CMIS).* CMIS also includes an SMI, which is more complex and substantially richer than that of SNMP. The more recent, enhanced version of CMIS is referred to as CMIS-E. CMIP and CMIS-E are specified in a series of ISO and CCITT specifications. For CMIP, the relevant document is ISO 9596: "Information Processing Systems—Open Systems Interconnection—Common Management Information Protocol," International Organization for Standardization, International Standard 9596, 1991; for the OSI structure of management information (MIM), the relevant specifications are ISO/IEC 10165-1, Information Technology—Open Systems Interconnection—Structure of Management Information—Part 1: Management Information Model, 1991; ISO/IEC 10165-2, Information Technology—Open Systems Interconnection—Structure of Management Information—Part 2: Definition of Management Information, 1992; and ISO/IEC 10165-4, Information Technology—Open Systems Interconnection— Structure of Management Information—Part 4: Guidelines for the Definition of Managed Objectives, 1991.

The OSI SMI was intended to permit truly object-oriented specification of management objects. This is in sharp distinction to the SNMP SMI, which contains—due to its intended interoperability with OSI management—many of the trappings of object orientation but none of the substance. Thus, the OSI SMI places great emphasis on facilitating *inheritance* of characteristics from one managed object to another. The OSI SMI also permits the definition of objects that are aggregates of simpler objects.

Like SNMP, the OSI SMI uses OIDs and, by default, encoding based on Abstract Syntax Notation (ASN.1),[5] another OSI standard. The SNMP and OSI representations of management information *are not equivalent*; however, considerable work has been done by the Joint Interoperability Task Force of Xopen and the NM Forum, culminating in recommendations (ISO/CCITT and Internet Management Coexistence (IIMC): Translation of Internet MIBs to ISO/CCITT GDMO MIBs, Draft 3, August 1993; and ISO/CCITT and Internet Management Coexistence (IIMC): Translation of ISO/CCITT GDMO MIBs to Internet MIBs, Draft 3, August 1993) that provide guidelines for converting between SNMP MIBs and OSI managed object specifications. The IIMC guidelines also deal with translation to and from object-oriented definitions suitable for use by the *Common Object Request Broker Architecture (CORBA),* which will be discussed later in this chapter. In translating into the OSI MIM from SNMP MIBs, the process can be nearly automatic; translating from the OSI MIM to SNMP MIBs, however, is more complex.[6]

CMIP is, in some sense, similar to SNMP; however, CMIP semantics enable the user to request a Get or a Set of an aggregate object, optionally with selection criteria applied. CMIP assumes an underlying connection-oriented OSI transport mechanism, which results in performance strengths and weaknesses that are, in many respects, the mirror image of those of SNMP. Management workstations tend to be limited in the number of connections that can simultaneously be maintained. Transmission will tend to be safe and efficient once established but could be problematic in a badly degraded environment. If a link were dropping, say, 20 percent of all packets

5. "Information Processing Systems—Open Systems Interconnection—Specification of Abstract Syntax Notation One (ASN.1)," International Organization for Standardization, International Standard 8824, December 1987.

6. Subrata Mazumdar, "Translation of SNMPv2 MIB Specification into CORBA-IDL: A Report of the Joint XOpen/NM Forum Inter-Domain Taskforce," July 1993; and Tom Rutt, "Comparison of the OSI Management, OMG and Internet Management Object Models: A Report of the Joint XOpen/NM Forum Inter-Domain Management Task Force," March 1994.

attempting to flow across it—which *has* happened on occasion at choke points in the public Internet, even though we try to avoid it—it is likely that the transport connection would break down, with the result that we would lose visibility into network devices on the far side of the degraded link.

For most readers, CMIP is of historical interest only. It continues to be used for certain telco switches but is rarely seen on the devices that you would be likely to use in an enterprise network.

15.1.1.3 The Telecommunications Management Network (TMN) Framework

The Telecommunications Management Network (TMN) is another ITU initiative that builds on the OSI management framework. We have seen that the OSI management protocols have, for the most part, failed to achieve critical mass in the marketplace. TMN, however, has immediate value as a framework for discussion, much as the OSI Reference Model is a convenient way to think about networks, even though many of the detailed protocols associated with OSI have become irrelevant. TMN takes a telco's business—and the network operational processes on which it rests—and characterizes them as comprising four layers.

Element Management Layer (EML). This is the lowest level, the level at which you manage individual network elements or devices. SNMP operates at the EML; when you poll a device to determine whether it is capable of responding, that is an EML process. Configuration management for individual devices is an EML process.

Network Management Layer (NML). This is the level at which you manage the operation of the network as a whole. Often, an NML activity entails many EML actions. For example, if a network device fails, we may see many distinct alarms. We use either automated or human diagnostic intelligence to recognize that there is a single root cause for multiple symptoms and to initiate appropriate remedial action. Similarly, if we wish to establish an end-to-end PVC through a Frame Relay network, we must alter the state of each switch along its path.

Service Management Layer (SML). This is the level at which the carrier manages service to the customer. Taking the customer's order, provisioning service to the customer in response to the order, responding to the customer's questions and problems (customer care), and customer billing all happen at this level. If you are designing an enterprise internetwork, you may not be conscious of a distinct SML, but it is there—it's just that your customers are internal.

Business Management Layer (BML). This is the level at which business planning occurs, including contract issues, legal and regulatory issues, capacity planning, and planning for service offerings. In general, these processes are not amenable to complete automation, but automated tools provide important and indispensable support to human decision makers.

15.1.1.4 TELNET, TFTP, and HTTP

A wag once remarked that the real network management protocol of the Internet is not SNMP; it is TELNET![7] There is more truth to this than most of us would like to admit. In many networks, engineers and network operators routinely log on to routers across the network, using the TELNET remote log-on protocol in order to determine their status and, possibly, to alter their configuration. In general, SNMP is not used to alter router configurations, because of its security limitations.

Since TELNET is based on connection-oriented TCP, it was at one time felt to be more secure than the UDP-based SNMP. Today, this position is not sustainable. Conventional TELNET, with a multiple-use password, is vulnerable to snooping. There are, however, numerous security-enhanced TELNET variants, each with its own pros and cons, that are preferable to raw TELNET.

Most routers support the use of the Trivial File Transfer Protocol (TFTP) to download configuration data. This can be preferable to the use of TELNET as a means of changing the configuration of a network device, because you can keep a copy of the configuration online and can download it again if something goes wrong. With TELNET, it is easy to lose track of the current state of a router as one operator after another fiddles with it.

TFTP is a simple, UDP-based stop-and-wait file transfer. This is inefficient in terms of time and network bandwidth in comparison with TCP-based FTP, but it is easy to support in the limited software environment of a router and is sufficient for simple downloads and uploads. As with TELNET, you must attend to potential security exposures. In fact, it can be a good practice, from a security perspective, to disable TFTP altogether until and unless it is needed.

HTTP, the protocol of the World Wide Web, is emerging as an important network management mechanism. It is increasingly common for the managed

---

7. Informal communication, John Day.

device itself—or an element management system associated with it—to provide a Web-based GUI by means of which an operator can interact directly with the managed device. This has a number of attractive features, including complete platform independence; the operator could be using a Windows system, a Macintosh, or a UNIX system, as long as he or she has a browser with suitable capabilities. And this approach could potentially also benefit from the various security features that are rapidly emerging for Web-based applications. As a result of the increased use of Web-based management, the Java programming language is becoming increasingly significant as a network management application development tool.

15.1.2 System Management

As previously noted, standardization in system management has been less successful than in network management. A few years ago, the *Open Software Foundation (OSF)* attempted to drive a comprehensive standardization of the entire system management space, along with complete integration with network management. The OSF attempted to produce a *Distributed Management Environment (DME)*, but this proved to be too ambitious an undertaking, and the effort failed.[8] The OSF ultimately released a very limited DME that represented an incremental advance over the then current state of the art in network management capability but failed to achieve the fully integrated system management solution that OSF had initially sought. Nonetheless, many of the underlying concepts of the DME were sound and have gradually been incorporated into other solutions.

The DME attempted to use a fully object-oriented approach to systems management. The DME was to follow the *Common Object Request Broker Architecture (CORBA)*[9] overall. Management information would be described in object-oriented terms, using a descriptive language, I4DL. The preexisting OSF Distributed Communications Environment (DCE) would provide underlying capabilities for distributing the management environment and for enabling communications among managed and managing systems.

Today, many ad hoc system management solutions use some combination of the OSF DCE and of other object-oriented techniques. The Tivoli management platform, for instance, is based on CORBA.

---

8. J. Scott Marcus, "Icaros, Alice and the OSF DME," Proceedings of the Fourth International Symposium on Integrated Network Management (ISINM), Santa Barbara, Calif., 1994.

9. Object Management Group, "The Common Object Request Broker: Architecture and Specification," OMG Document Number 91.12.1, December 1991.

The integration of network management and system management remains elusive. Indeed, one might wonder whether it is really as important as the industry once imagined it to be. In my experience, networks and systems are operated by different people, not only because different management tools are used but also because the knowledge and skills required to manage them tend to be significantly different. It may well be that there are no economies of scale in combining them until the underlying components have grown to look more alike than is the case today.

15.2 Operational Tasks

At this point, we should have a good understanding of the tool bag that we, as network designers, have available to us. How do we apply those tools to the tasks at hand? An awful lot goes into managing a network! We cannot hope to cover every aspect of managing your network, but we can provide some ideas and guidance for the more common tasks.

We will consider tasks, using the well-established FCAPS taxonomy developed as part of the OSI network management standardization process: fault management, or management of failures; configuration management; accounting; performance management; and security management. We will, where useful, further categorize these functions by TMN layers.

15.2.1 Fault Management

Fault management consists of the diagnosis and remediation of problems within the network. At the element management layer (EML), our basic tool for fault management is SNMP. Network management platforms, such as HP OpenView and Cabletron Spectrum, can display a topological map of our network and can alter the salience, such as color, of nodes or links to denote whether a given component is operational. For a network of modest size, this may be all that is necessary. A highly trained network operator can query components and interpret the observed symptoms to diagnose failures and will take action when necessary to dispatch field service personnel or to otherwise correct any problems.

In a larger network, we would generally prefer to use automated tools that can provide a Network Management Layer (NML) view. In a large network, it may be difficult for a human operator to understand the complex interrelationships among visible symptoms in order to grasp the underlying root cause. There may simply be too many events to deal with, particularly when a man-made or natural disaster strikes. And it may be difficult to recruit and retain a sufficient number of highly skilled human operators.

Carriers tend to make significant investments in custom-tailored systems to do just this. Typically, such a system will apply artificial intelligence techniques to winnow down the number of alarms presented to the operator and to correlate interrelated failure events. For the large enterprise network, a few systems of this type are available off the shelf, but they are generally complex to deploy and to customize.

15.2.2 Configuration Management

As previously noted, it is generally a bad practice to allow all of your operators and engineers to log on to routers and other network devices in order to alter their configuration as they will. You lose track of what the configuration of any particular piece of gear is at any given time. This loss of control can greatly complicate subsequent problem diagnosis. It also represents a potential security exposure. (You are, for example, potentially vulnerable to a disgruntled employee, and you may not have an audit trail of what he or she has done.)

In many cases, a better approach is to maintain the configuration of all devices in a centralized location—or, rather, two independent locations, to provide redundancy—and then to download the configuration when needed. Many organizations view this as a database problem. In many cases, it would be attractive to automatically generate configurations based on a database of circuits and their connectivity. You will generally need such a database, anyway, in order to make sense of accounting information, performance data, and the like, and potentially also to drive your fault management systems.

In recent years, tools have begun to emerge that attempt to automatically validate configurations. Cisco's NetSys is a particularly interesting example: It interprets multiple Cisco router configurations, looks for errors, and cross-checks them against one another for inconsistencies. This is another example of a tool that consolidates EML data from multiple network elements in order to generate a Network Management Layer (NML) view.

A special case of configuration management comes into play for the provisioning of new service. More broadly, we should consider adds, changes, and deletions of service. Each of these activities will be associated with numerous automated processes. In some cases, there may be manual processes as well, including on-site work by field service personnel. In each case, it is vital that you understand the business and operational processes involved and establish data models that adequately and appropriately represent what is going on.

15.2.3 Accounting

Accounting is the activity that enables billing. If you are a telco or any kind of commercial services provider, accounting is your life's blood! For an enterprise internetwork, accounting takes on a different yet nonetheless important flavor.

Switches tend to be good at accounting for traffic across virtual circuits. Internetworking devices, however, tend to be problematic. In general, you can get good statistics—not great ones—about the amount of traffic across a given router interface. It can be exceedingly difficult, however, to get information as to which traffic is going where, which is essential to the creation of a *traffic matrix*.

Current routers may provide raw data that captures end-to-end source/destination accounting information, but this data can be difficult to capture and to analyze. First, generation of the data is expensive in terms of the router's processing power. Second, the tables needed to store such data rapidly grow to be impracticably large. This, in turn, means that you need to frequently dump the data from your routers to a server in order to avoid running out of room for the table. Those frequent dumping operations generate more traffic on the network and still more load on the routers.

A complete traffic matrix could be very attractive for billing. As an example, transoceanic bandwidth costs easily an order of magnitude more than domestic fiber-optic bandwidth within the United States. Internet providers would like to bill you more for sending your data across the ocean. Indeed, one factor in the popularity of the first wave of (low-quality) Internet telephony has been billing distortions caused by the inability of Internet providers to properly reflect their transoceanic circuit costs in their charges.

Over time, it may become easier to get more granular accounting. Cisco's NetFlow offers the prospect of better accounting. Tag switching and other forms of Multi-Protocol Label Switching (MPLS) protocols (protocols that integrate levels 2 and 3 processing) all potentially offer the prospect of better and more granular accounting. However, it will take some time for these approaches to mature to the point where they are realistically deployable in large internetworks.

For all of these reasons, current practice among Internet service providers is to apply usage-based charges—if they are applied at all—only on the total volume of traffic to a customer's location rather than to selectively apply charges based on which traffic is going where. For dialup users, if charges are usage-based at all, they tend to reflect only the total duration of all sessions over the course of the month, not the traffic generated during those sessions. Some terminal servers provide product-specific accounting information of this type. My preference is instead to use information based on RADIUS.

RADIUS is a protocol whereby the terminal server queries an authentication server to validate that the user who wishes to log on is legitimate. The server answers yea or nay, based perhaps not only on whether the user ID and password were valid but also on whether the user in question has been paying his or her bills. Thus, RADIUS provides both *authentication* (verification that the user is who he or she claims to be) and *authorization* (verification that the user is entitled to use the basic service).

Many terminal servers also support optional extensions to the RADIUS protocol to provide *accounting* as well. The initial RADIUS protocol exchange happens at the beginning of a dialup session and authenticates the user, which is critical from a billing perspective. If we simply add a subsequent exchange at the end of the session, we have all the information that we need for session accounting. We just need to pair session-end messages with session-initiation messages to compute duration.

15.2.4 Performance Management

Many of the same statistics used for accounting can also be used for performance management, but they tend to be used in somewhat different ways.

Performance management has many practical aspects. Operations personnel may be interested in understanding what is happening *right now* with a given piece of equipment. This is an EML function that is largely a matter for a normal SNMP poller.

Network engineering personnel may be interested in somewhat longer-term performance or in understanding a more aggregated and accumulated view of what is happening with the network. They may want an NML view rather than an EML view. Often, this requires a more integrated view of the network, including a database of the network's topology.

Things get even more complex as we move to the BML level. To plan and to budget for growth over the coming year, we need a much more sophisticated level of understanding of the network. We need to trend both usage and capacity over long periods of time: weeks, months, or even years. We need to understand not only the topology of the network today but also what it was in the past when we took last week's measurements. This typically requires databases that integrate topology information with usage data and, ideally, with circuit cost data.

15.2.5 Security Management

How you approach security management will depend, to a considerable degree, on what services you offer, but we can draw a number of generalizations. The broader topic of security in general was covered at greater length in Chapter 13.

First, do not overlook the basics. The physical security of network components is paramount. Most devices implicitly trust anybody who has physical access to their dialup ports. Make sure that you know who potentially has access to your facilities, and make sure that you maintain a secure audit trail of each actual entry and exit.

If you use in-band management, consider carefully your exposure to users or customers. If you use out-of-band management, consider the risk of infiltration of the out-of-band network by outsiders. If you use dialup out-of-band management, consider the risk that an intruder will dial the number. (The mere fact that the number is unpublished—*security by obscurity*—does not provide sufficient protection.)

In all cases, consider carefully your exposure to the barbarians who may already be *inside the gates*. Over the life of your network, you may hire a hacker or two. How exposed are you?

A great deal has been written about selection of secure passwords for UNIX systems. Read it! It is equally applicable to router passwords. By all means, do not leave equipment configured with the passwords that the vendor assigned at the factory. Select meaningful passwords, and change them periodically. Better, avoid multiple-use passwords altogether and use instead a more secure scheme, such as challenge-response.

In general, firewalls and other security-oriented systems should offer as few unrelated services as possible, in order to minimize the risk of providing a foothold to a hacker.

15.3 Network Management in Perspective

As we have seen, numerous tools are available to the network designer today, but a dearth of comprehensive, fully integrated solutions exists. Why should this be? I like to think that we learn more from our failures than from our successes. If this were really true, designers of management systems should be extremely wise by now! Arguably, this is not the case. If we were to drive down the highway of integrated management system development, we would see that both sides of the road are littered with wrecks! The people who build these systems are not stupid. Why are there so few success stories?

To my mind, the high probability of failure largely reflects the fact that management of networked systems is a fundamentally difficult problem. And it is difficult in more than one way. This is not purely a technology challenge.

Management systems must, in some sense, mirror the operational processes they support. In the nature of things, two businesses will tend to evolve two sets of processes. Thus, building a completely general management platform to handle all conceivable organizations is a combinatorially intractable problem: You would have to accommodate too many different processes in too many combinations. Any successful system will limit itself to a tractably small number of combinations. Any system that overreaches, that tries to do too much, is destined to fail.

Validation of the Design against the Requirements

If you have followed the guidelines provided in the previous chapters, your network should, ideally, meet the full range of requirements. But is it, in fact, capable of doing everything that you intended? Does it fall short in some area, perhaps because of complex interdependencies in the design? Conversely, have you inadvertently "gold plated" other portions of the design, adding needless cost?

This chapter describes quantitative techniques that can be applied to validate the design when it is already at an advanced state, and also to tune it. Some of these techniques may also be useful earlier in the design process.

This chapter provides an overview of the basics of queuing theory and related mathematics. Queuing theory is a large subject, worthy of a textbook in its own right. My objective is not to make you an expert in queuing theory but rather to provide you with a basic understanding of the material and with insight into how internetworks react to load. In addition, this material should enable you to do simple analyses on your own, to interact productively with subject matter experts who specialize in network topological design and modeling, and to make productive use of commercial network design tools.

16.1 Performance

When we attempt to characterize system performance, it is generally in comparison to our expectations, whatever they might be.[1] Performance is not an absolute. When we seek to validate performance, we validate it against our objectives.

---

1. H. Kobayashi, *Modeling and Analysis: An Introduction to System Performance Evaluation Methodology* (Reading, Mass.: Addison-Wesley, 1978), pp. 5–6.

Whence came these objectives? No network exists in a vacuum. Our performance objectives are an aspect of the requirements definition process, as described in Chapter 3. They reflect application needs and other business or marketing requirements.

We would like our network to perform as well as possible; however, this objective must be viewed in the context of our other goals. Achieving our performance objectives is likely to be high on our priority list, if not at the top; however, improving greatly beyond that point may be far less interesting and may indeed not warrant the requisite incremental expenditure of money.

16.1.1 Measures of Performance

Typically, we measure the capacity of a data network according to a small number of metrics:

- *Throughput*—the maximum capacity of a link, or an end-to-end path through the network. Throughput is often expressed in *megabits per second (Mbps)*.

- *Delay*—the time it takes a data element to traverse a link or to traverse the entire network. Often, we speak of *round-trip delay,* the time it takes to traverse the network and then to return. As the network grows busy, packet-switching devices, such as routers, are routinely permitted to put packets on a waiting line, or *queue*. If we have designed too little capacity into the network, these queues can get big, and performance suffers. Delay is measured in units of time, such as milliseconds. We may use simple statistical measures, such as the *mean, median,* and *standard deviation* of delay, or we may use *quantiles,* such as the *ninety-fifth percentile*. Occasionally, we will be interested in the entire distribution of delay.

- *Loss*—the network may discard data that it is unable to carry successfully. Thus, there is no certainty that any particular data message will make it all the way through the network. In measuring loss—sometimes referred to as *packet drops*—we are determining whether the network has sufficient capacity to avoid congestion. In an undercapacitized network, packets will queue up until available memory is exceeded, at which point they will typically be dropped. Drops impact performance much more dramatically than queuing, in general, and consequently represent an important measure of the adequacy of a design.

- *Blocking probability*—the likelihood of connection failure. If you use a dialup online service, you are thoroughly familiar with blocking probability.

When you dial your online provider, you expect to hear the cheery sound of the modem on the other end of the line. How likely is it that you will get a busy signal, no answer, or another failure mode? These failures to connect are collectively referred to as the blocking probability, which can be expressed as a probability or percentage, or equivalently as a *P* grade, where *P* = 0.01 corresponds to a blocking probability of 1 percent.

16.1.2 Tools for Evaluating Performance

In general, we use two primary classes of tools to anticipate the performance of a computer network that has not yet been built: *queuing theory* and *discrete event simulation*. In an existing network, by contrast, we would instead typically take actual measurements and then analyze them, using statistical techniques.

Queuing theory is a mathematical discipline associated with the behavior of waiting lines, or queues. If you have ever waited to show your ticket to the agent at the airport, you know something about how queues work. The mathematics of waiting lines at the airport is essentially the same as those that pertain to datagrams passing through a router. As network designers, we benefit from decades of work on the part of the operations research community.

The other family of tools is based on *simulation*, the mathematical representation of a system. In *discrete event simulation*, we build a computerized model of our network, including its routers and links. Queues within our computer represent queues within the routers. The simulation could potentially work much faster than the real system; we need to keep track of how long an event will take, but we do not necessarily need to wait that long.

Each of these tools has its uses. The analytic techniques embodied in queuing theory can produce useful results quickly and provide a great deal of insight about the underlying relationships among the variables. Analytic solutions are available for many of the kinds of systems we care about; however, not all systems of interest have been solved.

Discrete event simulation can produce useful answers about *any* system but requires a fair degree of sophistication. A simulation result is a probabilistic sort of thing: If you run the same simulation multiple times, you will get multiple answers. This is not a problem for a competent analyst, who can develop statistical confidence intervals to ensure that the results are statistically significant. Nonetheless, the result is likely to provide only a crude approximation of how the network will respond to certain stresses. Moreover, the analyst likely has invested a significant amount of time getting there.

I have done a fair bit of discrete event simulation over the years. It can be helpful when you are designing new equipment or software, but, frankly, I have rarely found it useful in connection with network design in the large part. My feeling is that, for most network designers, analytic techniques are simpler, more practical, and sufficient for most needs.

In either case, it is essential that you characterize the system adequately and accurately. For both analytic and simulation models, GIGO (garbage in, garbage out) is the rule of the day. However, you do not have to dive into every minute detail of your network. Most of these details have negligible impact on how the network as a whole will perform. As you gain experience designing networks, you will develop an appreciation for those aspects that dominate the design versus those that are "in the noise," those that can safely be ignored. Concentrate first on getting the big stuff right. *Take the time to understand your network as a system; there is no substitute for understanding!*

This section provides a brief, nonrigorous overview of the basics of queuing theory. You might want to do some simple analyses on your own, with no tools more sophisticated than a spreadsheeting program required. For more complex tasks, you might be better advised to procure a commercial network design package. In that case, the following material will help you to structure your use of the tool correctly and to interpret the results.

16.1.3 Bandwidth

Have you allocated enough bandwidth to meet all requirements? For a network of modest size, particularly for topologies other than partial mesh, you can verify the adequacy of your design in terms of bandwidth with a simple spreadsheet. For more sophisticated applications, a commercial network design tool can be worthwhile.

- Have you allocated enough bandwidth to provide acceptable performance under conditions of normal usage, under the most intense traffic for which your performance commitments are relevant?
- Have you allocated enough bandwidth to provide acceptable performance—usually a more forgiving threshold—under conditions of an expected number of failed components—typically one?

You need to go back to your requirements to determine what your network is required to deliver. Again, performance is relative to expectations. You always want as much performance as possible, but you are not always willing to pay for it.

The adequacy or inadequacy of bandwidth is usually reflected indirectly in your estimates of queuing delay and dropped packets. If capacity is insufficient to carry the anticipated offered load, indefinitely long queues will build up. This queue buildup leads to queuing delays and ultimately to dropped packets, which will generally cause your network to fail to meet its objectives in terms of end-to-end delay.

16.1.4 Queuing Models, Delay, and Latency

As we have seen, queuing theory is one of the most potent arrows in the quiver of the network designer. Queuing theory is a general technique used to analyze waiting lines. For many years, operations researchers and industrial engineers used queuing theory to analyze waiting lines for bank tellers and airline ticket counters, as well as factory assembly lines. More recently, queuing theory has been applied to the performance of computer operating systems. The same methodologies are well suited to the modeling and analysis of packet data as it traverses a data network or an internetwork.

In this section, we consider the basic application of queuing theory to help you understand how to apply these techniques in the more straightforward cases.

Let's start by considering people waiting in line at an airport ticket counter. What are the essential behaviors?

- People enter, or *arrive at,* the waiting line and wait until an agent is available.
- People are *serviced,* perhaps in the order in which they arrived or perhaps according to another queuing discipline.
- People leave, or *exit,* the waiting line.

We will consider these processes in turn.

16.1.4.1 The Arrival Process

People arrive on a waiting line. A number of people (or datagrams) arrive per unit time. We generally use the Greek letter λ (lambda) to denote the number of arrivals per unit time (per hour or per second). Thus, the average inter-arrival time is simply $1/\lambda$.

Many arrival patterns are possible. One is a uniform arrival pattern, with each successive individual entering the line after a fixed interval of time—say, two minutes. This is an appropriate model for many real-world systems.

In computer networks, however, arrival patterns tend to be far more random and bursty. One of the most popular analytical models assumes a totally random arrival pattern, based on a mathematical abstraction known as the *Markov process*. A Markov process possesses the property of *memorylessness*. Knowing the behavior of a memoryless process in the past tells you nothing about how it will behave in the future. Thus, knowing that two people just arrived on the waiting line in the past minute has no influence at all on the probability that yet another person might arrive in the next minute.

Under a uniform arrival pattern, the interarrival times are constant. In a Markovian arrival pattern, the interarrival times are known to be distributed according to the *exponential* distribution, with a mean interarrival time of $1/\lambda$.

16.1.4.2 Under What Conditions Is It Valid to Assume a Markov Process?

The vast majority of theoretical work on queuing models has been based on Markovian arrival processes. For years, practitioners in many disciplines had known that they were getting good results with these models, even when the arrival processes were demonstrably far from Markovian! How could this be? This mystery was explained in the late 1970s, when Buzen and Denning[2] demonstrated that most of the results of classical queuing theory could be derived under far weaker assumptions than had previously been realized.

Nonetheless, the application of these queuing models to internetworks has come under attack in recent years from a somewhat unexpected quarter. A number of researchers demonstrated convincingly that live internetworking applications can generate traffic that is vastly more bursty than a Markovian model would lead us to expect.[3] These researchers claimed that the traffic demonstrated strong characteristics of *self-similarity*, meaning that the arrival rate at a given moment is not independent of what came before or of what is to come after; rather, it possesses a certain momentum—a tendency for high traffic at one instant to be followed by high traffic at the next. This represents an explicit contradiction to the memorylessness of the Markov process.

Self-similar traffic will tend to have significantly worse delay characteristics than the Markovian traffic traditionally assumed by queuing theorists. Many researchers have found self-similarity in Internet traffic; moreover, the research suggests that self-similarity should be observed at all time scales and traffic intensities.

---

2. P. Denning and J. Buzen, "The Operational Analysis of Queueing Network Models," *Computing Surveys*, September 1977.

3. See, for instance, W. Willinger, M. Taqqu, R. Sherman, and D. Wilson, "Self-Similarity Through High Variability: Statistical Analysis of Ethernet LAN Traffic at the Source Level," Proceedings of ACM SigComm, 1995.

This body of emerging theory must be taken seriously; nonetheless, it is not necessary to overreact. The theorists would tell us that self-similarity should apply to all volumes of traffic, both large and small; however, when I examine the distribution of a large aggregate of traffic over the course of time, I frequently find that the distribution is fairly smooth, more nearly consistent with what the classical models would predict.

Self-similarity would lead us to expect arrival patterns with a heavy "tail," and to predict increased delay as a result. Where the traffic is generated by large numbers of independent human users, perhaps the effects are mitigated—in any case, it seems to me that they are not dramatic in practice. Recall, too, that TCP/IP networks tend to be very robust and forgiving. Classical models may not perfectly describe the internetworking environment, but they nonetheless provide useful guidance.

As a practical matter, all that self-similarity means is that you must provide somewhat more "headroom" on your transmission paths than the classical models would otherwise lead you to expect, if you wish to avoid occasional periods when your users are unhappy with the performance of the network. You just need to be a bit more conservative in your planning and to keep a finger on the pulse of your particular network.

16.1.4.3 Markov Processes and the Number of Arrivals in a Given Time Interval

We are sometimes interested in knowing the probability of a given number of arrivals in a particular period of time. How likely is it that more than five people will appear in a single 5-minute period? These probabilities are governed by the *Poisson* distribution. Poisson distributions have important applications in manufacturing quality control: the number of defects per unit time.

Network designers implicitly use the Poisson distribution to estimate the required size for a pool for dialup users, as it can be used to estimate the probability that a given number of users will attempt to dial in over a given period of time. In order to avoid blocking, the number of dialin ports in the dialin pool must exceed the number of calls that must be simultaneously serviced.

The associated computation entails the use of the *Erlang B* formula, which assumes that calls either complete or go away. The Erlang C formula, by contrast, instead assumes that blocked calls queue up.

The probability of failure on completing a call is commonly denoted by a *P* value, where *P* is 1 minus the probability of success. For example, $P = 0.01$

reflects a probability of 0.01, or 1 percent, that call completion will fail, typically with a busy signal.

We express the intensity of traffic in a unit known as the *Erlang*, the product of the number of calls per unit time and the average hold time per call, expressed in the same units of time. Since the Erlang is the product of two numbers, one with a unit of time in the numerator and the other with the same unit of time in the denominator, the units cancel out. As a result, the Erlang is a simple, dimensionless number not associated with any units. It is just a number. You can think of it as a measure of the number of lines that would be needed to service calls in an ideal world in which each call came in at the perfect time.

Note that the number of Erlangs could be the same for a large number of short calls or for a small number of longer calls. If there are 100 calls a minute, with an average duration of 3 minutes, that represents the same number of Erlangs as 10 calls a minute, each held for an average of 30 minutes. It is 300 Erlangs either way. For the Erlang B formula, it makes no difference. All that matters is the product of the two numbers.

Instead of Erlangs, telephone people sometimes express traffic intensity in a unit known as centicall seconds (CCS). A CCS is the number of hundreds of seconds for which a line would be occupied per hour. Since there are 3,600 seconds in an hour, a line carrying 1 CCS of traffic would be busy one thirty-sixth of the time. Thus, there are 36 CCS in an Erlang.

We can use the Erlang B formula (or, equivalently, tables based on it) to determine exactly how many dialup ports we need to achieve a given P value. The Erlang B formula[4] is

$$B(a, n) = \frac{(a^n/n!)}{\sum_{i=0}^{n} (a^i/i!)}$$

where a is the number of Erlangs, n is the number of circuits, and $B(a,n)$ is the probability of blocking for a given number of Erlangs and a given number of circuits. Table 16-1 shows some sample Erlang B values.

Often, we are interested in determining the number of ports required to obtain a given P value for a corresponding number of Erlangs of traffic. We typically see families of curves, as shown in Figure 16-1. Each line represents the mean number of ports needed to achieve the desired P value.

---

4. J. A. Pecar, R. J. O'Connor, and D. A. Garbin, *The McGraw-Hill Telecommunication Handbook* (New York: McGraw-Hill, 1993).

Table 16-1: Probability of Blocking for Sample Erlang B Values

Circuits	Erlangs									
	1	2	4	8	16	32	64	128	256	512
1	0.5000	0.6667	0.8000	0.8889	0.9412	0.9697	0.9846	0.9922	0.9961	0.9981
2	0.2000	0.4000	0.6154	0.7805	0.8828	0.9394	0.9692	0.9845	0.9922	0.9961
4	0.0154	0.0952	0.3107	0.5746	0.7674	0.8791	0.9385	0.9690	0.9844	0.9922
8	0.0000	0.0009	0.0304	0.2356	0.5452	0.7594	0.8771	0.9380	0.9689	0.9844
16	0.0000	0.0000	0.0000	0.0045	0.1753	0.5258	0.7549	0.8761	0.9378	0.9688
32	0.0000	0.0000	0.0000	0.0000	0.0001	0.1286	0.5140	0.7525	0.8756	0.9376
64	0.0000	0.0000	0.0000	0.0000	0.0000	0.0000	0.0934	0.5074	0.7513	0.8753
128	0.0000	0.0000	0.0000	0.0000	0.0000	0.0000	0.0000	0.0673	0.5038	0.7506
256	0.0000	0.0000	0.0000	0.0000	0.0000	0.0000	0.0000	0.0000	0.0482	0.5019
512	0.0000	0.0000	0.0000	0.0000	0.0000	0.0000	0.0000	0.0000	0.0000	0.0344

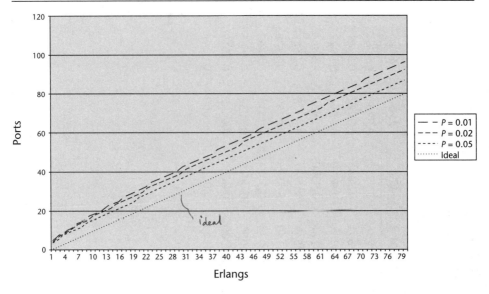

Figure 16-1: A family of Erlang B distributions.

In an impossible, ideal world, we would hope to need exactly one port per Erlang. The dotted black line in Figure 16-1 corresponds to that ideal state. In reality, things can never work out that way. The ratio between the number of Erlangs we are attempting to serve and the *required* number of dialup ports can be viewed as a measure of the efficiency of the system; as it approaches 1.0, we are approaching the ideal. To the extent that it diverges from 1.0, we are obliged to invest in additional ports in order to provide an acceptable *P* value, even though these additional ports may often be idle. Figure 16-2 depicts the ratio between the Erlangs served and the required number of ports.

The ratio of Erlangs per required port can be viewed as a measure of efficiency. It is immediately apparent that the ratio is low when the number of Erlangs served is low and is higher when the number of Erlangs served is high. This is yet another demonstration of the importance of economies of scale: *Large dialup pools are inherently more efficient than small ones.*

16.1.4.4 The Queuing Discipline

We usually think of a waiting line as being governed by the rule of first come, first served (FCFS). If we were waiting at an airline ticket counter, and someone who arrived after we did attempted to be served ahead of us, we would view this as a violation of the queuing discipline for this waiting line. But FCFS is not the only way to manage a queue, and it is not always the best way.

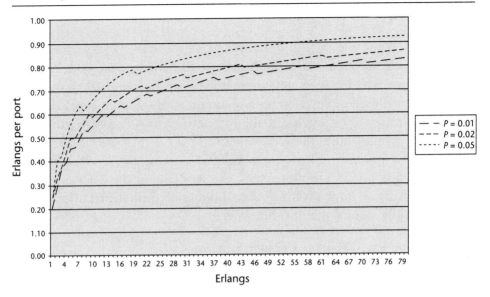

Figure 16-2: Ratio between Erlangs served and required number of ports.

We might choose instead to serve first the last request to arrive: a hallmark of a computer data structure known as a *stack*. We might also choose to process requests in random order.

Such scheduling disciplines have been extensively analyzed over the years, notably in the landmark work *Theory of Scheduling* by Conway, Maxwell, and Miller.[5] They demonstrated that among scheduling disciplines that ignore the expected time to process a given unit of work, FCFS is optimal, under the assumption that the total amount of work to be done is independent of the queuing discipline—that is, that the queue is *work-conserving*—in terms of minimizing expected wait time.

It turns out, however, that it is possible to do better. If you are overloaded with too many things to do, how do you typically respond? Most of us have a natural tendency to want to "clear the decks" by working through a number of short tasks first. Our intuition in that case is well founded: When we schedule first those tasks with shortest expected processing time (SEPT), we are doing what is generally optimal in terms of expected queuing delay among all queuing disciplines for work-conserving queues.

5. R. W. Conway, W. L. Maxwell, and L. W. Miller, *Theory of Scheduling* (Reading, Mass.: Addison-Wesley, 1967).

16.1.4.5 The Service Process

Let's return to our line at the airport. When we get to the head of the queue, we expect to be serviced. The airline ticketing agent assigns our seat. The service takes time. The server would, at full utilization, serve mu (μ) requests per unit time. Each request will thus require, on the average, a time of 1/μ.

These times will follow a distribution pattern. In some real-world systems, every request takes the same amount of time; these service times are said to follow a *uniform distribution*. In other systems, the service process is itself a Markov process; in these cases, the service time distribution will be exponential. If we have no idea what the service time distribution is, we would typically assume that it is Markovian.

16.1.4.6 Characterization of Queuing Systems

We often use a shorthand notation, attributed to Kendall, to describe queuing systems. In this notation, a queuing system is described by three basic attributes:

- the arrival pattern;
- the service pattern; and
- the number of servers operating in parallel.

For the arrival and service patterns, we use a D to denote a deterministic, or uniform, process; an M to denote a Markov process; and a G to denote a general, or undefined and unrestricted process.[6]

Thus, an M/D/1 has a Markovian arrival process, a constant (deterministic) service process, and a single server. An M/M/1 has a Markovian arrival process, a Markovian service process, and a single server. A D/G/2 has a deterministic (constant interarrival time) arrival process, an arbitrary service process, and two servers operating in parallel.

Straightforward, closed-form analytic solutions exist for many simple queuing systems and for many networks consisting of multiple simple queues. We now discuss some of the simplest and most useful analyses of queuing systems.

Analysis of Queuing Systems. One of the most fundamental determinants of the performance of any queueing system is the *utilization*. The utilization is defined simply as ρ, where $\rho = \lambda/\mu$.

---

6. D. G. Kendall, "Stochastic Processes Occurring in the Theory of Queues and Their Analysis by the Method of Imbedded Markov Chains," *Annals of Mathematical Statistics*, 1953.

ρ takes on values between 0.0 and 1.0. It can be thought of as corresponding to the utilization percentage: $\rho = 0.0$ represents 0 percent busy, and $\rho = 1.0$ represents 100 percent busy. In general, it is not meaningful to speak of $\rho > 1.0$, because a system cannot be busy more than 100 percent of the time. (Note, however, that there is a close analogy between ρ and the Erlangs that we discussed earlier. The number of Erlangs can indeed exceed 1.0, in light of the presence of multiple servers. For a dialup pool with a single port, the number of Erlangs of traffic intensity would correspond exactly to ρ, the utilization fraction of the single port.)

Queuing systems are often characterized according to the following quantities:

$\bar{Q}$ The mean number of elements in the queue

$\bar{N}$ The mean number of elements in the queue or in service

$\bar{S}$ The mean time an element spends receiving service

$\bar{W}$ The mean time an element spends on the queue

$\bar{T}$ The mean time an element spends on the queue and receiving service

From the previous definitions, it should be clear that

$$\bar{S} = 1/\mu$$

It is also the case that

$$\bar{N} = \bar{Q} + \rho$$
$$\bar{T} = \bar{W} + \bar{S}$$

Little's Law. One of the broadest and most general results in all of queuing theory is Little's law,[7] which relates the expected size of a queue to the expected wait time. Little established that under an extraordinarily wide range of assumptions,

$$\bar{W} = \lambda \, \bar{Q}$$
$$\bar{T} = \lambda \, \bar{N}$$

Analysis of M/M/1 Queuing Systems. The performance of M/M/1 queuing systems has been extensively analyzed. The average number of customers (or datagrams) in the waiting line is given by

$$\bar{Q} = \rho^2 / (1 - \rho)$$
$$\bar{W} = \rho / [\mu (1 - \rho)]$$

7. Kobayashi, op. cit.

Figure 16-3 shows how queue length and total number of customers (or datagrams) in the system increase as utilization of an M/M/1 queuing system increases. This demonstrates what our intuition already tells us: *The busier the server, the longer we are likely to wait for it.* As the utilization approaches 1.0, or 100 percent, queue length grows without bound, as does expected waiting time.

This analysis also sheds light on the probability of dropped packets. In general, a communications device will allocate buffer memory to hold packets that it is unable to ship over a transmission link. Depending on how a particular device is implemented, it may allocate memory for each link, a memory pool for the device as a whole, or a combination of the two. If the queue length grows to be greater than the number of packets that can be held in memory, the remainder must be dropped. Nothing else can be done with them.

If the system is saturated, it is clear that we will experience significant packet drops. The size of the queues will increase until memory is exhausted, at which point any subsequent attempt to queue more packets will result in packet drops.

In my experience, you are likely to see only modest rates of packet drops when link and processor utilization are less than 90 percent to 95 percent. If the arrival patterns were truly Markovian, you might see far fewer. The self-similarity of traffic corresponds to a greater degree of burstiness than Markovian assumptions would lead us to expect, and this burstiness means

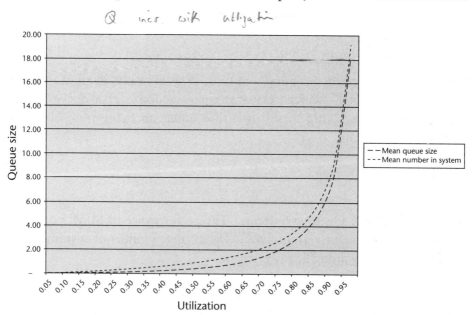

Figure 16-3: Queue size and total customers in the system as a function of utilization.

that the system may tend to become saturated for brief periods of time, even though capacity is adequate in general.

The performance of live internetworking systems tends, unfortunately, to be more complex than the preceding analysis would suggest. If packets are dropped, end-to-end mechanisms at the transport layer (TCP) will recover by retransmitting them, and flow-control mechanisms will be invoked on an end-to-end basis. In effect, there is additional buffering in the end systems at the edges of the network. A number of researchers are studying the performance of these end-to-end flows over the Internet, but we are a long way from having a solid, quantifiable basis for projecting their impact on any particular internetwork.

Analysis of M/G/1 Queuing Systems. As network designers, the arrival pattern is mostly outside of our control; however, the service process is something we can potentially influence, and it is not likely to follow the exponential distribution of service times that we would associate with a Markov process. We can relax the Markovian assumption regarding the service distribution, without sacrificing the ability to analyze the system. The Pollaczek-Khinchine formula[8] relates the utilization of an M/G/1 system to the expected values for such metrics as queue size and wait time, just as the formulae covered in the preceding section relate utilization to expected queue size and wait time for the simpler M/M/1 system.

The Pollaczek-Khinchine formula is

$$\overline{N} = \rho + \frac{\rho^2 \, (1 + C_s^2)}{2 \, (1 - \rho)}$$

Note the presence of the term C_S in this formula. This *coefficient of variation* of the service time distribution is defined as the standard deviation of service time, divided by the mean.

You can think of the coefficient of variation as a normalized measure of the variability of a distribution. If the distribution is a single constant, with no variability, the coefficient of variation is 0. For an exponential distribution, it is exactly equal to 1, which is to say that the mean and the standard deviation of an exponential distribution are equal to each other. A very bursty distribution will tend to have a coefficient of variation that is greater than unity.

If you substitute a value of 0 into the coefficient of variation in the Pollaczek-Khinchine formula, you will see that it becomes equivalent to the

8. H. Kobayashi, *Modeling and Analysis,* op. cit.

formula for an M/D/1, just as you would expect. If you substitute a value of 1.0, it becomes equivalent to the formula for an M/M/1. Again, this is just as we should expect: The M/D/1 and the M/M/1 can both be viewed as special, or degenerate, cases of the more general M/G/1 queuing system.

Figure 16-4 shows a family of M/G/1 curves, relating utilization to wait time. Each curve corresponds to a different coefficient of variation of service time. The data is based on expected queuing delays for a router or switch interface driving a T-3 (45Mbps) circuit. The service in this case is simply the time to "clock" the data onto the circuit, at 45Mbps; thus, the service time is a linear function of the datagram lengths. Once again, the case where $C_S = 0$ corresponds to an M/D/1 queuing model, that with $C_S = 1$ to an M/M/1 system. The cases with $C_S = 1.1$ or 1.2 accord closely to actual datagram lengths on the public Internet: largely a bimodal distribution of datagrams of minimum length versus 576 octets, with an increasing number of datagrams at an Ethernet frame size of 1,500 octets. Higher values represent traffic with datagram lengths that are scattered even more widely than that.

16.1.5 Propagation Delay

In any network, signals take finite time to propagate from one point to another. In a LAN, we often ignore this component, but it can be quite significant in a WAN. In fact, for networks operating at high speeds (above T-3,

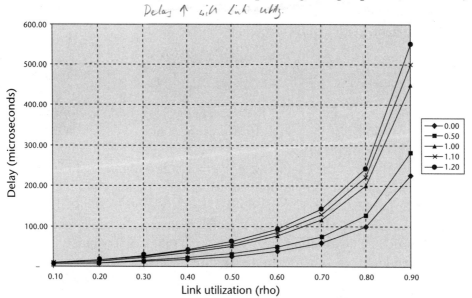

Figure 16-4: An M/G/1 queuing model. Distribution of total time (wait plus service) as a function of utilization and the coefficient of variation of service time.

or 45Mbps) and with distances of hundreds of miles, propagation will generally be the dominant component of network delay.

We tend not to think much about propagation delay. A customer once called me with a complaint. He had been measuring the round-trip between his data center in St. Louis, Missouri, and a router located in the same city. The response took just a millisecond or two. When he measured round-trip delay to one of our routers, located in the San Francisco Bay area, he found a round-trip time of some 35 milliseconds. He politely suggested that perhaps there was a problem with our router. As our colleagues at NASA like to say: *186,282 miles per second: It's not just a good idea, it's the law!*

When it comes to the speed of light, there is no way to "beat the house." It is simply going to take time to move the data from here to there.

It is easy to estimate propagation, but it can be difficult to compute it rigorously. The speed of light in fiber optics is somewhat lower than in a vacuum, and the speed of propagating a signal through copper is slower still. A trickier problem has to do with the length of the path: fiber-optic cables do not follow a straight line through mountains, over valleys, and under the ocean! Moreover, as a user of a carrier's circuit, you are not in a position to know how the circuit will be routed, nor will you necessarily be informed if that routing changes as a result of routine "grooming" of circuits on the part of your carrier.

As a rule of thumb, I generally estimate the effective speed of light as being about 0.5 C, or 93,000 miles per second, based on standard V&H mileage (as defined earlier in Chapter 2). In round numbers, think of it as 100 miles per millisecond. This corresponds to an expected round-trip time—based solely on propagation delay and ignoring any queuing delays—of about 70 milliseconds from coast to coast across the United States, which accords well with practice.

The fiber-optic path from St. Louis to San Francisco is likely to be somewhere between 1,500 and 2,000 miles. Multiply this by 2 to reflect the trips to and from the West Coast, and we should expect a round-trip delay of somewhere between 30 and 40 milliseconds. My customer's observation of 35 milliseconds was just where we should expect it to be.

If you need a better estimate of propagation delay, it may be preferable to measure it rather than to estimate it. Propagation delay should be constant, not variable; thus, if you take several measurements of round-trip delay (by using a tool called *ping,* for instance), the lowest result sets an effective upper bound on your propagation delay. You will want to do this over a single dedicated circuit, with no intervening routers or switches, if possible, in order to measure just the propagation through the circuit.

For still greater accuracy, take similar measurements to a device, such as a router, that is close at hand, just as my customer did with the router in St. Louis. Take the lowest result from that measurement as an estimate of constant delays not attributable to propagation delay, and subtract it from the measured delay to the distant router. This is about as good an estimate as you are likely to get.

16.2 Verification of Functionality

It would be nice to verify that the design carries all of the required protocols correctly, from a functional perspective, before the network has been deployed. Unfortunately, no general methodology will ensure in all cases that this is so. A few things, however, can help: independent review of the design, laboratory testing, and pilot deployments.

The *independent review* can be a key step. You want a fastidious scrub by people who are as competent as those who did the original design but who are not personally invested in your work. In terms of temperament, you generally do not want reviewers so caustic that they are unable to work with the design team or those who are too agreeable. Ideally, you want people who are objective and who can calmly and unemotionally present the unvarnished truth, as they see it, to the design team.

It can smooth the process considerably if the reviewers are people who already enjoy the respect of the design team. There are any number of reasons why some first-rate people might not have participated in the design team itself, including insufficient available time. These folks can be a valuable resource for the independent review. If you don't have people of sufficient stature within the organization, other than those who were already on the team, consider bringing in one or more knowledgeable outside consultants as reviewers.

Laboratory testing is a more complex issue. Testing prior to deployment is clearly a good thing to do; however, the chances are that you will not find all of the failure modes until you test under something approaching live conditions.

Pilot deployments can be particularly valuable. They represent a more forgiving environment than full-scale production yet still allow you to test what you are doing in a realistic environment, under real-world stresses. The pilot also has the potential to stress network management and other operational support systems, such as provisioning and customer care, in a way that laboratory testing generally cannot.

Among these options, the cost of correcting errors increases as you work your way down the list. The independent review is the cheapest and should be done first. The lab is the next most expensive and should therefore be done second. The pilot deployment is the most expensive of the three and should be done last; however, it is still cheaper to correct problems during the pilot deployment than it will be later, when the system is in live production.

16.3 Security

Validating the security design of your internetwork is among the most thankless tasks imaginable. In most cases, if your design works brilliantly, nobody will pat you on the back, because nobody will notice. If the design fails, you stand a greater chance of attracting notice—but perhaps not the kind of attention you want.

For the security design, it is particularly important that you undertake an independent review. In this case, you will want the review carried out by people who are subject matter experts in network security, not just in networking in general. At the risk of stating the obvious, you should be scrupulous in screening any consultants you might retain, since you will be exposing your network security design to the reviewers.

One approach that may be of interest derives from the old adage: "Set a thief to catch a thief." In recent years, we have begun to witness the emergence of people who will attempt to hack into your network, for a fee, in order to show you where the weaknesses might be. Again, you would want to assure yourself that you are working with trustworthy folks. I have not tried this approach myself, but it is quite possible that it will become commonplace in the coming years to hire professional, friendly network crackers.

16.4 Availability

Analysis of availability is closely related to that of performance. Commercial tools that model the performance of large networks often model failure probabilities as well.

16.4.1 Availability as a Function of MTBF and MTTR

Availability is usually expressed as a percentage: the time that the network was available for use, divided by the total time when it might have been available. Time used for scheduled maintenance is usually excluded from the numerator and the denominator of this division.

In the case of an internetwork, the definition can be a bit cloudy. In many cases, a service location has a perfectly good connection to a network backbone or an Internet service provider but is unable to reach certain locations of interest. For any given pair of locations, it is easy to state how availability should be defined between the two; however, it is difficult to arrive at a proper definition for all points accessible from a given location, which would be the more meaningful measure.

Returning to the general definition of availability, it is usually computed by using two key underlying quantities:

1. *Mean time between failures (MTBF):* The time, on the average, between successive failures of the component or service in question

2. *Mean time to repair (MTTR):* The time that will elapse, on the average, between the occurrence of a failure and the complete restoration of service

A simple computation of availability, then, is:

$$\text{Availability} = \text{MTBF} / (\text{MTBF} + \text{MTTR})$$

Why does this work? For a single outage, the network is available until it encounters a failure, which happens, on the average, after MTBF hours. The network is then unavailable until MTTR hours later. Thus, the numerator represents available hours, and the denominator represents total hours, just as we would expect.

In designing the network, there is always a temptation to think of availability as being solely a function of your network equipment and topology. In most cases, this is not so! The MTTR plays a key role in the formula; in fact, it defines how long you will be down, so it is largely responsible for the degree to which you are unable to achieve 100 percent availability. MTTR is often a function not of the equipment you choose but rather of the strategies you employ for field service and for deployment of spare parts. You can choose to mitigate the impact of MTTR by deploying a network with a very high degree of redundancy, but in doing so, you will tend to drive up your costs.

16.4.2 Computing Availability for Multiple Components

Computing the availability of a single component is trivial. Computing the availability of an entire network is more difficult. How do we do it?

16.4.2.1 Multiple Components in Series

Where we have multiple components deployed "in series" along a single path, the joint availability is easy to compute. Suppose, for example, that a customer is connected to an ISP with a router, a WAN interface card and a

LAN interface card in the router, a CSU/DSU, a serial line (dedicated circuit) from the phone company, and a CSU/DSU on the far side of the circuit. Reliability is assumed to be perfect from that point forward. This scenario is depicted in Figure 16-5.

In general, your equipment manufacturer can provide MTBF figures for any component. If there is significant field experience with the unit, they can provide figures based on that experience; otherwise, they should provide theoretical estimates, which are usually much more pessimistic. Assume for now that your MTTR is 4 hours for all of your components and that the availability of the dedicated local access circuit is 99.8 percent. Further assume that the probabilities are all mutually independent: A failure of one component does not alter the probability that another will fail. Under these assumptions, if the MTBF for the equipment is as shown in Table 16-2, the availability of each component and of the system as a whole will also be as shown. The service is available only if every component is available. Since the associated probabilities are assumed to be mutually independent, the overall availability is the *product* of the individual availability probabilities.

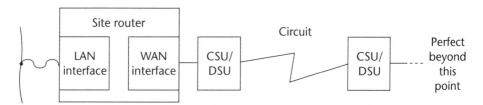

Figure 16-5: Computation of availability with multiple components in series.

Table 16-2: Computation of Availability for Multiple Components in Series

Component	MTBF (yrs)	MTBF (hrs)	MTTR (hrs)	Availability
LAN interface	15	131,400	4	99.997%
Router	20	175,200	4	99.998%
WAN interface	15	131,400	4	99.997%
CSU/DSU	18	157,680	4	99.997%
Circuit		—		99.800%
CSU/DSU	18	157,680	4	99.997%
Overall:				**99.787%**

Note that the dedicated local access circuit has a much lower availability than any of the individual hardware components. This is not a contrived example; that's the way that it usually works out. The overall availability is only slightly worse than the availability of the dedicated circuit. That, too, is no accident: The weakest component usually dominates the failure probabilities, if its availability differs significantly from that of the next weakest component. The strength of the chain is, to a large degree, the strength of the weakest link or links.

16.4.2.2 Multiple Components in Parallel

What happens when there are multiple components in parallel? Consider the case in Figure 16-6. Where we have multiple components deployed "in parallel," the joint availability is more complex to compute. Suppose, for example, that the same customer were connected to an ISP with two circuits in parallel connected to the single router, as shown in Figure 16-6. The single router has two WAN interface cards, each connected to a CSU/DSU, a dedicated circuit, and a CSU/DSU on the far side of the circuit. Assume that the carrier is providing physical diversity for the circuits and that all failure probabilities are thus independent.

In this configuration, the probability of available connectivity from the customer LAN through the router is still the product of the individual availabilities of those two components. We then compute the availability of each of the two paths from that point onward. The probability of availability from the router to the ISP is the probability that *one* of the two paths is available. This means that the combined path is unavailable only if both fail. The combined probability that both fail is the product of the probability that one fails (which is 1 minus its availability), times the probability that the other fails.

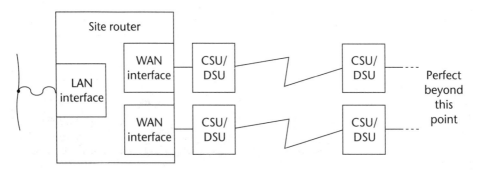

Figure 16-6: Computation of availability with multiple components in parallel.

That product represents unavailability; 1 minus the product represents the availability of the two paths collectively.

All of this sounds much more difficult than it is. In general, if you have two mutually independent paths in parallel and the probability of the former being up is A and that of the latter being up is B, the availability of the two together is simply

$$1 - ((1 - A) * (1 - B))$$

In tabular form, the example works out as shown in Table 16-3. In this case, the combined probability that one of the two paths is available is so close to 100 percent that the difference is masked at the number of decimal places shown in our spreadsheet. This is a substantial improvement from the previous example, where a single circuit provides an overall availability slightly less than its own inherent 99.8 percent availability.

This overall ability of 99.994 percent is much better than the previous example, with its 99.787 percent availability. This demonstrates the value of redundancy in the design; however, as designers, we must balance that advantage against the additional cost of a redundant configuration.

16.4.3   More Complex Analyses

We can iteratively apply the techniques described in the previous section to decompose and then describe a wide range of systems, including some very

Table 16-3: Computation of Availability with Components in Parallel

Component	MTBF (yrs)	MTBF (hrs)	MTTR (hrs)	Availability
LAN interface	15	131,400	4	99.997%
Router	20	175,200	4	99.998%
Combined:				**99.995%**
WAN interface	15	131,400	4	99.997%
CSU/DSU	18	157,680	4	99.997%
Circuit		—		99.800%
CSU/DSC	18	157,680	4	99.997%
Combined:				**99.792%**
Availability of at least one of the two paths:				**100.000%**
Overall:				**99.994%**

complex ones. In many cases, we want to conduct analyses that are more difficult to work through with such simple techniques. For example, suppose that our main router in New York were to fail, such that traffic from Boston to Washington had to route through, say, Chicago. Would we have enough reserve capacity all along the path to carry the load at acceptable levels of performance?

It you are doing a large, sophisticated network design, it is probably worth your while, in any event, to invest in commercial network design tools. We generally think of the primary mission of these tools as being to compute overall delay through the network and perhaps to help us with the placement of circuits. Many of those tools, however, can also help with availability analysis. For example, some tools can iteratively simulate the failure of each node (router) or link (circuit) in the design. In doing so, they compute the performance of the network in this degraded mode.

This analysis can be a very useful way of spotting problems with insufficient reserve capacity in the network design. For a network of any size, that task really requires automated support; it is impractical to do by hand.

The Management
Review Phase

17 Management Review: Financial Analysis

*T**he decision to build out a major network is a business decision, not a technical decision.* At some point in the life of any network design—and usually at many points—it will be necessary to review the design and its underlying assumptions in order to assure ourselves that what we are doing makes sense in the context of our overall organizational goals. Somewhere in our organization, someone is responsible for authorizing the expenditures that will bring this network to fruition.

In most cases, that someone is not us. It may be a senior executive or, more often, a group of executive decision makers. Engineering management may participate in this group, but it is rarely the case that engineering has the unilateral authority to create a major new network. That decision will be viewed, in most cases, as a *business* decision, driven by a concept of profit and loss for the organization as a whole. As such, the review is likely to focus on dollars and cents or their equivalent.

In general, those decision makers are going to need to be reassured that your network represents an appropriate expenditure of the organization's resources. If your organization is a carrier or an Internet service provider, the network may represent a direct revenue opportunity; if not, it may represent a means of expanding your primary business, providing better service to your customers, or driving down costs for your primary business. In all cases, management will want to weigh the benefits against the costs in a hard-headed economic way.

Many readers of this book will be engineers. Engineers have a natural tendency to view this management review process as an intrusion on the engineering function. In reality, however, the review process is a fundamental part of the job, and the questions that flow from this process are questions that we as engineers should be asking ourselves at each stage of the design process.

In most cases, management will review the business case for the network prior to launching the project and again prior to initiation of construction. In essence, the former takes place before the first chapter of this book; the latter, after the last chapter. Management is likely to do this whether you request it or not. It can be particularly valuable, however, to inject a formal management review at the close of the preliminary design phase. At that point, you are likely to be far enough into the design process to have a good understanding of the costs but to still be early enough to be able to readily accommodate midcourse corrections, if necessary. Moreover, you should, if possible, seek a budget allocation at that time; it enables you to proceed to the final design phase with a realistic understanding of what you will be able to spend and thus to adjust the design where necessary.

This management review will consider "soft" factors, but it is likely to be first and foremost an economic analysis. The new or improved network must be perceived as enhancing the organization's position in some way. It may support new services, which generate revenue. It may enable existing services to become more competitive, thus expanding revenue. It may enable the organization to reduce or avoid other costs. In any of these scenarios, there is some net gain to the organization, and this gain is, ideally, quantifiable. There is also a net cost to the organization, which is fairly easy to quantify. If the gain is likely to exceed the cost and if the cost is affordable, implementation of the network is likely to be viewed as a good thing; otherwise, not.

Let me apologize in advance to any readers who may have strong backgrounds in accounting or financial analysis. What follows has been intentionally simplified to make it easily digested by engineers with no formal background in these disciplines. In addition, it was written by an engineer who himself has no formal training in accounting. This material is intended merely to enable an engineer to have a more productive dialogue with a senior executive or a financial manager.

This chapter serves primarily to remind you to consider requesting a financially oriented management review when you get to this point in the design process. In preparing you for the management review process, we provide a few tips and pointers. Then we analyze the cost of a wide area internetwork, in light of usage trends. We also discuss revenue projections and consider cash flow over time. Finally, we arrive at the output of this process: your budget to proceed.

17.1 Cost Categories

At the most basic level, the network can be viewed as comprising the following major elements, in terms of cost: circuits and services, generally provided by carriers; equipment; labor; and facilities (buildings and related paraphernalia). In addition, there may be ancillary costs associated with new services. We will consider each of these cost categories in turn.

17.1.1 Circuits and Services

The cost of circuits and services was discussed at length earlier, but it may be useful to note again the things that are most easily overlooked. First, do not be tempted to focus solely on the obvious charges, such as the IOC mileage charge for inter-LATA private lines, and to neglect subtler, more complex charges, such as cross-connect fees (access connection, access coordination, entrance facility fees, and so on). Second, *do not neglect to consider taxes, especially local taxes!* These fees, which are omnipresent, may not play a critical role in comparing one service to another, but they are real costs that can be very important in understanding whether a particular service is profitable. In the United States, states and localities impose taxes on many telephony services, including dedicated circuits (leased lines). These taxes can vary greatly but generally average about 8 percent across the United States. Do not overlook them: Remember that 8 percent of a big number can yield a big number!

Your circuit costs generally include a one-time, nonrecurring charge for setting up the service or circuit and a monthly fee reflecting your use of the service. For the one-time fee, when you are looking at cash flow analysis, you will be concerned with the date when the fee is incurred or paid; for other forms of analysis, however, it may be more appropriate to spread the cost over the assumed lifetime of the circuit or service. This is a discussion that you will want to have with your financial people.

17.1.2 Equipment

Networking equipment can be purchased or leased. A variety of reasons might make leasing attractive to a particular organization, not least of which is that the lessor is stuck with all of the risk of the equipment's becoming obsolete. J. Paul Getty once remarked that one should own appreciating assets but should lease depreciating ones.

Analyzing the cost of leased equipment is easy: The lease will be associated with a predictable recurring cost and, typically, with some start-up costs. The analysis is not so different from that of a leased line.

In my experience, the vast majority of networking equipment is purchased. Once again, from a cash flow perspective, we would reflect the expenses when they are incurred, but for most other purposes, we would spread the costs across the assumed lifetime of the equipment, a process referred to as *amortization*.

This introduces a thorny problem. What is the useful lifetime of networking equipment? Historically, regulators in the United States held the telephone industry to incredibly long useful lifetimes for telephone switching gear. An assumed lifetime of 30 years would not have been uncommon. Today, a 30-year useful lifetime seems laughable for many data networking components. Core routers can become obsolete after as little as 2 or 3 years.

It is worth your while to put some thought into this. If you pick an unrealistically long lifetime, you will make your near-term financials look good—better, in fact, than they ought to look. The problem is that a day of reckoning is likely to follow. If you amortize equipment over 5 years but end up retiring it in the second year, 80 percent of the cost of that equipment will hit your books in that second year!

17.1.3 Labor

Labor can represent one third or more of your network cost, depending on the nature of the system you are deploying.

- **Engineering:** The design and planning group for a large network will tend to require a significant number of highly skilled—and thus expensive—people.
- **Network operations center (NOC) services:** Monitoring of the network to proactively detect problems and rectify them is an important task. If you are providing full service 24 hours a day, 7 days a week (often written 7 × 24) with your own personnel, you would typically need to continuously staff three shifts despite weekends, holidays, vacations, and sick time. The number of people you need will depend on the size, complexity, and dispersion of your network, but one way or another, you need enough people to provide around-the-clock coverage without burning your folks out.
- **Field service:** Where possible, you may attempt to have your users or customers deal with their own problems, possibly under the guidance of your field service organization. Sometimes, however, it will be necessary to fix equipment on site. That can be time consuming and expensive. You need to consider the mean time to repair (MTTR) that you are attempting

to achieve, and you need to determine how widely dispersed the field service organization might need to be to reach your sites within that time frame and to still have time to fix the unit!

- **Customer care:** How much hand holding do your users require? This can be a very labor-intensive activity.
- **Administration:** You are likely to have a fair number of folks involved in the administrative aspects of adds, deletes, and changes of service and also in accounting and billing.

This labor can be performed by your own employees, or it can be *outsourced,* contracted out to a third party. Outsourcing will generally provide you with greater predictability of costs. Your contractor will charge a handsome fee for this service; however, if the contractor's unit costs are better than yours—due, for example, to greater economies of scale—the net cost to your organization may nonetheless be attractive. Contract labor can also make sense for intermittent or one-time tasks. *You* might not have suitable work for those people when the job is done, but the contracting organization can simply sell their services to the next client. In costing outsourced projects, you should not forget to allocate the labor cost associated with having one or more of your own people properly managing the work done by the contractor.

In computing labor costs for your own employees, you will generally want to reflect these as *burdened* labor costs. This signifies that you are considering not only direct salary of these employees but also the cost of providing benefits, as well as the cost of office space, clerical support, and telephone and other utilities for the employee.

17.1.4 Facilities

You are likely to entail costs not only for rent but also for power to the building, physical security, and for many other things that do not immediately spring to mind as being part of network engineering. If you rent space from a carrier, you might be charged collocation fees. You might maintain a local POTS phone line for the convenience of any field service personnel who must visit a remote networking site. All of these cost money.

17.1.5 Ancillary Costs Associated with New Services

In estimating the benefits of new services, we need to keep in mind that they often introduce new costs beyond those associated with expansion of the network. For example, consider the cost of preparing reports to meet regulatory requirements that you are subject to by virtue of your entry into this new business. Where do those costs appear in your budget? We must be sure either to explicitly reflect all costs or else, equivalently, to consider incremental revenues net of those costs.

17.2 Expenses over Time

Networks grow, change, and evolve over time. Despite a temptation to price the network out as it might exist at a single point in time, any meaningful financial representation of the network must reflect not just a snapshot of the network but rather a continuum over time. The fundamental driver of this model is a projection of load as it is likely to vary over time. A key component of this forecast is generally driven by your marketing organization or, in the case of an internal network, by an organization responsible for forecasting internal usage. For an existing network, you will also have information reflecting historical trends in utilization.

In an ideal world, the forecasters would have already taken current trends into account, but this is not always the case in the real world. Thus, I have always found it useful to compare marketing forecasts to trend lines extrapolated from current data, in order to ensure that the variance between the two is adequately accounted for by new services and by other phenomena that would not yet be visible in trend lines based on measured data.

Consider, for example, Figure 17-1. We have taken the observed total bandwidth demands and have fitted an exponential growth curve to them, extrapolating that curve into the near future. Exponential growth corresponds to "compound interest": growth at a particular predictable percentage rate per unit time. Many networks exhibit exponential growth over time. The Internet grew exponentially at about 100 percent per year, by most measures, from the time of its creation in 1969 until about 1995, when the pace accelerated. For our example, suppose that marketing is predicting that three new services will ramp up, as shown in Figure 17-2. We might reasonably expect total demands to reflect the sum of traffic associated with new services, plus traffic associated with growth of the existing service, as shown in Figure 17-3.

This process provides an estimate of total traffic on the network, but it does not directly provide cost as a function of that growth. There are several ways to try to translate those traffic demands into costs, but we will focus on two: rigorous computation and linear approximation.

To rigorously compute the costs, you would need a design corresponding to each point in time of interest. Alternatively, you might achieve a good approximation of this by computing costs at a smaller number of points and

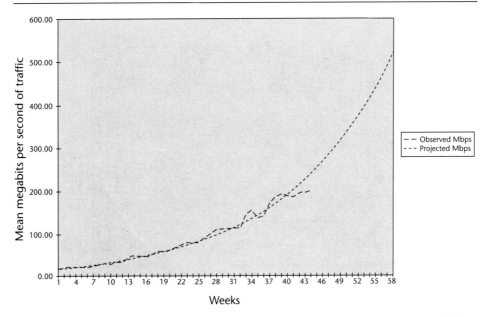

Figure 17-1: An extrapolated projection of traffic growth over time, based on measured data.

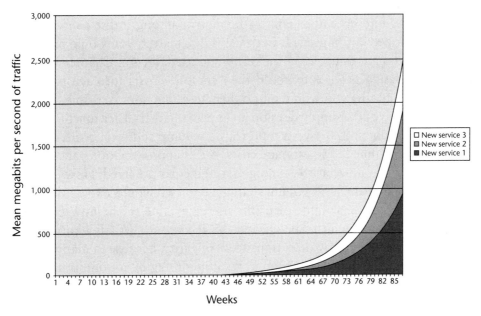

Figure 17-2: A marketing forecast reflecting growth of new application traffic over time.

Overall Forecast

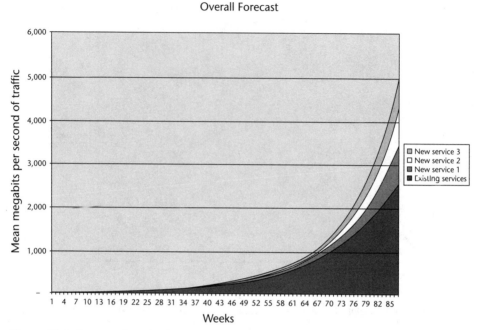

Figure 17-3: A comprehensive forecast. Growth of existing applications and creation of new ones over time.

then interpolating between them. You would need to translate your aggregate growth figures into an end-to-end traffic matrix among traffic sources and sinks, as described in Chapter 11. For each traffic matrix, you would produce a competent design, using either the techniques described in Chapter 11 or a commercial design tool. You would then compute costs for each of these designs, and typically you would graph them as a function over time.

An alternative is to simply develop an approximate transfer function, typically a linear function, between total traffic volume and total costs, and to use that transfer function to estimate costs. Is this approximation valid? If we use a linear function, we are assuming that unit costs are fixed. How do unit costs really relate to traffic volumes? In general, we would expect them to decline slightly as the volume of traffic increases, due to the now-familiar principle that things tend to be cheaper by the dozen. We also know that there are other noteworthy deviations from linearity, because in many cases, we have to buy things in large quanta, resulting in big discontinuities in our cost function as measured against traffic.

Nonetheless, we often find that total cost is *approximately* linear as a function of total traffic, over small operating ranges, and provided we are willing to squint our eyes a bit and ignore the fine detail in our data. If in doubt, you might rigorously work three or four designs in order to estimate the overall shape of the real transfer function between total traffic and total cost.

17.3 Revenues: The Benefits

At this point, we know how to estimate the cost of the network over time. What is the incremental revenue, or savings, that the network will produce over time? For a carrier or an Internet service provider, the new network will likely drive new services that generate revenue directly. For an organization that uses networking to enhance its ability to garner revenues in another way, the network might generate benefits either by enabling the primary business to expand, thus producing more gross revenue and, ideally, greater profits or, alternatively, by driving down the costs of providing existing services, thus enhancing profitability without necessarily expanding the business.

Computing the incremental *gross revenue* associated with a new service is usually simple enough: Multiply the effective market price at which you expect to sell the service by the number of units that you expect to sell. As the economists would say, we are interested in $p \times q$, price times quantity.

New services will generally necessitate new expenses, above and beyond those associated with expansion of the network. We need to keep our eyes on those incremental costs, in order to deduct them from gross revenues in order to obtain incremental *net revenue.*

In the previous section, we discussed the use of marketing forecasts over time. The same forecasts can provide the basis for estimating incremental revenues over time. Indeed, *it is critical that our cost and revenue forecasts be based on consistent data and consistent assumptions.* This may seem to be too obvious to warrant mention; however, cost projections are often done by engineers, whereas revenue projections are done by marketing types. As a result, miscommunications and inconsistent assumptions creep into the process far more readily than we would wish.

17.4 Profitability: Calling the Shots

For any given point in time, perhaps extending a few years into the future, we are now able to compute both the costs—often referred to as the *cost of goods and services*—and the incremental net revenue associated with the creation or expansion of the network we have in mind. How do we know whether building the network is a good idea?

If we take our incremental gross revenues at any given point in time and subtract our incremental costs from them, the result is our incremental *operating income*. We generally subtract from this a number referred to as *general and administrative (G&A)* overhead, which reflects, among other things, the cost of management and of sales and marketing. What is then left is incremental *net profit* before taxes. Figure 17-4 shows the relationships among these quantities.

Ideally, net profit will be a large positive number. If it is, we know that our design benefits our organization. If net profit turns out to be a negative number, we know that our design does not benefit our organization.

Net profit is often expressed as a fraction, or percentage, of gross revenues: the *margin*. If your organization is a commercial firm, you probably have guidelines about the margin that your firm expects of new initiatives. That is the yardstick against which the networking project will be measured.

We have seen that profitability is not static but changes over time. For a networking project, costs are usually front-loaded, whereas revenues ramp gradually over time. Profitability thus tends to improve over time. When you evaluate profitability over time, you are likely to get one of three outcomes, corresponding to Figures 17-5, 17-6, and 17-7.

Figure 17-5 shows a network-enhancement project that is profitable from the outset. This would be delightful, but it rarely happens in practice.

Columnist William F. Buckley once ran for mayor of New York City, with little prospect of winning. One day, an interviewer asked him what he would do if woke up on election day and found that he had been voted in. "Demand a recount," he replied without hesitation. Analogously, if you find yourself in the situation of Figure 17-5, the first thing that you should do is recheck your data for possible errors.

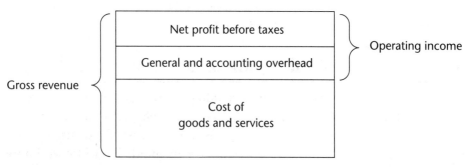

Figure 17-4: Gross revenue, cost, G&A, and net profit.

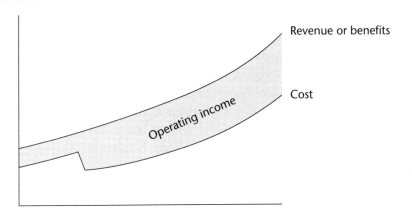

Figure 17-5: A networking project that is profitable from the outset.

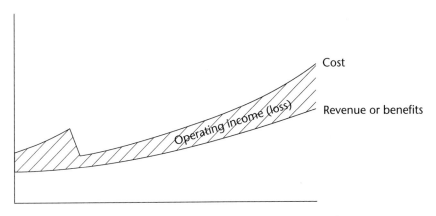

Figure 17-6: A networking project that is never profitable.

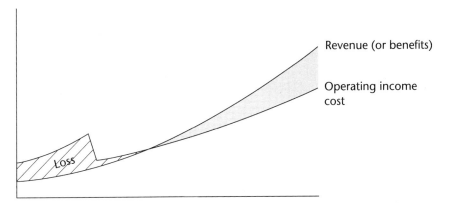

Figure 17-7: A project that becomes profitable after a period of time.

Figure 17-6 is just the opposite: The project is underwater from the outset and never breaks the surface of net profitability. In this case, you clearly have your work cut out for you. In general, it will be necessary to do one of three things: increase incremental revenue, drive down costs, or scrap the project. Do not be afraid to consider scrapping the project. If the project is a loser, it is far better to kill it at this early stage than to let it consume resources, potentially for years.

Figure 17-7 depicts the most common scenario. Net incremental revenues are initially less than net incremental costs but gradually overtake them, eventually generating strong positive results. This is often the case for the simple reason that, in all probability, you would not have invested the time and energy to get to this point in the design process unless you believed that the proposed network would eventually produce a net profitable result.

Key questions for the decision makers now become the following.

- How long until we achieve the break-even point on our run rate (the point at which the curves cross)?
- How deeply do we go into the hole before we reach that break-even point?
- At what point have we recouped the initial investment in this networking project?

These are serious questions. If it takes too long to reach the break-even point or if the total subsidy of the project before it hits break-even is too great, the project may be impractical, even if it appears to eventually generate net profits.

17.4.1 Hazards in Estimating Profitability

It is surprisingly easy to make mistakes in estimating the net benefits of one of these projects. Typical pitfalls include:

- Profitability represents the difference, sometimes a relatively small difference, between two big numbers. As any applied mathematician knows, relatively small errors in either number can produce a large relative error in the result.
- Costs are "hard" and are committed in advance; incremental revenues associated with new services are "soft" and uncertain. Shortfalls in revenue—caused by, for instance, overly optimistic forecasts—do not become obvious until it is much too late.
- As previously noted, costs are usually provided by engineering, whereas incremental revenues are usually provided by marketing. It can be exceptionally difficult, in practice, to ensure that cost and revenue forecasts are prepared with altogether consistent data and assumptions.

17.4.2 Dealing with an Insufficiently Profitable Network

As previously noted, if the network appears to take too long or cost too much prior to achieving break-even or does not generate enough net profit thereafter, you can opt to increase incremental revenue, drive down costs, or scrap the project. You generally want to be very cautious about increasing projected revenue. In my experience, marketing organizations are more likely to estimate high than low. In increasing the revenue forecast, you may be compounding the problem. If you "cook the books" to forecast revenue that is not, in fact, going to be forthcoming, the error may not be obvious until it is much too late. If you can legitimately increase the revenue forecast more so than cost, it may be appropriate to do so. You just need to be careful not to let wishful thinking cloud your judgment.

Driving down costs at this point is generally an excellent thing to do. Look for those $400 toilet seats! Where did you gild the lily? It's time to reach for the knife. Did you gratuitously add any features that are not, in fact, needed? Can some features that were optional in the requirements be eliminated without impact to the revenue stream? Could any nominally mandatory features be chopped without major impact to revenue? Could you get by with a smaller network footprint, or lower bandwidth? Did you drive a hard enough bargain with each of your suppliers? Can you persuade your carriers to drop one-time charges? Can you get significantly better rates on circuits or services by committing to hold them for a longer period of time or by committing to a large enough overall volume of purchases? Can you lease where you had intended to buy or buy where you had intended to lease? Can contractors do some aspects of the job more cheaply than your own people? Are there potential economies in the design that you failed to take advantage of?

Finally, when you have sliced every ounce of pork out of the design, if it is still not sufficiently profitable, it is likely that the project as a whole needs to be axed. This happens occasionally. It can be disheartening, but as previously noted, it is greatly preferable to kill the project at this point rather than later.

17.5 The Budget

If the financial analysis proves out and management agrees that the project has merit, you should, ideally, emerge from this phase with something very important: *a budget*. The budget represents the sum of money that your organization has agreed to spend to bring the network to fruition.

The budget does not represent a single lump sum. Rather, it is spread over the period when the network is under construction and perhaps also over the initial (often unprofitable) period of initial operation.

The deployment schedule is discussed in Chapter 18. One of your key tasks in establishing the deployment schedule will be to map it back to the budget. Usually, the deployment schedule drives the rate at which you spend money. Thus, the deployment schedule must be consistent with the broad framework established by your overall budget. Conversely, it may become possible to bound your budgetary time frames much more tightly once you have established your deployment schedule. Thus, it is often the case that we revisit the budget after the deployment schedule is in place, in order to provide more detail and finer granularity. In practice, these two aspects of the planning process interact closely.

More often than not, less money is allocated than appears to be required. The budgetary process often entails negotiation; the amount of money allocated may reflect not only the perceived cost-benefits of the new network but also the organization's overall ability to spend money at this time, the political standing of the project's proponents, and many other factors that we might want to think of as being extraneous to the value of the proposed network.

If your budget is insufficient, apply the knife before the ax. Revisit the cost-cutting measures discussed in Section 17.4.2. Consider whether it is possible to implement a more limited version of the project. Do revenues decline more or less than costs? In some cases, you can close a budget gap by slowing the rate of deployment, effectively spreading the expenditures out over a longer period of time. Finally, if you cannot reconcile the gap between the money you need and the money you have available, you must either attempt to renegotiate the size of your budget or shut the project down.

PART

IV

The Final Design Phase

18 Final Design: Overview

The design process now progresses to phase 4, its last predeployment phase. You have developed the basic design, you have a good handle on the costs of implementation, and your management team has authorized the project to go forward. Are you done? Hardly! To this point, your design is only conceptual. You need to put flesh on the bones.

> In creating an oil painting, an artist begins by "roughing in" large areas to reflect the broad outlines of the painting that is to be. The artist then adds successive layers of detail and refinement until satisfied with the overall result.

In particular, your design has reflected a good understanding of the available components, but you have not yet finalized your selection of carriers and equipment vendors. This is so because it is impractical, in most cases, to evaluate vendors and carriers against one another until you have a moderately detailed design in place to provide a context for that evaluation.

That selection process is at the core of the final design process. Once you have finalized your choice of vendors and equipment, you will need to revisit every aspect of the design to ensure that it still makes sense in the context of your overall network architecture. For example, the particular router that you selected may not support a feature on which you depended or may have fewer serial interface ports than you assumed. Your carrier may not be able to provide space or capacity at particular locations.

Finally, you will proceed to detailed physical engineering of your network, first at the generic level, then to a level of detail where you cope as necessary with the idiosyncrasies of each individual network location. At this point, you consider power and space requirements, physical connectivity among components (including out-of-band management access, if required), physical access for field service, and any requirements in terms of bearing capacity for the structure. Physical security for your facilities must be addressed, as well as your response to fires, earthquakes, and other natural and man-made disasters.

This book devotes very little page count to this physical engineering, and it is arguably not the most intellectually stimulating part of the design. Do not, however, be misled. *Physical engineering is likely to be the most time-consuming part of the job, and it is critical to your success.* In reality, it is more than just design; it entails the creation of specifications that will be used to build and deploy the network.

This chapter provides a step-by-step run-through of the major activities during the final design phase, in roughly the chronological order in which you would undertake them.

1. Review your assumptions. As a result of the financial review described in Chapter 17, you are probably obliged to make some changes to the design. More likely than not, you have been directed to simplify the design to make it cheaper. You may have been told to add capacity and features in some areas, and you may have been given the latitude to delete functionality in other areas.

So this is a time when you need to review the overall design. It is an excellent time to revisit the entire design and to look for possible disconnects among the numerous interrelated aspects of the design as a whole.

It is a good idea to take a hard look at your hierarchical layering of the network and your selection of transmission technologies. This may be the last point at which you can make changes without seriously impacting the physical build-out of the network.

2. Select your carrier or carriers. Now we come to one of the most profoundly significant choices that you must make: the selection of your carrier or carriers, the source of your wide area communications bandwidth. There is a natural tendency to think of carriers as providing undifferentiated commodity services and thus being fungible, or interchangeable. This is true to a point but not beyond that point.

No carrier today provides its own local access in every part of the world. In fact, no carrier today provides its own local access in all of the United States except by resale of other carriers' infrastructure. The unique footprint of each carrier may thus make one carrier more suitable than another.

Carrier services are similar to one another, but they are not the same. Even for the most standardized services, such as inter-LATA dedicated circuits, there are minor variations in the service description, in the carriers' quality and availability commitments, and often quite significant differences in the price and in the manner in which that price is computed.

If your organization is a carrier, your choice may seem to be a foregone conclusion. Even in that case, however, there is usually some selection process involved. First, your firm may not be able to provide access to all of the locations that you wish to serve, in which case you need to figure out how to reach the rest: Do you expand your own infrastructure, or do you procure services from competing carriers? Second, there may be instances where it is appropriate to use your competitors' services in preference to those of your own organization.

As a matter of business strategy, you need to determine whether you want to use one carrier or more than one. You may prefer the convenience of a single-carrier point of contact and responsibility, and it may also be the case that an exclusive relationship enables you to negotiate the most favorable possible deal. Alternatively, you may feel that using multiple carriers gives you the leverage you need in order to keep each of them on their toes and to ensure that you continue to get competitive terms and pricing throughout the life cycle of your network.

Chapter 19 provides a more detailed discussion of how to select carriers and of the Request for Proposals (RFP) process in particular.

3. Select your equipment vendors. At this point, you must also select the vendor for each significant piece of equipment. Once again, you must decide how many vendors you are willing to deal with. As with carriers, you may find it advantageous to work with more than one vendor; however, it is generally a bad idea to work with a great many vendors, because doing so complicates your management task and may also detract from the manageability and comprehensibility of the network as a whole.

Chapter 19 also provides pointers on your selection of an equipment vendor and provides specific guidance about the use of equipment-oriented RFPs.

4. Finalize your selection of backbone locations. Your selection of backbone locations may be influenced somewhat by your choice of carriers. This is particularly true if you are locating equipment into carrier points of presence (POPs), because your carrier may not have space exactly where you need it.

Your choices might also be influenced by changes in marketing requirements since you began the design, especially changes that flow from the management review envisioned in Chapter 17. This is a good time to take stock.

5. Complete your access design. The initial access design, as described in Chapter 9, necessarily made assumptions about the coverage and services available from your carrier. It also may have made assumptions about the capabilities of equipment used for access and concentration. Now that you have chosen your carriers and equipment vendors, you need to revisit the design.

6. Complete your concentration design. Analogously, your design for concentration reflected assumptions about backbone locations, access service locations, and equipment capabilities. Recall that the choice of single versus multiple homing of access locations is driven largely by reliability requirements; consequently, your choices could change now that you know the detailed MTBF characteristics of the gear and the committed availability figures for circuits and services. The methodology that you would use for computing availability under various scenarios appears in Chapter 16.

7. Complete your backbone topological design. If your backbone locations have changed, the topology is likely to need to change markedly. If cost or marketing considerations have shifted as a result of the management review, this might imply a significantly different traffic matrix, which in turn may imply a significantly different topological design for the network. Changes in the access locations or the concentration design can also influence the shape of the backbone.

If you have access to commercial tools for network design, you will want to bring them to bear at this time. They are particularly useful for evaluating partial mesh topologies (see Chapter 10). They are useful for sizing backbone links and are especially good at ensuring that there is sufficient capacity to still meet performance requirements when a single failure has occurred.

8. Complete your technical design. In the preliminary design phase, you took a first cut at a routing and addressing plan. You dealt with network management, security, and many other aspects of the detailed design. All of these will need to be refined, corrected, or confirmed.

To begin with, your choice of equipment vendors will influence the number of ports on each device, along with many other aspects of the detailed network topology. This is almost certain to necessitate revision to your IP address plan.

The routing plan may be impacted by features that these particular routers do or do not support. Network management will be influenced by the SNMP MIBs supported by the devices that you have chosen and by the facilities available for accounting, capacity management, and configuration management and verification. Infrastructure security is closely tied to the techniques that these devices provide for authentication and authorization of administrative personnel. All of these aspects will need to be reviewed from the perspective of a holistic understanding of the network design.

9. Optimize your design. The design is nearly complete. At this point, we go over it with a fine-tooth comb in order to cull out any needless costs. It is usually a good idea to look at the backbone topology to see whether it can be tightened up in any way and to consider whether more creative use of equipment or carrier tariffs might produce an adequate network at lower cost.

In doing so, you must strike a balance. Reducing cost is, in general, a good thing; however, not every apparent cost optimization really reduces total life-cycle cost. There is a constant temptation to tune the network to optimize for each specific special case. Within reasonable bounds, this may be fine; taken to extremes, however, it can make the network more complex and more difficult to understand and manage. Standardization of the design is essential to achieving operational economies of scale; special-case optimizations can interfere with this standardization.

10. Demonstrate that your design meets the requirements. Using the techniques already described in Chapter 16, we can verify the final design to ensure that it meets our criteria for end-to-end delay, dropped packets, throughput, availability, and delay in the face of failure of single or multiple components. We make minor refinements in the design, if necessary, to ensure that it meets our functional and performance requirements.

11. Create the physical design. We said it before, but it bears repeating: *Physical engineering is likely to be the most time-consuming part of the job. It is critical to your success.* Normally, we begin with "rack and stack" designs that reflect our generic network architecture. For each level in the hierarchical model of the network, we consider each kind of network location. For each, we prepare detailed design drawings to correct scale, showing the components to be used and the connections among them. In North America, we would typically orient these drawings toward either 19-inch or 23-inch equipment racks.

These drawings need to be more than just a wave of the hand. They have to be sufficiently detailed and accurate to enable someone else to manufacture the units and someone else again to maintain them. This implies the need for painstaking attention to detail.

The one thing that you can predict with confidence about any network—assuming that it is going to see actual use—is that it will evolve over time. Your designs will go through many revision cycles. *This implies the need for careful version control of the drawings.* It also requires careful management of the installed inventory of equipment deployed in the field; otherwise, it can be surprisingly easy to lose track of exactly what is where in your network.

Indeed, the engineers who work at this level need to be fanatical about attention to detail. The layout of components in the rack needs to carefully consider not only the dimensions of each device but also requirements to leave room for connectors, for ventilation, and for access by field service personnel.

Engineering for electrical power is of particular importance. Most failure modes take out just a single device or a single communications link. A failure of power generation can, potentially, take out an entire location, and with it a big chunk of your network. It is for this reason that carriers (who are very sensitive to the need for reliability) often design their facilities with dual power feeds at −48 volts DC, battery backup, and standby power generation facilities. Providing such highly reliable power is not cheap! These power requirements have implications for the generic rack designs and for the design of each facility.

Finally, the placement of racks in an overall configuration has implications in terms of the weight that the floor has to bear and also in terms of connectors between racks. The generic design needs to balance all of these factors in order to arrive at a good overall design.

Typically, the generic design will include any out-of-band access components, if your overall design employs them, and may also include intrusion detection. It may also include provisions for disaster recovery.

When the generic rack and stack designs are complete, we progress to detailed designs that take into account the characteristics of specific sites. In the interest of economies of scale, in terms of both manufacturing and field service, we would like to have as little variance as possible from the generic designs; unfortunately, it is rarely the case that we can totally avoid special-case adaptations.

These detailed designs reflect the placement of constellations of racks into individual physical locations. They must deal with power, air conditioning, and floor loading. If the standard rack configuration will not fit into a particular site, the detailed design must make appropriate accommodations.

Potential disasters need to be considered. For example, locations in California will typically need accommodations in anticipation of possible earthquakes.

Again, there is a tendency to underestimate the difficulty of preparing these detailed designs. For a large internetwork, the physical design could easily take several months to complete.

12. Develop a deployment schedule. All of the information necessary for deployment is now at hand. You can prepare a detailed schedule in preparation for deployment. Typically, you would want to use the same methodologies that you would to schedule any other large project. These are standard industrial engineering techniques that have been in use for decades.

A number of commercial tools on the market use the critical path method (CPM) to analyze project schedules based on dependencies between tasks, (where a dependency might indicate that a given task cannot begin until another task has completed. You specify the duration of each task, the dependencies among them, and the resources required. The tool can do most of the bookkeeping required in order to produce a schedule, and it may also be useful for tracking your progress against that schedule. Figure 18-1 shows a small segment of a CPM analysis.

Most scheduling tools can also produce an alternative view of the same data, known as the Gantt chart. A Gantt chart is basically a time line of activities. It is often shown with one time line for each of several resources, where a resource might be, for instance, a field service team deploying gear to your locations. The Gantt chart is simple and easily understood, and it has the additional advantage that you could provide a team or an individual with

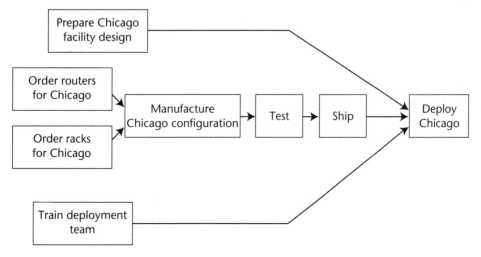

Figure 18-1: CPM analysis of a portion of a network deployment.

only the relevant portion of the Gantt chart. Figure 18-2 shows a Gantt chart equivalent to the CPM chart in Figure 18-1.

A few scheduling tools use a slightly more sophisticated algorithm known as PERT. Instead of providing a single estimate of task duration with PERT, you provide three: worst case, expected case, and best case. These provide an effective confidence interval for the duration of each task. The scheduling tool goes through the same computations that are required in CPM but provides additional information that can offer additional insight into the degree of potential risk in the overall schedule.

Using PERT adds significant complexity to the scheduling task. Is it worth it? PERT has its proponents, but most practitioners would argue that the benefits that PERT offers over CPM are warranted only for exceptionally large or complex projects.

A scheduling package will not automatically take into account every network implementation consideration. Neither PERT nor CPM inherently deals with geography or topology.

Your marketing requirements may not mandate that all locations be deployed at the same time. Your marketing department may feel, for example, that it is critical to deploy service to New York, Chicago, and Los Angeles and that other cities could wait. If so, you will generally want to build your schedule accordingly.

Potentially, these requirements interact with your network topology. For example, the circuit from Chicago to New York might have been designed to "touch down" in Cleveland. Do you build out Cleveland as part of a coordinated sequence with New York and Chicago, or do you instead do an interim deployment based on a circuit that bypasses Cleveland? One way or another, you will need to decide.

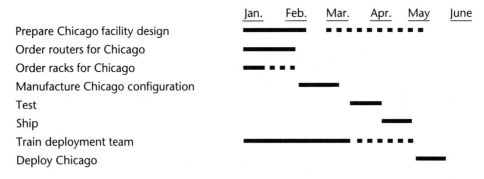

Figure 18-2: Partial Gantt chart analysis of network deployment in Figure 18-1.

Also, travel time and cost between locations is partly a function of geography. If you have a field service team in Cleveland on a Wednesday, it might be easy to do an installation in Detroit the next day but difficult or impossible to do one in Sacramento. Your schedules should consider the distance and the associated travel time between locations in order to minimize travel costs as well as wear and tear on your deployment teams.

Your budget may also place constraints on your deployment schedule. In general, you cannot deploy the network in a way that obliges your organization to spend money before the time period for which is has been budgeted.

13. Analyze your costs. It is advisable to review once again the costs and the anticipated benefits of your network at this time. Previously, you were working with generic estimates. At this point, you have chosen your carriers and equipment vendors and have finalized your designs. Consequently, your cost figures should be much more tightly bounded. The procedure you would use is as described in Chapter 17. In the course of this analysis, you would typically revisit the budget established as a result of the financial review envisioned in Chapter 17 and might apply tighter bounds to the time frames in which you expect to expend money.

19 Selection of Carriers and Vendors

We are ready to select key vendors for the network. These are important decisions, with many ramifications. In some ways, it would have been nice to have done this earlier in the process; however, it is often impractical to finalize this vendor-selection process until the design has been refined to a considerable degree. The reason for this is that the selection is to a significant degree a price/performance comparison; it is not meaningful to make the comparison independent of an understanding of what components and services will be used and how they will be used.

This chapter provides some brief background on the current market for telecommunications services and equipment. The industry is undergoing rapid consolidation; thus, the details of who does what are likely to change rapidly over the coming months and years. Nonetheless, it is helpful to understand who the players are and what they can do for you. Finally, we discuss the process by which you would typically issue a *Request for Proposals (RFP)* in order to benchmark the relative price/performance of carriers, systems integrators, or equipment vendors.

19.1 The Carriers

In nearly all cases, you are likely to obtain most or all of your connectivity from telephone companies, or common carriers, because they already have communication assets deployed, as well as the ability and the know-how to deploy new connectivity infrastructure where necessary. What follows is a U.S.-centric discussion of the carriers. In many parts of the world, regulatory policy is evolving rapidly. Where telephony was historically a government monopoly in most of the world, there is a strong tendency today to privatize it and to open it up to competition. Technological and market factors necessitate continuous modernization of the telecommunications infrastructure at a breakneck pace. Most governments recognize that competitive private enterprise is both more willing and more able than governments are to drive the necessary modernization of telecommunications infrastructure.

To understand carrier services, it is necessary to understand something of the regulatory environment, which is difficult, given that it is very much in flux today. The following discussion includes a great deal of historical information because it is impossible to understand the current regulatory environment without understanding where it came from and where it appears to be going.

19.1.1 Interexchange Carriers (IXCs)

In the United States, there has historically been a strong distinction made between *interexchange carriers (IXCs)*, which carry traffic between or among local areas known as LATAs, and *local exchange carriers (LECs)*, which carry traffic within a LATA and deliver it to IXCs for inter-LATA transport when required. Historically, AT&T was the only IXC. AT&T also had a substantial ownership stake in other companies of the Bell system, which included the predecessors of the dominant local exchange carriers in most of the United States. As a result of progressive deregulation over the past several decades, a number of new IXCs have emerged, notably including MCI, WorldCom (which acquired MCI in 1998), and Sprint. In each case, the availability of existing rights of way was essential to the start-up phase of the new IXC: In MCI's case, it was microwave facilities; in Sprint's, rights of way along the railroads, notably the Southern Pacific; and in WorldCom's, unused gas pipelines of the Williams Petroleum company.

Today, a new firm, Qwest, is once again running fiber-optic cable on a massive scale along railroad rights of way. On a more local scale, electrical utilities are wrapping fiber-optic cable around power lines, and state governments are burying it under the center medians of their interstate highways. So we are witnessing a simultaneous consolidation of traditional IXCs and the entry of new players on a regional and a national scale.

Meanwhile, the Telecommunications Act of 1996 has established conditions under which LECs can offer long-distance service. The *Regional Bell Operating Companies (RBOCs)*, those LECs that were previously part of the Bell system, will be permitted to carry customer traffic across LATA boundaries as soon as they can persuasively demonstrate that they have removed barriers to entry in the local markets in which they historically were dominant. None of the RBOCs has as yet been permitted to offer long-distance service in their traditional territory; however, they will ultimately no doubt be a significant force in this space.

A number of LECs that were not parties to the breakup of the former Bell system are already free to offer long-distance services and thus to compete with the IXCs. GTE, for example, is one of these. Southern New England Telephone (SNET) is, or was, another. These LECs are not subject to the same antitrust concerns and regulatory constraints as the RBOCs. In the two years following the passage of the Telecommunications Act of 1996, GTE signed up nearly three million long-distance customers. It also arranged for Qwest and others to provide it with a substantial nationwide fiber-optic infrastructure and is actively selling inter-LATA circuits and services on a significant scale.

SNET (Southern New England Telephone) was acquired by SBC (an RBOC) in 1998, and GTE is in the process of merging with Bell Atlantic, also an RBOC. At every level, the traditional lines are blurring.

In evaluating inter-LATA services from the RBOCs, it is particularly important to pay attention to the impact of remaining regulatory and business restrictions on their level 2 services: Frame Relay, SMDS, and ATM. The RBOCs tend to portray their services as blanketing their respective service areas. Today, this is only half true. Since they are still restricted from offering inter-LATA services, each LEC Frame Relay, SMDS, or ATM cloud operates as a purely *intra-LATA* island of connectivity. It is the customer's responsibility to build any necessary inter-LATA bridges between these islands. It is up to you, as the customer, to ensure that you thoroughly understand what they can and cannot do for you.

19.1.2 Local Exchange Carriers (LECs)

The breakup of the Bell system under a court consent decree known as the *Modification of Final Judgment (MFJ)* established seven regional holding companies (or RHCs), or "seven sisters": NYNEX, Bell Atlantic, BellSouth, Ameritech, U.S. West, Pacific Telesis, and Southwestern Bell (subsequently renamed SBC Corporation). Today, we typically refer to them as RBOCs. Each became the dominant carrier for about a seventh of the U.S. population. The initial intent was that they would all be of similar size. Their respective territories were as shown in Figure 19-1. Today, this map is primarily of historical interest. It is, however, helpful in terms of understanding the evolution of the system in the United States.

As part of the wave of consolidation that has swept the industry, SBC acquired PacTel, and Bell Atlantic acquired NYNEX. SBC then acquired SNET and is in the process of acquiring Ameritech; Bell Atlantic is in the process of merging with GTE, the largest non-RBOC LEC. Assuming that all

Figure 19-1: Historical territories of the former Bell Regional operating companies (RBOCs).

of these mergers are consummated, there will soon be four large LECs (SBC, U.S. West, BellSouth, and the as yet unnamed successor to Bell Atlantic and GTE) in place of the seven RBOCs plus GTE and SNET.

The RBOCs are by no means the only LECs. There are, in fact, hundreds of LECs, largely as a heritage of the era when the local phone company tended to be much more of a small, local "ma and pa" operation.

A few of the larger non-RBOC LECs are noteworthy. At some $21 billion a year, GTE was larger by most measures than any of the RBOCs prior to the recent round of consolidation. The former United Telecommunications, based in Kansas City, had been the largest LEC after GTE and the RBOCs. United Telecommunications was a major investor in Sprint and eventually bought out what had been GTE's share, thus becoming sole owner. At that point, it took on Sprint's name, which had far greater brand equity, and forsook the name United Telecommunications. Sprint continues to be a significant player in the LEC space.

In recent years, a number of companies have sprung up to compete with the LECs, primarily in metropolitan areas where the population density is highest. These *competitive access providers,* or *CAPs,* have built out local fiber-optic infrastructure in order to compete in the business-to-business marketplace. In general, the CAPs offer high-speed leased lines at the outset. Most do not offer local residential dial tone at all.

Most notable among these CAPs was Metropolitan Fiber (MFS), which was acquired by WorldCom, which then acquired MCI, becoming MCI WorldCom. Metropolitan Fiber built out large-scale SONET infrastructure in major cities throughout the United States, and had begun significant expansion in Europe. It also offered local dial tone in a few markets, notably the New York metropolitan area.

Next most significant is the Teleport Communications Group, or TCG, which has a close relationship to the cable industry. TCG was acquired by AT&T. Finally, we have Brooks Fiber, which tended to focus on second-tier markets. Brooks was also acquired by WorldCom, now MCI WorldCom.

The Telecommunications Act envisions the formation of a new breed of CAP, known as the *competitive local exchange carrier (CLEC)*. CLECs are similar in capability to CAPs and are permitted to offer both intra-LATA and inter-LATA services. The existing LECs that dominate their respective service areas are referred to as *incumbent local exchange carriers*, or *ILECs*. In some cases, the CLECs will be entirely new organizations; in other cases, existing LECs will establish CLECs to provide new services inside or outside of their established franchises.

Meanwhile, traditional IXCs have attempted to enter local markets. AT&T and MCI lost significant sums without achieving much market share. AT&T is now attempting to provide local voice service in a different way: It has acquired TCI and is attempting to acquire Media One, two of the largest cable TV operators in the United States, in order to offer voice and Internet access over cable.

All of this is taking place in a complicated regulatory arena, where the federal, state, and local governments interact in complex ways. The intent of the Telecommunications Reform Act was to stimulate competition in both the local and the long-distance marketplaces. The results have been somewhat mixed to date, and the prognosis is uncertain. As we have seen, the act touched off a wave of consolidation in the industry. In all probability, that wave has not yet spent its full force. Inter-LATA competition appears to have accelerated considerably, but intra-LATA has been slower to emerge.

19.1.3 Carriers of Cellular and Wireless Communications

The traditional system for cellular telephony in the United States is often referred to as a *duopoly,* a system of limited competition between two carriers. The limited bandwidth allocated to cellular telephony was generally provided to the ILEC for the area and to one other carrier or consortium of carriers.

In recent years, this system has been modified by new technologies and by new regulatory policies. New frequencies have been made available and auctioned off by the Federal Communications Commission (FCC) in support of new services, collectively referred to as *personal communications systems (PCS)*. Some of this bandwidth was obtained by traditional carriers, some by new, alternative carriers. The net result is that major markets in the United States will be served by perhaps as many as five or six cellular carriers in the coming years.

Also, a number of newer transmission technologies have enabled more efficient use of the existing airwaves than that achievable under traditional analog AMPS technology, which can be viewed as first-generation wireless technology. Notable among these are Time Division Multiple Access (TDMA), Code Division Multiple Access (CDMA), and, primarily outside the United States and Canada, Global System for Mobile communications (GSM). These newer technologies are collectively referred to as second-generation wireless. Still more advanced technologies, third-generation wireless, are thought to be on the horizon; however, the standardization process for them appears, at the moment, to be bogged down in political and business wrangling.

There has also been a movement to provide packetized data services explicitly over cellular telephony. Cellular digital packet data (CDPD) is particularly interesting in this regard; however, although the technical design was promising, the carriers were never able to price the service at levels that would make it more attractive than simpler alternatives, including the use of modems over conventional AMPS cellular telephony.

For many applications, wireline access has tended in the recent past to be cheaper and simpler than wireless. Wireless has always been attractive for applications that required untethered mobile access. In the future, cost-effective wireless fixed-access solutions have the potential to greatly expand their market share, at the expense of that of traditional wireline services. It is impossible today to predict with confidence how things will evolve, but improvements in wireless technology clearly bear watching.

If your application requires truly global reach, particularly if it requires global access to locations that are either remote or mobile, you may want to consider either geosynchronous or low earth orbit (LEO) satellite-based solutions, as discussed in Chapter 6. A number of systems are being deployed that could potentially be attractive for low- to medium-bandwidth access, and the Teledesic system, due for availability in 2002, could potentially provide high-bandwidth global access.

19.1.4 Nontraditional Carriers

A plethora of new carrierlike organizations have come into existence in recent years to offer connectivity. Usually, they are, in effect, providing low-cost bypass of the traditional telcos.

For example, it is increasingly common for the electric utility companies to run fiber-optic cable along their rights of way. It costs them very little to run more fiber than they themselves need; thus, they become a potential competitor to the ILEC.

In many cases, these organizations will have less operational sophistication than the established telcos, which have, after all, been providing these services for decades. Nonetheless, you may want to consider nontraditional services if they offer sufficiently attractive price/performance.

As an alternative to dealing with a nontraditional carrier, your organization might choose to *become its own* carrier. This is particularly true if your normal business requires that you maintain rights of way or other communication assets.

If you are an electric utility, for example, we have already noted that it is quite likely that there will at least be stretches of your power transmission network where you will want to run your own fiber-optic cable. Whatever your organization does, you should carefully consider whether the business you are in is such as to make it cost-effective for you to provide portions of your own infrastructure. It might even be possible to recoup some of your outlay by reselling surplus capacity on the network that you build.

At the same time, you must carefully consider whether it is cost-effective for you to operate those communication assets over time. If data communications is not a core competency for your firm, you need to consider the incremental operational costs and the intangible cost of potential distraction of management attention. In some cases, doing your own bypass might superficially appear to be a good deal but in fact is far more hassle than it is worth.

19.2 The Equipment Vendors

In the data communications industry, as among the carriers, we are seeing rapid consolidation. Within the past few years, Cisco has acquired numerous companies, including Stratacom (a leading vendor of Frame Relay/ATM switches) and a number of vendors of LAN switching technology; 3Com has acquired U.S. Robotics. Wellfleet (a router manufacturer) and Synoptics (a leading LAN bridging and switching vendor) merged to form Bay Networks, which was subsequently purchased by NorTel. And Ascend, the leading vendor of carrier-oriented terminal servers, acquired Cascade (a leading vendor of carrier-oriented Frame Relay/SMDS/ATM switches) and NetStar (a high-end router vendor) and is, in turn, in the process of being acquired by Lucent. Lucent had previously acquired Livingston (a terminal server vendor). Running counter to this trend, we see the emergence of numerous small start-ups as new technology creates new market niches.

This section attempts to provide some helpful hints as you approach the task of selecting your equipment vendors. Ideally, the general principles will be useful to you, even though many of the specifics will soon be out of date as events reshape this industry.

19.2.1 Routers

The router marketplace consists of a number of distinct categories. In broad terms, we can think of distinct markets for small remote-access routers, midsize routers, and large high-end routers. Cisco Systems plays a strong or dominant role in all segments of the market, but the segments play out somewhat differently.

Remote-access routers generally support one or two links at speeds of 56Kbps, or T-1, and connect them to a small number of LANs. These routers may provide ISDN or Frame Relay support on the WAN link. Increasingly, we are coming to view routers with one or two T-3 access ports in this category as well. Remote-access routers tend to be extremely plentiful, and it is therefore important that you procure them at a good price. There is less product differentiation at this end of the market than is possible at the high end.

Midsize routers provide a moderate number of ports and intermediate-speed connectivity. These routers might be used for the core of a small or medium-sized network or for traffic concentration in a larger network.

Large routers are used for the backbone of a large network. The boundary line for this category shifts over time, as the scale of the largest networks expands. Today, we might think of Cisco 75xx and 120xx routers and their competitors as being typical of this category. At present, we are witnessing the entry of a number of new players into this end of the market.

As you procure routers, you will want to carefully consider how willing you are to mix and match among vendors. In theory, routers from different vendors should be highly interoperable, particularly if you choose nonproprietary routing protocols, such as OSPF. In practice, however, you are likely to find that mixing vendors in the core of the network interferes with its manageability and increases your cost for operational support systems (network management). Mixing vendors on the remote-access side also impacts manageability, but less so in most cases.

19.2.2 Terminal Servers

Devices of a different class are used for large-scale concentration of dialup users, as described in Chapter 6. Ascend has traditionally been the market leader for carriers and larger ISPs in this space, but several competitors now have viable offerings.

For reasons that we explained earlier, the economics of dialup access argue strongly for highly concentrated solutions, combining both analog dialup and ISDN support. Further, it is likely that, in the near future, we will come to routinely expect these devices to also accommodate analog voice and to forward it using voice over IP (VoIP) capabilities.

A variant of this class of device is emerging, as carriers move to concentrate xDSL traffic. It is too soon to judge who the market leaders in this segment will be.

19.2.3 CSU/DSUs

CSU/DSUs are used to connect data communications equipment, such as routers, to high-speed serial lines, typically at speeds of 56Kbps, T-1 or T-3).

It is increasingly common for CSU/DSU functionality to be built into the data communications device. Thus, there is a tendency for the CSU/DSU to evolve from being a *product* to being a *feature*. We find examples of this in the channelized T-1 and T-3 interfaces of Cisco 75xx routers, in the corresponding interfaces of Lucent/Ascend/Cascade 8000/9000 Frame Relay switches, and in many small remote-access routers.

You may nonetheless find it necessary to procure some stand-alone CSU/DSUs. In doing so, it is helpful to remember a few things. First, the concerns we voiced earlier about mixing equipment from too many different vendors also apply to CSU/DSUs. Second, there is some tendency to forget that those embedded CSU/DSUs still have to be managed and that they can introduce compatibility issues with stand-alone units from other manufacturers. Third, in an international network, you must familiarize yourself with requirements for homologation (national approvals) for CSU/DSU equipment in each country in which you plan to operate: U.S. models will not necessarily be acceptable to the local authorities.

19.2.4 WAN Switches: Frame Relay, SMDS, and ATM

The market for Frame Relay, SMDS, and ATM switches has already converged to a significant degree. Nearly all ATM switch vendors provide an integrated solution for Frame Relay access, so you can connect your Frame Relay traffic over an ATM backbone. Few organizations choose to use SMDS these days, but if you wish to do so, some solutions support all three.

The way the market has evolved, many private enterprise networks tend to obtain Frame Relay services from a carrier rather than deploying switches themselves. If, however, you find it useful to deploy your own ATM switches, you should bear in mind that the incremental cost of also supporting Frame Relay access to those switches is likely to be low, and you should consider whether there are places where doing so would be beneficial to your network.

A number of vendors have tended to dominate the WAN switching market, including Ascend (formerly Cascade, now being acquired by Lucent), Newbridge, Northern Telecom, Fore, and Cisco (formerly Stratacom). Among these, Fore has tended to focus on enterprise solutions, especially for ATM LAN environments, while most of the others have placed greater emphasis on carrier-class solutions.

Mix and match is perhaps even more problematic for WAN switches than it is for routers. You have largely the same network management exposures, but you are likely to lose the ability to provision a PVC from end to end through your network if you use switches from multiple vendors. Also, the mechanisms that switches use to recover from link or interface failures are not interoperable; in general, if a link goes down between two vendors' switches, they will not be able to automatically recover from the failure.

19.3 The Request for Proposal (RFP)

We have reviewed the main options that you have as regards carriers and equipment vendors. How do you go about making an informed selection?

Selecting vendors is primarily a business decision and only secondarily a technical decision. As we have seen, there is some tendency for the various products and services to converge over time, to become commodities, to become more and more like one another. In most cases, you are striving to achieve the best price/performance you can.

Price will usually be a key decision factor. Consequently, you will want to let competitive market forces work for you.

The normal mechanism for doing this is to issue a *Request for Proposal (RFP)*, a document that tells potential suppliers what you expect to need, in what time frame. The RFP gives them a fair opportunity to respond with the best offer they can make.

We will first consider the business decisions that you need to make prior to issuing the RFP. We then describe the various kinds of RFPs, and close with a number of helpful hints in structuring the RFP.

19.3.1 Business Decisions

Before issuing the RFP, you need to think through what you are trying to accomplish.

- Are you looking to outsource the entire design and operation of the network?
- Do you understand exactly what you want? Do you have enough information to issue the RFP?
- How many suppliers do you want to deal with?
- What kind of supplier do you prefer? A systems integrator? A carrier? An equipment vendor?
- Will you issue a single RFP for all of your requirements or several specialized RFPs for specific aspects of your network?

Throughout the book, we have tacitly assumed that you are either designing the network yourself or else working closely with a systems integrator to do so. If you intend to outsource the *design* aspects of the job to a systems integrator, you would typically select the systems integrator early in the process—often by means of a very broadly phrased RFP process—and would then expect your systems integrator to follow essentially the same steps that we have provided up to this point, subject to your direction. For the most part, this is not the scenario that we are covering in this chapter, although much of the information about how to structure the RFP may be relevant. If you are outsourcing the construction and operation of the network but not the design, this is an appropriate point at which to do so.

It is important that you understand how tightly you want to constrain responses. As we shall see, a loosely defined problem lends itself to a loosely structured RFP, while the converse is true for a tightly defined problem. In the former case, you are still fishing for the information that you need to issue the RFP; in the latter, you are concerned primarily with price.

Who is integrating the system: you or a third party? You would ask much the same question if you were having a new house built: Would you prefer to retain a general contractor to oversee the whole job, or would you instead choose to play that role yourself? If your organization has strong project management and engineering skills, you might choose to integrate the network yourself. If not, you would be wise to pay someone to manage the job on your behalf. The systems integrator provides you with a single point of contact rather than requiring you to deal with a bevy of subcontractors.

A carrier may be able to serve as a systems integrator. Some have strong capabilities in this area; others might not. Reasons for asking a carrier to serve as your integrator might include the belief that you will get the best deal on communications infrastructure by procuring as much of it as possible from a single source or the knowledge or belief that the carrier's expertise is important to the success of the network.

There are also potentially valid reasons *not* to use a carrier as your integrator. You may want to procure services and circuits from multiple carriers, in order to retain bargaining leverage and independence—and, in this case, you probably want a systems integrator to impartially recommend the best carrier deals to you. Finally, there are cases in which the equipment vendor is capable of offering a complete, integrated solution. This may be attractive to you, particularly if you believe that a thorough understanding of the capabilities of the equipment is essential to your success.

If you are looking to retain a single systems integrator, you will generally want to procure the integrator's services through a single RFP process. Your integrator may very well end up issuing more detailed RFPs for specific elements of the project. If you are integrating the system yourself, you need to consider who the likely bidders are and whether they are capable of responding to a single RFP for all of the things that you need. It may be easiest for you to evaluate responses to a single RFP, but an overly broad RFP risks needlessly eliminating otherwise qualified bidders.

19.3.2 Types of RFPs

There are several distinct RFP-like documents that you might want to use.

- The *Request for Information (RFI)* typically asks vendors to describe their capabilities in a particular area. The RFI is sometimes used to set the stage for a subsequent RFP, especially in an area of technology that is still unsettled or in transition. An RFI usually does not request firm pricing and is not sufficient in and of itself to enable you to select a vendor. It gives your suppliers maximum flexibility in responding.
- The *Request for Quotation (RFQ)* is, in a sense, the opposite of an RFI. The RFQ is suitable for a request for something that you view as a highly commoditized service or product, where all that you want is price and availability information (and where you expect to make your selection largely based on price, subject to suitable availability). The RFQ discourages your suppliers from being creative in making you their best offer. You would use an RFQ rather than a more flexible form if you are confident that you know exactly what you want.

■ The *Request for Proposal (RFP)* can be viewed, in a sense, as a compromise between these two extremes, and it is the most frequently used of the three. The RFP invites bidders to provide a complete solution to a set of specified requirements. It affords them some latitude in designing a solution, but it requires them to submit pricing. The RFP, in conjunction with subsequent discussions with bidders, is usually sufficient to enable you to select suppliers.

19.3.3   Hints in Constructing an RFP

An RFP, as distinct from an RFI or an RFQ, provides a broad, functional description of your network and gives the bidder some latitude in responding. The RFP should give an accurate description of the network and should provide bidders with a level playing field, an equitable basis on which to respond. On occasion, there will be tension between these objectives. In most cases, there will still be some uncertainty in the design when you issue the RFP. Or you may be unwilling to provide full information to your bidders, for competitive or business reasons. Don't be overly concerned about possible inaccuracies in the RFP; *it is more important that the RFP be representative than that it be an accurate depiction of the network that you will eventually build.*

A colleague of mine once described the process of responding to an RFP, from the bidder's perspective, as being analogous to a take-home final exam in college. You have to give the best answer to the question that has been posed. If the exam were to pose a different question, you should provide a different answer. When it is time to deploy, you may be answering still another different question anyway.

On the other hand, the more restrictive form of the RFQ makes sense only if you can be reasonably accurate in describing the services that you will use.

Whether you use an RFQ or an RFP, you should try to be clear and straightforward in what you ask for.

Avoid "kitchen sink" requests. Many RFPs contain a list of technical standards that bidders are expected to adhere to. In some cases, those standards are large tomes, only a small portion of which is relevant to the bid. In other cases, the standard does not provide a clear indication of what you have to do to be in compliance. In still others, it may be possible to vacuously comply with a standard. In all cases, if you want your bidders to conform to a standard, make sure that you understand what the standard says, and provide enough guidance so that they know what you are asking for and why.

In creating an RFQ document, I typically create a document with three sections. The first is an overview or executive summary that explains, as simply as possible, what it is that we are trying to accomplish.

The second section describes procedures that I expect each bidder to follow. It describes the form of the intended response, how the response should be delivered, when the response is due, how to get answers to questions about the RFP (and whether the questions and answers will be made available to other bidders), and the planned schedule for any other relevant events, such as a bidders' conference. It may disclaim a commitment to procuring services based on the results of the RFP. You should also seriously consider setting a page limit on responses. I generally feel obliged to read every page that a bidder sends me, but consequently, I like to keep the bidders from going overboard in submitting standard "boilerplate" in their responses.

The third section typically contains explicit technical requirements and includes a network map and a pricing table (see Table 19-1). It is common to ask bidders to respond to your technical requirements in the same sequence in which you specify them, identifying in each case the RFQ section number to which they are responding.

There is no single right way to construct any of these documents. Large RFPs from the government can be complex. For instance, an entire volume might be devoted to pricing.

As a final helpful hint, I strongly encourage the use of *standardized pricing tables* for an RFQ or an RFP. Show your bidders exactly how you want them to price the response. Don't be overly concerned about stifling their creativity; as Picasso once said, "Form liberates." If you neglect to standardize the format for the cost portion of the proposal, you are likely to waste countless hours making sure that you are making a fair cost comparison among the responses (and even then, you are more likely to make mistakes). There is a tendency to pay insufficient attention to this aspect of the RFP, especially if you are a technical person by training rather than a business person. You should plan to put some careful thought into the format and structure of these pricing tables.

Table 19-1 provides a sample pricing format. Note that this would be meaningful only in conjunction with a detailed description of what exactly constitutes an acceptable technical solution, with a separate table providing street addresses, NPA/NXX information or both for each of the locations, and with clarification of what is meant by kilobits per second (Kbps) and the delay and loss characteristics at which the specified capacity must be provided. The particular characteristics of this trivial table correspond to the logical star design that appeared in Chapter 11. You may wish to refer back to Table 11-5 in Section 11.2.3.

Table 19-1: A Sample Pricing Table

From City	To City	Symmetric CIR (Kbps)	Inter-LATA		Intra-LATA		Other		Total		Available
			Monthly	One Time	Monthly	One Time	Monthly	One Time	Monthly	One Time	January 2000?
New York	Chicago	270									
New York	Los Angeles	380									
New York	San Francisco	190									

Index

Addison-Wesley Computer and Engineering Publishing Group

How to Interact with Us

1. Visit our Web site

http://www.awl.com/cseng

When you think you've read enough, there's always more content for you at Addison-Wesley's web site. Our web site contains a directory of complete product information including:

- Chapters
- Exclusive author interviews
- Links to authors' pages
- Tables of contents
- Source code

You can also discover what tradeshows and conferences Addison-Wesley will be attending, read what others are saying about our titles, and find out where and when you can meet our authors and have them sign your book.

2. Subscribe to Our Email Mailing Lists

Subscribe to our electronic mailing lists and be the first to know when new books are publishing. Here's how it works: Sign up for our electronic mailing at http://www.awl.com/cseng/mailinglists.html. Just select the subject areas that interest you and you will receive notification via email when we publish a book in that area.

3. Contact Us via Email

cepubprof@awl.com

Ask general questions about our books.
Sign up for our electronic mailing lists.
Submit corrections for our web site.

bexpress@awl.com

Request an Addison-Wesley catalog.
Get answers to questions regarding
your order or our products.

innovations@awl.com

Request a current Innovations Newsletter.

webmaster@awl.com

Send comments about our web site.

cepubeditors@awl.com

Submit a book proposal.
Send errata for an Addison-Wesley book.

cepubpublicity@awl.com

Request a review copy for a member of the media
interested in reviewing new Addison-Wesley titles.

We encourage you to patronize the many fine retailers who stock Addison-Wesley titles. Visit our online directory to find stores near you or visit our online store: http://store.awl.com/ or call 800-824-7799.

Addison Wesley Longman
Computer and Engineering Publishing Group
One Jacob Way, Reading, Massachusetts 01867 USA
TEL 781-944-3700 • FAX 781-942-3076